Resonant Learning in
Music Therapy

RESONANT LEARNING *in* MUSIC THERAPY

A Training Model to Tune the Therapist

EDITED BY
Inge Nygaard Pedersen, Charlotte Lindvang, and Bolette Daniels Beck

Forewords by Søren Willert and Helen Odell-Miller

Jessica Kingsley Publishers
London and Philadelphia

First published in Great Britain in 2023 by Jessica Kingsley Publishers
An imprint of Hodder & Stoughton Ltd
An Hachette Company

1

Copyright © Jessica Kingsley Publishers 2023

List on page 31 is reproduced from MacRae, 2019 with
kind permission from Amanda MacRae.
List on page 43 is reproduced from Nielsen & Kvale, 2004
with kind permission from Hans Reitzels Forlag.
The following are reproduced with kind permission from Barcelona Publishers: epigraph
on page 15 from Dileo, 2000; list on page 29 from Bruscia, 2013; table beginning page 287
and sections 'Presenting musical excerpts at the oral examination' on page 290 'Learning
from being a client and a therapist with the same partner' on page 293, and 'Transformation
from student-client to student-therapist' on page 294 from Pedersen, 2013; epigraph
on page 297 from Kilham & van Dort, 2019; epigraph on page 317 from Bruscia, 2019.

Front cover image source: Shutterstock®. The cover image is for
illustrative purposes only, and any person featuring is a model.

A CIP catalogue record for this title is available from the
British Library and the Library of Congress

ISBN 978 1 84905 657 1
eISBN 978 1 78450 218 8

Printed and bound in Great Britain by CPI Group

Jessica Kingsley Publishers' policy is to use papers that are natural, renewable
and recyclable products and made from wood grown in sustainable
forests. The logging and manufacturing processes are expected to conform
to the environmental regulations of the country of origin.

Jessica Kingsley Publishers
Carmelite House
50 Victoria Embankment
London EC4Y 0DZ

www.jkp.com

Contents

Foreword I

Søren Willert

I'm not a music therapist. During the period 1968–2006, I was attached to the Psychology Department at Aarhus University. In that context I happened to become actively involved in events leading, in 1982, to the inauguration of the Aalborg music therapy study programme. Since then and for the next 25 years I kept up close collaboration ties with Aalborg. I functioned as external examiner. For a substantial period, I was head of the external examiners' corps. Generally speaking, I let myself be drawn into all sorts of discussions about and support schemes for the department. I did this not because I had to, but because I wanted to.

The content area of this book, i.e., integration of a 'therapeutic track' in the academic study programme, formed one all-important reason behind my enthusiastic 'wanting to'. In 1982 I was, myself, doing small-scale teaching experiments of a similar nature. Some years before I had shifted from full-time to half-time university employment combined with a half-time job at our local Student Counselling Office. Suddenly to sense psychology from a *learner-by-doing* position instead of from a *learner-by-reading-thinking-writing* position felt like a revelation to me. I wanted psychology students to experience revelations like that. I set up workshops where students, working in training groups under my supervision, would do small-scale mutual counselling and joint reflection on their shared experiences. I was ever so thrilled when students, for example in their exam papers, reported that 'Now I *know* what theoretical concept X is all about. I've seen it. I've felt it.'

On the occasion of the music therapy programme's 25th anniversary I gave voice to my enthusiasm in a *Festschrift* article entitled *The World's Topmost Academic Study Programme*. On the one hand, the title was kind of a joke. 'Topmost' is a heavy word. I used it lightly, definitely not based on any objective, data-informed, world-wide rating procedure. On the other hand, the title was deeply felt, a personal, if not an objective, truth.

I'll present a highly abridged version of my 2007 praises. I'll continue with an even more abridged version of what Aristotle might have said, had he become acquainted with the Aalborg programme. I'll end up with briefly taking an 'Aristotelian look' at the Aalborg programme.

At my workshops, one part function of mine was norm-setting. In that capacity I would at times deliver the following exhortative speech to my students:

> At this course, we're not simply dealing with psychology as a body of knowledge about human beings as research objects *out there*. We're *rehearsing* psychology, and rehearsing it with *our own bodies*. Body and soul. Truth value, which reigns as all-important quality criterion at other courses, is here replaced by professional value. I'll give you one practice-based idea of mine, describing what professionalism may imply. It runs like this.
>
> Whenever you are practically engaged in some professional helping encounter, I require you to be, at any time, mentally prepared for receiving a tap on your shoulder followed by this simple question: 'What exactly are you doing right now, and how is that which you are doing linked with the overall helping task stipulated in the contract between you and the client?' Now, as you well know, because you have experienced it, practical helping work will often draw heavily on body-bound resources like gut feeling, tacit knowledge, and the like. Therefore, I'll grant you a time lapse of five to 10 seconds, allowing you to come to your rational senses before you answer. To complicate things further, I want your answer to cover three different assessment perspectives concerned with 1) theory, 2) ethics, and 3) aesthetics, respectively. Briefly put, 'theory' refers to such general understanding of the situation-at-hand as makes you believe your intervention will in fact be effective. 'Ethics' refers to such beliefs and values on your part as make you reasonably confident that your intervention, if successful, will do more good than harm. 'Aesthetics' refers to such experiential elements in your ongoing interaction with the client: sensing, gut feeling, and the like, as make you trustful that your relationship with the client is basically beneficial to the task at hand.

Now, as I might also mention to my students, the three assessment perspectives cited in my speech correspond exactly to the famous triad *truth*, *goodness* and *beauty* which, according to Plato, founder of Academia, the Western world's first university, constituted the essential qualities belonging to the ideal objects of knowledge. Thus, one implicit allusion from my speech would be that my profession-oriented workshops were in fact one of the *very few places* in the theory- and lecture-filled study programme where students got the *full* academic package.

This message comes out even more forcefully if, from Plato, we move on to Aristotle, who after Plato's death in 347BC left Academia, later to establish the Western world's university number two, the Lykeion. Aristotle adds an artisanship twist to Plato's thinking. This shows in his theory of knowledge. According to Aristotle, three kinds of knowledge are required for leading a virtuous life – as citizen or professional: 1) *Episteme*, corresponding to 'Theory': *episteme* gives answers to generalized 'what' questions; 2) *Tekhne*, methods knowledge, which is not included in Plato's triad: *tekhne* gives general answers to 'how' questions; 3) *Phronesis*, which is person- and situation-specific knowledge about goals to pursue: *phronesis* combines 'ethics' and 'aesthetics'.

I find it uplifting that the Aristotle triad corresponds exactly to those three parallel 'training tracks' which, together, make up the Aalborg music therapy programme: 1) an academic track having *episteme* in the foreground; 2) a music track developing students' technical competences, *tekhne*; 3) a therapy track guiding students' first steps towards acquisition of *phronesis*.

Reading Olav Eikeland's 2008 volume *The Ways of Aristotle* convinces me further that this coincidence is by no means accidental. Eikeland's meticulous scrutiny of Aristotle's oeuvre amounts to a scathing critique of today's academic culture. He summarizes his investigations by declaring that 'most of the much-too-didactical, and much too-isolated-from-practice schools of history, and their attempts to restrict learning to these settings must be considered as basic distortions and aberrations' (p.492).

In the introduction of this book, Dileo (2000) is quoted as stating that 'At the heart of music therapy is the person of the therapist'. According to Eikeland, Aristotle would gladly generalize this statement into 'At the heart of worthy intellectual work is *the person of the intellectual worker*'. At the Aalborg programme, staff persons collaborate with students as persons. If they didn't, they would betray the ethical obligations inherent in including the therapy track in the study programme. For staff, students are not empty vessels, i.e., heads to be filled with theoretical knowledge. Students are human beings who should be assisted and nourished in their process of changing their lives, body and soul, for the better.

Likewise, when moving around in the department premises you find students everywhere and anywhere – playing music, discussing, preparing exam papers, socializing. This is partly due to Aalborg University's strong PBL-tradition (Problem-Based Learning) which supports group work from the very beginning. It is also because the study programme involves students, not only intellectually, but also existentially.

References

Dileo, C. (2000). *Ethical Thinking in Music Therapy*. Barcelona Publishers.

Eikeland, O. (2002). *The Ways of Aristotle*. Peter Lang.

Foreword II

Helen Odell-Miller

At the time of writing this Foreword, the COVID-19 pandemic, which invaded most countries by 2020, is far from over. Despite this situation, which includes lockdowns, economic down-turns, and an apparent global increase in mental health issues, it is striking that music therapists have continued to develop clinical approaches, research, and train students across the world at a similar rate to periods outside the pandemic. New research has increased, and new knowledge in the mechanisms of music therapy, from improvisation to composed music, including approaches and techniques which draw upon technology, is developing.

This book demonstrates, above all, that both historical and established approaches and modern developments in music therapy are embedded within international music therapy training courses. The team at Aalborg University is a leader in this field, and through their writing in this book, members of the team demonstrate the importance of the integration of in-depth experiential learning in the training of students. Fundamental to this approach is the central concept of 'tuning the therapist'. The authors take great care to explain to the reader that this metaphor encompasses the training process of all the students' experiences.

I am personally pleased to have been invited to write this foreword, because I undertook my PhD at Aalborg University some years ago and was able to experience and learn from the team there. I witnessed first-hand the intensity of the clinical programme which emerges in the book. Master's students also have the rich opportunity to learn about research from the PhD research milieu, within the leading international PhD programme there.

Resonating throughout this book is a blended learning approach where students are collaborating with lecturers throughout their development as therapists, where the metaphor 'tuning the therapist' highlights authenticity of the student-therapist experience through embodiment, their developing musicality, and the importance of a deep sense of knowledge and understanding, including research-based learning at all levels.

I was reminded, whilst reading the book, of the potency and power of face-to-face musical and personal encounter, which can sometimes be lost during on screen learning during COVID lockdowns. The approaches emphasize the 'psychological-affective understanding of the phenomenon of tuning' where attuning to fellow trainees, and then to patients or participants, is much more than only physical motion. This process leads to the trainee music therapist becoming increasingly 'aware, present, adaptive, responsive and reflexive'.

These qualities are central to the development of music therapists, but also to the development of the profession. There is a global understanding, increasingly recognized, of the importance of the arts in medicine and psychological human development. Whilst I am writing this foreword, the World Health Organization is considering the value of the arts therapies, despite individual country cutbacks in funding for the arts in favour of STEM subjects (science, technology, engineering and maths). Some of the underpinning robust examples put forward towards the case for global expansion and recognition of music therapy have arisen from the long-established music therapy training education and research traditions at Aalborg University.

Musical skills taught at the core of the curriculum at Aalborg University include a wide range of music therapy approaches and techniques, including Mary Priestley's analytical music therapy approach taken forward by Inge Nygaard Pedersen, and Tony Wigram's music therapy improvisation approaches. The book describes innovative approaches by the Aalborg team, and also those arising from older, more established music therapy theory and practice. Always at the heart of these approaches is the person receiving music therapy, and the trainee's experience of practising music therapy. Three other skills not so rooted in musicianship are stated as key to the student training experience: understanding process within groups and individuals, organizational skills, and analytic and reflective skills. The book gets to the heart of the practice and theory of music therapy. Its contents will inform and inspire readers who train music therapists, employ them or work with them. The wealth of expertise, knowledge, and skill arising from one team in Aalborg University provides a legacy which will impact upon many.

Acknowledgements

Inge Nygaard Pedersen, Charlotte Lindvang, & Bolette Daniels Beck

We, the editors, would like to thank all the people who assisted us through the completion of this book.

First, we want to thank our colleagues of many years, Hanne Mette Ochsner, Ulla Holck, Niels Hannibal, Stine Lindahl Jacobsen, Sanne Storm, and Lars Ole Bonde, for their contribution to different chapters in the book.

Second, we want to thank our younger colleagues, Gustavo Gattino, Julie Ørnholt, and Jens Ingstrup-Anderson, for their dynamic feedback and review of the chapters.

It has been an important issue for us as the editors that all our colleagues are part of the process of writing this book and also part of a team, all of whom consider these disciplines to be an integrated part of the five years music therapy Master's programme at Aalborg University.

We also want to thank Søren Willert and Helen Odell-Miller for taking time to go through the text and write inspiring forewords from both a national and an international perspective.

Further, we want to thank Denise Grocke for her careful language wash of each of the texts and for creative suggestions when formulations could be clearer.

Finally, we want to thank Aalborg University for the support to the music therapy programme and music therapy milieu for the last 40 years and for supporting the integrative model of our programme over that time.

Introduction

Inge Nygaard Pedersen, Charlotte Lindvang, & Bolette Daniels Beck

At the heart of music therapy is the person of the therapist.

(Dileo, 2000, p.27)

The music therapy training programme at Aalborg University, Denmark, was established in 1982. The curriculum of the five-year BA/MA programme overall consists of three parallel 'training tracks': a therapy track, a music track and an academic (theory) track (Jacobsen, Pedersen, & Bonde, 2019). Each track includes a combination of different subjects. The therapeutic track has been integrated in the programme from the beginning in 1982 and it comprises personal therapy, individually and in groups ('training therapy'), and other therapeutic subjects including three supervised internships. The therapeutic track is mandatory, is paid for by the programme, and has equal status and weight compared to the other tracks. We want to emphasize that the therapeutic track cannot stand alone as a model *per se*. It is fully integrated with the other two tracks in the music therapy programme. Although the therapeutic training track is the focus of this book, it is important to keep in mind that it *must* sit alongside the music and academic tracks within the programme.

As the programme now approaches 40 years of experience of educating music therapists, it seems like an obvious task that the team of educators ask each other: How is it possible to share in the form of words how we are teaching the subjects in the therapeutic track? And how can we explicate the psychodynamic roots we sprout from, and the modern psychodynamic foundation that the education, specifically the training therapy, builds on today? Further, a generational handover is taking place, and with the founder of the programme, and a therapeutic teacher/ mentor for all Danish music therapists, Inge Nygaard Pedersen approaching retirement, the time has come for the team to collect and disseminate the many years of experiences concerning the specific training practice of the therapeutic track where students' unique and personal development is essential.

The main purpose of this book is to disseminate the practical and experiential type of learning that characterizes the therapeutic track, as well as the theoretical platform for these learning processes, and thereby we intend to fuse theory and practice.

The preparatory work for this book has been a long journey. From a professional viewpoint, the main reason is to be found in the current theoretical development in psychology and associated fields which challenges us in our thinking. Thus, the team of music therapy educators at Aalborg University has in recent years reflected on subjects concerning the complex theoretical ground we stand on today when we teach music therapy and specifically teach subjects that are part of the therapeutic track. We realize the importance of dialogue about how we understand psychodynamic concepts.

The first three chapters are designed to provide a historical and theoretical framework for the therapeutic training subjects called the therapy track in the Aalborg programme which are presented in the chapters that follow. In Chapter 1, three vignettes are used as an introduction to the rationale, concepts, and terminology concerning the therapeutic training that the programme in Aalborg provides. Chapter 2 presents the training programme in further depth and the learning contexts in Aalborg and explains the role of the music and the ethical concerns around the therapeutic training. Chapter 3 contains a theoretical platform for the disciplines in the therapeutic training track following a new paradigm in psychodynamic theory. Chapters 4–12 each provide a solid description of a therapeutic training subject from this track in the curriculum in Aalborg, with concrete examples and illustrations of the teaching and learning processes. Each chapter will reflect on how the therapeutic discipline in focus is linked to the other disciplines of the specific semester. Moreover, each chapter will clarify what competencies the students are expected to develop and provide reflections on how an ethical approach is woven into the learning process. Further, each chapter develops the theoretical outlook where it is deemed relevant.

To let voices from music therapy students be heard and provide the reader with lived experiences, the book contains many examples and vignettes from training therapy (with permission from the involved students).

The process of writing this book has been characterized by colleagues being sounding boards to each other, and by collaborative work and co-authorships in our team. The first three chapters particularly were shared and discussed with the whole team several times during the writing process. Still the 'we' in these three chapters refers to the three authors. All other chapters have been reviewed by one or two colleagues in the team.

In our team we acknowledge that it is hard if not impossible to 'separate the dancer from the dance': We are coloured by being a part of the practice that we want to disseminate. We wonder if it will be possible for us not only to revitalize our own understanding and teaching practice through the process of writing this book together – but also to stimulate reflection in others? Can we investigate and disseminate our own practice with sufficient clarity to shed new light on therapeutic training that reaches the mindset of a future generation of coming trainers and therapists?

The book is written for music therapy students in Denmark and for international music therapy trainers and students, for educated music therapists who are engaged in training formats of different kinds – as well as those planning and taking part in other arts and psychotherapy training programmes. It may also be inspiring in a theoretical or practical way to music therapists or other professionals who are engaged in various therapeutic processes. We hope that the book will contribute to the field of music therapy and perhaps facilitate interest, discussions, and research in training matters.

We see this book also as a step further from the book *Music Therapy Training Programmes in Europe: Theme and Variations,* edited by Stegemann and colleagues (2016). Their purpose was to demonstrate the progress towards formalized training in Europe and to draw a map of European music therapy programmes – including self-experience. Of 10 presented European programmes everyone has self-experience included in their programme, varying from being included in only one semester to three full years. The authors state in the introduction that: 'Fundamentally, self-reflective subjects should be offered in all training programmes, influencing and forming the personality of the students' (Stegemann *et al.,* 2016, p.7).

This present book offers a full description of how such learning processes have been developed and are performed at the programme in Aalborg.

References

Dileo, C. (2000). *Ethical Thinking in Music Therapy.* Barcelona Publishers.

Jacobsen, S.L., Pedersen, I.N., & Bonde, L.O. (eds) (2019). *A Comprehensive Guide to Music Therapy* (2nd ed.). Jessica Kingsley Publishers.

Stegemann, T., Schmidt, H.U., Fitzthum, E., & Timmermann, T. (eds) (2016). *Music Therapy Training Programmes in Europe: Theme and Variations.* Reichert Verlag.

CHAPTER 1

Tuning the Future Music Therapist

Charlotte Lindvang, Inge Nygaard Pedersen, & Bolette Daniels Beck

'Tuning the therapist' is a metaphor we have chosen to illustrate the art of training music therapists. How is it possible to tune the future therapist – the whole body of this unique, organic, susceptible, and sensitive instrument? If we accept this metaphor of the future music therapist as an instrument, we can imagine the many strings that the professional music therapist has, representing life experiences as well as educational and professional experiences. In the training context, it is possible to guide the future therapist to be aware of these strings and know about their conditions, strengths, and weaknesses – and of course to add new strings and to investigate how they oscillate and may come into play. Further, the instrument (the future therapist) has a soundboard which is sought to be developed through the student's therapeutic training towards a greater degree of holding capacity and relational capacity. According to the Cambridge English Dictionary to tune means 'to change a part of a musical instrument so that the instrument produces the correct sounds when played'.[1] When we use the concept of tuning as a metaphor in this book, we do not mean that the tuning that happens during training is intended to help a student playing or being 'correct'. It is not necessary to be like a Stradivarius violin, to be 'top-tuned' or be in perfect pitch as a music therapist. We use the psychological-affective understanding of the phenomenon of tuning rather than the physical-mechanical: Tuning can be seen as a process of being increasingly aware, present, adaptive, responsive, and reflexive. The therapeutic training process is related to the refinement of the individual student's inborn social skills, increasing the awareness of the students about themselves and their interaction with others, so that they can use themselves as well-tuned instruments when working with their future clients. It is also referring to the way the students' musical skills are gradually being fine-tuned to

---

1   https://dictionary.cambridge.org/dictionary/english/tune

be brought into play in a thorough, precise, and empathic way in the intensity of the intimate therapeutic interplay with other human beings.

We consider music therapy as a craft; it is not something that can be learned in theory exclusively – the craft must be trained, and the instrument fine-tuned – and the tuning continues as an ongoing process throughout the professional life as a music therapist (Willert, 2007). The competencies, knowledge, and skills that music therapists are obtaining through their training must be oriented towards the demands of the working life – the broad array of clients that the future music therapists are going to serve as well as the many different contexts they are going to enter. Taking the metaphor of tuning the therapist further, music therapists have learned to tune in to and be attuned with clients. Therefore, to start the chapter, three different vignettes from music therapy practice will be presented, illustrating different situations while improvising with clients. The underlying theoretical ground for the Aalborg training programme is rooted in psychodynamic theory, and therefore we will provide examples that are demonstrating how a psychodynamic-informed approach is used with both verbal and nonverbal clients (see a further description of psychodynamic theory in Chapter 3). The examples illustrate the importance of being present and self-reflective to meet the needs of the client. (The vignettes summarize our own experiences from practice and are partly fictionalized.)

Vignette 1: The music therapist offers a stable centre in the music

The music therapist is working with a client diagnosed with personality disorders and traumatic stress. The client starts improvising on the piano. The client alternates playing single tones in the high and deep register (avoiding the middle register), and the therapist is sensitively listening and discovers that there is no pulse in the music and that the tones are not linked together. The music therapist enters the improvisation on a separate piano and intuitively fills out the gap between the tones of the client and plays one repeated tone (d) at the middle part of the piano in a stable pulse like a heartbeat rhythm as an accompaniment during the whole improvisation. The tones of the therapist and client merge together and create harmonies that invite the players to focus inwards and listen, and the body language of the client shows intense concentration as if he is gradually becoming more absorbed in listening and immersing himself into the sounds. In the verbal conversation following the improvisation, the client expresses that he did not hear the therapist's music during the improvisation. However, he had a sense of a musical centre somewhere, that he felt drawn to and which he could move towards and away from (which was safe for him). He could now express in words that he needed a stable centre outside himself to allow himself to be grounded.

This vignette shows how the music therapist is able to listen carefully to the music of the client, and to find a position in a joint improvisation that offers a stable and predictable centre for the client. The therapist aims to bring the client from being not connected to being more connected to the music and the therapist, in a tempo he can choose himself. The music therapist is aware of the contact emerging through the musical harmonies between the therapist and client during the joint improvisation. The client validates this awareness: 'I did not hear the therapist's music, but I had a sense of a stable pulse in the music that I could move towards and away from.' He can sense and feel this in an embodied way without being cognitively aware of what the therapist is playing. The shared music serves as a mirror of the psychological process towards connecting. The therapist is trained to develop a sensitive listening attitude in order to hear and sense what the client could not yet verbalize as a conscious need before this joint musical experience.

Vignette 2: Attention to oneself as a therapist in the relationship with a client

The music therapist is arriving at the centre where his client is living. The client is a woman who is described as having neurodevelopmental disorders and has no verbal language. The therapist has just had a sad and exhausting experience at home and does not feel motivated to go to work today. The therapist is aware that he is a bit weary and that his own mood can influence the relationship and the joint music improvisation. He decides to take a few minutes alone doing voice and body exercises to regulate his energy and be better prepared for the client and for this session. The music therapist starts the session with the usual hello-song. Thereafter he gives himself time to just listen carefully to the client's sound and rhythm on the drum. At the same time, the therapist still feels his own state of mind but starts playing another drum slowly trying to be present with his client in the music. After a while, the therapist is drawn into the energetic musical dialogue that is developing and he is aware of the movement from being partly present to being fully present. The woman expresses through personal sounds and gestures that she is very excited about the music created and the music therapist senses both his own presence, the client's presence, and their mutual contact.

The vignette illustrates how the ability to be sensitively present and how the personal state of mind is something that the therapist is self-conscious about and takes responsibility for. This everyday situation demands an emotional flexibility on the part of the therapist. It is a common task for all therapists and health professionals to be able to contain their own emotions to be present with the person that they work with. When working as a professional helper it is sometimes a challenge to move between different types of tasks as well as moving from the private space to a professional space. The music therapist can use the music for self-regulation and thereby improve the ability to be grounded in the shared music with the client. The therapeutic training facilitates an awareness of the therapist's own state of being in the interaction on the emotional level which is especially important when working with clients without language.

Vignette 3: The music therapist is reflecting the inner state of the client

The music therapist is playing with an elderly client with dementia, who is not verbalizing much and rarely shows any emotions or response to the music. The music therapist is listening carefully to the client's sounds and body language in order to match, meet, and hold the client in the music. Suddenly, the music therapist gets a feeling of deep sadness, which she considers could reflect the client's inner state. She starts to sing and hum while being empathically related to the sad feeling, and the client plays softer on the instrument and tears come to his eyes. The music therapist sings and improvises phrases, addressing that the client is sad, and that it is okay. The client takes the therapist's hand, and they share eye contact. After the session, she tells the staff at the care home and the relatives what has happened, and they discuss whether this might be connected to the client's reaction to the recent loss of his wife which he has not been able to express until now.

This vignette illustrates how a music therapist can share feelings on a nonverbal level, which can lead to a deep release and give a possibility for the client to feel less isolated. The music therapist did not know exactly what caused the feelings to emerge but is trained to trust the importance of the moment and the power of the music to touch and embrace on an emotional level. According to psychodynamic theory, the process where the therapist is sensing something that is belonging to the client is called 'empathic countertransference', a concept which is further described in Chapter 3. To respond adequately to the client, the therapist is trained to be able to discriminate between her own feelings and the echo of the emotions of others that she perceives in her own body.

All three vignettes are examples of how a tuned music therapist might be working professionally. There are many more ways to describe what the therapist is doing to create a joint musical experience. Professional music therapists use themselves as people when they put themselves into play, concretely by listening, playing, and singing together with the people they work with. To be present as authentic people without being 'private' is an important part of the process of becoming 'tuned' as therapists. From a psychodynamic perspective the ability to move in and out of arousal levels and emotional states is crucial because the therapist takes an active part, as an empathic instrument or soundboard. Through the therapeutic training the music therapy students become prepared to use their own body sensation, nervous system, and cognitive ability as a tuning fork, in order to vibrate with and attune to the mood, condition, and context of the client. This kind of attunement can happen through singing together, through verbal communication, with musical sounds in improvisations, or through sharing a music listening experience. The development of the ability to reflect is also an extremely important area, as the music therapist moves between exploring/doing something and reflecting upon it. This oscillation is a process that music therapy students need to investigate and strengthen during their training.

Overall terminology

Before entering deeper into the background and rationale for establishing a therapeutic training track as part of an academic curriculum, we will clarify some of the words and concepts that we use throughout this book.

We are aware that there are professional terms applied in music therapy literature synonymously to represent the same meaning and, further, that music therapists use the same terms with slightly different meanings. As an example, Cohen (2018) discussed the difference in semantics of words like education and training in her book *Advanced Methods of Music Therapy Practice*, as developed in the US and UK. She noticed that in the US: 'training usually refers to clinical environments, such as the internship site or field placements, and education takes place at university. In the UK Music Therapy students receive training at university' (Cohen, 2018, p.66). In this book, we use the term 'music therapy training programme' for the university programme as a whole, and the term 'training' for all sorts and levels of training of music therapy students.

We use the term 'therapeutic training' as the overall concept for the cluster of disciplines in the therapeutic track of the Aalborg programme. The broad term 'experiential training' is applied as an umbrella term for all types of experiences and processes in the therapeutic track. We are in line with Bruscia (2014) when he formulates that experiential training basically requires that the student engage directly and with self-inquiry in the process. In the therapeutic track, development of the therapeutic skills and competencies is the primary focus of the experiential training. Self-inquiry in the form of various exercises is also embedded in the music and the academic tracks to support different learning aims – although the experiential training is not the primary focus in these contexts. We use the terms 'self-experience' and 'self-development' when we describe the students' learning processes related to the therapeutic track. It is important to emphasize that a huge part of the therapeutic training is an interpersonal process, and they experience and develop themselves in an intersubjective domain.

Two of the courses in the therapeutic track are called 'training therapy' in the Aalborg curriculum (see Chapters 5 and 8). These courses are close to but not the same as a 'personal therapy', since the students' processes are framed in a learning context, with the ultimate goal of being equipped to handle future music therapeutic tasks. In training therapy, the students enter a 'client position' over several sessions and they focus on their own authentic life story and life situation, and personal feelings are activated and shared during the training therapy course. The teacher of training therapy courses is called 'training therapist' when performing these disciplines.

Here we are in line with the Master's programme in music therapy in Augsburg where the same phenomenon is described in the following way:

> Personal development within the new and therapeutic method to learn differs from the pure self-experience in terms of therapeutic treatment. The training therapy accompanies the students on the path of a changed self-experience and self-reflection in preparation for their therapeutic role with the application of a medium, with a different function that is not familiar to most: music and its elements, but also possibly touches 'blind spots'. (Stegemann *et al.,* 2016, p.80)

In other courses on the therapeutic track, the students take turns in being in the client position (student-client), the therapist position (student-therapist), or the observer position, and the overall term for the staff members facilitating these courses is a 'teacher'. In individual and group internship supervision the teacher is called a 'supervisor'.

The student's experiences as a 'student-client' are considered indispensable and a prerequisite in relation to a gradual transition into the role as 'student-therapist'. The training processes are also functioning as a preparation for the continuation of personal and professional developmental processes after graduation.

Throughout the book all authors use the term 'client' when speaking about a person who is participating in music therapy. The term 'patient' is only used in quotations where the quoted author is applying this term. We use the term 'student' or 'student-client' when it is the student who enters the role of being a client. In the therapeutic training, we do not link the term 'client' or 'being in the client's position' with pathology, but simply with a specific learning context, where there is an asymmetric relationship. At the same time, we acknowledge a human equality between student and training therapist. We have a broad understanding of the term; a client could be any one of us, who seeks therapy, counselling, or other kind of help and support. And we believe that every client is an expert in their own life. Another term which is sometimes used in music therapy is 'user', which is referring to the person as an active participant, who is acting and not only receiving something from the other/the therapist. Acknowledging the positive connections between the term 'user' and the respect of the person's autonomy, we still find the term 'client' most appropriate. The term 'client' refers to the fact that the person needs something that the professional that meets the person has a responsibility and liability to consider. But often this means that the client takes an active part and develops self-agency together with the music therapist. We also use the term 'clinical work' synonymously with 'music therapy practice', as we think all music therapy practice is built on asymmetric relationships where a qualified music therapist takes care of a client in a specific professional frame for therapeutic processes, under the Code of Ethics.

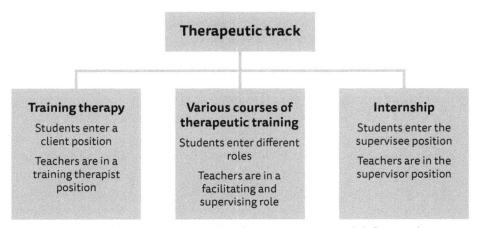

Figure 1.1: The therapeutic track with various courses and different roles

Below, we will argue for the importance and benefits of establishing a therapeutic training track as part of the music therapy training from different perspectives: an ethical perspective, a presentation of findings from studies of training therapy, and a brief outlook on therapeutic training concerning European training standards.

The therapeutic track
Ethical rationale for therapeutic training as part of an academic music therapy training programme

To create respect for music therapy as a profession, evidence and effects are often in focus. To meet the demands for high standards in both clinical practice and research, we need music therapists with strong empathetic and relational competencies. Therefore, we think it is imperative to keep interest and attention on the integrative training of students. The delivery of high-quality music therapy in, for example, the treatment of some of the most vulnerable citizens is dependent on a high quality of training. Furthermore, research studies in psychotherapy document that the quality of the relationship or alliance between the therapist and client is pivotal in relation to the outcomes (Hougaard, 2019; Jørgensen, 2004; Orlinsky, Rønnestad, & Willutzki, 2004; Rønnestad, 2006).

At a symposium about approaches and methods in experiential training at the World Congress of Music Therapy in Oxford in 2002, it was agreed by the participants that self-experience experiential training or personal therapy in music therapy programmes presents several ethical risks, but also that the ethical problems associated with *not* having any experiential training are far riskier (Murphy & Wheeler, 2005).

There are differences in training programmes all over the world concerning training therapy – if and how this training is integrated – and obviously many ways to prepare for the music therapy profession. The ethical questions that emerge in relation to an integration of a therapeutic track in the curriculum as we have in Aalborg will be further elaborated in Chapter 2.

The power relation

Music therapy students need to build experience and understanding concerning power relations between human beings. The Danish philosopher K.E. Løgstrup is known for his book *The Ethical Demand* (1956). Løgstrup suggests that even in our stances and attitudes we contribute to the lifeworld of our fellow human beings – we always influence each other and therefore we carry in our hands a responsibility for a part of each other's lives. According to Løgstrup it is a given fact that we have a power over each other which we must face and manage (Løgstrup, 1956).

No research offers a conclusive insight into music therapy students' original motivation for their studies. It is our experience that future music therapists usually choose the profession because of a wish to help other people and an urge to get their love for music into circulation with other people and not in an attempt to be powerful. But a strong desire to help may also have an underlying adverse cause and a therapeutic relationship always has a potential power dynamic (Møller, 2014). A client is entering therapy because they seek help, support, togetherness, change, etc., and even when we acknowledge that both parts contribute to the relationship, and learn from the interplay, a power asymmetry will remain. In music therapy the client is often not able to express themselves verbally, and this places an even greater responsibility on the therapist. Many music therapeutic tasks demand a high level of empathy and the ability to navigate in the 'language before language' – the sensory and emotional landscapes of communication – in order to carry this ethical responsibility.

'Ethical know-how'

The concept of Phronesis, as defined by Aristotle, refers to the capacity for practical judgement in concrete and particular situations, a kind of 'ethical know-how'. In the real world, situations happen that one could not have foreseen or prepared through theoretical or methodological perfectionism and Phronesis is therefore needed (Gallagher, 1993).

Therefore, we find that, regardless of which therapeutic theory or approach the therapist chooses, it is important to develop a psychic stability and resilience that ideally enables them to face and handle difficulties and complex situations without losing balance or energy, which could compromise the performance of Phronesis (Fog & Hem, 2009; Lindvang, 2010; Løgstrup, 1956). We define any attempt to work with music therapy as an ethical act including ethical know-how. In principle, the therapist sets up a safe space to make the relevant playing and interaction possible. The therapist must relate to the specific tasks and needs of the client or the group and the specific conditions of the concrete situation.

American professor in music therapy Cheryl Dileo emphasizes that it is impossible to think ethically without being aware of one's feelings, values, prejudices, virtues, and possible ethical blind spots, and that ethical thinking develops through self-awareness and self-exploration (Dileo, 2000). It is the experiences of one's own body, combined with the reflections and understanding on top of that, which pave the way to practical wisdom and an ethical practice.

As a group of professionals, music therapists do have ethical rules and standards to follow, to secure proper and decent behaviour, especially in relation to clients. But it is important that ethical rules are used in a reflective manner connected to the concrete circumstances (Fog & Hem, 2009).

The risk of burnout

In preparing the students for their professional working life as music therapists, it is important to build a capacity to listen carefully to their own needs. Music therapists often feel the client's feelings through the intimate, joint space created by the music, and as Rykov stated: 'We may be deeply affected by our patients' pain, loss, and hurt' (Rykov, 2001, p.190), and this openness and receptivity can lead to over-involvement, emotional exhaustion, and burnout (Rønnestad & Skovholt, 2012). In a review about burnout among music therapists (Gooding, 2019), findings indicated that music therapists are at average risk for burnout, and that emotional exhaustion was the most experienced dimension of burnout among music therapists. The study also points out that self-care strategies may promote resilience and lower the degree of experienced burnout. The review reveals that no studies have explored how former education and training may have an impact on music therapists' later experience of burnout. But in a global study from Orlinsky and Rønnestad (2005), most professional psychotherapists acknowledge the positive impact of their own therapy on their personal as well as on their professional lives. In another psychotherapy study it was found that therapists 'who had either received personal therapy previously, or were receiving personal therapy currently, reported more personal growth and positive changes, and less burnout' (Linley & Joseph, 2007, p.392). Thus, the therapist's own therapy may alleviate the emotional stresses and burdens inherent in the therapeutic profession.

In Lindvang's PhD-study focusing on Danish music therapy students' learning processes in the therapeutic track, it is pointed out in the analysis that therapeutic training develops and enhances the student's basic ability to take care of self, which is an important task since many therapists feel an urge to help others and risk ignoring their own needs. One student expressed it like this: 'I do need to nourish myself, I need to offer myself something, something that I can live on, on many levels, before I can be something for others' (Lindvang, 2010, p.260).

Therapeutic training as an integrated part of the music therapy programme raises the self-awareness of the future music therapist and builds a culture where listening to oneself and treating oneself with care is therefore an important prerequisite for professional work, which may reduce the risk of later stress and burnout. There is a need for professional self-care to cultivate the practitioner's resiliency. The student as well as the professional music therapist must learn to reach out for support, therapy, or supervision when needed (Lindvang, 2010; Rønnestad & Skovholt, 2012; Trondalen, 2016).

Previous research on training therapy, including music therapy as training therapy

In the introduction to the book *Self-Experiences in Music Therapy Education, Training, and Supervision*, edited by Kenneth Bruscia (2013), the following four foci for carrying out a self-experience pedagogy in the training of music therapists were described:

> 1) to impart knowledge and skill about how to practice music therapy; 2) to develop an understanding of how different methods of music therapy are experienced by clients; 3) to develop a capacity for deep empathy for clients; and 4) to develop self-awareness as a music therapist. (Bruscia, 2013, p.13)

The book includes several chapters describing experiential learning processes in music therapy and supervision. Two of the chapters are written by Hesser (2013a, 2013b), who has worked with music therapy self-experience groups in university pedagogics at NYU for more than 40 years. Hesser argued for the inclusion of self-experience of music therapy in training and throughout professional life:

> To go through an actual music therapy process ourselves can provide an essential type of experiential knowledge that cannot be obtained in any other way. The 'knowing' will be different, and this will directly affect our clinical practice. This personal experience creates a deeper understanding of the process of music therapy and empathy for what the client is experiencing. It prepares us to work more sensitively with others. (Hesser, 2013a, p.164)

These ideas are very much in line with the comprehensive description of music therapy students' training towards practice (Goodman, 2011). We will now present several research studies which focus on students' personal learning processes.

Studies on psychotherapy across theoretical schools and approaches agree on the importance of personal therapeutic experience for professional development of therapist identity and competencies (Geller, Norcross, & Orlinsky, 2005; Moertl *et al.,* 2017; Orlinsky & Rønnestad, 2005; Rønnestad & Skovholt, 2012). In two qualitative studies in psychotherapy in which the participants were at the end of their studies or newly educated, it was reported that students, through experiences of being in the client's position, developed both their ability to be grounded in contact with themselves *and* their empathic approach and understanding in relation to the people they met in therapy (Grimmer & Tribe, 2001; Murphy, 2005).

There have been similar findings in studies of music therapy training. In a survey of 45 music therapists from the Danish music therapy programme, who were working in different institutional contexts and with different client groups, the analysis concluded that therapeutic training had a significant influence on the development of reflexivity and competence to meet the client. Ninety-four per cent responded that 'they had been able to integrate their own personal experience from having been in the client position in their therapist identity' (Lindvang, 2010, p.51). In Germany, another alumni survey showed that the content of self-experience as a part of the education is considered especially important in relation to clinical work (Ruess & Bauer, 2015).

A survey investigating the inclusion of undergraduate music therapy education programmes in the US found only three out of 41 programme coordinators reported requiring personal therapy as part of the curriculum (Gardstrom & Jackson, 2011). The majority of coordinators of these programmes believed that such learning is inappropriate at an undergraduate level of education and training, citing both ethical concerns and pragmatic barriers. Yet, Jackson and Gardstrom (2012) found through qualitative analysis of reflexive journals that undergraduate students who participated in music therapy as clients found their self-learning to be of paramount importance. The following themes emerged from the data: Exploration/Insight into Self, Emotional Safety/Comfort, Musical Self-Expression/Creativity, Client Empathy, Connection to Others, Clinical Methods/Techniques/Structures, Validation/Acknowledgement, Selfcare, Ambivalence/Resistance.

Murphy (2007) explored experiential learning in music therapy education at Temple University through interviews. Murphy found that both the students and the professors estimated that the students learned more from experiences of being a client than from taking observer or therapist roles in the training context. To explore how music therapy students experience and describe their learning process from being in the client position, Lindvang (2013) interviewed nine voluntary Master's music therapy students from the Aalborg programme during their last semester. In the qualitative analysis a close connection between self-developmental processes and relational capacity emerged. Furthermore, it was illustrated how the students through training therapy acquired an embodied knowledge of being a music therapy client. This included how important it was for the therapeutic work to experience a basic trust in the relationship with the therapist and experiences of how it felt to be met in a sensitive and accepting way in the music. Several students described that the development of trust takes time and that it is not always easy to build that trust. Through the therapeutic training students also became aware that an ability to provide self-care might influence their future capacity to build therapeutic relationships and prevent burnout.

Watson (2005) explored British music therapy students' experience of change during training therapy. One of the students stated: 'It also helped me to become more patient as a therapist, since I saw within myself how difficult it is sometimes to change certain things' (Watson, 2005, p.14). Scheiby (1991) analysed the notes from a student during an individual training therapy in the Danish music therapy programme together with her own experience as a training therapist. The case study illustrates how music therapy training therapy serves a medium for self-development and transformation, as well as 'an experiential laboratory for gaining insights and skills essential for becoming a music therapist' (Scheiby, 1991, p.290). These skills were described as an understanding of the nature of the client–therapist relationship in music therapy, the discovery of different ways of using music as a tool in therapy, the development of the trainees' own musical language, and the disclosure of 'blind spots' in the students' self-awareness.

In a PhD dissertation at Temple University, USA (MacRae, 2019), the experience of having been trained in the specific discipline of Intertherapy (defined as InterMusicTherapy (IMT) among music therapists), following the advanced model of Analytical Music Therapy (AMT), was explored. Here the students take turns in being student-clients and student-therapists. The experiences were examined through questionnaires and interviews and analysed through the qualitative interpretivist research approach of Transcendental Phenomenology. In her findings MacRae concluded that, through IMT, the clinical skills of the trainees were influenced in the following ways: 'Developed empathy, enhanced therapeutic presence, recognition of how personal material influenced the therapy session, further development of self-awareness, and expanded musical creativity' (MacRae, 2019, p.ii).

Hence, although the number of studies is limited, previous research points to the fact that experiences of being in the client position is crucial for the embodied knowledge of how music therapy works on nonverbal and emotionally intensive levels, leading to insight and skills that enable the student to take on the role as a therapist in a qualified and ethical way.

Therapeutic training in music therapy training programmes in Europe

In this section we will briefly sketch the context around music therapy training standards in Europe concerning therapeutic training.

The EMTC (European Music Therapy Confederation) was founded in 1990 as a forum of professional music therapy associations (i.e., associations of qualified, practising music therapists) working actively to promote the further development of professional practice in Europe, and to foster exchange and collaboration between member countries. One of the foci for the EMTC has been the European Music Therapist Register (EMTR). The purpose was to ensure the recognition and protection of the professional title of the music therapist. A registration committee was established to formulate minimum standards for this music therapy register (De Backer, Nöcker-Ribaupierre, & Sutton, 2014). As far as we know, at the time of writing this book the EMTR has unfortunately not been continued. Therapeutic training was a part of the training recommended by the EMTC and a part of the EMTR standards. It is very difficult to get an overview of training programmes in Europe, not least if and how the many different programmes on different levels integrate therapeutic training as part of the programme. There is obviously a wide range in duration, quality, and therapeutic approaches between the offered courses, and it is difficult to compare them. It is an important topic for music therapy in Europe in the future to keep up educational standards and exchange between programmes (Schmid, 2014).

In 2015, the music therapy online journal *Approaches* published a special issue in collaboration with the EMTC: 'Music therapy in Europe: Paths of professional development'. This issue has two parts: Part I includes 16 articles covering many themes in relation to professional development including three articles about the role of the training. Part II presents short reports from 28 countries that outline the multiple paths of professional development of music therapy in the different EMTC member countries. The issue of *Approaches* highlights the diverse landscape of music therapy across cultures, the different histories and conditions, as well as financial and political priorities and needs in the regions, countries, and local communities. Drawing from local accounts, the editors of the issue of *Approaches* attempted to think globally: 'Although no thorough comparative study of the different professional pathways of development is attempted, some overall questions regarding training, education, research and recognition across different countries are raised' (Ridder & Tsiris, 2015, p.5). Therapeutic training was surprisingly not an issue in focus in the special issue on professional development. However, self-experience as a training element was mentioned by programmes from Austria, Latvia, Finland, Portugal, and Denmark. Further, the experienced music therapy programme leader Jane Edwards PhD reflects about the training context and the music therapy student in her paper and points out how important it is that course learning and personal development are integrated within the student's experience: 'When students have the opportunity to experience themselves as more than a selfless deliverer of services to future clients, their exponential growth pathway can be valuable and exciting' (Edwards, 2015, p.49).

In 2018–2019, the EMTC ran a survey among all the European training courses to collect information about the standards that are presently used for training. The EMTC planned to complete the analysis of the survey in 2020 and then the next step will be to find a common denominator for necessary competencies, core contents, and hours required in music therapy training to get minimum standards for qualification in Europe. In the EMTC survey self-experience was one of the 16 learning areas that was asked for, and the results may add information about the number of hours in the area of self-experience among the European training courses, for example. This work is still in progress. Results can be seen on the EMTC homepage, where a list of all training programmes in Europe, with information on level of graduation and language of instruction, can be found. The EMTC (2022) states: 'We know from experience that finding a music therapy training programme in another country, in a language you know, and at the level you need can be very challenging. Therefore we are in the process of compiling this table of searchable information about training courses in EMTC member countries. We hope it will help'. There is still a long way to go in order to find a common denominator for necessary competencies and to get minimum standards for qualification in music therapy in Europe. We hope this book will be helpful in this process.

In 2015, Lindvang and Pedersen distributed a questionnaire to all the music therapy programmes in Europe to investigate if and how these programmes integrate self-experience and training therapy into their curriculum. The questionnaire was sent to both private and state-run programmes, and to programmes at all levels, using the email addresses available at the EMTC webpage. All in all, the questionnaire was distributed to 95 possible participants. Twenty per cent responded and we ended up with 19 completed questionnaires from programmes at different levels, different lengths, and from different regions. The understanding of the terminology around therapeutic training differed greatly between the respondents. Unfortunately, the diverse landscape of music therapy training in Europe and the low number of participating programmes made it impossible to conduct any solid or valid comparisons.

After this opening chapter with vignettes that illustrated working situations for music therapists, an introduction to the concept of tuning, a presented ethical rationale for therapeutic training, and a brief outlook on therapeutic training in European music therapy, we will now present the context around the comprehensive therapy training at the music therapy programme at Aalborg University.

References

Bruscia, K. (2013). 'Self-Experience in the Pedagogy of Music Therapy.' In K. Bruscia (ed.), *Self-Experiences in Music Therapy Education, Training, and Supervision.* Barcelona Publishers.

Bruscia, K. (2014). 'Experiential Learning in a Classroom Setting.' In K. Bruscia (ed.), *Self-Experiences in Music Therapy Education, Training, and Supervision.* Barcelona Publishers.

Cohen, N.S. (2018). *Advanced Methods of Music Therapy Practice.* Jessica Kingsley Publishers.

De Backer, J., Nöcker-Ribaupierre, M., & Sutton, J. (2014). 'Music Therapy in Europe. The Identity and Professionalisation of European Music Therapy, with an Overview and History of the European Music Therapy Confederation.' In J. De Backer & J. Sutton (eds), *The Music in Music Therapy. Psychodynamic Music Therapy in Europe: Clinical, Theoretical and Research Approaches.* Jessica Kingsley Publishers.

Dileo, C. (2000). *Ethical Thinking in Music Therapy.* Barcelona Publishers.

Edwards, J. (2005). 'Possibilities and problems for evidence-based practice in music therapy.' *The Arts in Psychotherapy, 32*(4), 293–301. https://hdl.handle.net/1959.11/27802

EMTC. (2022). 'Training Programs.' EMTC. Accessed on 05/11/22 at https://emtc-eu.com/training-programs.

Fog, J. & Hem, L. (2009). *Psykoterapi og erkendelse. Personligt anliggende og professionel virksomhed [Psychotherapy and cognition. A personal matter and a professional company].* Akademisk Forlag.

Gardstrom, S.C. & Jackson, N.A. (2011). 'Personal therapy for undergraduate music therapy students: A survey of AMTA program coordinators.' *Journal of Music Therapy, 48*(2), 226–255.

Geller, J.D., Norcross, J.C., & Orlinsky, D.E. (eds) (2005). *The Psychotherapist's Own Psychotherapy.* Oxford University Press.

Gooding, L.F. (2019). 'Burnout among music therapists: An integrative review.' *Nordic Journal of Music Therapy, 28*(5), 426–444.

Goodman, K. (2011). *Music Therapy Education and Training: From Theory to Practice.* Charles C. Thomas.

Grimmer, A. & Tribe, R. (2001). 'Counselling psychologists' perceptions of the impact of mandatory personal therapy on professional development: An exploratory study.' *Counselling Psychology Quarterly, 14*(4), 287–301.

Hesser, B. (2013a). 'Music Therapy Group: Self-Experience in a University Setting.' In K. Bruscia (ed.), *Self-Experiences in Music Therapy Education, Training, and Supervision.* Barcelona Publishers.

Hesser, B. (2013b). 'The Transformative Power of Music in our Lives: A Personal Perspective.' In K. Bruscia (ed.), *Self-Experiences in Music Therapy Education, Training, and Supervision.* Barcelona Publishers.

Hougaard, E. (1996/2019). *Psykoterapi – teori og forskning* (2nd ed.) *[Psychotherapy – theory and research].* Dansk Psykologisk Forlag.

Jackson, N.A. & Gardstrom, S.C. (2012). 'Undergraduate music therapy students' experiences as clients in short-term group music therapy.' *Music Therapy Perspectives, 30*, 65–82.

Jørgensen, C.R. (2004). 'Active ingredients in individual psychotherapy – searching for common factors.' *Psychoanalytic Psychology, 21*(4), 516–540.

Lindvang, C. (2010). 'A field of resonant learning. Self-experiential training and the development of music therapeutic competencies: A mixed methods investigation of music therapy students' experiences and professionals' evaluation of their own competencies.' Doctoral dissertation, Aalborg University. Vbn. https://vbn.aau.dk/ws/portalfiles/portal/316410062/6465_dissertation_c_lindvang.pdf.

Lindvang, C. (2013). 'Resonant learning: A qualitative inquiry into music therapy students' self-experiential learning processes.' *Qualitative Inquiries in Music Therapy, 8*, 1–30.

Linley P.A. & Joseph, S. (2007). 'Therapy work and therapists' positive and negative well-being.' *Journal of Social and Clinical Psychology, 26*, 385–403.

Løgstrup, K. (1956/2010). *Den etiske fordring [The ethical demand]*. Klim.

MacRae, A.L. (2019). 'A phenomenological inquiry into InterMusicTherapy: An "experiential meeting place".' Doctoral dissertation, Temple University.

Moertl, K., Giri, H., Angus, L., & Constantino, M.J. (2017). 'Corrective experiences of psychotherapists in training.' *Journal of Clinical Psychology, 73*(2), 182–191.

Murphy, D. (2005). 'A qualitative study into the experiences of mandatory personal therapy during training.' *Counselling and Psychotherapy Research, 5*(1), 27–32.

Murphy, K. (2007). 'Experiential learning in music therapy: Faculty and student perspectives.' *Qualitative Inquiries in Music Therapy, 3*, 31–61.

Murphy, K. & Wheeler, B. (2005). 'Symposium of experiential learning in music therapy. Report of the symposium sponsored by the World Federation of Music Therapy Commission on education, training, and accreditation.' *Music Therapy Perspectives, 23*(2), 138–142.

Møller, L. (2014). *Professionelle relationer [Professional relationships]*. Akademisk Forlag.

Orlinsky, D.E. & Rønnestad, M.H. (2005). *How Psychotherapists Develop: A Study of Therapeutic Work and Professional Growth*. American Psychology Association.

Orlinsky, D.E., Rønnestad, M.H., & Willutzki, U. (2004). 'Fifty Years of Psychotherapy Process-Outcome Research: Continuity and Change.' In M.J. Lambert (ed.), *Bergin and Garfield's Handbook of Psychotherapy and Behaviour Change* (4th ed.). John Wiley.

Ridder, H.M.O. & Tsiris, G. (2015). '"Thinking globally, acting locally": Music therapy in Europe.' *Approaches, 7*(1).

Rønnestad, M.H. (2006). 'Fokus på psykoterapeuten – betragtninger om psykoterapiforskning og professionel udvikling' ['A focus on the psychotherapist – considerations on psychotherapy research and professional development].' *Mellanrummet. Tidsskrift Om Barn- Och Ungdomspsykiatri [The Space in Between. Journal of Child and Adolescent Psychiatry], 15*, 19–31.

Rønnestad, M.H. & Skovholt, T.M. (2012). *The Developing Practitioner: Growth and Stagnation of Therapists and Counselors*. Routledge.

Ruess, J. & Bauer, S. (2015). 'Questionnaire of the alumni survey for the music therapy training program at the University of the Arts, Berlin.' Unpublished diploma thesis, University of the Arts, Berlin.

Rykov, N.H. (2001). 'Facing the music: Speculations on the dark side of our moon.' *Journal of Palliative Care, 17*(3), 188–192.

Scheiby, B. (1991). 'Mia's Fourteenth – The Symphony of Fate: Psychodynamic Improvisation Therapy with a Music Therapy Student in Training.' In K.E. Bruscia (ed.), *Case Studies in Music Therapy*. Barcelona Publishers.

Schmid, J. (2014). 'Music therapy training courses in Europe.' Institut für Musik- und Bewegungserziehung sowie Musiktherapie Universität für Musik und darstellende Kunst Wien. Accessed on 29/11/21 at www.emtc-eu.com/european-surveys.

Stegemann, T., Schmidt, H.U., Fitzthum, E., & Timmermann, T. (eds) (2016). *Music Therapy Training Programmes in Europe: Theme and Variations*. Reichert Verlag.

Trondalen, G. (2016). 'Self-Care in Music Therapy: The Art of Balancing.' In J. Edwards (ed.), *Oxford Handbook of Music Therapy*. Oxford University Press.

Watson, T. (2005). 'Steering a path through change: Observations on the process of training.' *British Journal of Music Therapy, 19*(1), 9–15.

Willert, S. (2007). 'Psykologi som håndværk - psykologistudiet som håndværkeruddannelse? tre utopier og en brugervejledning [Psychology as a craft – the study of psychology as a craft education? Three utopias and a user guide].' In S. Brinkmann & L. Tanggaard (eds), *Psykologi: Forskning og profession [Psychology: Research and Profession]*. Hans Reitzels Forlag.

CHAPTER 2

Therapeutic Training in the Aalborg Music Therapy Programme

Charlotte Lindvang, Inge Nygaard Pedersen, & Bolette Daniels Beck

Therapeutic training embedded in an academic culture can benefit the learning processes and formation of the music therapist students in various ways. In this chapter we will introduce the specific background and curriculum of the music therapy programme at Aalborg University, Denmark, as an example of how therapeutic learning can be integrated into an academic programme. At first, we will present the historical background for this integrated programme, then we will introduce some of the theoretical learning principles that underpin the learning processes of the therapeutic track. Further, we will reflect on the role of the music in the music therapeutic training processes and finally elaborate on the ethical challenges connected to containing therapeutic processes within a university programme.

Historical background of the Aalborg music therapy programme

The music therapy programme in Aalborg was founded in 1982 as a four-year academic programme which was prolonged to a five-year, full-time programme in 1995. The pioneers who built the programme in Aalborg (Inge Nygaard Pedersen and Benedikte Barth Scheiby) both had a training background from the Mentorenkurs, Herdecke, Germany, in addition to being Masters in musicology. Mentorenkurs means a combination of being trained as a music therapist and as a future trainer in music therapy. It was a two-year full-time postgraduate programme. The heads of this Mentorenkurs, Professor Johannes Eschen (a trained music therapist in both Analytical Music Therapy and Nordoff/Robbins Music Therapy) and Dr Med Konrad Schilly (an anthroposophic psychiatrist at the Herdecke hospital where the programme was located), established a whole new programme structure, including training music therapy students in two distinctly separate music therapy approaches simultaneously. This was controversial at that time.

The two approaches were Analytical Music Therapy, as founded by Mary Priestley (Priestley, 1975, 1994), and Nordoff/Robbins Music Therapy, as founded by Paul Nordoff and Clive Robbins (1977). The pioneers (Mary Priestley, Clive Robbins, and Carol Robbins) were ongoing guest teachers at the Herdecke programme. Since the programme was a Mentorenkurs, the students were obliged to continually evaluate their training through 3–4 hours of weekly theoretical discussions in plenum. The intention of this intensive combination of training and programme evaluation was a first attempt to safeguard a high level of quality and a certain level of standardization of future European music therapy training programmes. The guest teachers were highly experienced and charismatic pioneers in clinical practice: Mary Priestley in mental health care and Clive and Carol Robbins in work with children suffering from developmental and communicative disturbances. The Herdecke programme integrated self-experience disciplines from Analytical Music Therapy (Group Music Therapy, Individual Music Therapy, Intertherapy, Psychodynamic Movement and Internship Supervision) and music training disciplines from Nordoff/Robbins Music Therapy (Clinical Improvisation, Improvisation Analysis) as weekly training disciplines.

For most students, the self-experience training specifically became very important and was the glue in finding a balance of being trained in two different approaches. The students were meant to integrate elements from both approaches, even if the pioneers of the approaches were not ready to communicate or share experiences mutually at that time. What the students learned through weekly theoretical discussions in plenum – in addition to everyday training in clinical practice and theory related to practice from two different approaches – was to clarify how each of the students personally would define art, music, health and pathology, therapy, and pedagogy in the future field of music therapy, and which theory of science they could resonate with. The pioneer teachers gave their answers to these questions during the training, except the question of theory of science. These answers were very different within the two approaches, and the students were faced with individual choices of ideas in all questions. Discussions on theory of science were facilitated by Eschen and Schilly to give the students a theoretical and philosophical overview of the different ideologies they were facing in the day-to-day training. Thus, it was not a programme where the students were intended to imitate their teachers but rather a programme of deep inspiration, which resonated with the statement of

Priestley in the first weekend she trained the students: 'Take from me what you can use and make it your own!' (Pedersen, personal notes, 1978). So, it was two very challenging and very exciting years for both the students and the teachers. Both Scheiby and Pedersen agreed that the self-experiential training integrated in a music therapy training programme was very fruitful. They could not imagine that this part of a training programme should be separated or excluded, no matter if the programme was at a Bachelor or a Master's level.

When the music therapy training programme was established at Aalborg University, Pedersen was its first employee in 1981. In preparing the programme, starting in 1982, she insisted on continuing this integration of a programme with equal weight on self-experience, musical training, and academic training, which was innovative and controversial for the university at that time. Scheiby strongly supported this idea; she was a teacher assistant until she had the second position in 1985. From the experiences in Herdecke, it was mainly the disciplines from Analytical Music Therapy that were transferred to the Aalborg programme, but clinical improvisation in a broader sense, with many different populations, was also included. It was the opinion of the two pioneers that all students would be best prepared for working in many different clinical areas through an integrated and broad-based programme, including therapeutic training with a focus on development of relational competences. To ensure that this kind of personal learning processes were performed in accordance with ethical criteria for university education, the programme was subject to a comprehensive evaluation by the Ministry of Education after six years of trial. The result was that the programme received full recognition and acceptance from the Ministry (FLUHU (EVM) Report, 1988). This approval gave the Aalborg programme favourable conditions in relation to implementation of therapeutic learning processes; for example, that students receive individual and group music therapy free of charge as a part of the training. At the same time this approval generated an ethical responsibility with regards to the implementation of the therapeutic subjects. Therapeutic processes are usually very personal and intimate, and a respectful understanding of the processes around the training and a high ethical awareness is necessary. The ethical concerns will be further elaborated later in this chapter, and throughout the book the authors will describe how the therapeutic disciplines are performed and handled with ethical care. It should be mentioned that specifically the employment of the late professor Tony Wigram in 1992 and Professor Lars Ole Bonde in 1995 added the needed balance in the equal weight of the three training tracks.

Concerning the balance between musical training and therapeutical training, we recognize what the educators in Vienna described regarding the development of their music therapy programme:

> The strong connection to psychotherapy is in particular influenced by self-conception of the second generation's music therapists as being 'therapists' – in contrast to being the doctor's musical auxiliaries. This paved the way for introduction of music therapy self-experience as a compulsory part of the curriculum in the 1990s. On the downside, the focus on psychotherapeutic methods and techniques led to a development where the music was at risk of fading into the background. Meanwhile, this tendency has levelled off, and the awareness of the importance of music as such in music therapy has risen again. (Stegemann & Fitzhum, 2016, p.31)

Since the music therapy programme started in Aalborg, Inge Nygaard Pedersen has continued to be engaged in the training programme, has shaped a number of experiential training subjects, and has developed and described the methodology and the theoretical understanding of self-experience as well as linked it to the work of the professional music therapists in numerous articles and book chapters (Pedersen, 1997, 1999, 2000, 2002, 2005, 2006, 2007a, 2007b, 2009), further as a co-author with Scheiby (1999) and Bonde and Wigram (Jacobsen, Pedersen, & Bonde, 2019; Wigram, Pedersen, & Bonde, 2002). Wigram developed a new therapy training subject, a group music therapy training format where the students learn by roleplaying; see Chapter 7 (Wigram, 1999). All the later trainers in the programme have contributed to and developed the original therapy training subjects. Lindvang has conducted research in music therapeutic learning processes (Lindvang, 2010, 2013).

Intertwining therapeutic, academic, and musical training

The recognition of the dynamic relationships that exist and develop in music therapy is the fulcrum for all types of music therapy methods that are taught at the programme in Aalborg. Basically, the aim is that the students develop a solid grounding and strength in their own being to expand the possibility to meet clients, users, or participants of all kinds. Further aims are that the students develop abilities to create relationships on different levels, according to the current needs of their future clients, and that the students develop a humility and awareness of their own limits and shortcomings.

The therapeutic experiences take place in a relational context with training-therapists, teachers, supervisors, and peers, which is of paramount importance for the learning processes. The culture of curiosity, reflection, and empathy in relation to the background, psychological functioning, and here-and-now experience of one another is considered as a basic ground. From there the trainers facilitate that the students build their music therapeutic competencies both in the specific therapeutic courses and in the study milieu, even though the tasks are very different in the many areas of learning. In the therapeutic training the students explore their own reactions and processes in music therapy, and especially in the group context, they also learn that their fellow students respond differently and have completely different processes. As Bruscia states, the most direct way for music therapists to learn the craft of music therapy is to experience it themselves. But therapy is not enough to become a good therapist – it is important that it is nested in an academic and educational culture (Bruscia, 2014). The embodied learning in the therapeutic track is important for the students' deeper understanding of psychological and philosophical theories, as well as it influencing the professional and personal development of musical and improvisational skills.

Through 40 years of teaching experiences and ongoing students' evaluations in the Aalborg programme, we see an overall advantage of integrating therapeutic training in the academic culture. The students' experiences from therapeutic processes grow together with the understanding of psychological and music therapeutic theories, as well as music therapy methodology and application. In this way the different kinds of learning processes inspire and fertilize each other. It is the coherence of the different subjects that together facilitate the students' preliminary professional identities. The intertwining of academic, musical, and therapeutic training from the very beginning of the educational process is one of the features of the Aalborg programme that distinguishes it from programmes or traditions where therapeutic training is a postgraduate or an advanced training process.

'Problem-based learning' at Aalborg University

Acknowledging the importance of how the therapeutic training is embedded in an academic and educational culture, we would like to present the specific overall learning principle of Aalborg University called 'problem-based learning'. In this tradition – which is applied at many universities in the world – a basic notion is that education is a lot more than acquiring knowledge, skills, and competences. It is also a process of formation, about how to relate to each other, and to the world; about how to use your knowledge, skills, and competences. Since Aalborg University was first established in 1974, all its university programmes have been based on problem-based learning (PBL) (Askehave *et al.,* 2015).

On all levels Aalborg University students work in groups applying problem-oriented methods in preparing independent projects of high academic standard based on authentic problems and questions within the area of their future profession. PBL provides the students with the possibility of developing their communication and cooperation competences as well as their abilities of working analytically and in an interdisciplinary way. The PBL learning principles go hand-in-hand with the overall intention of the music therapy training and we implement the PBL approach more or less in all subjects in our curriculum. The intention of PBL is that students understand (a part of) the world in a new way, a new light, or new perspective – it is a kind of learning that necessitates creative thinking, and such group work requires openness to experience and a willingness to engage in new ways of listening and playing together. Thus, PBL is a specific academic learning principle that fits well with the therapeutic track in the music therapy programme, with the aim of developing the students to be relationship-oriented in all aspects of their professional life and at the same time self-reliant, independent, and rooted in a realistic perception of conditions and contexts (Kolmos, Fink, & Krogh, 2004; Lindvang & Beck, 2015; Savery, 2006). In the education of music therapists, it is no less than crucial that the students build up an analytical, critical, and ethical consciousness and a strong self-agency to be able to take responsibility and make choices later in future work situations of high complexity.

Learning characteristics of apprenticeship

The academic training in the university is mostly a 'top-down' type of learning with lectures from the professors and reading relevant books and articles. The PBL tradition in Aalborg mentioned above facilitates that the students are also working independently, and their learning can also be characterized as a 'bottom-up' process through experience with authentic problems in their projects. Music therapy is not a traditional university area of study, in the sense that much learning originates from the student's personal and bodily experiences and a part of the knowledge acquired is 'tacit knowledge' (Polanyi, 1966). Basically, the music therapy education in Aalborg can be described as a combination of academic- and profession-based training (Willert, 2007). As the Danish philosopher Steen Wackerhausen (2004, 2005) has pointed out, in some professions the learning needs to be closely connected to personal development because the professional knowledge is a part of the person that will be unfolded later as participation in concrete clinical situations.

Following this line of thought the learning principles of the therapeutic track find support in another kind of learning paradigm than a traditional university academic paradigm (Pedersen, 1987).

Learning can be defined as a social practice which is situated in a specific context and culture. The rationale to build in an authentic music therapeutic practice as part of the training can be found in the learning principles from apprenticeship.

Based on Lave and Wenger's theory (1991) of situated learning and communities of practice, the late professor in psychology Steinar Kvale summarized the main characteristics of apprenticeship as follows: 1) 'Joint practice' which happens in a social organization, where the apprentice is slowly moving from peripheral participation to being a full member of the profession. 2) 'Acquisition of a professional identity' that happens gradually as the apprentice moves step by step towards the mastery of the profession. 3) 'Learning without formal teaching' that implies that the apprentice does a lot of observation and imitation of what the assistants and the master are doing. 4) 'Evaluation through practice': the apprentice continuously receives feedback, mainly in the concrete work situation, e.g., through the reactions from customers or co-workers (Nielsen & Kvale, 2004). These characteristics are also found in the act of implementing personal therapy processes in the music therapy programme in Aalborg.

1) 'Joint practice'

The music therapy milieu in Denmark is very small and, as mentioned, it has only one training programme and one organization for all professional music therapists and students. These two factors mean that the students are from the very beginning of their studies a part of the music therapy community, and they learn from participating in different events together with older students and newly educated and experienced professionals. At the onset of the therapeutic training, it is usual that the students participate peripherally or with a certain amount of caution. Gradually, during the years of training, they grow into the culture of self-inquiry and relational awareness and get deeper involved in a 'joint process' of learning and practice.

2) 'Acquisition of a professional identity'

The music therapy programme is clearly built with elements or building blocks, and the training develops progressively, from the students being in the client role to the students alternating between the client role and the therapist role in systematic training. Finally, the student has a four-month internship in the field, taking responsibility for music therapy interventions under supervision.

The culture of getting supervision thus becomes an integrated part of the professional music therapist identity.

3) 'Learning without formal teaching'

Part of the music therapy students' learning takes place without formal teaching during the therapy training courses. They observe how the training therapists listen, take initiatives, and respond to and guide the processes both in and outside the music, and they observe and empathize with their fellow students when they share their thoughts and feelings. They also listen to the supervisors and learn from the way they question and guide their fellow students.

4) 'Evaluation through practice'

The music therapy students get thorough feedback during all subjects of all three training tracks (academic, music, therapeutic). However, the feedback on the therapeutic processes is special; the students receive direct and personal feedback from their peers, the training therapists, the clients they meet in practicum, and their supervisors. In the close relational interplay, the student will experience how they influence others and how they are perceived and understood by others.

Lave and Wenger's theory (1991) focuses on apprenticeship learning as situated and implies that knowledge and learning are relational phenomena created in the joint practice and related to the concrete life and the specific culture that the participants are a part of. It is also possible to define apprenticeship as a more person-centred approach where the specific relationship between master and apprentice is the focus. In this context the master makes the profession visible to the apprentice through reflective practice (Dreyfus & Dreyfus, 2004; Schön, 1983). Both perspectives of apprenticeship learning build on the common principle of learning through practical experiences – earlier mentioned as a 'bottom-up' type of learning – characterized by entering and identifying with an established practice, and gradually making it one's own profession.

Learning through practice is an example of unconscious intelligence in relation to learning processes. There is a tacit aspect of an apprenticeship; one does not always know with the rational mind what one is learning in a given situation (Vedfelt, 2018). 'We can know more than we can tell' is a famous phrase from Michael Polanyi, a Hungarian-British chemist and philosopher who conceptualized the tacit dimension of learning and scientific knowledge (Polanyi, 1966, p.8). The music therapy students at the Master's level often express that now they see that a part of their former training was happening on a deep level of consciousness, which was ineffable for the person to express earlier in the training. In the Aalborg model elements of apprenticeship are indispensable to the training of future therapists and it is acknowledged that a part of the forming and learning – especially in the therapeutic training – is rooted in the body and is happening tacitly outside our conscious mind. Polanyi expresses it like this: '...tacit knowing...will be shown to form the bridge between the higher creative powers of man and the bodily processes which are prominent in the operations of perception' (Polanyi, 1966, p.7).

As mentioned above, one aspect of apprenticeship learning happens through close interaction with the master, in this context the training therapist, who is a kind of role model. A close relationship is developed between the training therapist and the student, and crucial learning can happen when the therapist and student succeed in repairing a conflict or misunderstanding which has emerged in the therapeutic relationship. It also happens that a student gets frustrated by their own shortcomings and limitations, which may be a natural and important part of a developmental process and not something to avoid or eliminate. The students explore themselves in new ways and they have the possibility of being inspired and enriched by the developmental processes of their peers. When students allow something that they did not know or were not aware of before to enter their consciousness, this paves the way for new learning. Learning will challenge the students' habitual relational patterns as well as the knowledge and prejudices they have in advance.

Embodied learning

In music therapy and many other social or health professions, the knowledge inherent in the professional's competence is not only mental or intellectual knowledge; it is a bodily knowledge as well (Wackerhausen, 2004, 2005), and therapeutic training involves the body. The basic feeling of self is rooted in the sensation of the body at a preverbal level (Stern, 2000, 2010) and therefore the body speaks a language before language – which is also called implicit knowledge. Our body is the centre of our being that connects us with others and the world around us; we inhale, and exhale, impression and expression happen in a constant exchange. It is a basic intention of the therapeutic training in Aalborg to support the student's development of a solid mindfulness towards bodily sensations. This kind of consciousness raises the awareness of one's own being as well as the ability to stay sensitive in a relationship. The work leads to a self-regulating capacity, which is of paramount importance to stay grounded while going with the flow of a therapeutic process. The bodily awareness also expands the capability to listen to the 'tacit information'. It requires a lot of training to be able to listen to the impulses, sensations, and reactions of the body in a way that can guide you in the therapeutic process. Awareness of body and voice is an important part of students' learning and formation process from the beginning of the training. The sound of our voice holds information about who we are and how we feel in the moment (see Chapter 6). These topics will be further elaborated in Chapter 3, in the discussions about listening perspectives and countertransference.

The role of music in the therapeutic training at Aalborg University

For music therapists, music is an important part of the communication in therapy that differs from the verbal exchanges. Music therapists are in general experts in the art of listening (Pedersen, 2000) and in meeting the client and creating a relationship through different musical experiences. An overall understanding of music in music therapy and in the therapeutic training will be elaborated in two different models below.

It is interesting that music has been used as a therapeutic tool since antiquity and maybe even further back in history. Ancient healing rituals including sound and music have survived in many cultures (Bonde, 2019), and practices of music listening to live music in ancient hospitals were used in Arab and Middle Eastern societies as early as 900 (Tucek, 2003). In the middle of the 20th century, the first pioneers of modern music therapy began to use music to assist injured soldiers from World Wars I and II and to work with children with disabilities. The pioneers realized that music could comfort, rehabilitate, and develop human beings on many different levels (Byers, 2016).

In Europe, one of the pioneers in music therapy was Juliette Alvin, from Britain, who worked with different client groups, and emphasized that music, body, and feelings are closely connected. Alvin said: 'The clinical approach to music is therapeutic in the full meaning of the term. It works in depth, applied to the medical or psychological treatment of physical, mental or emotional disorder' (Alvin, 1966, p.109). Wigram described her essential ideas of the importance of bodily reactions in music therapy: 'Music therapists need to understand human physiology and the way the body reacts to music and sound to fully grasp the influence of music within music therapy' (Wigram in Jacobsen *et al.* 2019, p.92). Alvin also emphasized that one 'needs to link the psychological effect of music with the physical effect', and she used the examples of shamans and witch doctors from primitive cultures to illustrate this idea (Alvin, 1966, p.192). Likewise, Bonde, in his book *Musik og menneske [Music and Man]*, emphasized that 'emotional effect from the music causes a bodily reaction or experience and every physical effect from sounds unavoidably produces a psychological response' (Bonde, 2009, p.68, our translation). Other music therapists have described music as a symbolic expression of the unconscious, and we will elaborate on this issue in Chapter 3. Music plays an indispensable role in the therapeutic training of music therapists: Through embodied experiential training the students gradually get to know the music therapeutic tools; they develop their listening skills and build trust in the power of music and the processes of music therapy (Lindvang, 2011). To exemplify the significance of the role of the music from the students' perspective, we will include some quotes from a study in which students were interviewed about their therapeutic learning processes (Lindvang, 2010). One music therapy student experienced music as being extremely important in the therapeutic training because the music made space for her to express herself and her different moods in situations where she otherwise would get stuck (Lindvang, 2010). Another student expressed: 'It has to be experienced, I think – you have to experience these therapeutic processes in the body together with the music, yourself, to really understand it...' (Lindvang, 2011, p.142, our translation).

In order to ethically apply music therapy with clients later on, it is important that music therapy students experience music as the means of expression and communication and experience sensorial or emotional transformation through the implicit musical being, acting, and relationship. Through self-experiences in the role of student-client, the students have the chance to learn how music can be the transformational vehicle in the therapeutic process. One student expressed his deepened understanding like this: 'Later the therapist made me aware of how interesting it was in this specific session that the music was the agent, it was the music that worked for me, and it was very interesting to discover this in the context of music therapy training' (Lindvang, 2010, p.204).

During the years of training the students develop their relationship with music and this may include a process of unlearning. The student sometimes needs to revitalize or reorganize their conception of and approach to music. Music is a part of the culture and historical context one belongs to; music is closely connected to memory; and music can be a marker of individual and/or subgroup identity. The students need to be conscious about their own musical history and how their music preferences developed – and they need to learn to be open to the musical taste and style of people from different cultures, places, and historical times. To be able to play with, accept, and contain different kinds of music is a very important prerequisite for their future clinical work, where they must adapt to many different client groups. Some clients might have damaged nervous systems and might need a slower tempo or a lower volume than would be natural for the student. Some clients might come from other cultures with very different music traditions or might need music from a time or genre different from the therapist's own preferred or well-known music styles. Through self-experience – as well as through musical training and practice as a part of the music track – the future music therapist can develop an adaptability to meet 'the other' both musically and personally.

Two models of understanding music

Here we will present two different models to illustrate how we understand the levels and areas of music in music therapy practice as well as in the training therapy.

In the discipline of music and psychology the understanding of music is divided into different levels in order to obtain an understanding of music and to define the meaning of music.

In a theoretical model from the Norwegian music therapist Even Ruud (1990, 1998, 2001), later unfolded by Bonde (2009), four levels with corresponding properties and effects of music are presented. These four levels are: 1) a level of physiology, 2) a level of syntax, 3) a level of semantics, and 4) a level of pragmatics (Jacobsen *et al.*, 2019, pp.34–35).

Table 2.1: Four levels of music with corresponding properties and effects (Bonde, 2009)

Level	Music	Focus	Effects
1. Physiology	Music is sound	The physical and psychoacoustic properties of music	…as vibrations/on the body: resonance, movement, vitality forms
2. Syntax	Music is language/ structure	Music and syntax: rules and generative principles	…as aesthetic phenomenon: experience of stylistic coherence and beauty
3. Semantics	Music is language/ meaning	Music and meaning: sources and types of meaning	…as existential and spiritual phenomenon: experience of mood, relevance, meaning
4. Pragmatics	Music is interaction	Musicking: music as a process, an activity	…as social and cultural phenomenon: play, ritual, community

1. Music is sound

At level one music is sound, a physiological phenomenon, which has an influence on our body related to the quality and effect of the sound and the current state of the body. This level is always active since the body is impossible to isolate from the sound environment, and the students in training therapy will accumulate many experiences of how their body is an ever-present gestalt in music therapy. This level relates to the neurobiological and neuroaffective understanding of the human being, which will be further presented in Chapter 3.

2. Music is language/structure

At level two music is understood as a language with its own 'grammar' and its own specific formation of meaning. At this level we need to know the 'codes' to describe the structure and to categorize the music. As a music therapy student, the development of an ability to tune into a specific kind of aesthetics or a specific structure of interactional pattern is a kind of syntactical level of music that needs to be trained in musical as well as therapeutic subjects in the curriculum.

3. Music is language/meaning

At level three the music is seen from a semantic perspective. The focus is on the semantic meaning, which is the personal meaning that you attribute to the music. This level is of high importance for the student-clients who will investigate how music touches and moves them emotionally and existentially. On this level the students reach a recognition of music as related to identity formation and feeling of self (Ruud, 2013). When students become aware through the personal processes in group therapy that the understanding of the meaning of the music is local and uniquely connected to each participant and to the context, they learn something important about music and receptive music therapy: A specific piece of music will never have exactly the same influence on different listeners. Listening is a subjective process, and the interaction between the music and the listener is essential for the results (Hannibal, Lund, & Bonde, 2013; Schou, Pedersen, & Bonde, 2011). Further, it is a common feature that students confront an *existential level* during the training therapy, for example deep fear or feelings of loneliness that may emerge through the musical interaction or music listening (Yalom, 2003). Death may also emerge as a theme when students share how it feels to lose a close relative. When students share for example a traumatic event with the therapist or the group, it is possible to use the music to meet and contain the student – and thereby reach an existential level of support that transcends the possibilities we have with spoken words (see Vignette 3 in Chapter 3). Music is also the agent that sometimes opens the student to an experience at a *spiritual level* in the therapeutic training. For example, it happens that students have strong and pivotal moments of unspeakable beauty in the music. Then tears may fall, or goosebumps spread all over – again connected to the bodily reaction the student delivers a level of remarkable presence here-and-now.

4. Music is interaction

At level four music is pragmatic, which means that music is understood as inter-action, and the focus is the music we take part in together (music = musicking). The music is a social phenomenon, expressed in humans playing together, per-forming together, conducting rituals together in the music. As a music therapy student, this is an important focal point to investigate in the training therapy since most music therapy practices have a pragmatic and interactional intention.

As formulated by Bonde (2009), the four levels should not be seen as isolated from each other and a student can obviously experience the music as musicking, as a social event, and at the same time recognize a specific aesthetic quality which may – in the next moment – lead to a spiritual opening. In the same way, a student may experience a musical improvisation as a strong experience on the semantic level in the beginning, where the purpose of the music is to investigate a childhood memory. While having a clear sense of the specific memory, the music gradually becomes more grounded in a steady pulse, and the student is now absorbed for a while in the experience of music as a physiological phenomenon and senses the warmth and strength in the feet. The meaning of the music is emerging in the complex and dynamic oscillation between the levels and those who participate.

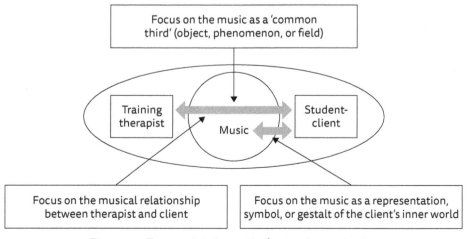

Figure 2.1: Focus points in music therapy improvisation
(Hannibal, 2007, authors' translation and modification)

Ruud's model might be supplemented by Hannibal's model (2007) which is more directly related to music therapy practice with a focus on improvisational music therapy. In the following we will apply this model to illustrate music therapeutic learning processes. Hannibal has suggested that the role of the music in music therapy improvisation can either be 1) music as a concrete phenomenon outside the participants, that they can relate to and share, 2) music as a relational area where the participants can express themselves and investigate their contact, or 3) music as a symbolic or metaphoric representation of the inner world, often facilitated by referential playing rules, like for example 'my inner child', 'a volcano', or 'a peaceful meadow'.

An example of the first level, where music is a concrete phenomenon to explore, could be that the student – who just started the course in individual training therapy – would like to improvise a kind of music that has a refreshing effect. The student tries out different instruments, the therapist does the same. Here the joint attention is the concrete phenomenon of instruments and of music, which can be explored and discussed even during the improvisation. The training therapist and the student-client can attribute different experiences and meanings to the music and thereby start to build a therapeutic relationship without being too close to begin with.

On the second level, music constitutes a relational space. An example from therapeutic training could be a group of students who investigate their level of contact in a musical improvisation. Here the students express themselves simultaneously in the music and may experience different aspects of being heard by the others or not, being a part of the group or not, etc. Music can be a powerful social intervention because music has the ability to create bridges between people who thought they were alone. The students are basically very motivated to play music together in the group training therapy. But it is at the same time a vulnerable arena for some of them to improvise freely together – at least in the beginning – since their former experiences of being a member of a group may be of a difficult character (transference phenomena are dynamically in play; see Chapter 3). The students most likely have different experiences which can be explored in music and further investigated in a verbal reflection if that is relevant in the context. Later in the process of the therapeutic training, students learn how to focus on the relation in the music and, for example, create holding with music, with a combination of an attitude of attention and care and the use of musical parameters such as a sustained pulse or repeated chord progressions and simultaneously they can match and imitate the music of the client (Wigram, 1999). (See Chapter 10 about Intertherapy and Chapter 7 on Clinical Group Music Therapy Skills.)

Concerning the third musical focus area, the music expression refers to music as an internal representation. It is a musical translation and interpretation of the student-client's inner landscape. It may be a process where the student-client expresses, for example, a perception of a strong body tension or emotion. Here a referential play rule like 'play the sense of your body tension just now' may facilitate that the student allows themselves to investigate the sensation or quality. The expression in the music helps to make the inner landscape audible and this experience can release a lot of tension in the moment. The process of expression may also facilitate recognition and understanding of the reasons behind the pattern of holding back emotionally and clarify the implicit content or meaning of the tension or emotion related to the personal history of the student-client.

Students' experiences in the music may be of a bodily, psychological, social, existential, and spiritual nature. As mentioned earlier, the different levels are difficult to separate in the real world of interaction; usually one level constitutes the figure and other levels the background, and it is a natural part of a therapeutic process that what is in front of the awareness may change as the process unfolds.

Communicative musicality

In the music therapy part of training, the students' relationship to music will adapt to a wider understanding of music than normally used in music education and society. Music therapy generally includes a wide array of musical forms and styles, but also an understanding of music as part of the communication between human beings. Thus, in this context 'musicality' is not understood as a special talent for playing music.

Infant researchers have found that the early interactive communication between caregiver and infant is characterized by musical qualities and elements. Professor of child psychology Colwyn Trevarthen and professor of music and psychoacoustics Stephen Malloch video-analysed infant-directed speech and found that the reciprocal preverbal dialogues had musical qualities, an innate 'communicative musicality' (Malloch & Trevarthen, 2009). The infants seemed to initiate, orchestrate, and maintain togetherness, communication, and pleasure with the caregiver in small narratives, building up to dynamic peaks with a nuanced sense of intertiming, suspense, tension, and release. 'Communicative musicality consists of the elements *pulse*, *quality* and *narrative*; those attributes of human communication, which are particularly exploited in music, that allow coordinated companionship to arise' (Malloch, 1999, p.32).

The infant research has provided extremely relevant knowledge to the music therapy profession with the concept and theory of communicative musicality as fundamental in all human interaction, regardless of culture, age, and verbal language skills (Holck, 2019, p.104).

This synchronized dance or 'dialogue' of small sounds and syllables between caregiver and infant, also called fatherese/motherese, seems to be a language that develops prior to the language that underlies the prosody and musicality of verbal speech, as well as body communication. The sense of timing, humour, and attunement in communicative musicality that is unfolded in the early part of life in the form of 'proto-narrative envelopes' (Stern, 1995) precedes the later development of verbal language and body language. While expressing and attuning to each other's mood and internal states in reciprocal interplay, nuances in micromovements, mimics, gestures, and tone of voice are shared. Hence, communicative musicality can be seen both as a language before language, but also as a basic part of all human communication – the musicality of human interplay.

It is important in training and supervised feedback to deliver embodied communicative signals to the music therapy students in a clear and sometimes augmented way. This can be a preparation for them to be able to engage future clients in the contact of musical dialogue or interplay, and also to work with clients who have challenged sensory systems and/or reduced communicative abilities.

Acknowledging communicative musicality as an important fulcrum in music therapy leads to the need for training the future therapist to possess: 1) a broad and spacious understanding of music that also embraces the level of communicative musicality, and 2) enough sensitivity and professional presence to engage and meet clients on pre-linguistic levels of communication. It is important that music therapy students have full access to the resources in their own communicative musicality, as well as that they build an awareness and consciousness about this basic level of human communication. During experiences of being in the client position, many students undergo a process of becoming more playful and able to build creatively on whatever happens in the musical interaction. For some students it is essential to experience that music therapy can help them to receive care and protection and to be mirrored through sounds and music. It is also an important issue for some students to let go of performing perfectly on their instrument or focusing on right and wrong in the musical interaction. In relation to the first model (see Table 2.1), some music therapy students need to loosen up the attention on the syntactic level to broaden their view on music and become more open to the semantic and pragmatic level which can sometimes be of a more or less chaotic character.

Through therapeutic processes, the students gradually fine-tune their sensitivity and listening skills and their awareness of and ability to act upon even the smallest nuance or change in the music. At the same time, the therapeutic process can give students a chance to expand their ability to stay present in the music also when they experience the sound or the music as unstructured, unpleasant, or boring. Developing sensitive listening skills and the ability to be present in chaos are different but equally important learning processes. Sometimes seemingly chaotic music contains important information. Later when the students are entering the role as student-therapist, the practical experiences and the supervision will further develop their competence and ability to analyse and understand what is going on in the music in music therapy.

Resonance

In continuation of our attempt to identify the role of music in the therapeutic training, we believe it is relevant to include the concept of resonance, which has been widely applied recently in many contexts such as in psychotherapy, sociology, and learning areas. Resonance is an acoustic/musical phenomenon that implies two systems relating to each other, for example two tuning forks with the same pitch that start to sound together when one of them is played. Resonance is also a psychological and social phenomenon. Then the re-sounding or oscillation can be expressed by the German synonym *Mitschwingung*, which may be directly translated as 'sympathetic vibration' between humans. Resonance may also refer to the phenomena of infectious emotional atmosphere in a group of people. Thus, the phenomena occur when a system/a person is met or affected by a frequency that matches one of its own frequencies – in a psychological sense one person may be affected by another person's mental mood when this in one way or another matches some of the person's own psychological experiences, feelings, or mood. Both types of resonance are involved in music therapy practice since we work in a field of people meeting and sharing in or through music. But we cannot in any simple way control the field of resonance between participants in therapy in the same way as when making, in a controlled manner, a tuning fork oscillate at specific frequencies. In music therapy, resonance is of course a complex phenomenon (Lindvang & Beck, 2015; Lindvang *et al.*, 2018; Rosa, 2019a). Langenberg used the term 'resonance' back in 1993 to illustrate that music can express something that the listener not only hears but resonates with, and she used the concept 'resonator function' to describe the personal instrument of relating and understanding by which the therapist resonates to the latent content of the music in therapy (Langenberg & Frommer, 1993).

Resonance, as a psychological phenomenon and concept used in a therapeutic context, has the interpersonal arena as subject area, and, in our understanding, resonance is a relevant term to use in music therapy and in our therapeutic training of students since it covers a broad spectrum of dynamics in our social field of learning. For example, it is essential that the students experience and realize when, how, and why they resonate with each other. The use of the concept in a therapeutic context is furthermore supported by the current knowledge about how human nervous systems are interrelated and are constantly affecting each other (see Chapters 3 and 5). In our modern understanding of psychodynamic theory, we acknowledge the neurological dimensions of human connectedness (Cozolino, 2002), and the relational and interpersonal phenomena is at the centre of our attention rather than the individual and intrapsychic gestalt alone (Binder *et al.*, 2006), and following this we do find the concept of resonance extremely relevant and applicable. The German sociologist Hartmut Rosa (2019a, 2019b) states that resonance is not an emotional state as such, it is a mode of relation that is neutral in respect to specific emotional content. Resonance has, in Rosa's understanding, to do with sensing the body and sensing and recognizing that expressions make impressions. It resembles a mode of relation that we seek to build in our students through therapeutic training; it is an approach of openness towards the other, and a readiness to meet the other (Lindvang, 2011). This implies that resonance is not to be understood as the opposite of dissonance – dissonance may be a part of a resonant field of learning, since a developmental environment is not without dissonance and conflicts. But we need to listen, to open our senses to what is there and to what is needed.

In the theoretical model from Ruud and Bonde mentioned above (see Table 2.1), four levels of music were presented. It is possible to combine the four levels (physiology, syntax, semantics, and pragmatics) with the concept of resonance, to illustrate the complexity of the phenomenon.

At the physiological level, resonance corresponds to the body's reactions to the pulse, the tempo, the frequencies, and the timbre of the music, for example when we can't help but go in tune with the tambour corps playing in the city streets (entrainment), or when a specific timbre gives us goosebumps. At the level of syntax, resonance occurs when we recognize the music, for example we know how the melody goes, or resonance may happen when we meet foreign music with curiosity and openness. At the semantic level, resonance can be described as a friendship between the music and the listener; the music holds a deep meaning, for example the listener may feel contained and protected by the music, or the music may facilitate a spiritual connectedness to something bigger than our rational mind can verbalize. When people play music together resonance develops at the pragmatic level; the participants listen to each other, follow each other, and share the lived experience with each other. As we acknowledge all four levels of resonance to be important in music therapy, they are also important to integrate in a music therapeutic learning process.

To reach the mode of being resonant demands – according to the Aalborg training programme – a solid self-experiential training where personal release of control and building of trust in the therapeutic process is necessary, as well as becoming aware of one's own vulnerable or blind spots. As Rosa states: 'To shift into a mode of resonance requires that we take the risk to make ourselves vulnerable. It conceptually requires that we let ourselves be touched, and even transformed, in a non-predictable and non-controllable way' (Rosa, 2019b, p.50). Further, it is important that students build empowerment and solid personal boundaries, since resonance demands that both parts are bounded gestalts – a resonant relationship requires that both can speak in their own voice, while also remaining open enough to be reached or touched by each other (Rosa, 2019a).

Overall, resonance is a broad and overarching concept and phenomenon, that we understand as referring to a mode of relation and to those waves which occur between humans on an unconscious level:

> Therapists...have to develop an openness to, and respect for, feelings and experiences that are quite unlike their own. The greater freedom they have to resonate to the unfamiliar 'keys' or dissonant 'harmonies' of others, the more it will enhance their receptivity to these unconsciously interactive cues that are often central to an understanding of patients. (Casement, 2014, p.83)

This prompts us to suggest the term 'resonant learning' to underline that the therapeutic training is embedded in the complex psychological processes of human relationships. This idea has already emerged in Lindvang's PhD thesis, titled 'A Field of Resonant Learning' (2010), in which the author focused on the students' experiences of their learning processes in the therapeutic track.

Ethical concerns around implementing therapeutic training in the curriculum

All the different learning processes presented above in this chapter demand a very high level of ethical consciousness.

The Aalborg programme provides a 'Handbook for students', which contains a lot of practical information and overall descriptions of the three tracks that constitute the education. It is emphasized that the personal therapeutic processes can be very demanding, especially because they are combined with intensive academic and musical training. In the literature it is reported that personal therapy can be a burden for the student-therapist (Macran & Shapiro, 1998), and many music therapy students in Aalborg sometimes find it challenging to contain fully the personal processes that have started in combination with studying theory, attending lectures, and training musical skills. On the other hand, students also find that the therapeutic space that is provided during their training is soothing and a personal support that makes it possible to manage the demands in other courses (Lindvang, 2010).

The students receive solid training through the alternations between the different ways of learning and expressing, which they will most likely benefit from in their future work as music therapists. Often employment requires that the therapist can navigate between different roles and tasks.

Boundaries

The issue of how the students manage to uphold boundaries between self-experience in group therapy and other parallel subjects and activities in the BA training is an important ethical concern. Since the self-experience training opens the student to personal and potential unconscious dynamics in the individual as well as between the students, it is a challenge to safeguard the boundaries around the therapeutic processes. The students must develop awareness of the different learning spaces with different kinds of learning objectives and learn to move between many different ways of being together. In Lindvang's study (2010), the boundary issue emerged in the interviews of students – exactly as an issue about the challenge inherent in changing roles, that you have to move in and out of as a student in music therapy.

The same holds for the educators, who are music therapists in other contexts: when they give lectures or lead an experience, they enter a role as teacher of the students and never as a therapist.

The process of learning to respect the different settings requires ongoing attention from the training therapists, teachers, and supervisors who lead the training, especially for the training therapist in the first semester, where everything is new to the students. Many of the students have never entered therapy before and therefore do not yet understand how intense an experience it can be and how valuable such experiences can be for developing an identity as a music therapist. It is also important that the programme helps make the boundary clear around therapy courses through guidelines that include the duty of confidentiality.

In line with the students, training therapists have a duty of confidentiality as well. However, if the training therapist deems it appropriate to pass on information regarding personal matters to the team and/or the chairperson of the study board, the training therapist will dialogue with the specific student, and they will find out how to pass on the sensitive information. This could happen, for example, in a situation where a student has tremendous personal problems and needs more support to be able to stay in the music therapy programme or needs advice concerning their future music therapy work.

All teachers who are training disciplines in the therapeutic track are part of the teaching team at the programme, which means that all parts of the students' training courses are taught by the same staff group. This choice calls for many ethical considerations, but it also secures close collaboration and coherence across the disciplines in the programme, and thereby high-quality standards of the training therapy.

We acknowledge that the process of formation that the student goes through is a result of learning across the many different courses, and the programme cannot and should not limit the student's developmental processes to the therapeutic space. The communicative culture of the whole programme may also influence the student's gradual move towards being a professional and ethically aware music therapist.

Supervision and parallel processes

We consider that the awareness of the therapist can be developed through a lifelong tuning and learning process. This can be supported and facilitated by continuous supervision. It is plausible that therapy as a part of training prepares for supervision in music therapeutic practice. One student who participated in Lindvang's study on students' learning processes stated: 'I don't think I could have been in meaningful supervision without being in training therapy' (Lindvang, 2010, p.53).

We also consider that the awareness of music therapy educators can be developed through a lifelong tuning- and learning process. To be part of a milieu where the experiential training is an integrated part calls for the educators to facilitate a culture where dynamic processes among colleagues are transparent and are taken care of. The team of educators need to investigate time and attention concerning the possible parallel processes (see Chapter 3) that may happen between students and teachers, and we need to be aware of the possible influences from organizational layers on the everyday life in the music therapy milieu. This means that sometimes the team of educators need supervision just as students do as part of their learning process. Seen from a family perspective, you cannot facilitate growth for children in a dysfunctional family. Our intention here is also to teach the students that music therapy work with future clients cannot be understood as a process detached from the institution or organization the clients are attending or living in.

Negative experiences

In a qualitative study by Grimmer and Tribe (2001) a group of recently qualified and trainee counselling psychologists was interviewed about the impact of mandatory personal therapy on their professional development. One of the four core categories of experience was about the development of empathy or resonating capacity through being in the client's position, but they also reported negative experiences from being in the client position. Several mentioned the experience of therapeutic interventions which they endeavoured not to replicate in their own practices.

Lindvang (2010) distributed a questionnaire to Danish music therapists to investigate how they evaluate the influence of their earlier self-experiential training on their current clinical competencies. Considering the qualitative comments given by respondents, only a few described negative experiences in relation to self-experience as a part of the programme. But the comments do point out and remind us that mistakes and inappropriate or insensitive interventions may happen where people interact – even in a therapeutic and educational setting with high ethical standards. Lindvang's interviews among students also revealed that some students had negative experiences during the therapeutic processes. One student reflected that the outcome of this was a deeper learning. Even though painful and negative experiences may be a part of many developmental processes in therapy, reported negative experiences should always cause reflection about ethics and responsibility around our educational practice (Lindvang, 2010).

The therapeutic training is mandatory

An ethical concern in relation to mandatory therapy in the music therapy training programme is that the student must follow the timing and progression of the therapeutic courses without consideration of personal needs. It is possible for a student to apply for a leave of absence due to personal reasons. But it is not possible to continue other parts of the training programme without the elements of therapeutic training.

A further issue that we are aware of is the fact that the possible uncovering of difficult material through the self-experience process may reduce effective participation of the student in other areas of the programme. If that happens the student is usually offered support to find a balanced effort between the tasks and challenges of the different areas of training.

The fact that we have implemented training therapy in our curriculum does not exclude the possibility, and in some cases the necessity, of recommending more intensive personal therapeutic work outside the training course. After all, there is a limited number of therapy sessions, which is supposed to develop the student's presence, awareness, and relational capacity as well as reflective competencies, but which is not in all cases able to heal the possible deeper personal wounds or traumas (see Chapter 3). Personal therapy as part of the training prepares the trainee therapist to be able to receive support from supervision and from further therapy when needed. In that sense the therapeutic track ensures or develops prerequisites in relation to a future ethical and self-caring attitude of the music therapist.

Evaluation

A third ethical dilemma concerning mandatory training therapy as a part of the training is that students must be evaluated due to requirements from the Ministry of Education to implement a certain number of exams in the curriculum. The student's participation in several of the subjects in the therapeutic track is completed with a written paper (5–8 pages) in which the student describes and reflects upon their process during the course. The examination is not done by the therapist but by someone outside the university. The grading (passed/not passed) is not an assessment of how well the student progressed during the personal process in therapy or other kind of evaluation of the content, but of the level of reflections presented in the paper. It is up to the students to determine what they include in the paper and how they synthesize their process. In this way the music therapy programme lives up to the formal requirements while at the same time letting the process stay confidential (Lindvang, 2010). It is our experience that students often find it a great learning process to go through their notes, drawings, summaries, videos, etc. to get an overview and gather the process into a coherent and meaningful narrative.

It can be a difficult matter when an educator is acting both as a training therapist and a teacher in other subjects (Payne, 2002). In the Aalborg programme this happens once in a while, and we are aware of the ethical dilemmas that may occur in such situations. In our curriculum it is defined that a training therapist cannot be an examiner in relation to the students. This is important because it prevents the role of a supportive training therapist to be mixed up with the role as an examiner – so that the student does not end up in a vulnerable situation where the personal knowledge of their life story and current issues are interfering with the professional judgement of academic or musical performance. When it happens that a former training therapist is a teacher in a small and limited subject on the Master's level, or the students choose a former training therapist as supervisor for the Master's thesis, the change of roles is always debated and clarified.

Ethical considerations are an indispensable foundation for educational practice which should be at the forefront of our consciousness and not left as a status of an appendix.

In each chapter of this book the authors will unfold the ethical questions and concerns in a concrete connection to the specific learning processes in focus.

An overview of the curriculum in Aalborg

The therapeutic track is run in eight out of 10 semesters and in three periods of practicum that are followed closely by supervisors. The students participate in both individual and group therapy and they are working with active as well as receptive music therapy methods during their self-experience in the therapeutic track.

In Table 2.2, the courses belonging to the therapy track can be seen together with the music and theory tracks.

The subjects are categorized in the three tracks, but as described above many of them have elements of therapy, music, and theory instruction included. The courses in the therapy track, which are directly related to self-experience and therapist training, are structured as a sequential process with increasing integration, reflexivity, and complexity during the five years of training. Under each of the courses in the therapy track, there is a note of the chapter in which the course is described in further detail (Chapters 5–12).

Table 2.2: Overview of music therapy courses

Year	Bachelor						Master's			
	First year		Second year		Third year		Fourth year		Fifth year	
Semester	1	2	3	4	5	6	7/1	8/2	9/3	10/4
Therapy track	Training Therapy: Group Therapy 1 (Ch. 5) Clinical Body and Voice Work (Ch. 4, 6)	Training Therapy: Group Therapy 2 (Ch. 5) Internship Observation (4 weeks)	Training Therapy: Group Therapy 3 (Ch. 5)		Clinical Group Music Therapy Skills 1 (Ch. 7) Clinical Body and Voice Work (Ch. 4, 6)	Clinical Group Music Therapy Skills 2 (Ch. 7) Internship (1 day in 12 weeks) Group Supervision of Clinical Music Therapy (Ch. 12)	Training Therapy: Individual Therapy (Ch. 8) Therapeutic Psychoanalytic Music Leading (Ch. 9)	Inter Music Therapy (Ch. 10) Guided Imagery and Music Level 1 (Ch. 11)	Internship (5 months) Clinical Supervision Individually and in Groups (Ch. 12)	Guided Imagery and Music Level 1 (Ch. 11)
Music track	Applied Musical Performance	Music Instruction 1	Voice Work	Music Instruction 2 Improvisation	Music Therapeutic Songwriting		Clinical Improvisation 1	Clinical Improvisation 2		
Theory track	Problem-based learning Music psychology	Observation and description of music therapy practice	Developmental psychology and neuropsychology Music and identity	Theory of Music Therapy and Research 1	Theory of Music Therapy and Research 2	Bachelor project	Advanced Music Therapy Theory and Therapy Theory Music Therapy Assessment	Advanced Music Therapy Theory and Research	Presentation and Communication of Clinical Music Therapy	Master's Thesis

Note: Some of the subjects are elective, such as music therapeutic song writing, music therapy assessment, music and identity, and GIM (which can be taken at 8th or 10th semester)

References

Alvin, J. (1966). *Music Therapy*. Hutchinson.

Askehave, I., Prehn, H.L., Pedersen, J., & Pedersen, M.T. (2015). 'PBL – Problem Based Learning.' Aalborg University. Accessed on 01/12/21 at www.aau.dk/digitalAssets/148/148025_pbl-aalborg-model_uk.pdf.

Binder, P.E, Nielsen, G.H, Vøllestad, J., Holgersen, H., & Schanche, E. (2006). 'Hva er relasjonell psykoanalyse? Nye psykoanalytiske perspektiver på samhandling, det ubevisste og selvet [What is relational psychoanalysis? New perspectives on co-action, the unconscious and the self]'. *Tidsskrift for Norsk Psykologforening [Journal of the Norwegian Psychologist Association]*, 43(9), 899–908.

Bonde, L.O. (2009). *Musik og menneske. Introduktion til musikpsykologi [Music and man. An introduction to music psychology]*. SamfundsLitteratur.

Bonde L.O. (2019). 'Music Therapy–A Historical Perspective.' In S.L. Jacobsen, I.N. Pedersen, & L.O. Bonde (eds), *A Comprehensive Guide to Music Therapy*. Jessica Kingsley Publishers.

Bruscia, K. (2014). 'Experiential Learning in a Classroom Setting.' In K. Bruscia (ed.), *Self-Experiences in Music Therapy Education, Training, and Supervision*. Barcelona Publishers.

Byers, K.L.H. (2016). *A History of the Music Therapy Profession: Diverse Concepts and Practices*. Barcelona Publishers.

Casement, P. (2014). *On Learning from the Patient*. Routledge. (First published by Tavistock, 1985.)

Cozolino, L. (2002). *The Neuroscience of Psychotherapy – Building and Rebuilding the Human Brain*. W.W. Norton & Co.

Dreyfus, H. & Dreyfus, S. (2004). 'Mesterlære og eksperters læring [Apprenticeship and the learning of experts].' In K. Nielsen & S. Kvale (eds), *Mesterlære. Læring som social praksis [Apprenticeship. Teaching as social practice]* (5th ed.). Hans Reitzels Forlag.

Grimmer, A. & Tribe, R. (2001). 'Counselling psychologists' perceptions of the impact of mandatory personal therapy on professional development: An exploratory study.' *Counselling Psychology Quarterly 14*(4), 287–301.

Hannibal, N. (2007). 'Relevansen af nyere psykodynamisk teori for det kliniske musikterapeutiske arbejde med psykiatriske patienter med personlighedsforstyrrelser [The relevance of recent psychodynamic theory in relation to clinically music therapeutic work with psychiatric patients with personality disorders].' *Psyke & Logos, 28*(1), 385–407.

Hannibal, N., Lund, H.N., & Bonde, L.O. (2013). 'Musiklyttepuder, lyd-bøjler og spillelister i behandlingen af psykiatriske patienter [Music listening pillows, audio-hangers and playlists in the treatment of psychiatric clients].' *Musikterapi i Psykiatrien Online [Music Therapy and Psychiatry Online]*, 8(2).

Holck, U. (2019). 'Communicative Musicality: A Basis for Music Therapy Practice.' In S.L. Jacobsen, I.N. Pedersen, & L.O. Bonde (eds), *A Comprehensive Guide to Music Therapy*. Jessica Kingsley Publishers.

Jacobsen, S.L., Pedersen, I.N., & Bonde, L.O. (eds) (2019). *A Comprehensive Guide to Music Therapy* (2nd ed.). Jessica Kingsley Publishers.

Kolmos, A., Fink, F.K., & Krogh, L. (2004). 'The Aalborg Model: Problem-Based and Project-Organized Learning.' In A. Kolmos, F.K. Fink, & L. Krogh (eds), *The Aalborg Model: Progress, Diversity and Challenges*. Aalborg Universitetsforlag.

Langenberg, M. & Frommer, J. (1993). 'A qualitative research approach to analytical music therapy.' *Music Therapy, 12*(1), 59–84.

Lave, J. & Wenger, E. (1991). *Situated Learning: Legitimate Peripheral Participation*. Cambridge University Press.

Lindvang, C. (2010). 'A field of resonant learning. Self-experiential training and the development of music therapeutic competencies: A mixed methods investigation of music therapy students' experiences and professionals' evaluation of their own competencies.'

Doctoral dissertation, Aalborg University. Vbn. Accessed on 01/12/21 at https://vbn.aau.dk/ws/portalfiles/portal/316410062/6465_dissertation_c_lindvang.pdf.

Lindvang, C. (2011). 'At gøre sig parat til det mulige møde [To prepare for the possible meeting].' *Tidsskrift for Dansk Musikterapi, 8*(2), 14–21.

Lindvang, C. (2013). 'Resonant learning: A qualitative inquiry into music therapy students' self-experiential learning processes.' *Qualitative Inquiries in Music Therapy, 8*, 1–30.

Lindvang, C. & Beck, B.D. (2015). 'Problem based learning as a shared musical journey: Group dynamics, communication and creativity.' *Journal of Problem Based Learning in Higher Education, 3*(1) (Special issue on PBL and creative processes), 1–19.

Lindvang, C., Pedersen, I.N., Bonde, L.O., Jacobsen, S.L. *et al.* (2018). 'Collaborative resonant writing and musical improvisation to explore the concept of resonance.' *Qualitative Studies, 5*(1), 4–23.

Macran, S. & Shapiro, D.A. (1998). 'The role of personal therapy for therapists: A review.' *British Journal of Medical Psychology, 71*, 13–25.

Malloch, S. (1999). 'Mothers and infants and communicative musicality.' *Musicae Scientiae, Special Issue 1999–2000*, 29–57.

Malloch, S. & Trevarthen, C. (eds) (2009). *Communicative Musicality: Exploring the Basis of Human Companionship.* Oxford University Press.

Nielsen, K. & Kvale, S. (2004). 'Mesterlære som aktuel læringsform [Apprenticeship as current teaching approach].' In K. Nielsen & S. Kvale (eds), *Mesterlære. Læring som social praksis [Apprenticeship. Teaching as social practice]* (5th ed.). Hans Reitzels Forlag.

Nordoff, P. & Robbins, C. (1977). *Creative Music Therapy.* John Day.

Payne, H. (2002). 'Arts therapies and psychotherapy training: An international survey.' *International Arts Therapies Journal, 2002.*

Pedersen, I.N. (1987). Musikterapi – en uddannelse under udvikling. Et nyt skud på stammen af universitetspædagogiske traditioner [Music therapy – a new shoot on the trunk of university pedagogical traditions]. Unpublished manuscript.

Pedersen, I.N. (1997). 'The music therapist's listening perspectives as source of information in improvised musical duets with grown-up psychiatric patients, suffering from schizophrenia.' *Nordic Journal of Music Therapy, 6*(2), 98–111.

Pedersen, I.N. (1999). 'Music Therapy as Holding and Re-Organizing Work with Schizophrenic and Psychotic Patients.' In T. Wigram & J. De Backer (eds), *Clinical Applications of Music Therapy in Psychiatry.* Jessica Kingsley Publishers.

Pedersen, I.N. (2000). 'Inde-fra eller ude-fra – orientering i terapeutens tilstedeværelse og nærvær [From inside or from outside – the therapist's orientation in therapeutic presence and attentiveness].' In C. Lindvang (ed.), Den musikterapeutiske behandling [The music therapy treatment]. *Musikterapi i Psykiatrien, Årsskrift 2*, 81–102.

Pedersen, I.N. (2002). 'Self-Experience for Music Therapy Students. Experiential Training in Music Therapy as a Methodology: A Mandatory Part of the Music Therapy Programme at Aalborg University.' In J.T. Eschen (ed.), *Analytical Music Therapy.* Jessica Kingsley Publishers.

Pedersen, I.N. (2005). 'At bruge musik til at håndtere modoverføring I individuel musikterapi i hospitalspsykiatrien [The use of music to cope with countertransference in individual music therapy in hospital psychiatry]. *Music Therapy in Psychiatry, 4*, 40–64.

Pedersen, I.N. (2007a). 'Countertransference in music therapy. A phenomenological study on counter-transference used as a clinical concept by music therapists working with musical improvisation in adult psychiatry.' Doctoral dissertation, Aalborg University. Vbn. Accessed on 01/12/21 at https://vbn.aau.dk/ws/portalfiles/portal/70261290/inp_2007.pdf.

Pedersen, I.N. (2007b). 'Musikterapeutens disciplinerede subjektivitet [The disciplined subjectivity of the music therapist].' *Psyke og Logos, 28*(1), 358–384.

Pedersen, I.N. (2009). 'Music Therapy Supervision with Students and Professionals. The Use of Music and Analysis of Countertransference in the Triadic Field.' In H. Odell-Miller & E. Richards (eds), *Supervision of Music Therapy: A Theoretical and Practical Handbook.* Routledge.

Polanyi, M. (1966). *The Tacit Dimension.* The University of Chicago Press.

Priestley, M. (1975). *Music Therapy in Action.* Constable.

Priestley, M. (1994). *Essays on Analytical Music Therapy.* Barcelona Publishers.

Rosa, H. (2019a). *Resonance. A Sociology of our Relationship to the World.* Polity Press.

Rosa, H. (2019b). 'Available, Accessible, Attainable. The Mindset of Growth and the Resonance Conception of the Good Life.' In H. Rosa & C. Henning (eds), *The Good Life Beyond Growth.* Routledge.

Ruud, E. (1990). *Musikk som kommunikasjon og samhandling. Teoretiske perspektiv på musikterapien [Music as communication and interaction. Theoretical perspectives on music therapy].* Solum Forlag.

Ruud, E. (1997/2013). *Musikk og identitet [Music and identity]* (2nd ed.). Universitetsforlaget Oslo.

Ruud, E. (1998). *Music Therapy: Improvisation, Communication, and Culture.* Barcelona Publishers.

Ruud, E. (2001). *Varme øyeblikke. Om musikk, helse og livskvalitet [Hot present moments. About music, health and quality of life].* Unipub Forlag.

Savery, J.R. (2006). 'Overview of problem-based learning: Definitions and distinctions.' *Interdisciplinary Journal of Problem-based Learning, 1*(1), 9–20.

Scheiby, B. & Pedersen, I.N. (1999). 'Inter music therapy in the training of music therapy students.' *Nordic Journal of Music Therapy, 8*(1), 58–71.

Schou, K., Pedersen, I.N., & Bonde, L.O. (2011). 'Musiklytning til patienter i skærmning. Pilot-undersøgelse på Musikterapiklinikken Aalborg Psykiatriske Sygehus [Music listening for vulnerable slightly isolated patients. A pilot study on The Music Therapy Clinic, Aalborg University Hospital, Psychiatry].' *Musikterapi i Psykiatrien [Music Therapy and Psychiatry], 6*(1).

Schön, D.A. (1983). *The Reflective Practitioner: How Professionals Think in Action.* Basic Books Inc.

Stegemann, T. & Fitzthum, E. (2016). In T. Stegemann, H.U. Schmidt, E. Fitzthum, & T. Timmermann (eds), *Music Therapy Training Programmes in Europe: Theme and Variations.* Reichert Verlag.

Stern, D. (1985/2000). *The Interpersonal World of the Infant: A View from Psychoanalysis and Developmental Psychology.* Basic Books.

Stern, D. (1995). *Et spædbarns dagbog [Diary of a baby].* Hans Reitzels Forlag.

Stern, D. (2010). *Forms of Vitality: Exploring Dynamic Experience in Psychology, the Arts, Psychotherapy and Development.* Oxford University Press.

Tucek, G. (2003). 'Altorientalische musiktherapie im spannungsfeld zwischen interkulturellem dialog und transkultureller anwendung. Vom traditionellen wissenssystem zum transkulturellen wissenstransfer [Ancient oriental music therapy in the field of tension between intercultural dialogue and transcultural application. From traditional knowledge system to transcultural knowledge transfer].' Dissertation, Faculty of Human and Social Sciences, Vienna University.

Vedfelt, O. (2018). *The Intelligence of the Unconscious – You Know More than You Think.* Kindle edition.

Wackerhausen, S. (2004). 'Det skolastiske paradigme og mesterlære [The scholastic paradigm and mastery].' In K. Nielsen & S. Kvale (eds), *Mesterlære. Læring som social praksis [Mastery. Learning as social practice].* Hans Reitzels Forlag.

Wackerhausen, S. (2005). 'Tavs viden, pædagogik og refleksion [Quiet knowledge, pedagogy and reflection].' In C.N. Jensen (ed.), *Voksnes læringsrum [Learning space for adults].* Billesø & Baltzer.

Wigram, T. (1999) 'Clinical Group Music Therapy. Techniques, Frameworks and Transitions.' In T. Wigram & J.D. Backer (eds), *Clinical Applications of Music Therapy in Developmental Disabilities, Paediatrics and Neurology.* Jessica Kingsley Publishers.

Wigram T., Pedersen, I.N., & Bonde, L.O. (2002). *A Comprehensive Guide to Music Therapy. Theory, Clinical Practice, Research and Training.* Jessica Kingsley Publishers.

Willert, S. (2007). 'Verdens bedste universitetsstudium... Musikterapistudiet som universitet-spædagogisk lærestykke [A champion university study... Music therapy as a university pedagogical doctrine].' Musikterapi-Uddannelsen 25 År, Festskrift. Aalborg Universitetsforlag.

Yalom, I.D. (2003). *The Gift of Therapy. An Open Letter to a New Generation of Therapists and Their Patients.* Piatkus.

CHAPTER 3

From Psychoanalysis to an Integrative Approach

THE THEORETICAL BACKGROUND TO THE AALBORG PROGRAMME

Inge Nygaard Pedersen, Charlotte Lindvang, & Bolette Daniels Beck

The idea of presenting the theoretical orientation in this chapter is to clarify and disseminate the way of thinking that underlies the experiential training in the therapeutic track at the Aalborg programme, and that permeates the musical and theoretical parts of the education at both BA and MA levels. The Aalborg music therapy programme overall is based on a psychodynamic orientation, but it is also integrative and eclectic and encourages educators, students, and researchers to familiarize with and draw on multiple theoretical frameworks. In our understanding, being psychodynamically oriented does not imply the dogma of psychoanalytic thinking.

We, the editors of this book, see it as important to consciously know and be able to base one's music therapeutic methodological approach on a theoretical ground; as it increases the clarity of planning and evaluation, it makes it easier to communicate with other professions and supports dissemination of the process and outcomes of music therapy.

We do not intend in this book to disseminate a theoretical model or a method representing the therapeutic training track alone, as this track is seen as an inseparable part of the whole training programme. However, we have experienced that the learning processes in the therapeutic training track specifically support the students' overall understanding of how the psychodynamic roots are a basic part of an integrative process of developing a music therapist identity. The three tracks are separated at the Bachelor level where the students learn basic tools musically (improvisational tools), personally (how to reflect on their own being and relationship with others), and theoretically (theories and research methods). At the Master's level, the basic tools from all three tracks are integrated in the students' experiences of being in the therapist role in many different situations and disciplines.

We intend to present the roots and further developments of a theoretical platform developed over almost 40 years, where some solid roots in our understanding of psychodynamic music therapy have survived changes in theory perspectives and paradigms. But the platform has also grown and integrated a diversity and variety of further different theoretical ideas. Cohen (2018) reflects on the history of development of theories in music therapy and she refers among others to Hanson-Abromeit (2015, p.28), where theory is defined as 'the foundation in which to design intentional interventions'. We can identify with this definition. Cohen also briefly describes how music therapy as a profession was established by practice pioneers who borrowed theories from other disciplines to underpin their practice. And still today there are different assumptions in the music therapy profession about whether music therapy practice should borrow theory from other disciplines or develop indigenous theories or both. Cohen points at Aigen as the one who:

> ...clearly delineates three stages in the development of music therapy theories: (1) the borrowing of theoretical ideas from other disciplines; (2) treatment models that developed from clinical practice; and (3) more indigenous and cross-disciplinary theories that are relevant to multiple models and forms of clinical practice. (Cohen, 2018, p.61)

As an example, Wheeler (1981) also advocated reliance on psychological theories and suggested that:

> It hopefully has become apparent that music therapy might progress more solidly if music therapists were to align themselves closely with a psychotherapeutic theory. Each theory has different assumptions about the nature of mental health and how to achieve it. Each has different implications for music therapy, and each will require further investigation to clarify its use in music therapy. (Wheeler 1981, p.15)

In this chapter we try to:

- Integrate roots from psychodynamic theory presented as basic assumptions

- Unfold descriptions of psychodynamic concepts following these basic assumptions

- Present theory derived from clinical practice during almost 40 years and indigenous and cross-disciplinary theories such as the listening perspectives, disciplined subjectivity, and resonance

We do not understand the three stages delineated by Aigen to be hierarchical, where one stage replaces the former. We think they remain and fertilize each other but also constantly influence each other. Consequently, some basic assumptions need to be replaced by new assumptions for the clinician to navigate in the integrated theory landscape. That is why we in this chapter present the historical and classical basic assumptions derived from psychoanalytic theory and we terminate the chapter with updated integrative basic assumptions.

Psychodynamic theory is complex because many different perspectives of theoretical orientations come together. Silverman, in a survey in the US in 2007, asked music therapists working in psychiatry about which approach they applied, and he found that 49.2 per cent answered with a psychodynamic approach, whereas only 5.7 per cent listed psychodynamic theory as their theoretical ground (Silverman, 2007). This points to the fact that it might be easier to use the psychodynamic concepts to understand single processes in clinical practice than to fully grasp, understand, explicate, and integrate the psychodynamic theory(ies) as a theoretical foundation.

As an example of the use of the isolated core concepts of psychodynamic theory, transference and countertransference (which we will unfold later in this chapter) applied and reflected in different approaches of music therapy was shown in the anthology *The Dynamics of Music Psychotherapy* (Bruscia, 1998), where representatives from analytical music therapy, Nordoff/Robbins music therapy (Nordoff & Robbins, 1977), and Guided Imagery and Music (GIM) therapy reflect on these concepts related to their approach (Isenberg-Grzeda, 1998; Turry, 1998).

A few music therapy theorists have attempted to embrace the huge task of embedding music therapy in a contemporary psychodynamic understanding. Early contributors to an overall understanding of psychodynamic therapy in music theory are, among others, Ken Bruscia (1998) and Susan Hadley (2003). With this knowledge in mind, and a humble attitude, we the authors now want to sketch an integration of relevant parts of the classic psychodynamic theory with relevant parts of recent intersubjective and neurologically based research on therapeutic relationships.

Psychodynamic theory lies at the roots of contemporary psychology and, as stated by Bornstein, can be a framework for the integration of a multitude of perspectives related to different needs in clinical practice:

Psychodynamic theory may be the closest thing we have to an overarching, all-encompassing theory in psychology. It deals with a broad range of issues – normal and pathological functioning, motivation and emotion, childhood and adulthood, individual and culture – and the psychodynamic perspective continues to have tremendous potential for integrating ideas and findings across the many domains of contemporary psychology. (Bornstein, 2019, p.11)

The history of the general psychodynamic approach is long and complex, with many side-tracks and theories developed over more than 120 years. It cannot be described in a simple way, and this chapter does not aim to unfold the historic development. However, we will try to build on some of the basic assumptions in the classical psychoanalytic theory and the successors of this theory, describe some of the adaptations of the central concepts to music therapy theory and practice, and form a bridge to the recent turns and theories that are used in modern music therapy thinking. Finally, basic assumptions for an integrated modern psychodynamic music therapy orientation are formulated.

The following four vignettes will exemplify teamwork and daily processes of teaching and learning practices based on a psychodynamic ground from the educators' as well as the students' point of view.

Vignette 1: Parallel processes between the team and the students

As psychodynamic-oriented educators in a music psychotherapy training programme we try to be aware of parallel processes between what is going on in the team and in the group of students, as well as in between these two groups, possibly reflecting processes in the university and society as a whole. This vignette illustrates how we try to develop our awareness and mutuality in the team of educators.

In our team we seek to acknowledge how the organizational situation and our well-being in the team influence our relationship with the students. At one of our biannual meetings in the team of educators and university employees, some of the educators shared their feelings of being worn out and sometimes not being able to keep track, confronted with the never-ending streams of emails and academic demands with high performance expectations. We reflected on how the educators' level of stress might be snapped up by our students because we are their role models. In the team we reflected on how we could maintain our culture as a team where we can be open, vulnerable, and supportive, and at the same time able to confront diversity and repair conflicts. We also discussed how we can lower our pressure on ourselves, take more care of our needs, and focus more on the core research that we love to do. We addressed jointly and with mutual support our wish to continue to build an inspiring and lively environment, where we can contain and support both the struggles and difficult processes and the creativity and enthusiasm of the students.

Vignette 2: Transformation and growth is a never-ending possibility

As psychodynamic-oriented music therapists we are committed to a lifelong learning perspective, acknowledging that our life (past, present, and future), and our different levels of consciousness, possess such a high degree of complexity that transformation and growth is a never-ending possibility. One of the educators in the therapeutic track shares the following:

> As a psychodynamic-oriented trainer, I am aware of how important it is that I am well prepared and fully present when I meet the students in the therapy room. I am aware of the solid framework of the therapy, the time frame, the ethical frames, and the framework of our curriculum. I am mindful of the students before I meet them, and I am aware of what happened last time we met. This day I felt a tension in my stomach – and I was aware that it might be a tension transferred from the students to me. In our last session a heavy silence characterized the group, without enough time and energy to investigate what this silence expressed. I felt a tension and discomfort in the hours after the session and I had a fantasy that there might be withheld anger or anxiety in some of the students. Now we had the time to investigate what happened last time, what thoughts and feelings they chose not to express. I tried to approach the theme with curiosity, and I invited the group members to share how they felt in the silence and reflections on why they did not break the silence. In the beginning it was difficult to talk about, but gradually the students found the courage to express themselves and it became clear that we were facing eight participants having eight different kinds of reflections and feelings around the silence. I was committed to the task of containing all the different positions that became audible. The group was surprised by how much material – feelings, stories, fantasies – was hidden in the silence. After this way of listening to each other there was a deep release of energy in the group, and a more relaxed atmosphere emerged. The group played a free improvisation – eager to sound together. After this session I felt the transformational process mirrored in my own mind and body. I felt calm and had a soft and warm feeling towards the group. This makes me think that each time a group becomes wiser about themselves and

each other I also become a bit wiser as a training therapist in the dynamic and moving process that our students undergo: I am a part of it – I cannot separate completely from it, even though my role is different than the students' roles.

Vignette 3: A safe therapeutic space

The third vignette illustrates from a music therapy student's perspective how a safe therapeutic space can facilitate a meeting between past, present, and future, and between the individual and the group. The vignette shows a ground-breaking experience from the very beginning of the training therapy. The student chooses consciously to do away with an old pattern of hiding true feelings and instead opens up to tell some painful memories and show the vulnerability behind a strong and humorous persona. The situation shows how powerfully the music can catalyse an (unforeseen) emotional release and a process of nonverbal sharing, and it pinpoints the transformational potential of being emotionally received and contained in a group:

> One of the things that affected me very deeply was when we got the task to bring a piece of music that meant something special to us. We were supposed to explain to the other group members what the music meant to us. I had no doubt. And yet. No one else before me had shared anything personal in the way I would like to do now. But I wanted to take the lead. Choose the path that would bring us closer together. I was tired of spending my entire life on pretence, and I refused to be once again superficially picking a random insignificant song that didn't mean as much as my chosen song did. Then it really hit me. What music can do. I had listened to that song countless times. Every time I had been squealing and singing along, and I do not remember that the song ever hit me the way it did that day when I shared it with the group. It was a significant learning process for me. The group nicely accepted what I told them about my past. I said that life has not always been easy to live. I told them how this song put things in perspective for me: It reminded me – and it still does – to take one day at a time. When the music started, I cried my eyes out. It surprised me. I wanted to hold back, but I didn't; I wanted people to see that it was okay to be sad, and I needed to feel that it was okay to be sad. And I really learned that it was okay. Right there. While listening to that piece of music, everything was okay. I was overwhelmed with emotions. Feelings that had been smouldering inside of me. Feelings about everything and nothing. In the group we all had to make a drawing of each other while we heard the personal songs. The drawings I got from my peers, I still look at today. They make me smile. People reflected exactly what I felt. They caught me, captured my feelings. Felt my feelings through the music. I really learned

what music therapy can provide. It was overwhelming, but absolutely amazing. People suddenly understood the way I was, in a whole new way. Without talking to each other, many new connections were formed that day.

Vignette 4: Overcoming countertransference in supervision

This vignette stems from the last year of the five-year course. During the long internship in the ninth semester, a student reflects on supervision and her experience of overcoming countertransference issues with an adult healthy client.

One client I experienced as particularly demanding, and this was overwhelming as I was a novice music therapist. After the third session, I realized that I had let the client control too much without me reacting to it. I felt uneasy about continuing the process, but this changed after I got supervision about the situation.

The supervisor asked whether I could connect the experience to other situations earlier in my life, where I have let people control and step across my boundaries and have had difficulty responding to it. I was able to connect it to situations from my childhood, and when the supervisor asked how it felt right now in my body, I felt a squeezed uncomfortable feeling located in the middle of the abdomen. I was invited to express this feeling through sound, and it was liberating to use the voice as it was directly speaking from the unpleasant squeezed feeling in the stomach. Suddenly it turned over to a feeling of strength and a sense of being grounded. Now I felt so strong, that everything could just come up, including this client whom I felt as demanding. So, although I also got verbal suggestions from the supervisor for being more directive in the future course of therapy, I did not need it, as the experience of strength and grounding now was settled within me from my core sound and singing. In the following sessions this new feeling of strength changed the dynamics of the relationship with the client, as I stood much stronger, open, and ready to meet her needs.

The process allowed me to see the problem in a different perspective. The experience of not being able to hear myself, but only 'the others', is an old pattern that I would very much like to change. I now know that there is a lot of power stored up that is available for me when this pattern is given air, space, light, and sound. This problem has thus given me a valuable learning experience and has been important in my process and development as a future music therapist.

These four examples are meant to be illustrative of how the students and educators work in a shared field of evolving consciousness based on a psychodynamic approach, and they will serve as concrete lived experiences forming a background for the review of theory.

Basic assumptions in the classic psychoanalytic orientation

The theory and method of psychoanalysis was developed by the physiologist Sigmund Freud (1856–1939), who contributed to the discovery of the brain neurons in his early career (Galbis-Reig, 2004), but is more renowned for his psychological theories. He was among the pioneers trying to understand pathological symptoms in connection with the environment and the life-history, building on earlier ideas of the existence of an unconscious mind (Olsen & Køppe, 1987). Based on clinical examinations of clients with 'hysteria', Freud hypothesized that unpleasant, shameful, and traumatic experiences were hidden in the unconscious mind and were expressed through somatic symptoms or emotional imbalance. (For a short introduction to Freud, see Storr, 2001; for a history of modern psychoanalytic thought, see Mitchell & Black, 2016; for a historical review of psychodynamic theory preceding psychodynamic music therapy, see Isenberg, 2016.)

In the following box a short synthesis of the basic assumptions in classic psychoanalytic thinking is presented (Bruscia, 1998; Gammelgård, 2011; Hadley, 2003; Karterud, Willberg, & Urnes 2013; McLeod, 2017; Olsen, 2002).

Basic assumptions in classical psychoanalytic thinking
1. Theory of the unconscious
The psyche manifests at various levels of consciousness. In the life of our psyche, some of our wishes, needs, and motivations are present at an unconscious level but show up in our actions, feelings, dreams, and thoughts or discloses in for example oversights and slips of the tongue.

2. The psyche is a tripartite system
Freud conceptualized two major models of psychic organization. First, a topographical model related to layers of consciousness: conscious, preconscious, and unconscious; later, a structural model related to the mental processes id, ego, and super-ego (1989/1923). The following three parts attempt to include both models:

1) *The id* (unconscious mind) contains material completely out of awareness such as all memories and innate instincts of the individual and species. The unconscious layer includes the so-called libido (according to Freud; primarily, the sexual instinct – which in his later work was broadened to also cover the 'self-preservation instinct' and renamed the 'life instinct') as well as unacceptable feelings,

self-destruction, and aggressive drives (also called the 'death instinct', as opposed to the life instinct). 2) *The ego* (conscious mind) contains material accessible in an everyday level of awareness and holds the individual's self-image and identity. It develops to mediate between the id and the external world (including the moral voice of the super-ego) as the decision-making component of personality. 3) *The super-ego* (conscious/unconscious) incorporates values, morals, and censorship mechanisms of society, which are learned from one's parents and others, and for example installs a sense of guilt when social injunctions are exceeded. The super-ego can sometimes be close to the id due to an uncompromising way of functioning from where the ego cannot flee.

In the first topographical model, the preconscious layer was situated between the unconscious and conscious, and contained material that is out of awareness but that could become conscious.

3. There are ongoing conflicts between different layers of consciousness

The conscious mind (the ego) has a regulating function and seeks to balance the impulses from the unconscious with the demands of reality, the need for personal safety and gratification, and standards of morality. These conflicts, and how they are re-enacted, play an essential role in the formation of the personality. The ego strength is important for psychological balance, e.g., the ability to handle and regulate aggressive impulses to avoid destructive behaviour, yet being able to carry out a healthy self-assertion or self-delineation.

4. Early imprint of personality

Childhood events have a great influence on adult life and shape the personality. Unique patterns of relating to the world are developed in early relationships and interaction with caregiver(s) and the original family.

5. The personality is developed through phases with specific conflicts and dilemmas

The development of the personality is the combined product of innate drives, motivations, character, and vulnerabilities we are born with and childhood experiences, such as the way we are raised and nurtured.

The human personality is shaped as the unconscious drives are modified by different conflicts at different times in childhood (i.e., during the Freudian five phases of psychosexual development: oral, anal, phallic, latency, and genital). Unresolved conflicts or 'fixation' in one of the stages was meant to influence adult function.

6. The past influences the present

A great part of our behaviour and feelings are affected and determined by unconscious factors and motives. Individuals learn from every experience they have and generalize what they learn from past situations to present ones. The patterns of relating imprinted in childhood are replicated in present relationships. For instance, in the case of early neglect, absence, or abuse, the child will develop patterns of relationship and strategies to psychologically survive and/or avoid anxiety that later can be problematic in adult relationships (such as dissociation, self-harm, or abusive behaviour).

7. Humans develop unique strategies to avoid inner tension and anxiety

Our psyche makes an effort to prevent unacceptable or threatening material in the unconscious from being conscious. We also use defence mechanisms as characteristic ways of coping whenever an experience threatens to destroy the delicate balance between what is repressed and what is in awareness. 'Resistance' is a concept that refers to a person's attempt to avoid painful feelings like shame and anxiety and, for example, resistance to therapeutic change is seen as a way of keeping the well-known psychic patterns in place.

8. Inadequate relationship patterns can be modified in therapy

Unconscious material can surface and be worked through in therapy, changing the level of conflict in the psyche, and allowing the ego to adapt to more adequate patterns.

9. Transference and countertransference are phenomena in therapy

Transference is a phenomenon that refers to feelings and sensations from past relationships which are directed from the client onto – but not originating from – the relation to the therapist (and/or the music). Countertransference is a similar dynamic of unconscious repetitions of psychic patterns – now enacted by the therapist. The analyst aims at staying neutral to provide a safe frame for the client's intense transference emotions. It is a precondition that the analyst has a personal therapy/ analysis to be able to handle the countertransference reactions in a thera- peutically beneficial way. The verbal interpretation of such mechanisms is important to engage the conscious mind in possible dynamic changes.

These basic assumptions are based on the classic psychoanalytic theory that has later been criticized and revised, and as described below, music therapists have also revised many of the original assumptions.

From psychoanalysis to a psychodynamic orientation

The psychodynamic orientation, as opposed to a classic psychoanalytic under- standing, is integrative, complex, and embraces all the many new concepts and ideas that were developed throughout the 20th century by Freud's students and successors, such as Jung's *theory of individuation*, in which the unconscious is seen as a creative source that also includes a collective unconscious of human archetypes, myths, ideas, and images (1981). The psychodynamic understanding also includes the *ego psychology* focusing on strengthening and developing ego competencies (Erikson, 1959, 1974; Hartmann, 1958; Rapaport, 1942), and the *object relations theory* focused on a subject's dependency on close relations to caretakers, as well as relations to outer objects, which could be persons, things, or places. The interactions with outer objects are thought to be internalized as inner objects and 'families of objects', and the different theories describe how psychological pathologies are rooted in imbalances between 'good' and destruc- tive inner objects (Fairbairn, 1952; Klein, 1932; Mahler, Pine, & Bergman, 1975). Attachment theory, as developed by Bowlby (1969), played a significant role in the understanding of the formation of secure versus insecure (ambivalent, avoidant, and disorganized) attachment styles. The attachment style depends on the qual- ity of the early bonding and relationship with one's primary caregiver. It predicts the way a person seeks support throughout life when feeling threatened and can have a lifelong impact on well-being and relationships. Winnicott, another of the object relations theorists, described 'the third area' as a transitional realm between the inner and outer world and between the caregiver and the child, where the child can experiment and sense its own being through playing; a symbolic space also used as a theoretical framework for music therapy in which the music therapist can create a substitute holding environment and playground for musical expression and exploration (Winnicott, 1971). Winnicott stated that the child does *not* primarily seek gratification of libidinal drives (i.e., hunger or pleasure), but rather seeks contact with the object (the primary caregiver). This was an important change of theoretical understanding of the development in childhood, as it honours the child's primary need for a relationship already from birth. *Self-psychology* (Kohut, 1971) also broke with traditional psychoanalysis and described the individual's integration of 'self objects', which were seen as inner representations forming an autonomous 'self-machinery'. Kohut described how the therapist's 'vicarious introspection' and empathy could enhance the development and integration of the self.

The relational and bodily turns

Realizing the meaning of the 'myth of the personal identity' (Sullivan, 1950) and 'the myth of the isolated mind' (Stolorow & Atwood, 1992), and acknowledging that earlier the focus primarily had been on the understanding and change of the intrapsychic world of the client, representatives of object relations theory and self-psychology increasingly understood the importance of a relational matrix as fundamental for human development. Greenberg and Mitchell categorized the new understanding as 'relational psychoanalysis', where interpersonal relations and object relations were bridged and emphasized (Greenberg & Mitchell, 1983). Further, with the theoretical contributions of Daniel Stern and many others (discussed later in this chapter), and the rapid development of neuropsychological research, a transition from a single person (monadic) psychology to a two-person (dyadic) psychology took place, acknowledging that we are 'born' into relationships and developed through relationships, rather than being separate individuals. The shift of focus towards intersubjectivity and co-constructed interactive processes, in which narrative dynamic issues and moment-by-moment negotiation of relatedness takes place, has been called the 'relational turn':

> ...psychoanalysis is making a profound change in the role of the analyst and in our understanding of therapeutic action. We emphasize, however, that both self- and interactive regulation are critical to our conceptualization of the relational turn from a dyadic systems point of view. (Beebe & Lachmann, 2014, p.402)

As one example of a music therapist who has integrated perspectives of the relational turn into her music therapy writings and research, we can mention the Norwegian music therapy professor Gro Trondalen. In the book *Relational Music Therapy: An Intersubjective Perspective,* Trondalen builds on phenomenological and hermeneutic philosophies and describes how the music therapeutic relationship is at the same time 'a frame and a relational possibility', allowing for the fusion of horizons (Trondalen, 2016). Trondalen emphasizes the significance of microprocesses and embodiment when 'moving along together' in the music therapeutic encounter and describes how the experience of musical intersubjectivity can lead to the creation of existential meaning on many levels. Another example is the Swedish psychologist and GIM therapist Katarina Blom, who in her PhD study builds on theories on intersubjectivity and change in psychotherapy. Blom points out that the music in GIM is a relational agent and her study contributes with knowledge on how the occurrence of clients' spiritual experiences in GIM can be prepared for through relational work (Blom, 2014). Blom is also a co-author of a book about intersubjectivity in professional care as well as in everyday life (Blom & Wrangsjö, 2013). The book emphasizes how nonverbal communication binds and connects us to each other as human beings. The theoretical foundation of this relational perspective is – as with Trondalen – more a paradigm than one single theory since several current psychological, philosophical, and neurobiological contributions are woven together.

Parallel to the relational turn, a bodily turn has taken place, focusing on implicit as opposed to explicit knowledge, and turning the attention to the 'bottom up' processes rather than 'top down' processes in human perception. Representatives for the bodily turn conceptualize an 'embodiment' (Merleau-Ponty, 1945/2010), and they point out that 'Somatic psychology' can be traced back to pre-Freudian Janet (introduction by Bühler & Heim, 2001), to Reich (1933/1974) and Lowen (1975). Recent development of bottom-up approaches such as body therapies (Boadella, 1987; Caldwell, 1996; Gendlin, 1996; Levine, 1997) and sensorimotor therapy (Ogden, Minton, & Pain, 2006) are all focusing on processes of bodily sensation and movement as fundamental in therapy rather than verbal conversation and cognitive insight.

One can also talk about an affective turn, a new acknowledgement of the significance of affect regulation and emotions in therapy. The emphasis on embodiment is being supported by neuroscientific research that also makes it possible to investigate interpersonal synchronization and empathy – as for instance the studies of brain-to-brain interaction and synchronization (Fachner *et al.*, 2019; Liu *et al.*, 2018).

These turns are of essential importance for music therapists who identify themselves as psychodynamic music therapists. This very brief presentation of psychoanalytic and later theories can be seen as a root formation of psychodynamic theory. In the following, the connection to music therapy theory will be presented, including how some of the basic assumptions are modified and renewed. After this part of the chapter, expanded descriptions of theories that have emerged in the relational, bodily, and affective turns will be provided.

Pioneers in music therapy and psychodynamic orientation

The pioneers in music therapy who first introduced a psychoanalytic way of thinking related to music therapy practice were Juliette Alvin and Mary Priestley, both located in London, and Florence Tyson from the US. While Tyson primarily wrote about psychodynamic music therapy based on her clinical experience in mental health, Alvin established a music therapy programme at Guildhall School of Music and Drama in London in 1968 and she 'developed a foundation model for improvisational music therapy between 1950 and 1980' (Wigram, 2019, p.189). Alvin, as a professional cellist, was deeply inspired by contemporary music, as for instance Stravinsky and the way:

> ...he broke the 'musical rules' in terms of harmony, melody, rhythm and form, and allowed us to make and experience a range of dissonant and atonal sounds that had previously been taboo. This opened the door for her development of free improvisation therapy, where clients and therapists can improvise without musical rules, and where the music can be an expression of the person's character and personality through which therapeutic issues can be addressed. (Wigram, 2019, pp.189–190)

Rachel Darnley-Smith in her PhD studied the ontology of music in music therapy and wrote about music in psychodynamic approaches where she identified that aspects of Alvin's work can be seen as a 'key to the psychodynamic foundations later developed by others in music therapy, in the first instance by Mary Priestley' (Darnley-Smith, 2013, p.65). Alvin's approach to improvisation was based on:

> ...a musical and personal openness to the client through a process of listening and freely responding... These features of listening and musical freedom underpin what might be called a 'psychodynamic attitude' in her playing; it is primarily improvisation that is intuitive and responsive to the client she is with. (Darnley-Smith, 2013, p.64)

In her free improvisational approach Alvin recognized the music as revealing of the whole personality of the client, both conscious and subconscious. In her book *Music Therapy*, Alvin argued that:

> The use of free rhythmical atonal improvisation liberates the player from obedience to traditional rules in tonality and musical form which he may not be willing or able to follow. He may let himself go on a musical instrument needing

no specific technique without offending any conversation and express himself directly often at a subconscious level, as one may do in art therapy... In the process, the patient can overcome his self-consciousness, his sense of fear, and reveal an untouched side of his inner life. (Alvin, 1975, pp.104–105)

Thus, the essential part of music therapy for her was the relationship between the client and the music and the way the music therapist could facilitate this relationship.

Mary Priestley was a professional violinist and she studied music therapy at Juliette Alvin's training course at the same time as she undertook a personal long-term psychoanalysis. She tried to combine her personal experience through a long-term psychoanalysis with her music therapy practice, and in a biographical study Hadley (1998) presents the close relationship between Priestley's life history and the therapeutic approach she developed (Pedersen, 2019). As Mary Priestley missed an emphasis on the self-developmental training of the students becoming therapists in her music therapy training, she:

> ...established a self-developmental, complementary training module for other music therapy educational programs as she felt they did not give the students a knowledge of and a focus on transference relationships and of the effect of the music therapist's way of being present in the clinical setting. (Pedersen, 2019, p.167)

Darnley-Smith describes that: 'Music, for Priestley, in improvised or composed form, was an expression or symbol of the unconscious' (Darnley-Smith, 2013, p.68). Priestley herself formulated that: 'the patient explores new pathways symbolically in the world of imagination but with bodily-expressed emotion in sound which gives her a safe toe-hold in the world of everyday reality' (Priestley, 1995, p.130). Mary Priestley, in offering her additional training, which she developed together with two music therapy colleagues at a large psychiatric hospital, was primarily concerned about adding an orientation tool for the therapist in the clinical work. She defines that the therapist's function in the client/therapist duet is twofold:

> He will, with his musical expression, contain the emotion of the client, matching her honest moods. He must also be alert to that inner voice from the client's unconscious: the countertransference and sometimes reproduce musically these feelings from the client's unconscious. (Priestley, 1994, p.11)

This is mirrored by Darnley-Smith when she reflects on the difference between the two pioneers, and argues that Priestley's approach:

...built on Alvin's in a particular way...as Alvin's case material and theoretical writings tend to focus upon descriptions of her work, providing an external viewpoint rather than a sense of involvement on the part of the therapist. Priestley, on the other hand, responded to the spontaneity of free improvisation in a deeply personal way and so gained an understanding of the possibilities of music therapy from 'the inside' of the experience, from the viewpoint of the client. (Darnley-Smith, 2013, pp.70–71)

Darnley-Smith also emphasizes that Priestley:

...understood that a therapist's own process of 'inner learning' is an essential tool for the work; she introduced into music therapy practice the necessity for the therapist's own music therapy, in order to gain at least a working understanding of their own unconscious, alongside the process of working with the unconscious of their patients. (Darnley-Smith, 2013, pp.71–72)

Ken Bruscia, professor emeritus in music therapy at Temple University, USA, is one of the later authors who has worked most intensively with psychodynamic theoretical concepts related to music therapy. In *The Dynamics of Music Psychotherapy,* he defines and exemplifies transference and countertransference related to improvisation, songs, and music imagery (Bruscia, 1998). Music therapy case studies related to psychodynamic theory are presented both in Bruscia (1998) and in *Psychodynamic Music Therapy: Case Studies* (Hadley, 2003).

In the following we will dive into different perspectives around central concepts of psychodynamic therapy as well as presenting original concepts from Inge Nygaard Pedersen's work, related to music therapy training.

Different perspectives on understanding the concept of the unconscious

Freud developed psychoanalysis as a science primarily to examine the unconscious through free-flowing associations by the client and a neutral position by the therapist. His successors emphasized that one can only examine the unconscious of another person through one's own unconscious, where empathy and intuition must be a first step of the clarification or interpretation process. Jung understood the unconscious as something independent and creative in the individual and in the culture. He distinguished between the personal and the collective unconscious, where the latter contained transgenerational experiences. While describing the unconscious he is cited by Jacobi as follows:

...the human being is in constant development and that creative unfolding processes of the unconscious are constantly expressing themselves in growth processes like a seed that follows its own rules when no artificial interventions take place. Thus, the unconscious can continually serve as a compensatory function being able to correct the conscious attitude constructively. (Jacobi, 1976, p.128, authors' translation)

A relational turn in understanding the unconscious

As previously mentioned, over the past decades a change towards a relational understanding – also of the unconscious – has emerged. The aim of obtaining insight into destructive dynamic drives, which was the aim in the classical psychoanalytic understanding, has been replaced by the aim of seeking meaning, contact, emotional vitality, and reciprocity as basic drives for human beings. This change also includes the understanding that all psychic phenomena occur and are maintained in an intersubjective field.

The understanding of working with the unconscious in a therapeutic setting has changed from an attitude stating that the client is primarily not motivated for change and will unconsciously resist attempts of help from the therapist to an attitude stating that the client is basically motivated for change. 'Resistance' in the new understanding can be seen as a secondary phenomenon emerging from earlier experiences of developmental efforts, where these were obviously rejected and not met by important others. These efforts have been attached to unconscious assumptions of danger. It is now assumed that intentions in the client's unconscious are directed towards growth, creativity, and need for contact. At the same time, it is assumed that human beings will be involved in inner conflicts and can end up being so overwhelmed by psychic pain that resistance is needed to protect the self. In a modern psychodynamic approach, it is acknowledged that the ability to be resistant, or in other words being self-protective towards changes, is in most cases a necessary resource to avoid further pain, being overwhelmed, and/or fragmented, until a new form of safety and empowerment paves the way to greater psychic awareness, openness, and flexibility (Thorgaard, 2006).

Where interpretation and insight were the tool and aim of the former attitude in psychodynamic therapy, a mutual change of the dynamic of the therapeutic relationship is the tool and aim of the current approach in psychodynamic therapy. Here the therapy process is basically interactive and intersubjective, and in choice of actions and directions the therapist must be informed by and make disciplined use of their unconscious. To be able to apply one's unconscious as an information source in therapy is a big part of the tuning process which concerns both mind and body.

A bodily turn in understanding the unconscious

It is widely recognized that our body holds a deep memory (Hvid, 2005; Levine, 2010a; Mindell, 1982). Former experiences are layered in the body, and music therapy students need to build up a self-experiential and embodied understanding of such bodily phenomena to be attentive to clients' bodily reactions during therapy and to be able to help clients with arousal regulation and emotional awareness, containment, and expression.

When the student learns to stay connected with the body and to listen to the language of the body, it is a way to cultivate curiosity and interest in the functioning of the body and mind. It is a step-by-step process of expansion of consciousness and a training to dare to meet what is beneath the surface. Through the training the students build a respect towards the bodily dimensions of human being and relating. It is not always a learning goal to make everything completely conscious, verbally explicated, and understood, but it is a goal to be familiar with being in contact with bodily experiences and to build up a competence to navigate in the complexity of unconscious information.

The unconscious described by music therapists

Music as a symbolic expression of the unconscious has been described by, among others, Priestley (1975, 1994); Tyson (1973 in McGuire, 2004); and Eschen (2002). They emphasize that content and issues from the unconscious can be both expressed, processed, worked through, and understood at both an unconscious and a conscious level. Priestley primarily emphasized improvised music in music therapy, whereas Tyson wrote about being aware of unconscious elements coming through in music-learning situations. Priestley understands improvised music as 'projective' in the sense that it is a manifestation of the unconscious.

Johannes Th. Eschen (2002) has written about the concepts of consciousness and the unconscious from the perspective of 'thinking processes':

- Primary process thinking: dream-like thinking processes where images tend to become fused and can readily replace and symbolize one another and ignore the categories of space and time

- Secondary process thinking: a way of thinking which obeys the law of grammar and formal logic and is governed by the reality principle

- Tertiary process thinking: thinking in creative processes (following Ammon, 1974, in Eschen, 2002), a state of mind where we can easily oscillate between primary and secondary process thinking

84

This oscillation can occur in a 'facilitating environment', where the ego boundaries are more-or-less open to the therapist and open to the un- or preconscious, to our emotions.

The American music therapist Florence Tyson also wrote back in the seventies that music can create a bridge from the inner world to the outer reality. She also mentioned how music can provide a safe way to give expression to inner feelings. Therefore, the main interest of the music therapist should be the inner life and reality of the patient.

Of course, today one could say that this main interest should be just as important for other art and psychotherapists.

These sources confirm the idea based in active music therapy that expressing oneself through musical improvisation can reveal unconscious material and offer an opportunity for sharing inner landscapes and expressing oneself in a creative and ambiguous language (Hannibal, 2014). The psychodynamic therapeutic training usually applies an understanding of music as a process of expression and meaning more than a product. Music is primarily understood as a part of the participants, and only seldom as something objective outside the participants. In an interview from 1980 Mary Priestley stated: 'Music is an expression of what is in the player, you cannot divorce the two' (Mary Priestley. Interview by Pedersen and Scheiby, 16.08.1980).

Improvisational music can – sometimes all of a sudden – bring the players in an altered state of consciousness and in a feeling of being led by the music instead of 'me playing the music' (Priestley, 1994). An example is Priestley describing:

> Sometimes when the therapist and patient are improvising there comes a moment where the music starts to change its quality so that it begins to hold the therapeutic couple. The therapist may feel that the music has become greater than the two of them and then he feels that it is playing him. In fact, instead of being the player he feels that he has become the instrument. At such a time there might be an alteration of consciousness with the act of playing the music. ... The two players are strongly united in, but overshadowed by, the music. One comes out of such an experience altered, one has lost some of one's constricting individuality and gained a feeling of a greater breadth of being. (Priestley, 1994, pp.320–321)

She claims though that such experiences are by-products of the improvisation and 'in no way essential for good therapy to take place' (Priestley, 1994, p.324). It can offer experiences of tolerable closeness or of tolerable joy, which can be extremely needed by the client. She also explains that such experiences 'form an extension of the normal tuning process...both the individual tuning of the therapist and patient and their tuning one to the other so that emotions may be responded to and resonated, when desirable' (Priestley, 1994, p.324).

We, the editors, think that such 'extraordinary' experiences, as described above, can be an essential part of a tuning process, although such experiences can never be planned.

We don't think that solely harmonious music or what could be defined as aesthetically beautiful music can generate this feeling of being taken over by the music. Surrendering to musical expressions of strong emotions like rage or anxiety can also give the players an experience of being closely together and the feeling of being overshadowed by the music.

Music can also be a means of exploring unconscious relationship patterns and variations as stated by Bruscia:

> The process of replicating and generalizing past relationships is a creative one, very much like music. We do not merely play the same piece over and over in exactly the same way (which is impossible); we recreate it differently each time, depending upon the situation, or we create a new piece using techniques or previous styles we learned previously. (Bruscia, 1998, p.xxiii)

In receptive music therapy here exemplified by the Bonny Method of Guided Imagery and Music (GIM) (Bonny, 2002; Grocke, 2019), the traveller listens to music in an altered state of consciousness and, again, a sort of fusion can happen where the experience is that the music takes over and leads the person to transformation and deep personal change (Grocke & Moe, 2015).

One of the primary sources to understand the content of the unconscious is in dreams. In active music therapy, dream images can be further explored by using them as the focus of music improvisation. In receptive music therapy methods such as GIM, music listening in an altered state of consciousness allows the client to access unconscious material in an 'awake dream state' through the experience of imagery such as visual, emotional, and kinaesthetic experiences. Bruscia has described how a psychodynamic orientation can conceptualize treatment processes in GIM for instance related to possible transference to music and to the therapist (Bruscia, 2019, p.312).

These descriptions by well-known music therapists illustrate the complexity of what the students need to learn during their therapeutic training: Music is multimodal and reaches human beings on many levels; there is an ongoing interchange between what is awakened by the music, the physical signals in the body, the images or memories, the sense of self, and the cognitive understanding of what is going on. To meet all the levels of personal development a range of active as well as receptive methods are applied in all the subjects of the therapeutic track at the Aalborg Programme, which will be elaborated in the following chapters of this book. Verbal interaction is also applied to raise the level of reflection in relation to experiences in the music.

The psychological level of the music in the therapeutic training often reaches unconscious and deeply seated emotions of the student. Music can evoke feelings and memories, and students learn to use music to express needs, feelings, and longings. The early psychological attachment and interactional patterns may be audible in the student's improvised music and thereby the music is an arena for repairing and rebuilding appropriate patterns.

Listen to myself, listen to the client

Drawing from a psychodynamic orientation, training in 'listening perspectives' and 'listening attitudes' are basic elements in the development of the music therapist's tuning and identity formation. Pedersen has described different listening perspectives and listening attitudes as the therapist's tools for orientation and information. A listening perspective can be described as the therapist listening simultaneously to:

- A foreground – the patient's here and now presence and expression

- A background – the patient's split reality (often a reality with very strong emotions). (Pedersen, 1997, 2002, 2019)

It involves listening to the field of tensions and movement (or the lack thereof) between these two polarities – the foreground and the background. The last perspective is possible only when the therapist is simultaneously listening to how they are influenced by being in this specific relationship here and now.

As part of the therapeutic training process the students learn to differentiate between the two listening attitudes and learn to oscillate between the two during simultaneous listening. The first listening attitude can be identified as an allocentric attitude where the therapist listens with full awareness directed towards the client and resonates deliberately and authentically with the client's physical presence in the room (the foreground) (Fog, 1995). The second listening attitude can be identified as an almost embodied, flowing, inward state of listening that ensures more distance from the client – an egocentric attitude where the therapist listens primarily to their own perceptions and is not directed towards the client, while at the same time making relatedness possible at a very sensitive level (the therapist perceives something that also belongs to the client, the background). The therapist is in a state of acute sensitivity and 'increased preparedness' and strives to be open to all nuances of vibrations that might flow between the therapist and the client and which are captured by the therapist (Pedersen, 2019, pp.79–80).

Disciplined subjectivity

Therapeutic training is important to prepare and tune the future therapist for a complex situation, where an openness and sensitivity towards the other must walk hand-in-hand with a clear self-perception.

Applying such strong sensitivity as described above requires the therapist to be disciplined in their way of relating to the client. The concept of neutrality as described by Freud (the therapist should be a neutral screen for the client to project on to, which implies to ideally keep their own reactions away from the concrete situation) is not applicable in music therapy or in a relational under-standing of therapy. Pedersen (2007b) has defined disciplined subjectivity as a replacement for neutrality: Disciplined subjectivity is defined as being subjec-tively present and at the same time resonant to the client's universe. This means that the therapist is acutely sensitive and attentive and can move in and out of the transitional space. The Danish psychologist Jette Fog has conceptualized the therapeutic relationship as 'separated in connectedness' and the application of disciplined subjectivity we see as an example of how the therapist can work towards this concept (Fog, 1995).

This sensitivity is necessary for the therapist to:

- Perceive the vibrations (non-verbal sensations) of which the therapist is a part

- Take responsibility for not being overwhelmed by the vibrations/emo-tions/experiences of which the therapist is a part

- Be aware of and take responsibility for the transitional space of which the therapist is a resonant part

- Be committed to continuously finding ways of understanding the pro-cesses that take place in the transitional space of which the therapist is a part (Pedersen, 2000, 2007, in Pedersen, 2019, p.80)

These tasks often include an expanded understanding of time and consciousness. It takes lifelong training and tuning to be present with vitality in many fields of awareness simultaneously activated.

Training processes concerning listening perspectives and listening attitudes and disciplined subjectivity are important for the future music therapist to be able to cope with the phenomena of transference and countertransference.

Transference and countertransference

Transference and countertransference are two important concepts in the psychodynamic perspective of music therapy. Bruscia (1998) has written comprehensively on both transference and countertransference, and he has moved forward from Freud, who 'originally tried to explain transference phenomena as an enduring mental structure or dynamic that resides within the client – as strictly intrapersonal' (Bruscia, 1998, p.22). Bruscia defines transference as follows:

> A transference occurs whenever the client interacts within the ongoing therapy situation in ways that resemble relationship patterns previously established with significant persons or things in real-life situations from the past. Implicit is a replication in the present of relationship patterns learned in the past and a generalization of these patterns from significant persons or things and real-life situations to the therapist and the therapy situation. Essentially, the client re-experiences in the present the same or similar feelings, conflicts, impulses, drives, and fantasies as she did with significant persons or things in the past while also repeating the same or similar ways of handling and avoiding these feelings, persons and situations. (Bruscia, 1998, p.18)

Hannibal (2000) in his PhD thesis identified preverbal interaction structures in clinical improvisation in music therapy, and from these preverbal interaction structures he could identify the transference relation in clinical improvisation in music therapy. Hannibal showed that Stern's theoretical concept of preverbality could be used as a common theoretical basis concerning an action and an interaction perspective to describe relational patterns in both verbal and musical interactions, and that transference patterns in the verbal context emerge in the musical context and vice versa. He also concluded that both conflict and other relational patterns (of different qualities) emerge in the musical context (Hannibal, 2000).

In line with the concepts of Stern (1995), Hannibal talks about schemas instead of generalizations (a concept of Bruscia's). Hannibal concluded that his study confirmed the basic assumption of the Danish professor in psychology Esben Hougaard, who stated that:

> The interpersonal relation in the clinical improvisation is structured by preverbal relational schemas, which has been developed on the basis of being together with significant others. It is therefore a transference phenomenon, due to the fact that

all interpersonal relationships have a transference quality, as personal perception is based on schemas. (Hougaard, 1996, p.161, our translation)

Many years passed before Freud became curious about the countertransference of the therapist – a concept defined as the therapist's unconscious reaction towards the client's transference. So, transference and countertransference were originally understood as unconscious reciprocal phenomena in therapy.

Concerning working with transference and countertransference, in classical psychoanalytic treatment, the therapist was expected to hold a neutral position towards the client and thus offer a screen for the client's transference reactions. Similarly, countertransference was regarded as a phenomenon the therapist should aim at avoiding or controlling, as originally described by Freud. Later, it was regarded as a phenomenon which could be very informative and clinically applicable if applied (disclosed or acted out in the music) at the right timing and with the right intensity. Post-Freudians such as Thomas French and Erika Fromm (1964) emphasized that one had to be present in the flow of one's own countertransference long enough to be able to withdraw and objectively make an interpretation. Patrick Casement (1985) emphasized what is later seen as a more modern model, that the analyst always must make use of an 'inner supervisor', as the analyst will never be able to be totally objective in interpretations of the field of transference in the therapeutic relationship (Vedfelt, 1996). Paula Heimann (1950) argued that the concept of countertransference refers to all emotions the therapist is feeling in relation to the client, as she thinks the differentiation between emotions occurred in response to the real relation, and emotions which are transference phenomena are very difficult to distinguish both concerning the therapist (countertransference) and the client (transference). She points out that the emotional response from the therapist to the client is one of the most important tools in analytical work, and she understands the countertransference as an important tool to examine and explore the unconscious of the client. She claims that the aim of self-experience for the therapist is to be able to sustain the emotions emerging in the relationship. If the therapist can sustain these emotions and subordinate them to the therapeutic work, the therapist can function as a mirror for the client. A basic preconception is that:

> ...the unconscious of the therapist understands the unconscious of the patient and this attachment at a deep level comes to surface in the form of emotions experienced by the therapist in their answers to the patient – in his/her countertransference. (Heimann, 1959, in Langs, 1990, p.141)

Heinrich Racker (1968) was the first to distinguish two different positions in the countertransference reactions, namely the positions of 'concordant identification' and 'complementary identifications'. These positions were further developed by Mary Priestley (1975/1994). She identified them as:

1. Empathic countertransference (e-countertransference) where the therapist can identify with emotions or sensations coming from the client, that the client is unaware of.

2. Complementary countertransference (c-countertransference), which implies that the therapist identifies with former caretakers or relatives from the client's past, as the client unconsciously relates to the therapist similarly as to the former caretakers. Through c-countertransference the therapist can unconsciously repeat behaviours from certain persons in the client's past. It is very important for the therapist to be sensitive to and aware of their own countertransference reactions and to use them constructively to change negative relational patterns in the therapeutic relationship.

In both cases the task of the therapist is to aim at keeping a deep and lasting contact with themselves to be as aware as possible of both countertransference reactions towards the client. Racker writes:

> The awareness of countertransference by the therapist creates the cornerstone to identify the unconscious trials by the patient to repeat unconscious relationship patterns. This awareness can lead to an interruption of the vicious circles and create the possibilities of internalizing a more positive result with the therapist. (Racker in Tansey & Burke, 1989, pp.25–26)

Bruscia (1998) also wrote comprehensively about countertransference – how to understand the signs of it and how to uncover and work with countertransference. He invited six different music therapists representing different music therapy approaches to write a chapter on their understanding and use of countertransference, and it is clear in these chapters that the psychodynamic concept of countertransference exceeds definitions and limitations of different music therapy approaches. Bruscia understood the concepts of transference and countertransference in a broader context to cover all emotions and sensations resonating between the therapist and client which is in line with our current understanding. We consider both concepts as very important tools of information to understand the underlying dynamics between the therapist and client or in the group. Also, we consider that transference and countertransference are connected and mutually influencing these dynamics (Pedersen, 2007a). This understanding has been further developed within the relational psychoanalysis (Binder *et al.*, 2006), where it is emphasized that the awareness of transference patterns should be directed towards the emotions of both the client and the therapist as it is a relational issue, and it is a mutual task to uncover the unconscious communication taking place in this specific relationship. Here, the therapist of course can draw from experiences from self- and other therapeutic experiences and most often will be the leader on this mutual journey. But the perspective on the relationship is a two-person intersubjective dynamic focus, and not a focus solely on the intrapsychic dynamic of the client. In contemporary psychodynamic psychotherapy a 'development' is understood as finding a new pattern in the relationship, a third way, which creates more flexibility and freedom for both the client and the therapist.

Both concepts and their interconnectedness thus are important in therapeutic learning processes. (For further descriptions of the history of countertransference, see also Pedersen, 2007a.)

Parallel processes in supervision

Parallel processes are an important learning process in self-experience and experiential training. This phenomenon includes that, most often, unconscious processes, which are unfolding between client and therapist, can unfold as a repetition between the supervisee and the supervisor in the supervisory process. Ogden (2005) describes how awareness of subjective fantasies and emotions by the supervisor can help clarify unconscious interpersonal processes between the supervisee and the client. Ogden kept calling the phenomenon 'reflection processes' after Searles who first defined this concept in 1955 (Ridder, 2013), although many other psychotherapists applied the concept 'parallel processes'. Watkins (2010) describes the concept as an enwidening of the Searles concept and thus he claims it should be called parallel processes. Some discussion went on among theorists concerning whether the phenomenon covers such processes only one way from client to therapist to supervisor, or whether these processes can unfold in reverse. Today the concept of parallel processes is applied to both definitions (Jacobsen, 2005).

In education, parallel processes in supervision can be an important source of information for the ongoing learning process as well as for the supervision of therapy.

The psychodynamic approach in the light of new theoretical developments

As already mentioned, experiential observation and video analyses of interaction between infants and caretakers informed the relational turn, where the focus shifted from looking at the internal psychological processes to the intersubjective processes of the early development. The American psychologist Andrew Meltzoff (1990) experimentally investigated infants 42 minutes after birth and found that the newborn infants were able to remember and imitate facial expressions (such as movements of the tongue), not as a result of reflexive imitation, but intentional and goal corrected. By repeating the interactions, he found that the infant compares a motor action against an internal memory, schema, or representation of what was previously seen. The infant uses cross-modal translation from a visual input (the other's facial expression) to its inner proprioceptive sensation of its own face, bodily movements, and sounds, establishing the first sense that 'you are like me' in form and in timing. The correspondence between infant and caregiver forms an appreciated and playful interaction that is the fundamental intersubjective matrix for the recognition of identity and development of the infant self (Meltzoff & Moore, 1998).

The British emeritus-professor in child psychology and psychobiology Colwyn Trevarthen analysed video recordings of early interaction between mother and child (Trevarthen, 1998). Later he worked together with Steven Malloch, a professor in music and psychoacoustics, who coined the term 'communicative musicality' (see also Chapter 2) describing the intimacy and loving interconnectedness in the preverbal dialogues that is unfolding through musical concepts such as timing, melodic contour, turn taking, narrative, and rhythm (Malloch & Trevarthen, 2010).

The American child psychologist and psychoanalyst Daniel Stern likewise based his self-theory on observation of the mother–infant dyad and the interactions that take place in the real world (Stern, 1985/2000). These real-world observations stood in contrast to earlier psychoanalytic studies, where an emphasis on the inner world of the infant and the hypothesis of the infant's inner symbolic preverbal representations was based on older children's and adults' memories. Stern also rejected theories of phased development including, for example, a 'symbiotic or an autistic phase' (Mahler, Pine, & Bergman, 1975), as it did not fit with the observed fluency of development in the competent, active, and communicative infant. Stern formulated a theory of the infant entering successive domains of relational experience, each building on top of the other, called 'intersubjective domains', that would remain intact for the rest of life. Out of five domains three are implicit and nonverbal: the sense of the 'emerging self', the 'core self', and the 'subjective self'; and two are verbal: the 'verbal self' and the 'narrative self'. Stern described the preverbal experience as a subconscious, tacit, and procedural knowledge, that he called the implicit knowledge, in contrast to the verbalized explicit knowledge. Repeated and similar experience of being with another (the daily rhythms and sensations of interplay and interaction) was thought to build prototypical procedural schemata in the child, termed RIGs (representations of interactions that have been generalized), that is related to early attachment patterns (Hannibal, 2019; Stern, 1985/2000). Stern later named the RIGs 'ways of how to be with another' (Hannibal, 2007).

Stern was interested in the sense of reality that comes before the development of language and words, which he saw as limited to the stream of experience in the implicit domains. To come closer to a description of the perspective of the infant in the preverbal domain, Stern developed the concept 'dynamic forms of vitality' (2010), which focus on the shape, contour, liveliness, and intensity, or the 'how' of the interaction rather than on the content ('why' or 'what'). 'Affective attunement' (Stern, 1985/2000) describes a process, where the mother/father matches the dynamic forms of vitality (intensity, rhythm, form, and timing) in the infant's gestures and sounds of expression. The affective attunement process intends to create a sense of shared experience and an experience of community. A co-regulation is taking place, and a communication of what can and cannot be shared, that shapes the infant's later expectations of social interaction.

Based on this theory, Stern developed ways of working in the implicit realms in psychotherapy together with the Boston Change Process Study Group (2010). They build on the idea that therapeutic change, in adults as well as children, is taking place in the relationship in the here-and-now interactions and in the implicit domain. This is radical compared to the general thinking that therapy is about verbalization, reflection, interpretation, and insight in the unconscious processes. Working at the 'local level', a process of continuously fitting in with the other can lead to 'present moments of meetings' where important new ways of being together can be experienced. These moments happen spontaneously, and can be emotionally laden, or be an opening to a more coherent way of being together. Stern himself advocated for music therapy and other arts-based psychotherapies as important ways of working in the nonverbal domain (Stern, 2010), where the musical form of vitality is the basic form of interaction and communication, that reach deeply into the implicit patterns of the client and the therapeutic dyad.

Stern's theory has been widely adopted in the psychodynamic theoretical landscape of music therapy (Hannibal, 2019; Holck, 2019; Trondalen, 2016). As music therapy researcher Susan Hadley expressed it:

Modern infancy research and affective neuroscience have thus brought about a paradigm shift in psychodynamic thinking that has particular significance for music therapists, given the quasi-musical characteristics of early communication and empathic interpersonal relations that continues throughout the lifespan. (Hadley, 2003, p.9)

Attachment

Patterns of attachment develop early in life and can continue to influence romantic relationships, family relationships, and even the generalized basic trust towards peers and the life condition itself. Following up on Bowlby's studies, recent literature points to the attachment style as penetrating and fundamental to our way of living (Hart, 2018b; Mikulincer, Shaver, & Phillip, 2003; Sutton, 2019).

The unconscious bodily communication in face-to-face dialogues between mothers and infants was investigated by Beebe and Lachmann (2014), who used a detailed microanalysis to uncover how insecure attachment patterns can be observed in the moment-to-moment self- and interactive processes of related-ness. In order to repair early attachment wounds in therapy, it is important that the therapist is trained to be aware of micromovements and bodily mirroring such as turning the head away, imitation patterns, and micro attunement. The training of music therapists integrates several measures to train this sensitivity, by working with sound and bodily awareness, by watching and reflecting on video recordings of their own training therapy sessions, and by carrying out micro analyses of video recordings of other music therapists as part of project work. Entering the personal processes in music therapy, the students have the possibility to experience and investigate their attachment style and habitual relational patterns. Through the structure and repetitiveness of music, as well as the empathic and holding attitude of the training therapist, it can be possible to find enough safety to let go of tension or fear and access moments of resonance, connection, and openness to develop a new experience of being in the world.

Perspectives from current trauma theory

An increased focus on the role of trauma in mental illness as well as in medical conditions has developed in the past decades. This has led to an increased under-standing of the importance of being aware that trauma can be re-experienced in the treatment situation, and of the role of dissociation for self-protection.

There are many different types of trauma and degrees of traumatization that demand different treatment approaches. The recovery process is usually based on empowerment of the trauma survivor and the restoration of relationships, and common to all treatment processes is the importance of a good working alliance between therapist and client. Common for most trauma treatment approaches is the adherence to Herman's three phases of trauma treatment: establishing safety, retelling the story of the traumatic event (grieving the losses), and reconnecting with others (Herman, 1995). Many modern trauma treatment methods also incorporate the rebalancing of the autonomic nervous system (ANS), with the aim of working inside as well as on the edges of the client's 'window of tolerance,' and thereby gradually increase its flexibility. Knowing the psychobiological defence mechanisms related to life-threatening experiences allows for the tracking of both active defences (fight and flight) and immobilizing responses such as freeze, faint/shut down, and playing dead, and for supporting the client when they go into a bodily experience of any of these responses during the therapy.

Treatment of developmental trauma inspired by a psychodynamic orientation investigates the childhood relationships, where neglect, loss, and emotional, physical, or sexual abuse originally took place, as well as into the current relationship patterns and problems, and the defences that prevent the client from uncovering unconscious parts of the trauma reaction (Spermon, Darlington, & Gibney, 2010). Another way to describe the unconscious content belonging to traumatic experiences is to talk about *dissociation*, where the traumatized individual, due to the overwhelming character of the trauma, splits up the psyche for self-protection.

> ...when trauma strikes the developing psyche of a child, a fragmentation of consciousness occurs in which different 'pieces'...organize themselves according to certain archaic and typical (archetypal) patterns...one part of the ego regresses to the infantile period, and another progresses, i.e., grows up too fast and becomes precariously adapted to the outer world. (Kalsched, 1996, p.3)

There are different theories of dissociation, one of them called the 'theory of structural dissociation' inspired by Pierre Janet, which describes how split off parts of the personality present as different states or parts in life which can be totally separated and unaware of each other or have some interconnectedness (van der Hart, Nijenhuis, & Steele, 2006). These parts can, for instance, be different child parts, showing up in treatment with different needs and voices. In the treatment process increased integration, presence, connection, and acceptance is supported, also of so-called 'perpetrator parts' that can seem aggressive and abusive but often hold self-defence impulses that were adequate in the original context. By hearing and working with all parts, a more coherent psychological system can be created.

Several recent theories of trauma and trauma treatment have emphasized the importance of working with a bottom-up approach addressing trauma symptoms through nonverbal and implicit pathways (Levine, 2010a; Porges, 2010; Rothschild, 2000; van der Kolk, 2015). Van der Kolk has contributed to the understanding of how trauma memory is stored in the body, and how it often can be inaccessible for the conscious mind and verbalization. He suggested that effective treatment of trauma must be based on the regulation and synchronization of body and mind. Likewise, the principles for trauma treatment developed by Peter Levine (1997, 2010) build on the idea that it is not the traumatic incident that creates trauma, but the way incomplete defence actions (such as fight and flight) energetically are stored up in the nervous system, creating disturbing physical and psychological symptoms. Levine described how trauma treatment can be based on a tracking of discharge and defence actions through a thorough sensation of the body in the co-regulated and resonant therapeutic dyad, where a *pendulation* between activation and deactivation (the two branches of the autonomic nervous system (ANS)) is monitored or guided by the therapist. This procedure is securing a gentle process where fragments of trauma reactions are processed on the bodily level, so that the nervous system gradually can discharge the energy, unfreeze, and become more flexible. Levine advocated for the use of vocalizing, where sound and vibration are ways to enhance vitality, strength, and sensation in the body. Making music together is also seen as a way to reinforce the social connection and reduce the withdrawal and isolation often seen in traumatized individuals (Levine, 2010b).

Stephen Porges presented a theory of 'neuroception', where he described the ongoing appraisal of danger versus safety in the human nervous system (Porges, 2003). By analysing physiological measurement of heart rate variability, he found that humans have two parts of the parasympathetic system: a) the well-known dorsal vagal part responsible for freeze and immobilization as self-protection, and b) the ventral vagal system connected to the 10th cranial nerve (the vagus nerve), that is connected to the 'social engagement system'. The ventral vagal system is activated by face-to-face communication where activation of the eyes, ears, and facial muscles influence the vital organs (heart, stomach, lungs) and help to calm down stress and anxiety (Porges, 2003). Porges also found that the function of the auditory system is dependent on neuroception, and that both singing and music in the same range as the human voice can provide a calming effect (Porges, 2010).

Music therapy theory which specifically integrates these neurobiologically informed trauma treatment principles is primarily found in Guided Imagery and Music (GIM) literature (Beck, 2015; Beck *et al.*, 2018, 2021; Körlin, 2010; Maack,

2012; Rudstam *et al.*, 2017; Story 2018), as well as in a broad range of music therapy and community music therapy approaches building on drumming, improvising, singing, and moving to music (Auf der Heyde, 2012; Borcson, 2012; Osborne, 2012; Stewart, 2010). Music therapy can be a powerful method for a safe expression of fear, rage, sadness, and loss connected to traumatic experiences, and it is also a way to explore and build up positive emotions, vitality, empowerment, connectedness, and playfulness. Music listening can generate inner experiences of hope, comfort, and connection to positive memories and can help with the regulation of arousal and fear.

During the therapeutic training, music therapy students become more aware about their own history and they are encouraged to work through their own problematic life experiences. They can also be advised to continue in a personal therapy outside the programme, but this will be their own decision. In specific and rare cases where students through therapeutic training might be faced surprisingly with serious traumatic experiences, they will be carefully encouraged and advised about how they can work on becoming familiar with their own reactions and can be prepared for sensitively being able to contain these experiences in future work with clients who have had traumatic experiences. Gradually the students are trained to meet the self-defence responses that are characteristic of trauma in a sensitive way, and to provide a careful framework with respect to their future clients' boundaries and tempo. Many of the clients that music therapists are going to serve will have experienced multiple traumatic events and will have different degrees of dysregulation in the autonomic nervous system. This means that they will be unable to calm themselves when agitated, or unable to get into an active and mutual communicative state when in low activation, or even be in freeze or dissociative states. The students learn to provide a holding and grounding structure with their music and to create listening experiences that are fitted to the window of tolerance of their specific client, so that they can create a safe space which is not too demanding or overwhelming.

There are many ethical issues connected to therapeutic work with severe early abuse and developmental trauma. Psychotherapists still grapple with the problem of accuracy of trauma memory, as it is now well known that the brain edits and rewrites memories constantly. It is recommended to the students to work with the client's symptoms and memories as they are presented, with an intention of support and empowerment without judging or interpreting, and with a focus on improvement of the client's here and now function in life. To work with traumatized children, and traumatized clients without verbal language, reduced cognitive skills, or few psychosocial resources, the students learn to use the music as a way of providing trauma-informed care, and to uphold a moment-to-moment attunement and awareness of bodily changes. These are advanced skills that build on many stepping stones during long-term therapeutic training.

Neuroscientific research in relation to psychodynamic theory

Instead of a cognitively oriented brain research that focuses mainly on the processes taking place inside the brain, the *enactive brain paradigm* or *'embodiment of mind'* maps persons in relationships and in the environment, looking into processes of connection between brain, body, environment, and relationships, and as such it is a good framework for describing many levels of brain processes in music therapy (Thompson, 2007).

The therapeutic training integrates neurobiological research that supports the use of music therapy to regulate brain processes, stress states, and attachment processes. Music therapy students learn about relevant neurobiological research during their theoretical subjects, but they are also encouraged to integrate this knowledge in their understanding of their therapeutic training, and to learn to describe their practice on various levels. In this section, some examples of research underpinning the relevance of music therapy and psychodynamic-based interventions will be provided. Some researchers have tried to find evidence for the existence of an unconscious mind. In the results of four experiments led by Shevrin's study group, where participants were presented with conflictual subject-specific stimuli (hearing phrases connected to unconscious conflicts derived from clinical casework), electroencephalographic (EEG) measurements identified alpha synchronization, known for its inhibitory function, and related it to the existence of a brain mechanism of unconscious defence (Bazan, 2017).

Psychodynamic neuroscience research describes metapsychological models and the neurobiological basis of topics such as empathy, embodiment, and emotional conflict (Fotopoulou, 2012; Northoff, 2011). Markova, Nguyen, and Hoehl (2019) discussed the underlying neural structure of entrainment in infant-directed singing and touching, and how dyadic emotional contact in early childhood has been found to stimulate the capacity of arousal regulation in the growing child. A review of physiological response and frontal EEG asymmetry in infants and adults indicated that insecure attachment is related to a heightened stress response and impaired emotion regulation (Gander & Buchheim, 2015).

Brain research has demonstrated that the brain continues to create new neural pathways and alter existing ones to adapt to new experiences, learn new information, and create new memories; this is referred to as neuroplasticity (Oberman & Pascual-Leone, 2013). This contradicts earlier beliefs stating that we are determined to stay in fixed patterns and behaviours founded in childhood. It has been found that use-dependent change in the brain takes place through a change of actions and experiences (Kleim & Jones, 2008). This is promising for therapeutic processes and supports the focus on dynamic relationships and the importance of creating new experiences of attunement and synchronization in the therapeutic space. It also emphasizes the importance of supporting the client to carry out new actions and behaviours in everyday life.

Neuroscientific research can be related to the students' learning processes both in the short term (chemical changes in the brain and mood regulation) and the structural changes in the brain that are changing over time when the students improvise on a daily basis during five years of training.

The possible positive role of music in music therapy has been supported by neuroscientific research (Christensen, 2012, 2017). Music has been found to engage a multitude of regions in the brain simultaneously, such as sensory processes, attention, memory-related processes, perception-action mediation, multisensory integration, activity changes in core areas of emotional processing, processing of musical syntax and musical meaning, and social cognition (Koelsch, 2009). Music interventions are connected to instant neurochemical changes related to pleasure and motivation (Chanda & Levitin, 2013; Cheung *et al.*, 2019; Ferreri *et al.*, 2019). Music also influences the stress and immune defence systems and hormones connected to prosocial behaviour such as oxytocin (Harvey, 2020; Kreutz, Quiroga Murcia, & Bongard, 2012). Several researchers have indicated that the dopaminergic effects are connected to musical expectation, and the release of opioids is connected to actual experience of the strong emotional experience of music (Barbano & Cador, 2007; Chanda & Levitin, 2013; Gebauer, Kringelbach, & Vuust, 2012; Kringelbach & Berridge, 2009). A review of functional neuroimaging studies on music and emotion concluded that music can modulate activity in brain structures that are known to be crucially involved in emotion (Koelsch, 2014).

With the development of new neuroimaging techniques, neuroscientists have been able to study different types of whole brain networks and connectivity rather than focusing on single regions of the brain. Resting state networks (RSNs) such as the default mode network (DMN) are spontaneous, synchronous, low-frequency oscillations observed in the brains of subjects who are awake but at rest. Music listening seems to activate the DMN that is connected to mind wandering, reflection, and introspection (Reybrouck, Vuust, & Brattico, 2018). Interestingly, studies on music listening in persons with schizophrenia showed increased connectivity in the DMN (He *et al.*, 2018). Receptive music therapy with verbal clients is a combination of inward focusing on music and externally focused verbal integration. The central executive network (CEN) is connected to executive functioning and verbal learning, and the salience network (SN) is connected to emotional processing. In posttraumatic stress disorder and other conditions where numbness or dissociation has blocked the flexibility or blurred the shift between the networks, music therapy can be seen as restorative because it can activate DMN networks and provide clear shifts between this network and other networks (Lanius *et al.*, 2015).

Following the realization of the significance of social and relational connection, neuroscientists have begun to investigate interbrain synchronization during interpersonally coordinated action studying adaptive timing, motor sequencing, and special organization of movements, as well as anticipatory and attentional processes that enable rhythmic joint action and interaction (Keller, Novembre, & Hove, 2014; Zatorre, Chen, & Penhune, 2007). How these functions and underlying brain structures are related to 'extended hyper-brain networks' is still not clear. A study on choir singing showed that the vocalizing patterns of singers are coupled to their respiratory and cardiac oscillations (Müller & Lindenberger, 2011), another that the brains of pianists performing a musical duet correlated to piano MIDI signals (Zamm *et al.*, 2019), and in studies of improvising guitarists it was found that 'brains are swinging in concert': brain signals were oscillatory in nature and were characterized by specific spectral peaks, indicating the temporal structure in the synchronization patterns between guitars and brains (Lindenberger *et al.*, 2009; Müller & Lindenberger, 2019; Müller, Sänger, & Lindenberger, 2013). In a dual EEG study of a GIM session, Fachner and colleagues (2019) found similar emotional processing in the therapist and guide related to moments of specifically intense imagery in the session.

New psychodynamic approaches related to neuroscience

Several authors have integrated the understanding of stress and resilience, neuroscientific findings, and psychodynamic thinking. Allan Shore has called the new focus on brain-mind-body a paradigm shift in psychotherapy – from a left-brain conscious cognitive verbal orientation to a right-brain affective unconscious orientation (Shore, 2019). When working with clients with severe relational trauma, where affect and stress regulation capacity is disturbed, the focus on attachment, affect regulation, and right-brain to right-brain mutual synchronization and joint interpersonal action is especially important.

Another example of a new approach that integrates psychodynamic theory with modern neuroaffective science is Fosha's accelerated experiential dynamic psychotherapy (AEDP), where the therapist creates a secure attachment relationship to the client and helps to track emotions that were previously too overwhelming. The client is helped to have a complete emotional experience, and afterwards reflect upon the experience; this is called a meta-therapeutic processing. Fosha sees the 'transformance drive' as a wired-in capacity for growth and healing. The therapist works actively with psychodynamic defence mechanisms that prohibit the emotions from coming to the surface (Fosha, 2000; Fosha, Siegel, & Solomon, 2009). The Swedish psychologist Katarina Blom has worked with relational modes in Guided Imagery and Music and integrated the work of Fosha in her emotional relational approach to GIM (Blom, 2014).

Susan Hart, a Danish psychologist, has integrated trauma theory, attachment theory, neurobiology, and the theory of the triune brain (MacLean, 1990) into the 'neuroaffective therapy model' that includes three different levels of intervention: the autonomic, the limbic, and the prefrontal level (Hart, 2018a, 2018b). Her standpoint is that it is necessary to address problems in the basic regulation and attention as well as the emotional/limbic area before cognitive understanding and integration can take place. In client groups with impaired cognitive functions, it is still possible to intervene at the autonomic and limbic levels and thereby increase their life quality. Because of the nature of music as an embodied and emotionally evocative art form, applying receptive and active music therapy methods can be seen as a unique way of accessing the deeper layers of the brain and the nervous system. Music listening and music-making with a therapist can be used to mirror and regulate autonomic and limbic processes in the client on a micro level, a very intensive way of interaction and contact, which develops new pathways and structures in the brain, as well as new types of experiences and actions (Lindvang & Beck, 2017).

Mentalization

Mentalization-based treatment (MBT) was developed for borderline personality disorder and has been described particularly by psychologist Peter Fonagy and psychiatrist Anthony Bateman (Bateman & Fonagy, 2012, 2016). Over the last 20 years the mentalization-based approach has been applied to many different treatment areas as well as educational settings and mentalizing capacity is now understood as something close to the very core of our humanity (Fogtmann, 2014; Skårderud & Sommerfeldt, 2013).

The theory behind the concept of mentalizing is based on the understanding of the influence of the early attachment relationship and the neuro-biological and psychological theories as described above. The approach in mentalization-based therapy is also grounded on an interdisciplinary integration of evolutionary theory, psychoanalytic/psychodynamic thinking, systemic thinking, and more. The aim of mentalizing therapy is to enhance a mentalizing process, foster mirroring, offer validation and detailed inquiry, investigate misunderstandings, support affective responsiveness, and to develop the capacity for reflection. Mentalization is not a static skill, but a dynamic capacity which is affected by the person's level of stress and arousal especially in relational contexts (Bateman & Fonagy, 2012).

In the manuals for MBT the focus is on the therapist's mentalizing capacity (Karterud, 2015). One of the key factors in the manual is to monitor if and how the therapist can be in a 'not-knowing' stance during the interaction with the client(s). In contrast to being the expert who interprets the client, as in classical psychoanalysis, the therapist adapts a curious attitude and stays open to different perspectives and aspects of an experience. The therapeutic approach in MBT focuses on adopting an investigative dialogue with the client, building trust in the therapeutic relationship, and on creating coherence between the client's bodily and emotional being, thoughts, and understanding of themselves.

It is at the core of the students' learning processes in the therapeutic track that they develop their mentalizing capacity understood as the ability to imagine and to empathize with for example the needs, wishes, and emotions that are connected to the way people are and the way they act. It is a very human capability that underpins our everyday life together – without this capacity we would not have a robust sense of self and be able to socialize (Fonagy *et al.,* 2002). 'Seeing oneself and others as agentive and intentional beings driven by mental states that are meaningful and understandable creates the psychological coherence about self and others that is essential for navigating a complex social world' (Bateman & Fonagy, 2016, p.5).

Music therapy students do possess a certain level of mentalizing capacity when they start their training, but they usually need to develop, strengthen, and refine this capacity to become a professional therapist. If human beings are under stress or feel anxiety in a situation, we are likely to struggle with a reduced capacity to mentalize in these moments. Working as a therapist requires a mentalizing capacity that is as stable as possible – despite the emotional difficulties you meet and even if the person you work with, or your colleague, has lost their ability to mentalize. Misunderstandings and difficulties in communication happen but are possible to repair with a mentalizing attitude.

A well-developed mentalizing capacity resembles reflection on a high level where you both feel and think in a clear way. It is a sophisticated level of information processing in the brain that implies a vital connection to the bodily senses as well.

Strehlow and Hannibal (2019) argue that the mindset of the music therapist is the most important factor in facilitating mentalizing in music therapy. The therapist is concerned with the here-and-now and participates and engages in a verbal as well as musical interaction. In both modalities implicit as well as explicit mentalizing qualities may unfold. Strehlow and Hannibal divide mentalization into four layers, starting with an implicit level where the interaction in musical improvisation is performed in an implicit way, and moving to an explicit level in musical improvisation, where the words are being thought while playing. At the third layer, the therapist reflects verbally with the patient after the improvisation at an explicit mentalizing level, and finally there is a layer defined by the way the therapist talks with the patient during the verbal reflection. These layers can be seen as something common in all psychotherapy processes.

These layers are recognizable in the context of training therapy for music therapy students. In the students' training processes, they work with mentalization on an implicit level, for example, while they listen to, feel, and relate to each other as they participate in a shared improvisation. They also work with their mentalizing capacity on a more explicit level, as for example in a verbal dialogue, looking for coherence and meaning in what they just expressed together in the music (Lindvang, 2017; Strehlow & Hannibal, 2019).

A bridge from psychodynamic theory to the students' training processes

In our attempt to comprehend the many dimensions of the theoretical cross-field between therapy theory and learning theory we, the authors, would like to briefly mention Ole Vedfelt, a Danish psychotherapist and theoretician in the psychology of consciousness. Vedfelt has contributed to the field with an integrative approach to psychotherapy by formulating a contemporary and spacious meta-theoretical framework (called cybernetic psychology) which aims at embracing the complexity of the unconscious and the therapeutic relationships (Vedfelt, 2001, 2018). Vedfelt acknowledges the significant contribution related to exploration of the unconscious made by both Freud and Jung but found:

> ...a model was needed that was capable of uniting the advantages from Freud and Jung's intrapsychic theories, with a theory of the psyche as an open system – a theory ready to describe levels and states of consciousness and with a balanced understanding of body, mind and soul relation. (Vedfelt, 2001, p.299, authors' translation)

We, the authors of this chapter, acknowledge this viewpoint of integrating the intrapsychic theories with a theory of the psyche as an open system. This is a theoretical platform for us when we emphasize the *relational perspective* as a vehicle for an integration of elements of the classical and the new orientation in psychodynamic understanding.

According to Vedfelt, human beings do consecutively receive a lot more information than they are capable of comprehending while being in a normal rational state of consciousness.

In an analysis of students' therapeutic learning processes, Lindvang (2010) used the theory of cybernetic psychology as one of the analysis approaches and found that the therapeutic training processes develop the students' perceptional responsiveness: The students learn to use different sources of information and modalities in the human contact, for example bodily sensory information and images, and to connect these with what they hear and see. In Vedfelt's cybernetic terminology this corresponds to the development of a 'supramodal space' (Lindvang, 2010, 2013, 2015). A supramodal space is a multidimensional psychic space with access to several modes of experiences, and with a capacity to collaborate with associative networks, through memories, feelings, body sensations, etc., and to treat a huge amount of information. The ability to contain many sorts of information simultaneously is called the 'supramodal ability'. According to Vedfelt, it is highly important in the development of the trainee therapist to train this creative and partly unconscious human ability, in order to reach a level of very quick treatment of information, getting access to as whole and coherent a picture of the concrete client and of the dynamic process as possible (Vedfelt, 2018). Self-experience in music therapy training gives the student important non-intellectual experiences of navigating in a supramodal space, for example in the music improvisations. The theory about a supramodal space may be comparable to the earlier formulated tertiary process thinking (see earlier in this chapter); a creative state of mind characterized by an easy and quick oscillation between different levels of consciousness.

The psychodynamic concepts as described in this chapter are based on an awareness of a broad spectrum of layers of consciousness, including altered states of consciousness (listening perspectives, disciplined subjectivity, transference issues, and parallel processes). In psychodynamic-oriented music therapy, the therapist acknowledges that the participants or clients and the therapist are in a shared process of both conscious and unconscious communication, and of implicit and explicit mentalization. In musical improvisation or in listening to music in an altered state of consciousness, it is possible to tune in to the deeper layers of our being, such as our deep sensory and emotional processes, and through that open for the investigation of other streams of information than the cognitive and rational mind deliver.

It is also important that students become aware of and respect that our consciousness is like an ocean with innumerable streams of impulses we do not even perceive in an everyday state of mind. And that they experience in their own body how music can be a way to reach deeper levels of our being and a way to get in contact with the supramodal ability, also called unconscious intelligence (Vedfelt, 2009, 2018). The students are trained to listen, in a psychodynamic sense, to what they meet on as many levels as possible in a given situation or context. They learn to listen to the sound, the speed and rhythm, the facial and bodily expression, as well as to the content, melody, or form. From the very beginning our students are asked to observe themselves as well as others and they develop a bidirectional consciousness which means that they learn to contain themselves as well as the other (person, context, etc.) at the same time.

Training therapy as an educational aspect of becoming a psychotherapist is a tradition going back to Freud. At that time, the analysis of the trainee therapist, known as the 'training analysis', was considered to be the most important component in training to become an analytical therapist (Hougaard, 2019). Today most psychotherapy training programmes acknowledge and require self-experience as an aspect of therapeutic training. Although many therapists, including psychoanalysts, no longer work with clients as Freud did, his wisdom on matters of therapeutic training nowadays is an accepted part of most therapeutic practice (Geller, Norcross, & Orlinsky, 2005).

Concerning the therapeutic learning processes for music therapy students at Aalborg University we have chosen to keep an integration of self-experience simultaneously with other learning processes (musical, academic). We find that the different teaching processes fertilize each other. Research shows that future therapists find that learning through self-experience processes and supervision is highly important for the quality of their future clinical practice (Lindvang, 2010; Orlinsky & Rønnestad, 2005). These learning processes need to be both individual and in dyads and groups where the students have a chance to build the necessary trust to really sense and understand themselves and meet themselves in the mirror of and interaction with the other/s. They can experience if and how possible abandonment and inner conflicts might influence their directedness towards growth, creativity, and need for contact. It is an important developmental step for the students to be able to make disciplined use of their subjective unconscious through sensations, feelings, and inner imageries as an orientation tool in a (future) clinical music therapy practice. These processes are time-consuming, and this is why the therapeutic training processes are implemented through all years of the training programme in Aalborg (Bachelor and Master's level). During the students' personal developmental processes, it is crucial that they learn to acknowledge their own and others' inner landscape as enriching resources where deep creative sources of energy circulate. When emotional conflicts or problems are left behind with no attention it may turn into a dry area, or a frozen lake – i.e., a part of the landscape where the energy is bound and solidified. Then the student needs a safe, supportive, and guiding space in order to find courage in meeting those darker, lonely, or painful places inside. On the other hand, it may be extremely important for a student to experience that it is possible to let go of being tied to problems, let go of the intention of solving, and turn the attention in the direction of new inputs. Together with the training therapists, co-students, teachers, and supervisors the student takes steps along the five years of training and education towards a strengthened understanding of the complexity of the psyche and towards a deeper trust in new relational possibilities.

According to psychodynamic theory an important element in self-development is to experience frustration, and the basic understanding of learning in the traditional psychodynamic view is therefore that a certain dosage of frustration can motivate learning, because the student will begin to search for alternatives and new knowledge to grow (Hermansen, 2005). In the music therapy students' therapy processes the teachers and therapists apply a modification of this way of thinking as they seek to create a safe and open space to promote learning – they do not seek to *cause* frustration, but they do show interest in the dynamics of frustration and support inquiry into realms of tension and conflict since such investigations may lead to new ways of understanding and relating to self and others (Gilmore & Anderson, 2016). As described above in the section about mentalization, it is a core element to nourish students' courage, curiosity, and investigating attitude.

Other theories that can be applied to psychodynamic theory

In an integrative approach, streams or rivers from different theoretical landscapes blend and merge. Although the theoretical river delta is a complex landscape, it is also satisfying and encouraging that we now have more languages, concepts, and tools to describe the music therapeutic reality.

Today music therapists are employed in many different contexts. Many projects have emerged where music therapists use their competencies in various situations, such as creating social communities through health musicking, training people in neurological functions with music, and teaching health care staff how to apply music in their work, for example in difficult care situations. Furthermore, music therapists are employed in hospital contexts, where they implement music and music therapy interventions during medical procedures. We consider it to be important that music therapists who work in all these different contexts do have therapeutic self-experiential training, even if the primary focus is not on the therapeutic relationship. The music therapists still need to be aware of clients' levels of attachment and to stay resonant and empathic in relation to the levels of sensitivity and arousal in every client, participant, or group. The music therapists also need to contain and process the interpersonal dynamics that happen in the groups or the projects and be prepared for continuous self-inquiries.

With this said, we also acknowledge that music therapists working in institutions and settings are guided by specific theories other than psychodynamic theory. Music therapy can be described with the use of many different perspectives and concepts, and we find it important to be able to speak the language of the workplace, community, or research centre. As already mentioned, a psychodynamic foundation is useful for the ability to relate and create a therapeutic contact even in a setting where the main theory is built on cognitive behavioural thinking and practice, body and gestalt-oriented theory, existential therapy, systemic therapy, narrative therapy, etc. There can be clashes, but even the clashes can drive new development of insight and sharpness in the way we work as well as good discussions with peers.

Basic assumptions for a modern integrative psychodynamic music therapy

Psychodynamic therapy is built on a history of ideas and development where the therapeutic relationship is at the centre. At the beginning of this chapter, we presented a list of basic assumptions in Freudian psychoanalysis, and now, to sum up the chapter, we will list what we currently formulate as basic assumptions in a modern psychodynamic-oriented music therapy in the form of principles and concepts. The assumptions are meant as underlying ideas for performing many different music therapeutic methods and techniques across client populations, diagnoses, and needs.

1. A developmental understanding

Rather than being determined by early imprinted relational patterns human beings carry all earlier experiences but have a continuous potential for change throughout the course of life. This potential is connected to an innate drive for development and unfolding towards agency, individuation, social connection, and healing. Both in cases of healthy development and in cases of functional impairment or illness, inner resources can be strengthened, and there can be a possibility for developing towards recovery, increased capacity for self-regulation, and higher levels of integration. In music therapy, this understanding implies that musical activities are applied to work with obstacles and challenges, and to support the potential for change and development. Change can also include accepting oneself – and thereby providing a change in self-perception.

2. A relational orientation

A human being is developed and formed through the interplay and mutuality in their early close relationships as well as later relationships. The quality of life for most human beings is deeply dependent on forming and joining relationships, families, groups, and communities. Thus, a development of relational capacity and communication or the experience of an attuned interplay will influence the general well-being and sense of vitality. In music therapy, it is possible to build contact and provide experiences of safe attachment in a trustful relationship through nonverbal embodied interactions in the here-and-now. Musical interaction (listening, voicing, or playing) can support, intensify, and develop the relational interplay, and can be used to explore the roles of and communication between the participants.

3. Human communication is basically musical

Early communication between infant and caregiver is based on an innate, embodied, joyful form of interaction and companionship that has musical features such as rhythmic dialoguing, playing with tension and relief, melodic intonation, and using sounds in a playful way. This communicative musicality continues throughout life to be an intrinsic part of human communication. Communicative musicality is the language before language that enables music therapeutic interplay between therapist and clients with or without verbal language skills. In musical nonverbal communication, the ability to mutually tune into a field of contact and to synchronize on deep bodily and social levels makes it possible for experiences of resonance. Resonance can emerge in a dynamic relationship, and can be achieved through an interpersonal, affective interaction.

4. Human consciousness is complex

The body-mind-environment-time can be seen as an ecological multidimensional interacting system. For each human being, this system includes different personality traits and states, where the body-mind is in a flow between conscious and unconscious states as well as explicit and implicit experiential modes. In the music therapeutic context, we can move in and out of consciousness states, move between linear time and a sense of timelessness, move back and forth in the personal history, and thereby provide integrative experiences. Thus, a therapeutic relationship can include an expanded understanding of time and consciousness – a meeting point between past, present, and future – where earlier relational experiences can affect the present and present experiences can affect the relational experiences of the future. Furthermore, in music therapy it is possible to provide access to experiences of expanded states of consciousness, sharing ineffable moments of existential being.

5. The unconscious affects the life of human beings

The unconscious of each human being must be understood in a cultural, historical, and personal context. The unconscious can be seen as a huge ocean with depths, subcurrents, and dynamic processes beneath the surface. It can contain repressed material (things that are not acceptable or not containable for the rational mind), or unexpressed material (things that we know about ourselves but cannot yet express), and it includes bodily stored memories and experiences that are not easily accessible. The unconscious is also a creative reservoir which supports and vitalizes our life through dreams, meditation, music listening and improvisation, and other deep states of contemplation. Unconscious material is a mixture of intrapsychic dynamics, understood as subjective personality and character, and ways of seeking relationship with others, understood as intersubjectivity. Music therapy has a potential to access and uncover unconscious material such as fixated relationship patterns, sensations, feelings, and memories, because of its affordances for nonverbal, embodied, and affective experiences. In the music therapeutic relationship, it can be important to investigate what is empowering the therapy process, which fears must be embraced, which resources need to be retrieved, which ideas and creative impulses need a space to flourish, and which issues need to be contained, addressed, and expressed.

6. Transference and countertransference in the therapeutic relationship

Transference is a way of understanding a client's unconscious, relational, and interactional patterns in the therapeutic relationship; patterns that have been developed through past relationships and life experiences (childhood as well as adulthood). These patterns can be transferred through musical, bodily, or verbal interaction and communication. Countertransference is the therapist's unconscious reactions to these patterns: It can originate from the therapist's own life experiences and/or be an empathic resonance with the client. These reactions can, when recognized, be an important source of information for the therapist to get to know which relational patterns are present in the therapeutic process, also when working with nonverbal clients. Although the therapeutic relationship is asymmetric, both the unconscious of the client and the therapist contribute to the encounter. The music therapist needs to be continuously concerned with embodied awareness, mentalization, and meta-reflection, and the therapist's thorough preparation, self-reflection, and supervision is necessary to become aware of and capable of containing and coping with transference and countertransference dynamics in the therapeutic processes in an appropriate way.

7. Awareness of the needs of the client/group

Music therapy is carried out with respect for the client's culture, musical preferences, worldview, gender, race, religion, aspiration, and personal life goals and with a professional understanding of the specific problems or challenges of the client. In a psychodynamic-oriented approach, the specific takes precedence over the general; the specific client with a specific history and life situation, the specific therapeutic relation, and the specific therapeutic moment is essential. The therapist has a responsibility and an ethical obligation to try to meet, understand, and respond to the client's lifeworld, problems, and needs. In some situations, it is the client who leads, in other situations it is the therapist who takes the lead – always with a humility towards the complexity of knowledge and truth of each individual, group, or culture. Thus, the therapist seeks to be sensitive and inclusive, while attuning to the musical expression and identity of the client.

8. Self- and co-regulation

A human being is influencing the environment and is also influenced by the environment, which includes other human beings. In human interaction it is possible to regulate ourselves and each other. With some clients who have difficulties with self-regulation, music therapy can establish a dyadic regulation where music can be used consciously to reinforce an increase or decrease of arousal. Regulation of arousal can be a necessary prerequisite for enabling the client to be present in the communicative musical process. The music therapist can work with regulation on a macro-level by managing the structural framework of the sessions, creating a tranquil and safe environment, and a predictable structure in the session, for example with musical opening and closing rituals, and play rules for improvisation. On a micro-level, the music therapist can work with emotional regulation and arousal regulation through attunement to and synchronization with the tiny details of sounds or movements in the here-and-now, using musical parameters such as pulse, sound quality, and tempo.

9. Mentalization is an important relational capacity
Mentalizing capacity enhances the human self-regulating system, develops introspection and self-reflection, and qualifies empathy and social interaction. This capacity grows from intersubjective experiences throughout life and especially through early processes of attachment to primary caregivers. A mentalizing approach seeks to meet and regulate the level of arousal. When it is meaningful and possible for the client it can enable or develop attention to affective states as well as assist the client in containing and understanding emotions and thoughts. A key point in mentalization is to see or listen to oneself from the outside and others from the inside which can happen through musical interaction. In music therapy, the playing is audible, which enables clients to investigate their expression and contribution to the relationship on an implicit level. For verbal clients this can be followed up by an exploration of intentions and reactions on an explicit level. An important focus for the mentalizing music therapist is to apply a curious sensitive attitude and to be emotionally available when investigating feelings, thoughts, and behaviours during the therapy process.

The learning process of music therapy students
Metaphorically the student will gradually develop like a tree: Creating foundation in being connected to and aware of one's own roots as well as sensing and being aware of the interconnectedness to others through the rooting. Next to this, finding inner balance and strength in a trunk with a solid bark, which refers to

the capacity of being well-defined, though still permeable. Gradually the student will unfold and expand the treetop, with many branches, leaves, flowers, and fruits – representing the experience and expertise that the training has built up in a mixture with life experience. When graduating the harvest is to be shared with the world and in the years to come nourish the ground and growth of future music therapy in a cyclic movement.

Following and facilitating the students' personal and professional growth during their education is an exciting task and a special gift. Each of the students need to find their own path of development. It is striking how the educational process on one hand makes their uniqueness increasingly clear: their upbringing and family background, their personal characteristics and relational patterns, their life experiences and health conditions, their specific interests and competences, etc. On the other hand, they gradually become a part of a group of music therapy students and a part of a wider music therapy community where people share interests and have so many things in common. The students learn a specific language, a certain perception of music and of therapy, and they go through a cultural adaptation to the profession.

When we link the developmental approach to the educational process of music therapy students we move into a field where therapy and learning are closely related. Gradually the student develops an identity where being a human, a person, is merged with being a professional. The student develops both in a vertical and in a horizontal dimension: In the vertical dimension the student trains the ability to stay grounded and embodied with a clear connection between sensations, emotions, and thoughts, and in many cases with an open mind in relation to existential and spiritual dimensions of being a human. In a horizontal dimension the student trains to find balance between impression and expression in relationships and to broaden the horizon to contain and understand the differences and complexities of human beings.

References

Alvin, J. (1975). *Music Therapy* (rev. ed.). John Clare Books.

Auf der Heyde, T.M. (2012). 'Interpersonal rhythms disrupted by a history of trauma: An in-depth case study of analytical music therapy.' Doctoral dissertation, City University of New York. Semantic Scholar. Accessed on 02/12/21 at www.semanticscholar.org/paper/Interpersonal-rhythms-disrupted-by-a-history-of-An-Heyde-Christine/bf2245a4d8c423 72aa432e7899447945088134df.

Barbano, M.F. & Cador, M. (2007). 'Opioids for hedonic experience and dopamine to get ready for it.' *Psychopharmacology, 191*, 497–506.

Bateman, A.W. & Fonagy, P. (eds) (2012). *Handbook of Mentalizing in Mental Health Practice.* American Psychiatric Publishing, Inc.

Bateman, A.W. & Fonagy, P. (2016). *Mentalization-Based Treatment for Personality Disorder. A Practical Guide*. Oxford University Press.

Bazan, A. (2017). 'Alpha synchronization as a brain model for unconscious defense: An overview of the work of Howard Shevrin and his team.' *The International Journal of Psychoanalysis, 98*(5), 1443–1473.

Beck, B. (2015). 'Guided Imagery and Music (GIM) with Clients on Stress Leave.' In D. Grocke & T. Moe (eds), *Guided Imagery and Music (GIM) and Music Imagery Methods for Individual and Group Therapy*. Jessica Kingsley Publishers.

Beck, B.D., Lund, S.T., Søgaard, U., Simonsen, E. *et al.* (2018). 'Music therapy versus treatment as usual: Protocol of a randomized non-inferiority study with traumatized refugees diagnosed with posttraumatic stress disorder (PTSD).' *Trials, 19*, 301.

Beck, B.D., Meyer, S.L., Simonsen, E., Søgaard, U. *et al.* (2021). 'Music therapy was noninferior to verbal standard treatment of traumatized refugees in mental health care: Results from a randomized clinical trial.' *European Journal of Psychotraumatology, 12*(1), 1–15.

Beebe, B. & Lachmann, F.M. (2014). *Relational Perspectives Book Series. The Origins of Attachment: Infant Research and Adult Treatment*. Routledge/Taylor & Francis Group.

Binder, P.E., Nielsen, G.H., Vøllestad, J., Holgersen, H., & Schance, E. (2006) 'Hva er relasjonell psykoanalyse? Nye psykoanalytiske perspektiver på samhandling, det ubevisste og selvet [What is relational psychoanalysis? New analytical perspectives on interaction, the unconscious and the self].' *Tidsskrift for Norsk Psykologforening [Journal of the Norwegian Psychologist Association], 43*(9), 899–908.

Blom, K.M. & Wrangsjö, B. (2013). *Intersubjektivitet: det mellanmänskliga i vård och vardag [Intersubjectivity. The inter-humanity in work and everyday life]*. Studentlitteratur.

Blom, K.M. (2014). 'Experiences of transcendence and the process of surrender in Guided Imagery and Music (GIM): Development of new understanding through theories of intersubjectivity and change in psychotherapy.' Doctoral dissertation, Aalborg University. Vbn. Accessed on 02/12/21 at https://vbn.aau.dk/ws/portalfiles/portal/316470580/Katarina_Martenson_Blom_Thesis.pdf.

Boadella, D. (1987). *Lifestreams. An Introduction to Biosynthesis*. Routledge.

Bonny, H. (2002). *Music and Consciousness: The Evolution of Guided Imagery and Music*. Barcelona Publishers.

Borcson, R.M. (2012). 'Survivors of Catastrophic Event Trauma.' In L. Eyre (ed.), *Guidelines of Music Therapy Practice in Mental Health*. Barcelona Publishers.

Bornstein, R. (2019). 'The Psychodynamic Perspective.' In R. Biswas-Diener & E. Diener (eds), *Noba Textbook Series: Psychology*. DEF Publishers. http://noba.to/zdemy2cv

Boston Change Process Study Group (BCPSG) (2010). *Change in Psychotherapy. A Unifying Paradigm*. Norton.

Bowlby, J. (1969). *Attachment and Loss, Vol. 1: Attachment*. Basic Books.

Bruscia, K. (1998). *The Dynamics of Music Psychotherapy*. Barcelona Publishers.

Bruscia, K. (2013). 'Self-Experience in the Pedagogy of Music Therapy.' In K. Bruscia (ed.), *Self-Experiences in Music Therapy Education, Training, and Supervision*. Barcelona Publishers.

Bruscia, K. (2019). 'A Model of Clinical Supervision.' In M. Forinash (ed.), *Music Therapy Supervision* (2nd ed.). Barcelona Publishers.

Bühler, K.E. & Heim, G. (2001). 'General introduction to the psychotherapy of Pierre Janet.' *American Journal of Psychotherapy, 55*(1), 74–91.

Caldwell, C. (1996). *Getting Our Bodies Back*. Shambhala Publications.

Casement, P. (1985/2014). *On Learning from the Patient*. Routledge.

Chanda, M.L. & Levitin, D.J. (2013). 'The neurochemistry of music.' *Trends in Cognitive Science, 17*(4), 179–193.

Cheung, V.K., Harrison, P.M., Meyer, L., Pearce, M.T., Haynes, J.D., & Koelsch, S. (2019). 'Uncertainty and surprise jointly predict musical pleasure and amygdala, hippocampus, and auditory cortex activity.' *Current Biology, 29*(23), 4084–4092.

Christensen, E. (2012). 'Music listening, music therapy, phenomenology and neuroscience.' Doctoral dissertation, Aalborg University. Vbn. Accessed on 02/12/21 at https://vbn.aau.dk/ws/portalfiles/portal/68298556/MUSIC_LISTENING_FINAL_ONLINE_Erik_christensen12.pdf.

Christensen, E. (2017). 'Hjernens og kroppens perceptioner, emotioner og netværk i relation til musikterapi – en introduktion til aktuel forskning [The perceptions, emotions and network of the brain and body in relation to music therapy – an introduction to current research].' In C. Lindvang & B.D. Beck (eds), *Musik, krop og følelser. Neuroaffektive processer i musikterapi [Music, body and emotions. Neuroaffective processes in music therapy]*. Frydenlund.

Cohen, N.S. (2018). *Advanced Methods of Music Therapy Practice*. Jessica Kingsley Publishers.

Darnley-Smith, R.M.R. (2013). 'What is the music of music therapy? An enquiry into the aesthetics of clinical improvisation.' Doctoral dissertation, Durham University. Accessed on 02/12/21 at http://etheses.dur.ac.uk/6975.

De Backer, J., Nöcker-Ribaupierre, M., & Sutton, J. (2014). 'Music Therapy in Europe. The Identity and Professionalisation of European Music Therapy, with an Overview and History of the European Music Therapy Confederation.' In J. De Backer & J. Sutton (eds), *The Music in Music Therapy. Psychodynamic Music Therapy in Europe: Clinical, Theoretical and Research Approaches*. Jessica Kingsley Publishers.

Erikson, E. (1959). *Childhood and Society*. W.W. Norton.

Erikson, E.H. (1974). *Dimensions of a New Identity. Jefferson Lectures in the Humanities*. W.W. Norton.

Eschen, J.T. (2002). *Analytical Music Therapy*. Jessica Kingsley Publishers.

Fachner, J.G., Maidhof, C., Grocke, D., Pedersen, I.N., Trondalen, G., Tucek, G., & Bonde, L.O. (2019). '"Telling me not to worry…" Hyperscanning and neural dynamics of emotion processing during Guided Imagery and Music.' *Frontiers in Psychology*, https://doi.org/10.3389/fpsyg.2019.01561

Fairbairn, W.R.D. (1952). *Psychoanalytic Studies of the Personality*. Routledge and Kegan Paul.

Ferreri, L., Mas-Herrero, E., Zatorre, R.J., Ripollés, P. *et al.* (2019). 'Dopamine modulates the reward experiences elicited by music.' *Proceedings of the National Academy of Sciences, 116*(9), 3793–3798.

Fluhu (EVM) Rapport. (1988). Høgenhaven, A.K. Det Faglige Landsudvalg for Humanistiske Uddannelser [The National Humanistic Research Council]. Unpublished report. **[AQ]**

Fogtmann, C. (2014). *Forståelsens psykologi – mentalisering i teori og praksis [The psychology of understanding – mentalization in theory and practice]*. Samfundslitteratur.

Fonagy, P., Gergely, G., Jurist, E.L., & Target, M. (2002). *Affect Regulation, Mentalization, and the Development of the Self*. Other Press.

Fosha, D. (2000). *The Transforming Power of Affect: A Model for Accelerated Change*. Basic Books.

Fosha, D., Siegel, D., & Solomon, M. (eds) (2009). *The Healing Power of Emotion: Affective Neuroscience, Development and Clinical Practice*. W.W. Norton & Co.

Fotopoulou, A. (2012). 'Towards a Psychodynamic Neuroscience.' In A. Fotopoulou, D. Pfaff, & M.A. Conway (eds), *From the Couch to the Lab: Trends in Psychodynamic Neuroscience*. Oxford University Press.

French, T. & Fromm, E. (1964). *Dream Interpretation: A New Approach*. Basic Books.

Freud, S. (1989). 'The Ego and the Id (1923).' *TACD Journal, 17*(1), 5–22.

Galbis-Reig, D. (2004). 'Sigmund Freud, MD: Forgotten contributions to neurology, neuropathology, and anesthesia.' *International Journal of Neurology, 3*(1).

Gammelgård, J. (2011). 'Love, drive and desire in Freud, Lacan and Proust.' *International Journal of Psychoanalysis, 92*(4), 963–983.

Gander, M. & Buchheim, A. (2015). 'Attachment classification, psychophysiology and frontal EEG asymmetry across the lifespan: A review.' *Frontiers of Human Neuroscience.* doi:10.3389/fnhum.2015.00079

Gebauer, L., Kringelbach, M., & Vuust, P. (2012). 'Ever-changing cycles of musical pleasure: The role of dopamine and anticipation.' *Psychomusicology, Music, Mind and Brain, 22*(2), 152.

Geller, J.D., Norcross, J.C., & Orlinsky, D.E. (eds) (2005). *The Psychotherapist's Own Psychotherapy.* Oxford University Press.

Gendlin, E. (1996). *Focusing-Oriented Psychotherapy.* Guilford Publications.

Gilmore, S. & Anderson, V. (2016). 'The emotional turn in higher education: A psychoanalytic contribution.' *Teaching in Higher Education, 21*(6), 686–699.

Greenberg, J.R. & Mitchell, S.A. (1983). *Object Relations in Psychoanalytic Theory.* Harvard University Press.

Grocke, D. (ed.) (2019). *Guided Imagery and Music: The Bonny Method and Beyond* (2nd ed.). Barcelona Publishers.

Grocke, D. & Moe, T. (eds) (2015). *Guided Imagery and Music (GIM) and Music Imagery Methods for Individual and Group Therapy.* Jessica Kingsley Publishers.

Hadley, S. (1998). *Exploring Relationships Between Life and Work in Music Therapy: The Stories of Mary Priestley and Clive Robbins.* Temple University. ProQuest Dissertations Publishing, 9911013.

Hadley, S. (2003). *Psychodynamic Music Therapy: Case Studies.* Barcelona Publishers.

Hannibal, N. (2000). 'Præverbal overføring i musikterapi: Kvalitativ undersøgelse af overføringsprocesser i den musikalske interaktion [Preverbal transference in music therapy. A qualitative examination of transference processes in the musical interaction].' Doctoral dissertation, Aalborg University. Vbn. Accessed on 02/12/21 at https://vbn.aau.dk/ws/portalfiles/portal/316434842/niels_hannibal.pdf.

Hannibal, N. (2007). 'Relevansen af nyere psykodynamisk teori for det kliniske musikterapeutiske arbejde med psykiatriske patienter med personlighedsforstyrrelser [The relevance of recent psychodynamic theory in relation to clinical music therapeutic work with psychiatric patients with personality disorders].' *Psyke & Logos, 28*(1), 385–407.

Hannibal, N. (2014). 'Implicit and Explicit Mentalisation in Music Therapy in Psychiatric Treatment of People with Borderline Personality Disorder.' In J. De Backer & J. Sutton (eds), *The Music in Music Therapy. Psychodynamic Music Therapy in Europe: Clinical, Theoretical and Research Approaches.* Jessica Kingsley Publishers.

Hannibal, N. (2019). 'Daniel Stern's Theories on the Interpersonal World of the Infant, Change in Psychotherapy and the Dynamics of Vitality.' In S.L. Jacobsen, I.N. Pedersen, & L.O. Bonde (eds), *A Comprehensive Guide to Music Therapy.* Jessica Kingsley Publishers.

Hansen-Abromeit, D. (2015). 'A conceptual methodology to define the therapeutic function of music.' *Music Therapy Perspectives, 33*(1), 25–38.

Hart, S. (2018a). *Brain, Attachment, Personality: An Introduction to Neuroaffective Development.* Routledge.

Hart, S. (2018b). 'Psychometric properties of the Emotional Development Scale: Investigating reliability and validity including corrections with the Marschak interaction method and the neuroaffective mentalizing interview.' Doctoral dissertation, Aalborg University. Vbn. Accessed on 02/12/21 at https://vbn.aau.dk/ws/portalfiles/portal/291314084/PHD_Susan_Hart_E_pdf.pdf.

Hartmann, H. (1958). *Ego Psychology and the Problem of Adaptation.* International Universities Press.

Harvey, A.R. (2020). 'Links between the neurobiology of oxytocin and human musicality.' *Frontiers in Human Neuroscience.* https://doi.org/10.3389/fnhum.2020.00350

He, H., Yang, M., Duan, M., Chen, X. *et al.* (2018). 'Music intervention leads to increased insular connectivity and improved clinical symptoms in schizophrenia.' *Frontiers in Neuroscience, 11*, 744.

Heimann, P. (1950). 'On countertransference.' *International Journal of Psychoanalysis, 31*, 81–84.

Herman, J. (1995). *Trauma and Recovery.* Basic Books.

Hermansen, M. (2005) *Læringens univers [The universe of learning].* Klim.

Holck, U. (2019). 'Communicative Musicality: A Basis for Music Therapy Practice.' In S.L. Jacobsen, I.N. Pedersen, & L.O. Bonde (eds), *A Comprehensive Guide to Music Therapy.* Jessica Kingsley Publishers.

Hougaard, E. (1996/2019). *Psykoterapi – teori og forskning* (2nd ed.) *[Psychotherapy – theory and research].* Dansk Psykologisk Forlag.

Hvid, T. (2005). *Kroppens fortællinger [The stories of the body].* Modtryk.

Isenberg, C. (2016). 'Psychodynamic Approaches.' In B. Wheeler (ed.), *Music Therapy Handbook.* Guilford Press.

Isenberg-Grzeda, C. (1998). 'Transference Structures in Guided Imagery and Music.' In K. Bruscia (ed.), *The Dynamics of Music Psychotherapy.* Barcelona Publishers.

Jacobi, J. (1976). *C.G. Jungs psykologi [C.G. Jung's psychology].* Gyldendal.

Jacobsen, C.H. (2005). 'Supervisors interventioner ved parallelprocesser [The interventions of the supervisor by parallel processes].' *Matrix – Nordisk tidsskrift for psykoterapi, 22*(4), 354–369.

Jung, C.G. (1981). *The Archetypes and the Collective Unconscious.* Princeton University Press.

Kalsched, D.E. (1996). *The Inner World of Trauma: Archetypal Defences of the Personal Spirit.* Routledge.

Karterud, S. (2015). *Mentalization-Based Group Therapy (MBT-G): A Theoretical, Clinical, and Research Manual.* Oxford University Press.

Karterud, S., Wilberg, T., & Urnes, Ø. (2013). *Personlighedspsykiatri [Personality psychiatry].* Akademisk Forlag.

Keller, P.E., Novembre, G., & Hove, M.J. (2014). 'Rhythm in joint action: Psychological and neurophysiological mechanisms for real-time interpersonal coordination.' *Philosophical Transactions of The Royal Society B Biological Sciences, 369*(1658), 1–12.

Kleim, J.A. & Jones, T.A. (2008). 'Principles of experience-dependent neural plasticity: Implications for rehabilitation after brain damage.' *Journal of Speech, Language, and Hearing Research, 51*, 225–239.

Klein, M. (1932). *The Psychoanalysis of Children.* Hogarth.

Koelsch, S. (2009). 'A neuroscientific perspective on music therapy.' *The Neurosciences and Music III – Disorders and Plasticity: Annals of New York Academic Science, 1169*, 374–384.

Koelsch, S. (2014). 'Brain correlates of music-evoked emotions.' *Nature Reviews Neuroscience, 15*, 170–180.

Kohut, H. (1971). *The Analysis of the Self.* International Universities Press.

Körlin, D. (2010). *Music Listening, Imagery and Creativity in Psychiatry: Guided Imagery and Music (GIM) and Creative Arts Therapies (CATs) in Stress Disorders.* Lambert Academic Publishing.

Kreutz, G., Quiroga Murcia, C., & Bongard, S. (2012). 'Psychoneuroendocrine Research on Music and Health: An Overview.' In R.A.R. MacDonald, G. Kreutz, & L. Mitchell (eds), *Music, Health, and Wellbeing.* Oxford University Press.

Kringelbach, M.L. & Berridge, K.C. (2009). 'Towards a functional neuroanatomy of pleasure and happiness.' *Trends in Cognitive Sciences, 13*(11), 479–487.

Langs, R.L. (1990). *Classics in Psychoanalytic Technique* (rev. ed.). Jason Aronson, INC.

Lanius, R.A., Frewen, P.A., Tursich, M., Jetly, R., & McKinnon, M.C. (2015). 'Restoring large-scale brain networks in PTSD and related disorders: A proposal for neuroscientifically-informed treatment interventions.' *European Journal of Psychotraumatology, 6*, 27313.

Levine, P. (1997). *Waking the Tiger: Healing Trauma: The Innate Capacity to Transform Overwhelming Experiences.* North Atlantic Books.

Levine, P. (2010a). *In an Unspoken Voice. How the Body Releases Trauma and Restores Goodness.* North Atlantic Books.

Levine, P. (2010b). 'Trauma, rhythm, contact and flow.' In J.V. Loewy & A.F. Hara (eds), *Caring for the caregiver: The use of music therapy in grief and trauma.* The American Music Therapy Association Inc.

Lindenberger, U., Li, S.-C., Gruber, W., & Müller, V. (2009). 'Brains swinging in concert: Cortical phase synchronization while playing guitar.' *BMC Neuroscience, 10,* 22.

Lindvang, C. (2010). 'A field of resonant learning. Self-experiential training and the development of music therapeutic competencies: A mixed methods investigation of music therapy students' experiences and professionals' evaluation of their own competencies.' Doctoral dissertation, Aalborg University. Vbn. Accessed on 03/12/21 at https://vbn.aau.dk/ws/portalfiles/portal/316410062/6465_dissertation_c_lindvang.pdf

Lindvang, C. (2013). 'Resonant learning: A qualitative inquiry into music therapy students' self-experiential learning processes.' *Qualitative Inquiries in Music Therapy, 8,* 1–30.

Lindvang, C. (2015). 'Kompleksitet i læreprocesser og terapi [Complexity in learning processes and in therapy].' In T. Hansen (ed.), *Det ubevidstes potentiale: Kybernetisk psykologi i anvendelse [English edition in review: Potentials of unconscious intelligence – Redefining the unconscious in psychotherapy, creativity and learning].* Frydenlund.

Lindvang, C. (2017). 'Udvikling af samhørighed og mentaliseringskapacitet gennem læreterapi i grupper [Development of cohesion and the capacity of mentalizing through group training therapy].' In C. Lindvang & B.D. Beck (eds.), *Musik, krop og følelser. Neuroaffektive processer i musikterapi [Music, body and emotions. Neuroaffective processes in music therapy].* Frydenlund Academic.

Lindvang, C. & Beck, B.D. (eds) (2017). *Musik, krop og følelser. Neuroaffektive processer i musikterapi [Music, body and emotions. Neuroaffective processes in music therapy].* Frydenlund Academic.

Liu, D., Liu, S., Liu, X., Zhang, C. *et al.* (2018). 'Interactive brain activity: Review and progress on EEG-based hyperscanning in social interactions.' *Frontiers in Psychology, 9,* 1862.

Lowen, A. (1975). *Bioenergetics.* Penguin Compass.

Maack, C. (2012). 'Outcomes and processes of the Bonny Method of Guided Imagery and Music (GIM) and its adaptations and Psychodynamic Imaginative Trauma Therapy (PITT) for women with complex PTSD.' Doctoral dissertation, Aalborg University. Vbn. Accessed on 03/12/21 at https://vbn.aau.dk/files/68395912/Carola_Maack_12.pdf.

MacLean, P.D. (1990). *The Triune Brain in Evolution: Role in Paleocerebral Functions.* Plenum.

Mahler, S., Pine, M.M.F., & Bergman, A. (1975). *The Psychological Birth of the Human Infant. Symbiosis and Individuation.* Basic Books.

Malloch, S. & Trevarthen, C. (2010). 'Communicative musicality: Exploring the basis of human companionship.' *British Journal of Psychotherapy, 26*(1), 100–105.

Markova, G., Nguyen, T., & Hoehl, S. (2019). 'Neurobehavioral interpersonal synchrony in early development: The role of interactional rhythms.' *Frontiers in Psychology, 10,* 2078.

McGuire, M.G. (2004). *Psychiatric Music Therapy in the Community. The Legacy of Florence Tyson.* Barcelona Publishers.

McLeod, S.A. (2017). 'Psychodynamic approach.' SimplyPsychology. Accessed on 03/12/21 at www.simplypsychology.org/psychodynamic.html.

Meltzoff, A. (1990). 'Foundations for Developing a Concept of Self: The Role of Imitation in Relating Self to Other and the Value of Social Mirroring, Social Modeling, and Self-Practice in Infancy.' In D. Cicchetti & M. Beeghley (eds), *The Self in Transition: Infancy to Childhood.* University of Chicago Press.

Meltzoff, A. & Moore, M.K. (1998). 'Infant Intersubjectivity: Broadening the Dialogue to Include Imitation, Identity and Intention.' In S. Braten (ed.), *Intersubjective Communication and Emotion in Early Ontogeny*. Cambridge University Press.

Mitchell, S.A. & Black, M.J. (2016). *Freud and Beyond: A History of Modern Psychoanalytic Thought*. Basic Books.

Merleau-Ponty, M. (1945/2010). *Phenomenology of Perception*. Routledge.

Mikulincer, M., Shaver, P., & Phillip, R. (2003). *The Attachment Behavioral System in Adulthood: Activation, Psychodynamics, and Interpersonal Processes*. Elsevier Academic Press.

Mindell, A. (1982). *Dreambody: The Body's Role in Revealing the Self*. Routledge.

Müller, V. & Lindenberger, U. (2011). 'Cardiac and respiratory patterns synchronize between persons during choir singing.' *PLoS ONE, 6*(9), e24893.

Müller, V. & Lindenberger, U. (2019). 'Dynamic orchestration of brains and instruments during free guitar improvisation.' *Frontiers in Integrative Neuroscience, 13*, 50.

Müller, V., Sänger, J., & Lindenberger, U. (2013). 'Intra- and inter-brain synchronization during musical improvisation on the guitar.' *PLoS ONE, 8*(9), e73852.

Murphy, D. (2005). 'A qualitative study into the experiences of mandatory personal therapy during training.' *Counselling and Psychotherapy Research, 5*(1), 27–32.

Nordoff, P. & Robbins, C. (1977). *Creative Music Therapy*. John Day.

Northoff, G. (2011). *Neuropsychoanalysis in Practice. Brain, Self and Objects*. Oxford University Press.

Oberman, L. & Pascual-Leone, A. (2013). 'Changes in Plasticity Across the Lifespan: Cause of Disease and Target for Intervention.' In M.M. Merzenich, M. Nahum, & T.M. Van Vleet (eds), *Changing Brain: Applying Brain Plasticity to Advance and Recover Human Ability. Progress in Brain Research*. Elsevier.

Ogden, P., Minton, K., & Pain, C. (2006). *Trauma and the Body: A Sensorimotor Approach to Psychotherapy*. W.W. Norton.

Ogden, T.H. (2005). 'On psychoanalytic supervision.' *International Journal of Psychoanalysis, 86*(5), 1265–1280.

Olsen, O.A. (2002). *Psykodynamisk leksikon [Psychodynamic dictionary]*. Gyldendal.

Olsen, O.A. & Køppe, S. (1987). *Freuds psykoanalyse [Freud's psychoanalysis]*. Gyldendal.

Orlinsky, D.E. & Rønnestad, M.H. (2005). *How Psychotherapists Develop, a Study of Therapeutic Work and Professional Growth*. American Psychology Association.

Osborne, N. (2012). 'Neuroscience and "real world" practice: Music as a therapeutic resource for children in zones of conflict.' *The Neurosciences and Music IV: Learning and Memory, 1252*(1), 69–76.

Pedersen, I.N. (1997). 'The music therapists' listening perspectives as source of information in improvised musical duets with grown-up psychiatric patients, suffering from schizophrenia.' *Nordic Journal of Music Therapy, 6*(2), 98–111.

Pedersen, I.N. (2000). 'Indefra eller udefra – orientering i terapeutens tilstedeværelse og nærvær [From inside or from outside – The therapist's orientation in therapeutic presence and attentiveness].' In C. Lindvang (ed.), *Den musikterapeutiske behandling [The music therapy treatment]. Musikterapi i Psykiatrien. Årsskrift 2*. Musikterapiklinikken, Aalborg Psychiatry/Aalborg University.

Pedersen, I.N. (2002). 'Self-Experience for Music Therapy Students. Experiential Training in Music Therapy as a Methodology: A Mandatory Part of the Music Therapy Programme at Aalborg University.' In J.T. Eschen (ed.), *Analytical Music Therapy*. Jessica Kingsley Publishers.

Pedersen, I.N. (2007a). 'Countertransference in music therapy. A phenomenological study on counter-transference used as a clinical concept by music therapists working with musical improvisation in adult psychiatry.' Doctoral dissertation, Aalborg University. Vbn. Accessed on 03/12/21 at https://vbn.aau.dk/ws/portalfiles/portal/70261290/inp_2007.pdf.

Pedersen, I.N. (2007b). 'Musikterapeutens disciplinerede subjektivitet [The disciplined subjectivity of the music therapist].' *Psyke og Logos, 28*(1), 358–384.

Pedersen, I.N. (2019). 'Analytical and Psychodynamic Theories.' In S.L. Jacobsen, I.N. Pedersen, & L.O. Bonde (eds), *A Comprehensive Guide to Music Therapy* (2nd ed.). Jessica Kingsley Publishers.

Porges, S.W. (2003). 'Social engagement and attachment: A phylogenetic perspective.' *Annals of the New York Academy of Sciences, 1008*, 31–47.

Porges, S.W. (2010). 'Music Therapy and Trauma: Insights from the Polyvagal Theory.' In K. Stewart (ed.), *Symposium on Music Therapy and Trauma: Bridging Theory and Clinical Practice*. Satchnote Press.

Priestley, M. (1975). *Music Therapy in Action*. Constable.

Priestley, M. (1994). *Essays on Analytical Music Therapy*. Barcelona Publishers.

Priestly, M. (1995). In T. Wigram, B. Saperston, & R. West (eds), *The Art and Science of Music Therapy. A Handbook*. Harwood Academic Publications.

Racker, H. (1968). *Transference and Countertransference*. Hogarth.

Rapaport, D. (1942). 'Freudian mechanisms and frustration experiments.' *Psychoanalytic Quarterly, 11*, 503–511.

Reich, W. (1933/1974). *Character Analysis*. Farrar, Straus & Giroux.

Reybrouck, M., Vuust, P., & Brattico, E. (2018). 'Brain connectivity networks and the aesthetic experience of music.' *Brain Sciences, 8*(6), 107.

Ridder, H.M.O. (2013). 'Hvordan parallelprocesser og kreative metoder skaber indsigt i supervision [How parallel processes and creative methods provide insight in supervision].' In I.N. Pedersen (ed.) *Kunstneriske medier i supervision af psykoterapi. Indsigt og vitalitet [Artistic media in supervision of psychotherapy. Insight and vitality]*. Aalborg Universitetsforlag.

Rothschild, B. (2000). *The Body Remembers: The Psychophysiology of Trauma and Trauma Treatment*. W.W. Norton & Co.

Rudstam, G., Elofsson, U., Søndergaard, H.P., Bonde, L.O., & Beck, B.D. (2017). 'Trauma-focused group music and imagery with women suffering from PTSD/complex PTSD: A feasibility study.' *Approaches, Special Issue, 9*(2), 202–216.

Shore, A.N. (2019). *Right Brain Psychotherapy*. Norton.

Silverman, M.J. (2007). 'Evaluating current trends in psychiatric music therapy: A descriptive analysis.' *Journal of Music Therapy, 44*(4), 388–414.

Skårderud, F. & Sommerfeldt, B. (2013). *Miljøterapibogen. Mentalisering som holdning og handling [The Environmental Therapy Book. Mentalization as Attitude and Acting]*. Hans Reitzels Forlag.

Spermon, D., Darlington, Y., & Gibney, P. (2010). 'Psychodynamic psychotherapy for complex trauma: Targets, focus, applications, and outcomes.' *Psychology Research and Behavior Management, 3*, 119–127.

Stern, D. (1985/2000). *The Interpersonal World of the Infant: A View from Psychoanalysis and Developmental Psychology*. Basic Books.

Stern, D. (1995). *Motherhood Constellation: A Unified View of Parent-Infant Psychotherapy*. Basic Books.

Stern, D. (2010). *Forms of Vitality: Exploring Dynamic Experience in Psychology, the Arts, Psychotherapy and Development*. Oxford University Press.

Stewart, K. (ed.) (2010). *Symposium on Music Therapy and Trauma: Bridging Theory and Clinical Practice*. Satchnote Press.

Stolorow, R.D. & Atwood, G.E. (1992). *Contexts of Being: The Intersubjective Foundations of Psychological Life*. Analytic Press, Inc.

Storr, A. (2001). *Freud: A Very Short Introduction*. Oxford University Press.

Story, M. (2018). 'Guided imagery and music with military women and trauma: A continuum approach to music and healing.' Doctoral dissertation, Aalborg University. Vbn. Accessed on 03/12/21 at https://vbn.aau.dk/ws/portalfiles/portal/412824655/PHD_KMS_E_pdf.pdf.

Strehlow, G. & Hannibal, N. (2019). 'Mentalizing in improvisational music therapy.' *Nordic Journal of Music Therapy, 28*(4), 333–346.

Sullivan, H.S. (1950). 'The illusion of personal individuality.' *Psychiatry, 13*(3), 317–332.

Sundberg, N. (2001). *Clinical Psychology: Evolving Theory, Practice, and Research.* Prentice Hall.

Sutton, T.E. (2019). 'Review of attachment theory: Familial predictors, continuity and change, and intrapersonal and relational outcomes.' *Marriage and Family Review, 55*(1), 1–22.

Tansey, M.J. & Burke, W.F. (1989). *Understanding Countertransference. From Projective Identification to Empathy.* The Analytic Press.

Thompson, E. (2007). *Mind in Life: Biology, Phenomenology, and the Sciences of Mind.* Harvard University Press.

Thorgaard, L. (2006). *Relationsbehandling i psykiatrien I–V [Relationship-based treatment in psychiatry I–V].* Hertevig Forlag.

Trevarthen, C. (1998). 'The Concept and Foundations of Infant Intersubjectivity.' In S. Bråten (ed.), *Intersubjective Communication and Emotion in Early Ontogeny.* Cambridge University Press.

Trondalen, G. (2016). *Relational Music Therapy: An Intersubjective Perspective.* Barcelona Publishers.

Turry, A. (1998). 'Transference and Countertransference in Nordoff-Robbins Music Therapy.' In K. Bruscia (ed.), *The Dynamics of Music Psychotherapy.* Barcelona Publishers.

van der Hart, O., Nijenhuis, E.R.S., & Steele, K. (2006). *The Haunted Self: Structural Dissociation and the Treatment of Chronic Traumatization.* W.W. Norton & Co.

van der Kolk, B. (2015). *The Body Keeps the Score. Brain, Mind, and Body in the Healing of Trauma.* Penguin Publishing Group.

Vedfelt, O. (1996). *Bevidsthed. Bevidsthedens niveauer [Consciousness. The levels of consciousness].* Gyldendal.

Vedfelt, O. (2009). 'Cultivating feelings through working with dreams.' *Culture & Psyche, 3*(4), 88–102.

Vedfelt, O. (2018). *The Intelligence of the Unconscious – You Know More than You Think.* Kindle edition.

Watkins, C.E. (2010). 'Psychoanalytic constructs in psychotherapy supervision.' *American Journal of Psychotherapy, 64*(4), 393–416.

Wheeler, B. (1981). 'The relationship between music therapy and theories of psychotherapy.' *Music Therapy, 1*(1), 9–16.

Wigram, T. (2019). 'Free Improvisation Therapy: The Alvin Model.' In S.L. Jacobsen, I.N. Pedersen, & L.O. Bonde (eds), *A Comprehensive Guide to Music Therapy.* Jessica Kingsley Publishers.

Wigram, T., Bonde, L.O., & Pedersen, I.N. (2002). *A Comprehensive Guide to Music Therapy.* Jessica Kingsley Publishers.

Winnicott, D.W. (1971). *Playing and Reality.* Routledge.

Zamm, A., Palmer, C., Bauer, A.R., Bleichner, M.G., Demos, A.P., & Debener, S. (2019). 'Synchronizing MIDI and wireless EEG measurements during natural piano performance.' *Brain Research, 1716*, 27–38.

Zatorre, R.J., Chen, J.L., & Penhune, V.B. (2007). 'When the brain plays music: Auditory-motor interactions in music perception and production.' *Nature Reviews Neuroscience, 8*(7), 547–558.

CHAPTER 4

Three Personal Being and Communication Spaces

A PROTOTYPE EXERCISE

Inge Nygaard Pedersen

Introduction

In this chapter I will present a prototype exercise titled 'Three Personal Being and Communication Spaces', which I have developed over several decades. It is an exercise that has grown into a basic exercise for all psychotherapists, including music therapists, to raise their awareness of how they ground and position themselves in relation to others, both in everyday life and in therapeutic relationships. At the Aalborg music therapy programme, the exercise is further applied as a kind of self-assessment for the students, in that they are taught in this exercise for one whole day in the first week of their first semester and again at the end of the fifth semester. In the first semester, the students often notice issues about themselves, which they want to bring in, explore, and process through their group music therapy training as student-clients throughout the first to third semester (see Chapter 5). At the end of the fifth semester, when they are taught again for one day with a repetition of this exercise, the exercise mirrors their personal growth in all three spaces. The exercise thus can be used as a mirror for the therapeutic training processes they have gone through from the first to fifth semester of their study. Because of this multi-layered function of the exercise, it has been given a chapter of its own.

Today this exercise is a part of the discipline 'Therapy-Related Body and Voice Work' (see Chapter 6), a discipline in the therapeutic track of the music therapy programme at Aalborg University. The exercise described in this chapter is taught for one whole day during the first week of study. The discipline 'Therapy-Related Body and Voice Work' includes this day and a further four whole workshop days in the fifth semester. In the fifth semester the exercise described here is repeated on the first of those four days.

This discipline has been gradually developed during many years, from the time when it was titled 'Psychodynamic Movement'. This chapter, together with Chapter 6, describes this discipline as a whole. The aim of the discipline is described as follows by Storm: 'It offers the student the possibility of learning something about the pre-conscious bodily awareness by studying the phenomenon of the body experience through the practice of *listening* and *observing*' (Storm, 2013, p.62).

I will start the chapter with a short historic view of the development of the discipline 'Psychodynamic Movement' during three generations. Then follows a presentation of the rationale behind and learning aims of this specific prototype exercise 'Three Personal Being and Communication Spaces', leading to a detailed description of the conduction of this exercise in the therapeutic track of the music therapy programme at Aalborg University. Additionally, I will bring a thematic analysis of themes derived from students' reports on this exercise during seven years. Finally, a theoretical platform underpinning an understanding of the multiple potentials of this prototype exercise will be presented.

Historic view of Psychodynamic Movement

The term Psychodynamic Movement was originally created by the English music therapist Mary Priestley (1925–2017) back in the seventies as a 'part of her clinical work with long-term psychotic/schizophrenic inpatients at St Bernhard's Hospital London during the seventies and eighties' (Pedersen, 2002, p.190).

As a former music therapy student in the music therapy mentor course in Herdecke, Germany (see Chapter 2), I was introduced to this discipline as a student-client, and I was also introduced by Priestley to the clinical use of the exercise as a trainee, in my internship while visiting St Bernhard's Hospital for six weeks in 1979. The core of the discipline Psychodynamic Movement is: 'improvised movement by one or more persons on an agreed topic, accompanied by one or more persons who follow and interpret the movements in a parallel instrumental/voice improvisation. This is also called *improvised movement to improvised music*' (Pedersen, 2002, p.191).

Overall, the discipline Psychodynamic Movement included four parts that lasted approximately two hours (Priestley 1975).

In the first of the four parts:

all group members were sitting in a circle while the group leader addressed the whole body mentioning all body parts...in a 'tighten' and 'relax' repetition of verbal phrasing. The idea of this part...was to make the group members pay attention to different body parts and to different experiences of tension and relaxation. (Pedersen, 2002, p.191)

In the second part, and with no verbal exchange concerning the first part, the group leader selected two different pieces of music for so-called *free dance*, often two pieces of music with polarities of mood. The group members were encouraged to move freely to the music following the body signals arising from listening to the music. The idea here was to establish an inward connection to the body and to let the sensations evoked by music listening be a resonator for associations and feelings. Just after this movement improvisation, the members were given time and space for verbal reflection for the members to express their experiences.

In the third part, a common topic, emerging from the previous verbal reflection, was created by the group leader. This topic became the focus of the next improvisation – the real *improvised movement to improvised music.* The improvised music was carried out by a co-therapist, or one or more students who were instructed to follow and interpret the movements. The other group members were told to move freely with eyes closed (if possible), being inspired by the announced topic. They were further told to listen to their body and let the body tell them how to move during the musical improvisation. After the improvisation, a further verbal reflection round was established, where the members had a chance to share and reflect their experiences, and to have feedback from the group leader and other group members. The group leader often gave exploratory questions, such as 'You seemed to explore a lot of feelings – was this the way you felt it yourself?' (Pedersen, 2002, p.193). The idea of this section was to give the group members a chance to connect to, resonate with, and explore their personality through the body as the basic tool of inner experiences. The accompanying musical improvisation might provoke, contain, or reinforce the experiences. The group members could simultaneously benefit from being in a group, where they could explore their need for distance and closeness, their mutual inspiration of movements, or mutual sensations and feelings being present in the room.

Finally, the fourth and last part included a *lay down with closed eyes relaxation exercise*, where the group leader initially made a quick test of running through all body parts as an introduction; for example: 'be aware of "a certain part of your body" and allow yourself to relax this body part' (Pedersen, 2002, p.193). A co-therapist/student improvised relaxation music for this final part. The idea was to enhance the awareness of the body and specific body parts in a relaxed state for the group members, and to let go of problems confronted during the improvisation through body relaxation. This last part of the exercise was meant to give the participants a possibility to feel eventual tensions from their dancing experience in their body, and to encourage them to trust that the body can help contain these tensions during relaxation.

From 'Psychodynamic Movement' to 'Therapy-Related Body and Voice Work'

Psychodynamic Movement as a discipline has been developed further through three generations. An overview of this development is presented in the table below:

1978–1980	Mary Priestley was teaching in Herdecke, and already here she did not bring a co-therapist for her training course for the students in Psychodynamic Movement; instead, she instructed and used one of the students in the student group.
1979–1980	Benedikte Barth Scheiby[1] and the author developed and taught the discipline Psychodynamic Movement in addition to Priestley's courses in Herdecke.
1982–1990	Scheiby and Pedersen (the author) taught the discipline at the music therapy programme in Hamburg – at the Hochschule für Musik und Darstellende Kunst, and at the music therapy programme at Aalborg University.
1990–1996	The Hamburg teaching course in Psychodynamic Movement was continued by Pedersen and Professor Dr Susanne Metzner from Germany.
1996–	All three of us adapted to teach the discipline alone (Pedersen in Aalborg (DK), Metzner in Magdeburg (G) and Scheiby in New York (USA, till 2018)) due to economical restrictions.
2005–	At Aalborg University, I (the author) had a chance to re-establish a co-partnership in teaching this discipline in a partnership with external Associate Professor Sanne Storm, PhD (from the Faroe Islands). From this year, we retitled the discipline 'Therapy-Related Body and Voice Work'.

The development of the discipline Psychodynamic Movement mostly consisted of adding more elements to the discipline, and the scheduled time of the discipline grew from two hours to three full successive days each half year at its highest. These elements were inspired from different additional educations by the developers (Pedersen, a relaxation, movement, and massage education; Scheiby, a postgraduate training in bioenergy; and Metzner, a yoga and other styles of movement training). Thus, the development of the discipline by Pedersen and Scheiby added the following elements:

---

[1] A friend and fellow-student from Mentoren Course, Herdecke, Associate Professor at Aalborg University 1985–1990 and from 1991, adjunct faculty member at New York University.

1) awakening; 2) warming up; 3) energy work; 4) body analysis; 5) psychodynamic movement, 6) relaxation/massage. The development of the discipline by Pedersen and Metzner added the following elements: 1) tuning in – individual/group member, 2) centring – chaos/harmony; 3) the inner child – the inner parents; 4) the inner partners – female/male – authority/empathy; 5) submission/borders – symbiosis/separation; 6) parting – individual/group member. (Pedersen, 2002, pp.196, 202)

The added elements and teaching forms of these developmental steps of the discipline Psychodynamic Movement through two generations are described in detail in Pedersen (2002, pp.190–215).

In the third generation of developing the discipline it was retitled 'Therapy-Related Body and Voice Work' and more weight was given to the human voice part of the discipline, as Storm had undertaken several voice training courses and developed a voice assessment tool (VOIAS) disseminated in her PhD thesis (Storm, 2013).

Today the discipline 'Therapy-Related Body and Voice Work' still covers a one-day course at the beginning of the first semester and runs over a block of four days at the end of the fifth semester. Storm and I collaborated on and planned the course as a whole. I teach the exercise included in this chapter at the beginning of the first semester, and also at the first day of the teaching block in the fifth semester. Storm teaches the last three days in the teaching block in the fifth semester (described in detail in Chapter 6). Often, we followed each other's teaching days on a voluntary basis, as they are very inspirational and we gained a lot of impressions of the challenges and developments of the students.

It was in 2005 that I started to unfold the exercise 'Three Personal Being and Communication Spaces' for a whole day's work.

Teaching aims of the exercise 'Three Personal Being and Communication Spaces'

Concerning the prototype exercise 'Three Personal Being and Communication Spaces', there is a specific focus on psychic, private, and social dimensions conducted as inner and outer spaces experienced with closed eyes. The term 'space' (the private space, the social space, and the soloist space) is applied, because it is a self-experiential exercise, where the concrete sense of inner and outer spaces is in focus.

The teaching aims of this exercise are formulated broadly in the syllabus of the music therapy programme at Aalborg University as part of the teaching aims for the discipline 'Therapy-Related Body and Voice Work' (see Chapter 6). The overall aim is basic training in and consciousness about applying body and voice as something embodied for the future music therapist in music therapy clinical work.

Specific for the exercise 'Three Personal Being and Communication Spaces', this training prepares the students for the following purposes and competencies:

1. Being able to orientate oneself in the nonverbal field concerning closeness and distance

2. Experience one's own possibilities and challenges in being present in and expressing oneself from the three different spaces in order to identify personal working issues for group music therapy for each student (in the first semester)

3. Reflect on one's embodied and vocal resources and challenges concerning entering therapeutic (verbal and nonverbal) dialogues and the establishment of contact in relationships in psychodynamic-oriented music therapy (in the fifth semester)

I have didactically reflected on the purpose of this exercise in earlier publications (Pedersen, 2000, 2002, 2007b, 2014). Back in 2002, I stated that this exercise is an important element in training music therapists, where the students learn to listen to and be familiar with themselves from within, and especially learn to be familiar with an inner presence, that can be recognized by the student as 'my private space'.

The exercise is conducted in student dyads, where one student improvises through the voice (and eyes closed) and another student intuitively paints while listening to the voice sounds from the student partner. The painter works with eyes opened. A formalistic separation is implied between what the voice improviser has experienced from inside with eyes closed, and what a partner fellow student has experienced from outside with eyes open, while the latter is listening and painting. It is the responsibility of the voice performer to be aware of, reflect, and integrate whatever possible from what the two students share and explore in their verbal dialogue after the improvisation, where they share experiences from two different fields of experiencing (experiences from giving voice from inside and experiences from listening from outside).

In future clinical situations for the students, it is mostly not possible or realistic to separate the perception from within and the perception from outside that clearly. As expressed by the English professor and art therapist Arthur Robbins, it is about being aware of if I, as a therapist, am present from within or partly from outside my perception of an inner centre, and being aware of using this as a compass for what kind of work I am into just now. For the therapist it is crucial to 'try to sense the direction and the nature of the energy: if it comes from deep inside or from outside' (Robbins, 1998, p.19). He writes that he is aware of a raised perceived experience of his body, simultaneously with a state of 'being present'. He points out that, if one part of the therapeutic relationship is not fully present, the aim of the treatment is to try to make both parts present simultaneously. This ability can't be expected to be present in the client. Therefore, the therapist has to make use of a 'disciplined subjectivity' (Pedersen, 2007b, 2014) in their way of being present (see Chapter 3).

The American psychoanalyst Patrick Casement talks about the therapist's resonance as something which is dependent on an ability to both adapt to what is personal for the therapist and what comes from the patient. He points out that each therapist has to learn to stay open to the other person's 'being different' and develop an ability to respond on an interactive emotional level in relation to, or in spite of, the cognitive understandings of the emotions. He expresses this in musical terms, such as giving resonance to unknown 'tunes' or dissonant 'harmonies' in other persons. He considers this as necessary to raise the therapist's receptivity by extending the field of emotional susceptibility (Casement, 1987). I, the author, identify an extra sensitive listening attitude by extending the field of listening susceptibility (see Chapter 3). For instance, the therapist does not only listen with the ears, but with the body as a whole. She further does not only listen to somebody else or to herself. She listens to herself listening to the client (Pedersen, 1997, 1999).

In training, the main purpose of the exercise 'Three Personal Being and Communication Spaces' therefore is to tune the awareness of the students, so they can resonate to both known and unknown tunes with a stable connection to one's private space – also when the student is present in the field of awareness in the other spaces being conducted through the exercise. The experience of being centred is extended to be fluctuating in all three imaginary 'being present' and communication spaces.

Performance of the prototype exercise 'Three Personal Being and Communication Spaces'

As mentioned earlier, it is important to emphasize that the conduction of this prototype exercise in the first and fifth semester is an exact repetition. Both workshop days start with a deep relaxation exercise followed by warming up exercises for at least one hour, before this prototype exercise is conducted with the group of students. The students are guided to connect to a partner and to work in dyads.

Each dyad chooses an A and B person. The role of A is to stand with eyes closed and to express the sensations and experiences of the three imagined spaces through voice improvisation to make the experiences audible and embodied. The role of B is to sit opposite to A and to listen carefully and let the sounds from the three spaces be formed with crayon colours into a painting for each space. The A students are guided by the group leader to stand in a circle of fellow A students with faces towards the centre, closed eyes, with good distance between the students. They are further guided to find a balance in the body in the standing position. The B students are guided to sit on the floor inside the circle just in front of their standing A student partner with three pieces of paper and colours.

Then follows the instruction of *the private space*, where the A students are told to imagine a private space inside the body and around the body. They are told to imagine a space where they can recharge themselves if they have been very much present in the universe of others. The A students are also told to imagine that it can be a space where they can hide themselves if they want to avoid other people. The A students are told to express vocal improvised sounds from their experience of this space. The A students are encouraged to keep their own private sounds, even if they can hear and maybe feel seduced by the sounds of the other A students.

The B students are guided to listen to the sounds of their partner and simultaneously make a painting for each of the three spaces in the exercise. They are encouraged to let the sounds from the partner flow out through the fingers in colours and forms on a piece of paper. They are told to turn the back of each painting upwards after each of the three spaces. This is because the A students are not expected to directly watch the paintings, when having terminated the voice improvisation of all three spaces and when opening their eyes, until A has narrated their experiences obtained through voice improvisation with closed eyes from inside.

Each of the improvising spaces are directed for a length of time by the group leader, who clearly beats a drum signalizing the start and stop of the improvisation of each of the three spaces. The mean time is about 10–15 minutes per space.

In the transition from the private space to the social space, the A students are told to let the sounds resonate in the body and to be aware of how it felt to be present in and express their private space; and, finally, to be aware of how far their private space reached out.

During the instruction of *the social space*, the A students are told to listen to and express their experience of being related to the other participants through vocal sounds. They still have their eyes closed. They are encouraged to be aware that they can be inspired by or inspire the others and that they can build sound pictures together – only the fantasy sets borders for possibilities. Often dialogues arise, which lead the participants away from just being inspired by others and into a simultaneously mutual dynamic flow in the sound space, with several variations of tempo, pitch, dynamics, etc. In the instruction, it is emphasized as very important that the students are aware of not losing connectedness to the private space, even when the sound improvisation is at its highest. If a student senses that the contact with the private space is lost or even feels like disappearing into the total sound picture, it is suggested to the student that they take a short break in the voice improvisation to re-establish the connectedness to the private space. Also, in this second part of the improvisation, partner student B, sitting in front of student A, is listening with open eyes and creating a simultaneous painting inspired from the sounds of the voice sounds from A.

After the drum has terminated the social space, the A students again are guided to keep their eyes closed and to let the sounds resonate in the body. They are further guided to be aware of how it felt to be present in and being in dialogues with fellow students in the social space. Finally, they are guided to try sensing both the private and the social spaces and the transition between them, also when they are not expressing them in sounds.

The instructions for *the soloist space* emphasizes that the A students are allowed to take up and fill out space with their vocal sounds, without paying attention to the fellow students, who have the permission to do the same. They are encouraged to imagine they are standing on the stage in a big concert hall, and imagine they have permission to find their unique way of filling this hall with their voice sounds so they can be heard from the back rows and farthest corners of the hall.

They are further told to be aware that the sound may move as much inward as outward, that they can have a feeling of being part of a sound bar. It is also emphasized here that it is very important that the A students keep connected to the private space, even if the sound expression might be at a high volume, so the perception of filling out that amount of space is centred from within the private space. The focus in this part of the improvisation is not about listening to the others – rather it is on being able to be familiar with manifesting oneself clearly and significantly, without losing the ability to listen to oneself from deep within. Partner B is sitting in front with open eyes painting the sound space of the A student partner.

After the drum has terminated this third and last part of the improvisation, the A students are guided to stand with closed eyes for a little while and to let the sounds resonate in the body. They are further guided to perceive all three spaces and the transitions between them with closed eyes and without expressing them in sounds.

The verbal reflection on the experiences through all three spaces of this exercise starts in dyads with A and B, where they are guided that A initially narrates about experiences from within with closed eyes. Then they can start to mutually look at and find a meaning in what the painting may show about the experiences by both A and B students. At the end they are told to write notes on a piece of paper, where A writes briefly about what was the most important experience in each of the three spaces for A, and B writes what B imagines was the most important experiences for A in the three different spaces. The painting and B's written notes are given from B to A as a ritual present.

After this verbal dyad sharing, a switching of roles between the two students takes place, and the improvisation in three parts is repeated, as described above, with student B as the voice improvisator and student A as the listening painter.

After the second verbal sharing in dyads, the prototype exercise is terminated in a verbal sharing plenum. Each student is acknowledged by the group leader in sharing the most important experiences in each of the three spaces to the group leader and the group of fellow students, and simultaneously shows their drawings. After the first performance in the first semester, the students are encouraged to reflect, after having shared in plenum, if there are issues in their experiences that might inform what they want to focus on in the group music therapy courses throughout the first to third semester (see Chapter 5).

The group leader collects all paintings and written notes from all students after the first semester course day to make a copy and return the originals to the students. The copies are stored in a locked cupboard until the fifth semester in case the students lose their original material in the meantime.

At the end of the second performance of the exercise in the fifth semester, each student is given the possibility to compare paintings and log notes from the first and the second participation in the exercise, and to notate differences appearing in their two participating experiences. This is an additional reflective part of the verbal dialogue of the second performance of the exercise. Their notes from reports and summing up of the exercise will further guide the students for their developmental processes towards becoming a professional music therapist.

After having attended both workshops during the first and fifth semester, the students have to write a self-reflective report, with a minimum of five and a maximum of eight pages, on their experiences of the participation in the discipline 'Therapy-Related Body and Voice Work', where this exercise covers two of the six workshop days. As guidelines for the report, the students are told to focus on:

1. Their overall impression of and experience of the discipline

2. The choice of one or two exercises, where they share their experiences in detail

3. The student's idea of how this chosen exercise/s can be of benefit for future clinical work

Summaries of some students' experiences of the exercise – a thematic analysis of 37 student reports

Out of a pile of student reports over seven years of teaching, 37 reports deal specifically with this exercise, chosen as one of the two demanded exercises (in point 2) of the guidelines for the report (see above). After having read the 37 reports several times, I defined six overall themes and started to underline key statements of self-experiences deductively and place them under the following defined six themes. For each of the themes, I wrote a short text summing up the essence of the key statements connected to each of the themes.

Theme 1: Overall experiences (11 key statements)

Theme 2: Experiences from the private space (14 statements)

Theme 3: Experiences from the social space (15 statements)

Theme 4: Experiences from the soloist space (16 statements)

Theme 5: Differences in experiences from first to second performance (22 statements)

Theme 6: Possibilities of application of experiences and the exercise in clinical practice (13 statements)

Overall, I found 89 key statements, with the highest number related to the fifth theme concerning differences in experiences from first to second performance.

In the following I will present the six composite themes, a few summarized key statements for each theme, and then a composite statement summing up the essence of the key statements of students' self-experiences which connect to the theme. Some of the essences will be presented from a first-person perspective, to bring the experiences to life. All statements were originally in Danish and translated by the author.

The first theme: Overall experiences

I want to bring a summarization of a key statement from one student report as this statement covers elements from composite key statements.

> By having a wire into our inner space simultaneously as being present in the outer space, a realization is created for how much and how little it is possible to take up space. It is an exercise mirroring our ability to stay to oneself and further to be aware, how much one influences and is influenced by others. It is paramount that the private space is given full attention first, to enable ability of sensing our own borders, ability of containing, sensitivity for entrainment, power, weakness, and vulnerability in togetherness with other people.

The key statements placed under the theme of overall experiences of the exercise, I have summarized by partly quoting, partly rewriting, student statements into an essence:

> This exercise guides one to listen inward and outward at the same time and to be aware of shifts between the three different spaces. It creates a platform for authentic sounds and for the possibility of us as participants to open our senses to inner and outer layers of oneself and others; and it mirrors one's way of being and one's condition in all three spaces. An important focus is on one's own borders and the borders of the others, as the exercise trains the awareness on borders. Awareness of one's private space, as trained in the exercise, promotes abilities of presence and empathy by a future music therapist. The use of voice improvisation of the experiences of the spaces creates other realization possibilities, than just visualizing the spaces. The voice expresses the unconscious and body and voice are intertwined.

The second theme: Experiences from the private space

Most of the key sentences under this theme are from the experiences related to the first workshop. This private space mirrors the different conditions of students when performing the exercise and often in the following verbal sharing life issues emerge, which they were more or less aware of. These issues can provide information as to what may be important for the students to address in their group and individual music therapy in the therapeutic training track. Some students find this space especially very peaceful, while others can feel very insecure and have a hard time in this space. The different experiences reported here support an existentialistic theory on two poles in human dimensions underlying this exercise, and the work for each student is to find a way of being able to be present in both poles and able to move flexibly between them as a progression.

I want to present two summarized key sentences each representing one polarity (see later in the chapter):

> In the private space we can experience a very big need to sense safety. The voice improvisation was cross-borders, like being exposed to a partner, a feeling of being tensed and insecure.

> It was easy to get into the private space, and very comfortable in there. The border was very clear, and also, there was a clear perception of the size of the space. We could be ourselves in our private space.

Some of the students who find this space peaceful and comfortable may feel uncomfortable in either of the two other spaces. The essence of all key statements under the theme of experiences from the private space is presented here in a first-person perspective to come closer to the statement as a whole:

> It is difficult to contain and to stay to myself in the private space and it feels unpleasant. An insecure feeling on how the partner will receive my sounds is present, and this makes me think too much. I can feel peace, but simultaneously I feel isolated. Connection to the body is fundamental for being present in the private space. I can also experience this space as a sanctuary, where I can be in a feeling of flow and keep my focus inward, which gives me a peaceful and personal surplus of energy. I can feel my essence here, without a demand on mirroring it in other people. To be familiar with this space strengthens my social space.

The third theme: Experiences from the social space

Most of the key statements are likely from the first performance of the exercise, whereas the experiences from the second performance from all three spaces are collected in the sixth theme concerning differences in experiences of the two performances.

The following two summarized key sentences exemplify different experiences of taking part in the voice expression of the social space at the first performance, which also mirrors polarity:

> From the beginning it is okay to participate in the social space, but it is impossible to avoid being distracted by the sounds of the others. It is a feeling of not

'speaking' the same sound language as the others. It is difficult to participate actively – it is easier to keep listening and trying to keep in contact with the private space.

The social space felt really good, and a clear feeling of being based in the private space was present. During the improvisation in interactions with the other fellow students, a need emerged to come back to the private space – a need of safety. If the others came too close, a safety could be found without problems in the private space.

An essence of the total number of key statements under the theme of the social space is also presented in a first-person perspective here, and sounds as follows:

I easily get disturbed by the sounds of the others in this space, and I lose contact to my own self. I have my awareness constantly directed outwards, and I get insecure if I am not part of a dialogue. I am aware of adapting myself towards the others, or I am busy running away from contact with the others. It is difficult to keep a contact to both the private and the social space at the same time – it is either/or. I really enjoy the interplay, and I can share and examine impressions and expressions in the shared sound space. It is important to have my own self present in the social space, and I feel like the way from the private space to the soloist space has to pass through the social space.

The fourth theme: Experiences from the soloist space

Most key statements under this theme again belong to the first performance. This space is a challenge for many students, and some do not understand the meaning of doing it at the first performance. They do not feel a need to be in centrum or to drown out the others. Also, this theme includes polarities in the key statements, which produce working issues for personal music therapy during the programme.

It was rather cross-borders to be present in the soloist space, and really unpleasant. A need to run away or to start crying emerged, and a feeling of being forced to do something unpleasant. A panic reaction almost came through in between... It became clear that outshouting others creates a really unpleasant feeling. Also, the voice felt pressed in the situation – like being tensed to listen to.

In the soloist space an inner primordial woman was found right away. The sounds and the songs, which came out through the voice, were simple and powerful. No dissimulation was needed. No thoughts about the sounds came up – it just floated out... It presented a picture on inner resources and power to be pulled on.

The overall essence, covering all key statements under this theme, from a first-person perspective sounds as follows:

It is difficult to stay present and to find my own sound in the total sound picture in the soloist space. I feel a need to disappear, the experience is cross-border and I feel like being under pressure. I have the courage to break self-made limitations and I challenge the anxiety by taking my space. I feel pleasure in improvising freely, and I play around with childish expressions free of responsibility and consideration. I can be in a flow and let go of control, and I am not concerned about my sounds being heard by others. I feel like expressing my primordial voice sound, a core sound, directly connected to the private space. The direct contact to the private space in the soloist space and the movement between the spaces makes me feel more whole and gives me a better feeling of personal integrity.

The fifth theme: Differences in experiences from first to second performance

This theme gathered the most key statements, and these statements are not presenting polarities at the same level as the other themes. Almost all 22 statements present experiences of positive changes for the students; only one statement expresses no change. I want to bring three summarized statements here, as these statements were rather unfolded in the reports, and they express the students' abilities of self-reflection after the second performance of the exercise.

The exercise clarified different working issues for the personal therapy and gives an awareness of patterns in interaction with other people. It also gave an awareness of wishes for which patterns to change. This exercise has promoted this awareness since the first performance of it – awareness of when other people are crossing one's borders, and when it is a need to clearly say 'no' instead of withdrawing oneself.

An insecurity dominating the first performance has been replaced by a self-security. The private space still takes up a lot of space in the inner world, but it is no longer a hiding spot to hide oneself from the surroundings. It has transformed to a secure base, a space where it is possible to seek peace and quietness. It can give a rest from the expectations of others and nurse oneself and one's values.

It was much easier to stay present in the private space the second time – much easier to leave out the sounds of the others, and stay to one's own sounds, when wanted. It was also much easier to open up and listen, when wanted... Even more important was the fact that, in the soloist space, there was a feeling of breaking through with the voice. Suddenly and totally unexpected, not caring at all, that it might not sound as intended to sound. A feeling of totally letting go of the head, voice, control, thoughts, and anxiety. Like singing in high heaven – to be present. To be in one's body. To be the person I am.

It is important here to mention that the changes are not coming from this exercise alone, but from the longitudinal work on personal processes in *group music therapy* (see Chapter 5) through three semesters in between the first and second performance of this exercise. This second performance of the exercises serves as a mirror for the students, where they can re-experience the spaces and compare their experiences from the first and second participation. Through the many years, the repetition of this exercise has overall been a positive experience for all students.

The essence, covering all of the statements to the theme concerning differences between first and second performance from a first-person perspective, sounds as follows:

I am better connected with my feelings, and I do not need so much control. I am proud of being able to keep my personal sounds, and I feel more like expressing a core voice sound, which is also my base. I experienced a real contact with the others in the social space, and in the soloist space sounds came out of me, which I did not know about. A solid contact to the private space makes the social and soloist space freer, and it also makes me conscious that I am expressing my own personality and I need to act myself – not to wait for others to act. I have moved from being more guided from outside to being more guided from inside. My experience of no change between the two performances can be an expression of being well integrated or of stagnation in my personal development.

The sixth theme: Possibilities of application of experiences and the exercise in clinical practice

The students overall consider this exercise to be useful both for themselves as future music therapists and for different client populations. A couple of longer summarized key statements illustrate these considerations:

To be familiar with our private space and our role in the social and soloist space is very important in relation to the roles you as a therapist can meet and enter in clinical practice. To be able to withdraw and to find our centre in the private space in a given situation, where it can be difficult to follow the client, can be crucial for our ability to get close to or to make a distance to the client. It is also important to be able to move further out in our attention from the safe private space/centre, and simultaneously keep our identity and safety there, in being social and turned towards the client in our awareness. It is specifically important to remember how our own experience in the performance of the exercise was, and how emotional and personally challenging and cross-borders it can be for others, to be present in and to express these three spaces through the voice. A helpful training to obtain a better empathy and ability to resonate deeply with future clients in situations where they have difficulties in finding or feeling their private space or the opposite, if they have difficulties in daring to move out from the private safe space.

Experiences of border problems in this exercise are really important to progress with this kind of work. It has been very important to be able to set limits to others, seen from the perspective of being a future music therapist. If our private space is without boundaries, it is difficult to know when you are present by yourself or by the client. This would make the future therapeutic work less effective, and probably it would be difficult to survive this work for a long time, if there is not a clear experience of a private space, from where to charge energy and return when needed.

The essence of all the citations to this sixth theme

This exercise mirrors competencies of being present in and shifting focus between the three personal being and communication spaces; it also raises the ability of building and staying in relationships with a focus on opening/closing borders, giving/taking awareness, and transference conditions. A stable contact to one's private space helps in developing a professional therapist, who can also function as a secure anchor for the client. The exercise creates awareness of the ability of the voice to create and support experiences of being and the ability to mirror inner physical or psychological blockages. The exercise will be useful for clients with mild psychological and psychiatric problems including eating disturbances, and it will be useful for counselling work on self-experience. It can help human beings to be better connected to their emotions and to identify relational patterns and resources.

The many key statements unfold the student's experiences of this exercise and the polarities of each space. Most of the citations from the fifth theme on differences of the first and second performance show that the students have changed from one pole to another; still a real progression includes the movement and fights in movements between the poles as described later on in the chapter.

A theoretical platform for the prototype exercise 'Three Personal Being and Communication Spaces'

This exercise offers an opportunity to develop an awareness of who I am, how I have developed, how I relate to others, how unconscious stored memories might influence my ability of setting borders, to be in social communication without losing my feeling of who I am – and finally how I can be authoritative in an authentic way. The essences of the thematic analysis reflect both themes related to the person as a self, turned inward in awareness and being present in a perceived private space, and the person in relation to others. Another opportunity offered is to develop awareness that being self-contained in a perceived private space is a prerequisite for being able to be authentically present in a perceived social space and in a perceived soloist space. The theoretical platform of the 'Three Personal Being and Communication Spaces' is therefore in line with the psychodynamic understanding described in Chapter 3, that 'the personality is biologically settled by both the character and the temper of the single person, and socially shaped by close relationship experiences with attachment figures. In addition, the personality is modulated by psychologically overwhelming experiences through one's life. Thus, the psychodynamic approach highlights unconscious processes and self-awareness integrated with a biological, psychological, and social understanding of contemporary neuro-affective and developmental psychology.'

Experiencing a perceived soloist space in the exercise is a challenge for many students. Many of them have been raised with a perspective of not taking too much space, or a perspective of always being polite and thinking about others before thinking about oneself in social situations. In work with different client groups, it is often a need that the therapist can take a clear leading role in a natural authoritative way to help the client progress.

Further, an existential theory growing out from the roots of psychodynamic theory as a theoretical platform is useful in understanding the benefits of this exercise. The exercise focuses on the participant's personal embodied experience of being present and expressing themselves through voice sounds. The personal experiences are based on different inner sensations and imageries of spaces (a private space, a social space, and a soloist space), and on personal experiences of being related to oneself and to others in the different spaces.

Existentialistic theory is concerned about human beings' lived experiences in life and about psychological development of human beings from an existential perspective (see Chapter 3).

A specific existential understanding of human development is offered by Van Deurzen (1999), who, from a holistic perspective, identifies four existential human dimensions called the physical dimension, the social dimension, the psychic dimension, and the spiritual dimension. She also offers an idea of polarities in each of these dimensions. This idea of polarities suggests that human development is taking place in dynamic inner fights in human beings between a positive and a negative pole identified in all four dimensions.

Table 4.1: Four existential dimensions (Van Deurzen, 1999, p.143)

Polarities in existential dimensions	Positive pole	Negative pole	Value of being in-between
Physical dimensions	Life, health, richness, desires	Death, illness, poorness, pain	Safety
Social dimensions	Belonging, acceptance, love, admiration	Isolation, rejection, hate, judgement	Recognition
Psychic dimension	Integrity, identity, perfection, trust	Disintegration, confusion, defectiveness, doubt	Autonomy
Spiritual dimension	Meaning, soul-peace, aim, the good	Meaningless, guilt, hopelessness, evil	Wisdom

Existential dimensions related to the prototype exercise 'Three Personal Being and Communication Spaces'

I find it meaningful to transfer Van Deurzen's idea of positive and negative polarities within each of the three spaces and also to transfer Van Deurzen's suggestion that human development is taking place in dynamic inner fights in human beings between a positive and negative pole in different dimensions of life. I would add that inner dynamic fights also take place in human relationships. The thematic analysis of the students' reports document very clearly their experiences of many such fights between inner dynamic forces related to both their self-picture and their relational experiences.

I have identified two poles in each of the three spaces from experiences through many years of teaching students in this prototype exercise. I have further applied this model in assessing work with ambulatory clients in mental health, together with my colleague Prof. Lars Ole Bonde (Pedersen & Bonde, 2013). We have defined the poles in the following way.

Table 4.2: Three Personal Being and Communication Spaces (Pedersen & Bonde, 2013, p.22)

Poles of polarities in the Three Personal Being and Communication Spaces	Negative pole	Positive pole	Value of the *in-between forces* understood as a continuum
The private space	Hide oneself, feel unreal, anxiety, confusion, self-devaluation	Feel alive, real, containing, self-caring, self-conscious	Level of identity and feeling of self-esteem
The social space	Feel outside, isolated, jealous, rejected	Give/take, flow, playing, setting natural borders	Level of experience of feeling demarcated
The soloist space	Take place unconsciously, artificial authority, giving up, demanding	Feel powerful, integrated, natural authority, persevering, flexible	Autonomy

This model, where positive and negative polarities in the Three Personal Being and Communication Spaces are identified, is a frame of understanding both personal developmental steps and a frame of understanding developmental steps in relation to others. This frame of understanding can be applied both for identification of music therapy students' steps of development in the therapeutic track and as a frame of understanding steps of development for clients in counselling work or clinical work with mental health clients on an ambulant basis with mild to moderate mental health issues.

For music therapy students participating in the teaching process of this exercise questions arise, such as how they can position themselves in relation to clients in order for the clients to be able to get into a process of fighting between inner dynamic forces as an alternative to be fixed in one of the poles.

As an example, a different position for the student-therapist is called for if the client is fixed in a negative pole in the private space than if the client can move in a flexible way between the poles. Therefore, the overall idea of the therapeutic training track – and in this chapter specifically the exercise 'Three Personal Being and Communication Spaces' – is to prepare the students to move between the spaces, and to be familiar with both negative and positive poles in each of the spaces, without being overwhelmed. These movements can be challenging for people suffering from low self-esteem, problems with setting boundaries, anxiety, and poor feeling of autonomy.

From clinical practice I have experienced myself that, to get in contact with clients suffering from autism or autistic features, I need to be positioned for a longer time in my own private space and wait for a natural meeting possibility. I cannot expect the client to be able to establish a contact with me under pressure from me, if I position myself in the social space. Also, in work with people suffering from psychosis, I have experienced that I sometimes need to position myself in my soloist space to be able to follow and meet another person in a hallucinated reality. Here it is very important that I stay in contact with my own private space to avoid both of us floating around without either of us being grounded. If I expect the person suffering from hallucinations to meet me in 'my realistic world', I might lose any possibility of establishing a contact between us.

To sum up this exercise, it can be seen as a frame around other training disciplines in the therapeutic track. It provides the students with a possibility to mirror their feeling of being grounded, feeling of being familiar with setting natural borders, and feeling of being aware of their position in relationships and awareness of self-appearance. The setting is very structured but still the individual experiences and expressions are very personal and unique. The teaching of this exercise is subject to the ethical rules as described in Chapter 2 and the presentation of students' experiences in this chapter is only possible due to informed consent by the students.

References

Casement, P. (1987). *Lyt til patienten [Listen to the patient].* Hans Reitzels Forlag.

Pedersen, I.N. (1997). 'The music therapist's listening perspectives as source of information in improvised musical duets with grown-up, psychiatric patients, suffering from schizophrenia.' *Nordic Journal of Music Therapy, 6(2),* 98–111.

Pedersen, I.N. (1999). 'Music Therapy as Holding and Re-Organizing Work with Schizophrenic and Psychotic Patients.' In T. Wigram & J.D. Backer (eds), *Clinical Applications of Music Therapy in Psychiatry.* Jessica Kingsley Publishers.

Pedersen, I.N. (2000). '"Inde-fra eller ude-fra" – orientering i terapeutens tilstedeværelse og nærvær. ["From with-in or from with-out" – An orientation in the presence of the therapist].' *Musikterapi i psykiatrien online (MIPO), 2000 (1),* 97–109.

Pedersen, I.N. (2002). 'Psychodynamic Movement: A Basic Training Methodology for Music Therapists'. In J.Th. Eschen (ed.), *Analytical Music Therapy.* Jessica Kingsley Publishers.

Pedersen, I.N. (2007a). 'Counter transference in music therapy. A phenomenological study on counter transference used as a clinical concept by music therapists working with musical improvisation in adult psychiatry.' PhD dissertation. Institute for Communication and Psychology. Aalborg University. Accessed on 06/12/21 at https://vbn.aau.dk/ws/portalfiles/portal/70261290/inp_2007.pdf.

Pedersen, I.N. (2007b). 'Musikterapeutens disciplinerede subjektivitet [The disciplined subjectivity of the music therapist].' *Psyke & Logos, 28(1),* 358–384.

Pedersen, I.N. (2014). 'The integration of a Self-Experience Track in the Education and Training of Danish Music Therapists: The Aalborg Model'. In K. Bruscia (ed.), *Self-Experiences in Music Therapy, Education, Training and Supervision.* Barcelona Publishers.

Pedersen, I.N. & Bonde, L.O. (2013). 'Musiklytning og indre billeder: At sytrke identitets- og salvværdsfølelsen gennem "musiklytning og indre billeddannelse" for ambulante psykiatriske patienter [Music listening and inner imagery: To strengthen identity and self-esteem through music listening and inner imagery].' *Musikterapi i psykiatrien online (MIPO), 8(1),* 17–41.

Pedersen, I.N., Lindvang, C., Holck, U., & Jacobsen, S.L. (2014). 'Læreterapi og terapeutiske færdigheder [Training therapy and therapeutic competencies].' In L.O. Bonde (ed.), *Musikterapi: Teori, uddannelse, praksis, forskning. En håndbog om musikterapi i Danmark [Music therapy: Theory, education, practice, research. A handbook on music therapy in Denmark].* KLIM.

Priestley, M. (1975). *Music Therapy in Action.* Constable.

Robbins, A. (ed.) (1998). *Therapeutic Presence – Bridging Expression and Form.* Jessica Kingsley Publishers.

Storm, S. (2013). 'Research into the development of voice assessment in music therapy.' PhD dissertation. Department of Communication and Psychology. Aalborg University. Accessed on 06/12/21 at https://vbn.aau.dk/files/316401121/Sanne_Storm_Research_into_the_Development_of_Voice_Assessment_in_Music_Therapy.pdf.

Van Deurzen, E. (1999). *Eksistentielle dimensioner i psykoterapi [Everyday mysteries – existential dimensions of psychotherapy].* Hans Reitzels Forlag.

CHAPTER 5

Group Training Therapy

Charlotte Lindvang

*We are a network more than we consciously know and in a group with
many communicative exchanges and emotional resonances, we have
a unique and multifaceted possibility to move and to be moved...*

This chapter focus on therapeutic learning during the discipline 'group training
therapy' (GTT) in the Aalborg curriculum, where the students are participants,
engaging in a group process during three courses spread over one-and-a-half
years. The chapter first introduces the overall setting of the discipline and
presents music therapy methods that are applied. Further, considerations concerning ethics and the specific role of the training therapist are presented. Then
all three courses are reviewed in separate sections presenting the educational
context and learning objectives for each course followed by an elaboration of
therapeutic learning areas at stake: In the 1st course: 'security and trust'; in the
2nd course: 'emotional and relational awareness'; and in the 3rd course: 'mentalization and new horizons'. To elaborate the progression of the learning processes,
the chapter describes selected salient developmental themes that students get in
touch with during the three courses. Vignettes and citations from music therapy
students illustrate the vitality and dynamics of the themes and paint a picture of
a discipline that provides the students with some of the initial building blocks in
becoming a music therapist. The essence of these building blocks is experience of
the therapeutic potential of group processes, the ability to listen to oneself and
to others, and to explore, express, and reflect in music and in verbal dialogues.

Finally, the chapter presents theory that underpins the therapeutic approach and methods applied in this discipline.[1]

Introduction

Group training therapy (GTT) is a special learning environment, where the student enters a position as client and group member in a music therapy process. GTT is a mandatory part of training in Aalborg. A music therapist who is highly experienced in group therapy, and has relevant further education such as GIM, acts as the group therapist (called a 'training therapist'). The training therapist is conducting a learning process that constitutes a groundwork for a future professional *integrated and experienced identity* as a music therapist (Lindvang, 2013, 2015; Pedersen, 2002). Thus, GTT differs from any therapy group outside university concerning context, content, and purpose. GTT also differs from other learning arenas inside the university. More than acquisition of skills and proficiency, GTT provides a space that allows students to experience and express themselves and be moved by each other as the processes of contact and communication unfolds. GTT offers a calm pace and pauses with silence inviting students to move into contemplation and deep listening. GTT aims at expanding students' ability to be present and open to what is at stake, including meeting and investigating differences and difficulties as the following vignette illustrates (the number at the end of the vignette refers to an overview of music therapy methods applied in GTT, which is presented later in the chapter):

Vignette 1

One way to start a session in GTT is to guide the students to sense their body, their breath, and connect to a sense of a centre inside the body. From there, participants let out the sound of their voice. The training therapist instructs the students to focus on the bodily felt sense of their voice and from there gradually move into the shared vocal space. In one group, some of the students expressed from the beginning of the session that they were tired after an intense week with other teachings. The common voice improvisation – in which the training therapist participated in order to follow and mirror the students

---

[1] This chapter presents vignettes composed by the author/training therapist based on the memory, notes, and excerpts from some of the students' final assignments in GTT. The quotes represent, with written permission, six students from different cohorts.

– became sensitive and soft and characterized by low volume harmonious and disharmonious sounds. After the improvisation, verbal exchanges followed: 'It was like walking through a winter landscape, first alone but then hand in hand with the group', 'I felt a relief that we allowed the sensitivity', 'Maybe the improvisation was an illustration of how tired we are, but it was beautiful', 'This improvisation gave me a sense of acceptance and I feel that I am more ready for the day now' (see Table 5.1; A1).

Placement in the training programme

GTT has been part of the Aalborg curriculum since the programme started in 1982. The discipline had different formats over the years, but for the last 15 years, GTT has been established as three courses placed in the first three semesters of the Bachelor's degree in music therapy. The intention of placing this training at the onset of the Bachelor's degree is to let the students develop a practical knowledge about music therapeutic processes from the beginning as well as build up understanding of clients from the lived experiences of being in the client position themselves. Furthermore, the group process gives the students a special in-depth knowledge of each other, which allows them to build trust in each other – something that they can carry with them during their studies.

Scope

GTT consists of 18 full days, six days each half-year for one-and-a-half years, scheduled as two days in a row, three times during the semester, and contains about 110 meeting hours all together. Two days in a row gives the possibility of letting go of everyday tasks and building up concentration and intimacy in the group work. The groups ideally consist of 6–10 participants; it is necessary to split them in two groups if the cohort is larger than 12 students.

Theory supporting the approach in GTT

The theoretical contributions presented later in this chapter constitute selected areas from the huge landscape of group therapy theory. These contributions underpin the therapeutic approach in GTT at Aalborg University and add to the general theoretical background for the therapeutic track presented in the first three chapters of this book.

Meta-reflections and theoretical discussions sometimes come up at the end of a day with GTT. The discussions connect to what the students have experienced during training and the training therapist plays an active role in explaining theoretical underpinnings on a level that students can comprehend. Students are also advised to study group therapy literature related to GTT. However, theoretical teaching is not applied as a direct part of GTT. GTT seeks to develop an 'action-borne knowledge' which is also known as the principle of 'learning by doing' formulated by the American educational reformer John Dewey (Dewey, 1938). Learning happens through self-experience and participation in a relational and practice-oriented learning arena (see Chapter 2). Certainly, a professional identity gradually emerges from the intertwining of theory and practice during the five-year training programme – but in GTT the primary focus is to provide students with first-hand bodily felt experiences of themselves and others, of group dynamics, and of music therapy.

The setting of group training therapy

This section will describe the time, space, and roles of both students and training therapist including the ethical obligations on both parts.[2] Most of the students have never tried to be part of a therapy group before. Phenomena of anxiety among the students are quite usual, for example pre-perceptions of what group therapy is, fear of being forced to expose oneself, or fear of the unknown and non-controlling aspects of the process. To enable development of a sense of trust in the group, the students are informed prior to starting the sessions about the reason for having training therapy as part of the curriculum, the overall setting and experiential approach, and what is expected from them in this context.

Time

Usually, a therapy day lasts from 9.00 am till 4.00 pm. The routine is to have a lunch-break of one hour, and a short break of 10–20 minutes, both in the morning and during the afternoon. It is important that everyone respects the timing of the day and of the breaks to secure the common group energy and raise concentration.

It is a basic task to build up or to strengthen the students' sense of time and timing in music therapy. The group starts and ends precisely at the time that is scheduled and students learn about time in therapy through repeatedly seeing

---

2   See also Chapter 1, where we present the ethical rationale for having training therapy as a part of the academic curriculum, and Chapter 2, in which we present the overall ethical concerns around this implementation.

how the therapist navigates the time factor as a part of the setting. During the three courses in GTT, the students start to be timekeepers themselves, for example when they work in small subgroups, and experience how to combine attention on time with the attentiveness in the processes that take place.

Vignette 2

In one group, it became clear that some of the group members had difficulty being ready for the time after the breaks. One of the group members took up this issue and the training therapist supported an exploration of what it might express and how it influenced the group environment. The dialogue led on to reflections on the fear of making mistakes in relation to the group's norms and there was now an opportunity to work further with the theme right/wrong in the group process, for example by examining this through a joint improvisation. This investigation set some energy free and raised the awareness of each other in the group. There was an agreement in the group to take care of the group time by taking responsibility for being accurate (see Table 5.1; A12).

The training therapist keeps the timing in the sessions and accommodates variations and shifts between different ways of being together, in music, in bodily work, in meditation, in verbal reflections, etc. This alternation helps stay focused and concentrated during long days in the therapy group and furthermore provides a basic training in moving between different modes and forms of expression in music therapy.

Space

It is important to secure the room as a therapeutic space during the therapy day – also during the breaks where some students stay in the therapy room in order to rest, or to write in their notebooks. The space has a circle of chairs fitting the number of participants. If someone is missing it is a ritual to start and end the day having their empty chairs to represent them, to confirm that they are still a part of the group even though they are absent. Further, the room is equipped with many different instruments to have various possibilities of expression and evoke various sensations and emotions in each group member. In addition, a stereo to listen to recorded music is available. To make space for body movement, chairs and instruments are removed.

Student roles and ethical obligations

According to the description of GTT in the curriculum, the students are expected:

- To participate in all therapy days and actively participate in the group process

- To keep a notebook/diary on a regular basis and during the course (usually we devote time to writing in the notebook a couple of times during the day)

- To deliver written assignments when asked by the training therapist

- To comply with the ethical guidelines

The students follow the ethical guidelines for the GTT course described in the curriculum; the work is confidential, which means that the students should respect the frames and the limits around the process; they cannot continue the therapeutic process after the session or course is over. This is a delicate balance, since it is also natural for the students to develop their relations in their everyday life as student peers. The students are encouraged to be aware about the ethical challenges around the therapeutic processes that happen as a part of their training and to reflect and discuss in GTT if they have difficulties in finding the limits and the right ethical balance. It is a continuous learning process to balance between building supportive relationships outside GTT and at the same time protect and take care of what they share and discuss inside GTT. It is important for the future music therapist to learn to distinguish between different kinds of spaces and tasks. When the novice therapist enters practicum later, they need to go in and out of their role as music therapist and to be aware about ethics in the concrete situations: what kind of interaction suits what kind of space (see Chapter 12 on supervision).

Training therapist role and ethical obligations

The role as training therapist is to guide the group through learning areas and towards learning objectives described in the curriculum, and as a part of that facilitate a space for musical and verbal interaction. Especially in the first course, the training therapist plays a prominent role in order to secure the setting and make clear what the group is working with, structure musical improvisations as well as verbal discussions, or to regulate the energy or intensity in the group. If inappropriate dynamics happen in the group, the training therapist redirects the attention, facilitates investigation, and helps the group to reflect and become wiser about what is happening inside the individual and between them. Through experiencing the processes and watching the training therapist, students gradually build knowledge as a kind of situated learning without formal teaching (Lave & Wenger, 1991; Nielsen & Kvale, 2004; see also Chapter 2). The training therapist keeps a structure and directs the process during all three courses. However, students usually become more active as group members and they fill the space, which the training therapist facilitates, more freely and more personally, as the courses proceed.

During all three courses, the training therapist usually starts the group session by summing up what the group was working with last time – and possibly points to themes that the group could continue from the last group session. The intention is to create a common place to start from, to build continuity between the therapy days and to build the history of the group and its members.

During each therapy day, the training therapist offers a framework for verbal interactions, which can be in the form of structured rounds where students take turns, or it can be in the form of an open shared reflection space where the group can speak freely for a certain period.

The training therapist has different roles during music improvisations depending on the intention and context of the specific improvisation. The training therapist sometimes enters music improvisations or body movement when the objective is to open up the space at the beginning of a session or to regulate the energy of the whole group, for example if the energy is low after a lunch break. During the third course, where students take turns being in the centre of the group process, the training therapist takes an active role in an improvisation together with the group (see the example later in this chapter). However, the most common role is to facilitate the group members' interaction as well as facilitating the group to develop its own formation and way of expressing and functioning, and therefore the training therapist is usually the active listener and observer to the creative expressions in the group through improvisation, movement, or painting.

It is essential to build up and safeguard a relationship characterized by openness and trust between the group and the training therapist to create conditions that nourish authenticity in the group. The training therapist can also make mistakes or misunderstand, and repairing interventions are common. The training therapist seeks to contain the group and each individual with empathy and a caring atmosphere. In the final assignment, a student reported an experience of the relation between group members, the training therapist, and the group by the end of two training therapy days:

Our training therapist completed a body relaxation by humming quietly while we were all laying on the floor. I got the imagery that we were all instruments in instrument boxes with beautiful soft lining in different colours. The training therapist gently opens all of us in each session. When we are open, we can all strike each other's strings. Everyone can be heard, and everyone can be played. My group strikes strings and melodies I did not know that I have. I find new sounds and melodies in the others. The training therapist lets us sound together and fade out when the time is up – always closing us gently down again (see Table 5.1; B2/B12).

The training therapist is not a part of the group on an equal level to the students. On the other hand, the therapist is not outside the group either, since being together with the group involves the therapist, whose professional background, personality, musicality, experience, and nervous system is actively present during the work.

The training therapist has a duty of confidentiality. The training therapist passes on general comments concerning the dynamics of the current groups in the programme to the rest of the team once a year, but the training therapist does not disclose any individual themes to the team unless there is an urgent need to do so (see Chapter 2).

If needed, in between the therapy days, a student can always contact the training therapist. The premise is that student and training therapist agree on how to bring the items of their dialogue back to the group. Sometimes the processes in GTT can open up psychological issues that cannot be treated inside the group and the training therapist occasionally suggests or recommends students seek help – eventually in the form of individual therapy – outside the training programme.

The training therapist does not appear at any point in the music therapy training programme in the role as an examiner for the student unless the student chooses the training therapist, for example, as supervisor of the final thesis, which will include an examiner role. It does happen that the group therapist enters other roles across the programme, and such changing roles will be articulated to the students.

The training therapist is supervised by an approved supervisor specialized in psychodynamic-oriented group therapy, who is not a part of the music therapy milieu.

Music therapy methods

The training therapist applies music in many ways in GTT. Overall, both active and receptive methods are in play during all three courses. Through music, the group can investigate and clarify the mood of the group that may be hard to illuminate with words (Davies, 2015). The training therapist can choose to bring in music to open up as well as conclude the processes that happen in the individual and between the group members. Whether actively listening, playing, or moving, music can be a here-and-now catalyst for mentalization processes in the group. In a joint improvisation, the mentalization takes place implicitly when the group members listen to, feel, and relate intentionally to each other through the music (Hannibal, 2014). At the same time, what happens in music can inspire the verbal reflective space, where meaning and coherence can be debated in a joint conversation about the experiences in the music (see Chapter 2 for elaboration of the music, specifically the use of improvisation, in the therapeutic track). Vignettes and citations from students in this chapter illustrate how the music is woven into each GTT session in the group. Sometimes students find that music is a safer and larger space for expression than verbal exchanges: 'Playing together has given a sense of eternal speaking time to everyone, where we can talk at the same time, in different ways, and still be heard.' Another student commented on the inner expansion connected to a music listening: 'I am surprised how the music was felt in my whole body like a river that flowed inside' (see Table 5.1; B5).

Table 5.1 gives an overall view of the most common music therapy methods that the training therapist applies in order to meet the learning objectives of GTT. The table is generated by the author having collected and created an overview of exercises over a number of years. During the chapter, examples refer back to the specific methods (written numbers in brackets). Most examples refer to column A and B. However, the attention to the bodily sensations and experiences in relation to music is a common feature during all kinds of processes in GTT. Further, the training therapist applies specific exercises (column C), in which students investigate how music affects their body and they start to allow a bodily expression that flows from the inside and out – and to distinguish this way from when they move with the attention on how they look. The intention is that students become more comfortable in their body, more sensitively listening to their body as well as bodily expressive. Awareness of the body continues in all practical training specifically in body and voice work (see Chapter 6).

Table 5.1: Music therapy methods during three courses of group training therapy

A: The training therapist facilitates musical improvisation with instruments and/or voice in order to:	B: The training therapist applies music listening to pre-composed or live music in order to:	C: The training therapist introduces different exercises with body and music:
1. Meet each other in music, e.g., as a way to start the session	1. Facilitate presence, e.g., as a way to start a session (mindful listening)	1. To mirror each other, e.g., in a couple
2. Investigate the group 'temperature' here-and-now	2. Support guided relaxation, pre-composed music, or therapist playing/singing	2. To let the body follow different instruments in a piece of music
3. Regulate the temperature/level of arousal in the group	3. Create a calm atmosphere while writing in the logbooks (background music)	3. To facilitate grounding, e.g., move to a rhythmic piece
4. Investigate specific themes (applying a thematic playrule, e.g., 'a safe space')	4. Initiate a shared discussion on a theme, e.g., 'self-compassion' after the listening	4. To prepare for work on emotions: move to selected music that expresses (aspects of) an emotion
5. Investigate group dynamics (applying a playrule, e.g., 'investigate leading and following')	5. Support a free (individual) imagery to music, e.g., based on a specific theme, which is in play	5. To regulate the energy or emotional arousal up, e.g., to open to joy, or down, e.g., to calm the body and mind
6. Investigate specific emotions, e.g., 'anxiety' or 'anger'	6. Let the students share self-selected music as a way to tell the group about themselves	6. To open to playfulness; follow each other in the group, taking turns to be the leader while music inspires the movement
7. Manifest in music what was shared in words	7. Regulate the energy/arousal level in the group	7. To make a co-student move using an instrument or voice
8. Allow for free expression and investigation; no rules	8. Explore commonalities and differences in a reflection in the group after listening	8. To express the vitality forms of the music with the body (body-listening)

9. Allow for investigating new roles in the group	9. Support a guided fantasy (talk-over)	9. To work with body-expression following the immediate impulses in the body
10. Investigate relations in music (applying a musical playrule, e.g., 'find a common pulse')	10. Support focus on the breath (music breathing)	10. To express with the body what others in the group express in a music improvisation or vice versa
11. Allow for opposites to meet and interact, e.g., need for structure vs need for freedom	11. Facilitate interactive group GIM, either group-fantasy, where they take turns telling a story, or guided group co-imaging based on a current theme in the group	11. To be in touch with each other, e.g., a soft massage on shoulders to soft background music
12. Support a current theme of an individual member or the group	12. Round off a session and let the music help to integrate the process	12. To let a co-student or the training therapist touch with hands in order to support a student in, e.g., establishing grounding, providing arousal regulation, comfort or healing during music listening

Learning areas during the three courses of GTT

Before stepping into further explanation of the context and content and the students' realm of experiential learning during the three courses of GTT, Figure 5.1 gives an overview of learning areas and salient developmental themes that students move through. The three overall learning areas and nine developmental subthemes have arisen through triangulation of the curriculum, the present author's thematic analysis of their own notes from being in the position as training therapist, as well as of students' written reports from 2015 to 2020.

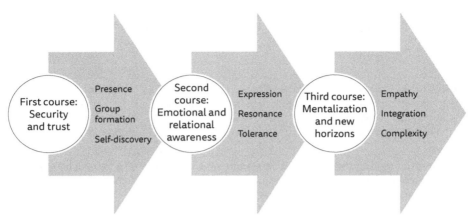

Figure 5.1: Learning areas and developmental themes

Below, each semester (course) will be presented separately. In all three sections, there will be 1) a referral to the context and connection to parallel courses in the training programme, and 2) a description of selected developmental themes unfolded in GTT illustrated with examples and quotes from students.

A theoretical section follows the review of all three courses.

First course: Security and trust
GTT seen in context and relation to other (parallel) learning areas
At the beginning of the Bachelor's degree programme students need to get to know what the music therapy training at Aalborg is all about and to get to know each other, build up a relationship in the group, and ground themselves in the new context. This reality supports the focus of the first course in GTT, which is to build up a group identity as well as build up trust and safety in the group as the process develops. Security and trust are not goals as such, but are a prerequisite for the learning that follows – in this first course the work is, for example, aimed at developing body awareness and encouraging playfulness. The process is also intended to expand the students' listening skills and their mutual attention towards each other. For example, students discover that they do not experience safety and trust in exactly the same way. In line with the Aalborg curriculum, Table 5.2 lists the most important therapeutic learning areas and the learning objectives in the first course of GTT. The salient developmental themes – presence, group formation, and self-discovery – are elaborated below.

Table 5.2: Learning area, learning objectives, and developmental themes, first course

Learning area: Security and trust

Learning objectives:
- Get to know the framework of group training therapy in music therapy
- Developing level of attention, mindfulness, and listening skills in the group process
- Develop a sense of grounding and centring
- Expanding body awareness
- To explore and express oneself authentically through music and in words
- Establishing a basic sense of trust and security in the group
- Share the personal experiences of the group therapy process with the group

Salient developmental themes:
- Presence
- Group formation
- Self-discovery

Parallel to group therapy, the students engage in a theoretical and musical learning process that begins with the theoretical subject *music psychology* where they develop insight into the key theories of music as a psychological, social, and cultural phenomenon. The musical subject *applied musical performance* is a practical music training in working consciously with musical parameters in order to accommodate the needs of others. These theoretical and musical courses go hand-in-hand with the lived experiences in GTT: In the training therapy, the students start to experience and develop their awareness about sensations and feelings in themselves and in their peers, and they start to exercise the ability to reflect on these experiences. Alongside this, they start to develop their relation to music in new directions.

Developmental themes during the first course

Presence

Presence is a prerequisite for contact and therefore a crucial learning area in the therapeutic training of the students. It is an important training to stay present while the group moves up and down in energy level and while moving between inner and outer attention and between different modalities/modes of expression. The training therapist guides the students into an immersed sensing where subtle nuances in their bodily and auditory presence gradually develop, and they are repeatedly encouraged to meet whatever they sense and experience with curiosity and care.

As an introduction to group therapy, we often listened to soothing music and were guided by the training therapist to relax the body, create grounding, and practise 'getting present' in the room and in the group. I experienced that we as a group needed to attune to each other – we came from all sorts of places and experiences, and now we had to gather in a common focus – the training therapy (see Table 5.1; B1).

Often the training therapist directs the attention to the breathing. Attention on the breath facilitates grounding and contact with the whole body and increases the presence in the here-and-now (see also Chapters 4 and 6). In training therapy the students also work with their presence and grounding through guided visualizations, moving to music, and through music improvisation, where the focus is, for example, to find a common pulse in the group.

Feeling safe and secure in the group is closely connected to the level of presence students can provide. If the students feel insecure in the group, it influences their openness and ability to let go of control and surrender to the therapeutic learning process.

Group formation

In some of our cohorts of students, the training group is very heterogeneous in terms of age and amount of life and work experience. This gives the group members an authentic chance to investigate what happens when differences meet and to learn what it means to be in different existential phases of life. Respecting the diversity in the group is an important part of the building of safety. The training therapist acts as a role model in showing how to contain the diversity in the group.

For safety to grow, it is necessary to allow expression of insecurity in the group. Usually, the students have different experiences of participating in groups. Some students may have traumatic experiences from former groups; it may be from childhood bullying in school or from working in places where they were humiliated in front of colleagues, etc. With such underlying emotional material, it is understandable if students step into the training therapy with caution. For some students it is just very new to them to express their thoughts and feelings in a group and they need time to open up to the opportunity of sharing and being expressive. Again, the training therapist shows patience and acceptance.

The training therapist offers exercises that engage the group members in nonverbal interaction with each other and the group formation partly takes place in the music improvisation. While listening to the students improvising in the first course, the training therapist commonly hears how students seek to find a common way of expression, how they synchronize and adapt to each other to create a safe and shared musical space. As a student expressed: 'I felt it as very liberating that it was also music and not only our words that could be used to connect us to each other' (Table 5.1; A1/A7).

It is furthermore an important task for the training therapist to teach the students how to engage in verbal dialogues in a therapeutic way. The students learn from listening to how the training therapist intervenes verbally and they learn verbal skills through exercises where they are supposed to, for example, summarize what another group member said and also acknowledge and validate what the person speaks about – without offering their own opinions or experiences in the conversation. It may feel a bit artificial for the students to begin with, until they each find their own 'melody'. It is sometimes a matter of unlearning some habits of commenting, judging, or distracting each other in verbal exchanges. The students need to develop their listening capabilities as well as discover their authentic curiosity. In this way, the students start to learn how to support themselves and their peers.

Self-discovery

Through each step in the group formation, the students get to know themselves and each other from new perspectives. Each participant investigates how safety and security feels in the body. Guided by the training therapist, who eventually chooses music to support the exercises, the group commences with visualizations of safety, both as a bodily felt sensation, and as an inner image of a safe place, and later of a safe person (Table 5.1; B5/B9). One student described an important event from the training group where she sensed her own inner space during a simple bodily exercise in which she was guided to lean back on the training therapist's hands that were held against her back. The feeling of leaning against someone (here the therapist) was safe to her, and slowly she leaned forward again into a position that felt more upright. The student physically felt in a new and different way how it is to stand on one's own two feet, to be grounded in the body, and at the same time stand openly in front of the group (Table 5.1; C12).

At the beginning of the first course in GTT, the students write an essay about some of the important relations they have had and have in their current life. It is first a text they write to themselves with the intention of making a space for some initial reflections about their own life. The training therapist reads the text from each student and all the essays from the group constitute a kind of background knowledge for the group therapist. The reflections prepare the students for processes in the therapy group where they will be inspired to and asked to share life experiences. As such, the writing is a reflective stepping stone in the growing understanding of how former and current relations are contributing to the formation of our identity in the here and now.

Another student task in the first course is to present themselves to the group by a single piece of music. They bring a selected piece of music, in order to share something personal with the group. The group listens to try to understand the person's perspective and unique relation to the chosen music – not to analyse or judge the music in any way. While they listen to the music, they each make a spontaneous aesthetic response in form of a drawing or poem (Table 5.1; B6). After listening the training therapist facilitates a dialogue among the students with focus on the aesthetic responses. In the final assignment, a student looked back and reflected:

> I brought a song that reminded me of my father whom I lost when I was an infant. The process in the group contributed to a more solid sense of identity in me. It happened that I acknowledged in this process that what I feel is important. I got a clearer feeling of whom I am. ... A fellow student made this drawing for my song 'Last Train to London',[3] which illustrated a red sports car driving towards the horizon on a long straight road with no traffic or houses for miles around. It was a perfect match with the feeling I had, even though it was hard for me to define the feeling, this drawing just fit into my universe. Even though the drawing had no visual features in common with my story, it reflected something from my inner reality. That drawing is very clear to me even today.

As the student undergoes the process of choosing the music, presenting the music to the group, and talking about a part of themselves or a part of their life, they are embarking on the journey of self-discovery. As the vignette illustrates, it is simultaneously an onset in the process of experiencing interaction and empathic resonance in the group.

By the end of the first course, the students are asked to think about what personal developmental themes they have discovered are important for them to work with during the next year of the training therapy in the group. The themes are, for example, 'find ways to be more expressive, both in words and music'/ 'develop my patience with myself and my peers'/'investigate silence and pauses both in music and in the group discussions'/'dare to use my main instrument in the group therapy improvisations'/'dare to be honest and not be ashamed of myself'. Later in the group therapy process, the students can return to the working theme and reflect on it from a new point of self-exploration.

---

3   A song by Electric Light Orchestra.

Second course: Emotional and relational awareness
Context and relation to other (parallel) learning areas

Beginning the second semester in February, the students are in a new situation; they are more settled, and they know a lot more about what it takes to study music therapy at Aalborg University. Concerning the group therapy, on the one hand, the students usually feel safe since they know the other group members and the training therapist, and they know how the group works. On the other hand, they need some time to ground themselves in the training therapy group again after about a three-month break with exams.

The overall theme of the second course in the training group is to create conditions for the students to express and understand more about different moods and emotional states, as well as to investigate relations and relational patterns. The students are encouraged to open up more, in order to be in deeper touch with each other and the music. The students learn to express feelings both verbally and musically, and thereby get more visible in the group as the unique persons they are. Usually, experiences of resonance happen in the group as the members recognize themselves while they listen to each other, and a growing group cohesion emerges. Table 5.3 lists the most important therapeutic learning areas of group therapy in the second course and the learning objectives in line with the formulations in the Aalborg curriculum. The salient developmental themes – expression, resonance, and tolerance – are elaborated below.

Table 5.3: Learning area, learning objectives, and developmental themes, second course

Learning area: Emotional and relational awareness

Learning objectives:
- Expand the emotional awareness and emotional contact with self and others. Experience affect regulation
- Develop knowledge and understanding of own resources and potential areas for development in relation to emotional processes
- Build experiences in expressing oneself musically in the group within the setting of training therapy
- Develop knowledge and understanding of relational patterns linked to the experiences from the group therapy process
- Reflect on the relationship and dynamics between the individual and the group
- Develop awareness about the dynamics of the group and be able to describe its development

Salient developmental themes:
- Expression
- Resonance
- Tolerance

Parallel to the second course in training therapy, the students continue developing musical competencies in launching and leading a group of people in playing music together (*Music Instruction*). Besides that, they have a course in *Observation and Description of Clinical Practice*, which implies one month of *internship*, where the students will leave the university and observe executive music therapists in different clinical contexts, and thereby get a close insight into music therapy practice. The students will learn to separate descriptions from interpretations and learn how to analyse sounds and music from clinical practice. The training in the group therapy, where students are observing each other and developing a more detailed awareness about what they see and hear and how they feel and think, mutually supports the practicum experiences. In group therapy they learn to listen to each other without analysing or judging; they learn how to be attentive and create a space of emotional containment.

Developmental themes during the second course
Expression
As a part of the therapeutic training in Aalborg, students work intensely with improvisation (see Chapter 2 for more detail). Usually, the students are skilled in different types of music and have been playing their main instrument for many years when they enter music therapy training. Thus, it can be a challenge for them to express themselves spontaneously when directed by, for example, a simple play-rule and the mutual listening to each other in the group (Table 5.1; A10). Some students will need time to change their attentional focus towards, for example, emotional expressions and dynamic movements in the group (Table 5.1; A2/A6). Gradually the students experiment and discover new possibilities.

In one exercise, students listen to classical music selected by the training therapist and they translate the vitality dynamics of the music to movements with their body, while a fellow group member observes and makes a drawing of the forms of vitality that are expressed (Table 5.1; C8). Later students move into a thorough investigation of different feelings, such as anxiety, anger, sadness, and joy. Here the students are invited to examine their own history and knowledge of these feelings through exercises and verbal sharing, and the group works to express them in music, including examining the different qualities, intensities, and colours each emotion may have (Table 5.1; A6).

Students usually have an intimate relation to music closely related to their emotional life. Yet, the process in GTT provides them with the possibility to widen, nuance, and strengthen this relationship. To facilitate deeper understanding of emotional and mental states in oneself and in others, an open mind or a kind of curiosity is a prerequisite. The training therapist applies different music therapy methods (see Table 5.1; e.g., A4, A8, B8) to invite the group to investigate the phenomenon of open mind/curiosity as a prelude to an immersion in the emotional realm.

It is important to encourage students' ability to be playful in order to expand their expressive and communicative creativity. However, being innovative in the group may be difficult because of fear of not being accepted. Sometimes a group is holding back their expressions, for example, in fear of saying, doing, or playing something that does not fit in the context. Some group members might be impatient, and they express frustration about the silence and verbalize their longing for their peers to open up, share, and, for example, play louder in the music. A similar dynamic theme that emerges is to question how much space each member can be awarded or take:

We had a talk about silence in our group that led to a deeper understanding of each other, as it turned out that the silence for some could seem noisy and almost awkward while others enjoyed the silence. For me, this discussion meant a lot, especially in relation to my personal process around being afraid that I take up too much space in the group. I think that since our talk we found a good balance in giving and taking space, and gradually I felt more comfortable in the silences and found a balance and a harmony in my need for sharing.

Often the students come to a recognition about the paradox that the space seems to grow bigger when someone in the group dares to take up space by expressing and sharing authentic feelings. However, it is equally important for the coming student-therapist to experience that it is sometimes a difficult task to express and communicate how you feel. For example, students start to understand that some members in the group have had experiences of being misunderstood when they have tried to express their feelings in other contexts. In one group, the students came to acknowledge that a fellow student had not been *allowed* to express feelings in the childhood family. If there is sufficient security and trust in the group and a culture where you can explore together what is at stake, in the individual and between the participants, the students may experience that it is possible to create change through new experiences of expressing and sharing. Through musical improvisation, some themes can be redeemed and renewed; other themes can be contained and possibly become conscious through verbal reflections in the group.

Resonance

In the training group, there is an extensive network of relationships as a student described:

> In group therapy, I definitely learned a lot through experiencing my own reactions to the rest of the group members, and through my emotional reactions to how the therapist tackled what I brought up, and what the others brought up, and also by seeing the others' reactions to each other.

When the group members feel safe and they start to share more with each other, they are at the same time deepening their attention and having experiences of resonance at a bodily level. A student describes her impression 'that several of the group members have experienced bodily reactions such as goose bumps, palpitations, tension, sweating, crying, etc., and more mental reactions, imagining what it is like for the person telling their story'.

Little by little, the students' differences become more visible, as well as their commonalities. An emotional recognition often takes place – something the students have not previously understood about themselves begins to take shape by means of the resonance. They experience how they as group members are affective mirrors to each other and how emotional resonance vibrates in the group. Gradually the members see each other in a broader perspective, and a mutual respect emerges. Connected to a music listening experience where the training therapist guided a fantasy about entering a garden as a 'talk over' piece of music (Table 5.1; B9), one student reported:

> I revisited the garden of my grandmother, it was touching to see all the details, and I realized from a new perspective how much effort and love she had put into this garden, every flower, every plant... I was surprised when we shared our experiences afterwards that several of my peers had similar experiences. ...and I felt this shared appreciation of our grandparents tied us together in a whole new way.

The common group improvisations, as well as the shared listening, is an important part of the resonant learning arena. In the music, or after listening to music, the students affect and inspire each other. A student expresses it like this: 'To me, the music has helped me to get a deeper understanding of the others in the group and their feelings. The improvisations have created resonance inside me and between my fellow students and me' (Table 5.1; A9/A11).

The students have different things to learn. Some are good at listening to others and need to orient some of the attention to themselves; they need to listen to their own heartbeat and to give acceptance to themselves equivalent to what they offer others. Some students are able to allow expression of their own thoughts and feelings but find it harder to keep attention in a listening position.

Tolerance

Tolerance can be understood as a psychological state where you are able to contain yourself and your feelings as well as others and their feelings. In GTT, the training therapist supports students to work explicitly on their psychological flexibility and ability to move in and out of emotional states and ability to regulate emotional arousal. They work with their tolerance towards themselves, as one of the students explains:

> I must admit that I have found it difficult and challenging to work with my emotions. To feel an emotion, to unfold it, describe it with words and in sound – in general; relate to it. I know very well that it is about the fact that it can be somewhat risky to me to move along that path. Therefore, it is much easier to talk about the feelings of others. Nevertheless, this learning about myself gives me a broader perspective in relation to my future role as a music therapist.

One of the learning objectives is to be able to endure and tolerate intensive emotional states, mental imbalance, or disagreements in the group. Disharmony or misattunements may happen in the group – then the therapist will help the group to become aware and to talk about it or investigate it musically to rebuild trust and therapeutic alliance (Table 5.1; A12). However, it is not always possible or appropriate to examine and share emotions in the group here-and-now. The group process, where many different needs are taken into account, offers the students the possibility of extending their tolerance threshold – which is different than repressing what is going on inside. A student wrote in the final report:

> An important focus for the group was that, even though we are one group, there are still many different emotions and experiences represented. Although most members of the group experienced an atmosphere or an improvisation in the same way, there has been room for someone to experience or mean something else. The group taught me something about humility and patience in relation to other people's stories and experiences.

The learning intention is to strengthen students' understanding, acceptance, and tolerance towards themselves and others including the fact that people are different, feel and express differently, and need different things in their life.

Third course: Mentalization and new horizons
Context and relation to other (parallel) learning areas
The focus in the last phase of the group therapy process is to further develop and integrate body awareness, emotional awareness, and the ability to reflect verbally and musically in the group. Through the process, the students expand their perception and understanding of the mutual influence in the group. They are now more confident and ready to receive the opportunity to practise dynamics and to experiment with letting go of old patterns and try out new ways of being and acting in the group.

The mutual trust and the group coherence are growing while the form of the session changes to a mentalization-based therapy where group members take turns being in the centre of the process in the group. The students are developing their mentalization capacity (see Chapter 3), which involves a living contact with what is going on at sensory and emotional levels, as well as a higher level of understanding and recognition of differences in the group concerning history, personality, emotional needs, and ways of experiencing and expressing. They open up to new horizons as they see themselves, the group, and the learning process more clearly connected to their further learning processes and future as music therapists. Table 5.4 illustrates the overall learning area and learning objectives, as formulated in the Aalborg curriculum. The salient developmental themes of empathy, integration, and complexity are elaborated below.

Table 5.4: Learning area, learning objectives, and developmental themes, third course

Learning area: Mentalization and new horizons
Learning objectives: • Express and articulate, in a nuanced way, emotional and relational experiences in music as well as in words • Development of empathy, towards co-students and towards themselves, as well as to people outside the therapy room • Identify and apply basic mentalization: investigate, seek understanding, and make sense of the emotions and experiences of themselves and other group members • Participate with authenticity in a mentalization-based framework; be able to share relational events/situations in detail and to apply music in the process • At a basic level, be able to assess own resources, boundaries, and developmental potential in relation to a future as music therapist

Salient developmental themes:
- Empathy
- Integration
- Complexity

Parallel to the group therapy in the third semester, students focus on the theoretical subject *Developmental Psychology and Neuropsychology*. One student stated in the final group therapy assignment that there was a connection between the parallel learning areas:

> In the reading material on the anatomy and physiology of the brain as well as various theorists, I see training therapy in a new light. The broad understanding of the fact that development is possible at all ages throughout our life. There has been a development for me and for the group as a whole in the three courses of training therapy; it is possible to practise something new, to change something, to create new networks in the brain or repair something that has been 'broken' or out of balance, may it be relational, bodily, or mentally.

The acquiring of knowledge of central theories of (neuro-)developmental psychology in the formation of personality and identity strengthens the students in their capacity to understand the processes in group therapy. Vice versa, the development of their mentalizing capacities acquired in group therapy strengthens their ability to grasp the theory in an embodied way. Further, students' musical competencies develop in the module *Voice Work*, which is a basic practical music training of the students' skills in vocal techniques and improvisation. The students also follow the module *Music and Identity* that has a psychological focus on how music influences identity formation and life history. This course includes the students writing their personal musical autobiography. There is a clear link between the musical autobiography and the reflective work in group therapy with the common emphasis on the students' development of insight in their own history, personality, and developmental potential. In group therapy as well as in *Music and Identity*, the students expand their horizon and their empathy as they acknowledge the uniqueness of their co-students, how different their backgrounds and current life situations are, and how manifold the relations to music are.

Developmental themes during the third course

The training therapist introduces a specific structure of the group work where the students, by turn-taking, experience being the centre of the group's attention in order to work more in depth with a self-chosen relational theme. This way of working with the group is a format inspired from MBT-G, mentalization-based therapy in group (see theoretical reflections below). The gradual building of presence and the ability to listen and express from the beginning of GTT make the students ready to take new steps during the third course in the training therapy.

Empathy

The music in the training therapy becomes an arena for the development of giving and receiving empathy. The group becomes a place for the students to generate new experiences that can contribute to a repair of previous negative relational experiences, for example in the form of missing empathic responses or emotional misattunement. Such personal developmental processes influence the development of the group, and vice versa, as a student explains:

> New steps in the development have often come after a declaration of trust in the group that the group has lived up to – one or more in the group has dared to be fragile, and the group has shown itself mature enough to empathically embrace what was shared and to reflect verbally or improvise together on it (Table 5.1; A12).

In this third course of GTT, the group members' task is to contribute with relational and emotional events where they experience problems mentalizing (see Chapter 3). It can be situations in which emotional reactions are overwhelming and hard to understand, relational events where they experience intense feelings that are difficult to handle or let go of, etc. The students embark on developing their mentalizing capacity, which implies they need to be investigative, to be open to feelings and thoughts, to be non-judgemental, to be interested in new aspects and new angles, and to apply this attitude towards themselves as well as to the other group members and to every dynamic that emerges between them in the group. These abilities are essential in terms of understanding and later leading group processes as a music therapist.

What usually emerges in the group in this format is a high level of empathy. Through engagement, and curiosity towards intentions and needs behind appearances, the students practise placing themselves in the shoes of their fellow students. When the individual participant shares a personal history and a relational event, the training therapist guides all group members to be active and make use of elements from former learning in GTT. They listen carefully to the narrative, they practise wondering and to ask open questions, they practise acknowledging, validating, and offering affective mirroring as they show their empathy. During such a session in the group, they can all contribute with ideas of how to use the music closely related to what the person in the centre would like to *investigate* further in the music or *get* from the music or need to *express* in the music. If needed, the training therapist supports the group in identifying how the group can empathically be with the person in the music. Sometimes, but not always, the training therapist takes part in the improvisations and the role in the music depends on what is at stake for the individual and the group. For example, the training therapist can take a lead in the group expression if the individual needs energetic support in expressing anger and the group seems to hold back too much (Table 5.1; A3/A6). They can also be an active conductor who stops the improvisation one or several times during the improvisation in order to have a dialogue with the individual in the centre, and from that dialogue, direct the group work in a direction that is helpful to the individual. In the following example, the training therapist participates on an equal footing with the group of students. In the final assignment, a student described the empathic and mentalizing experience in the music like this:

I tried to describe a very important pilgrimage I did, shortly after the sudden death of a close relative, where meeting other pilgrims with whom I had a strong attachment helped to make the unbearable a little bit easier to bear. After telling the group about these experiences and about my longing to continue the pilgrimage with these people, the training therapist suggested that we could try to make a musical improvisation with me as a pilgrim and the others in the group as well as the therapist as my fellow pilgrims. Thus, the group was a picture of the people from my journey who had supported me very much by simply being present and walking with me at a steady pace. In the improvisation, the group kept a stable pulse corresponding to a stride tempo and apparently laid a harmonious bottom. I chose the xylophone, where I played melodies that sometimes fitted well with the others' playing and inter-twined in the pleasant hiking mood, and sometimes I took some spontaneous 'runs' on my instrument, where I just played loose, wild, and out of pulse and completely outside the frame. The group continued in their steady going and I felt very accommodated and supported. It was as if the improvisation gave me a place to be with all my sorrow, pain, and despair. A place where I could express some reactions and at the same time be safe, knowing that the others would keep 'walking' in a stable and empathetic way (Table 5.1; A7/A12).

Integration

Besides the new structure of the sessions in the third course, the format continues to alternate between verbal group discussions, spontaneous improvisations, and exercises that focus on integration of body and mind. Sometimes the group improvise and afterwards seek words to describe what they experienced in the music and through reflections reach a new level of understanding of self and group (Table 5.1; A8). Alternatively, they improvise in order to translate and further investigate in music and bodily interactions what they have discussed verbally (Table 5.1; A7). Gradually students' many different experiences in body, emotions, and thoughts may become more connected. They begin to develop the ability to be aware of themselves and the others at the same time, and the ability to create meaning and coherence in what they feel and experience and in relation to what others feel and experience.

During the process of GTT, the student may have experiences that come into the light of understanding at a later stage. One student looked back and reflected about the theme that she focused on while being in the centre of the group work, which also illustrates the integration between body and mind, individual and group:

> I chose to work with self-care focusing on getting better at noticing my own needs in the here-and-now so I can take a break to avoid reaching extreme fatigue... When I sit and read through my logbook, I think that my discovery of this self-care theme comes from the fact that I have become better at giving in to the physical exercises (Table 5.1; column C) and I have become aware that I am not always in touch with my body. ... The group played an improvisation for me in the end. In the music, I could feel the group better than in the verbal exchange. I was very grateful for that and really felt like they had given me something. I was touched by that (Table 5.1; A12).

From an ethical point of view, self-experiential learning spaces are essential in music therapy training. Students' level of self-awareness and self-care influences the level of sensitivity towards others, including future clients, and may prevent stress and burnout in their future as a music therapist (Orlinsky & Rønnestad, 2005).

It is a milestone when students get to the point in the group process where they acknowledge that they could not have walked this kind of learning path alone. When the third course is ending, many students formulate that they do not think it would have been possible to reach the same level of emotional integration without the help from the group.

Complexity

Students in training groups move through a growth process that is complex – where therapy and learning will gradually come together as a whole. The group is a space that gives the students opportunities to interact and learn from each other and thereby expand their horizon: their view and understanding of themselves and of others. Thus, training therapy is strengthening the 'mentalizing muscles' of the students. They bring up personal themes from their life outside the group that the group works with, and furthermore, the here-and-now experiences in the group become material to learn from for all members of the group. This means that the field of resonance and learning spans the individual history, the group history, and the here-and-now events. Directing the attention to what is happening in the individual and in the group here-and-now is usually an authentic, intense, and direct way to develop students' mentalizing capacity. Furthermore, a here-and-now event like a group improvisation may evoke feelings that are not only connected to what happens in the music here-and-now, but also to what happened 'there-and-then'. Each group member has personal reasons, needs, and intentions that colour the experience of the concrete event. The goal is that students experience from the inside that it matters what and where we come from and understand how every person or group is composed in the complexity of past, present, and future. The therapist facilitates these investigations across time and places by exemplifying and encouraging presence and reflection.

Group therapy theory that underpins GTT
The group's healthy potentials

Psychodynamic group therapy has developed into many variations since the German-British psychiatrist and group analyst S.H. Foulkes founded the classic group analysis in England in the 1940s. Foulkes had a very optimistic view of the potential therapeutic capacity of the group, and he formulated the famous mantra: 'trust the group'. Foulkes emphasized the human need for social engagement and tendency of adjusting to each other as well as the group's healthy potentials through the mutual support between the members (Foulkes, 1948/1983). This thinking supports the basic understanding in the Aalborg programme that the group possesses creative and healing potentials and enhances the development of awareness, empathy, and insight of the students, which is fundamental in relation to the future work as a music therapist.

The theoretical foundation of group analysis is integrative, based on various disciplines – primarily psychoanalytic theory and systems theory. Foulkes described the group as a complex field of essential phenomena like mirroring (the group as a 'hall of mirrors'), resonance, and context (Bechgaard, 1994). In group analysis, the path to knowledge, insight, and change is the free discussion and the concrete interaction between group members (Bechgaard, 1994). In GTT, both verbal and musical interaction are applied and the training therapist seeks a balance between structured exercises and time for free exploration and improvisation. Each time the group meets, the training therapist prepares an overall theme and a structure for the day, in accordance with the objectives defined by the educators and the study board in the curriculum of the Bachelor's degree programme. The metaphor from Foulkes about the therapist as a 'conductor' fits the role of the training therapist in the Aalborg programme. The training therapist facilitates a therapeutic space for the group and encourages each of the group members to participate through listening, expressing, and reflecting. Every group has its unique and dynamic process of learning within the structured setting.

Foulkes was inspired by humanistic Gestalt psychology and used the concepts 'figure' and 'ground' to illustrate that there is a dynamic relation between individual and group-as-a-whole in group analysis. In GTT, the focus is the group as a whole, while acknowledging the individual student. According to Foulkes and his systemic thinking, it is not possible to reduce the group to the sum of individual members: the group is *more* than a collection of individuals. Foulkes invented the concept 'group matrix', which is described as a maternal form or a psychological network in which all the individual and collective processes meet and interact (see also Chapter 9). The matrix has such a strong influence on the group that the concepts individual and collective are no longer opposites of each other (Karterud, 1999). Foulkes stated that 'each individual – itself an artificial, though plausible, abstraction – is basically and centrally determined, inevitably, by the world in which he lives, by the community, the group, of which he forms part' (Foulkes, 1948/1983, p.10).

Neurologic perspectives on groups

Foulkes used the central nervous system as an analogy to the vital life of the group, in which each group participant constitutes a neuron in the neural network (Bechgaard, 1994). Seen from a neuropsychological perspective, no nervous system is an island. The human nervous system changes and develops continuously because of interactive experiences throughout life (see Chapter 3), thus also as a result of psychotherapy in groups (Cozolino & Santos, 2014). Further, all who participate in a group affect the others, and are affected by the others, in the here-and-now. The group is a network more than the members consciously know and, in a group with many communicative exchanges and emotional resonances, a unique and multifaceted possibility to move and to be moved is provided. Thereby, the members can gradually expand the flexibility and adaptability of their nervous system and strengthen their empathy (Badenoch & Cox, 2010; Hart, 2017; Lindvang, 2017). Likewise, it is possible to train students' ability to move up and down in arousal during the processes of GTT and develop a calm and stable baseline in the autonomic nervous system. In the face of strong emotions and stressful situations, that most likely will happen both in GTT and in later practicum experiences, students need to be able to establish grounding and balance (Badenoch & Cox, 2010).

Little by little, music therapy students become aware of how much they influence each other – and thereby start to realize how much they can influence future clients solely by their way of being present in the room. Experimental studies show that when people experience pain and witness other people in a painful state some of the same areas of the brain are active (Rosenørn & Petersen, 2012). This points to the fact that in a group it may happen that the participants get overwhelmed by the pain of others if they are unable to accommodate and regulate their own nervous system and empathic resonance (Coutinho, Decety, & Silva, 2014). This is the background for the very thorough immersion in sensing the body and training the ability to self-regulate performed in GTT. Concerning the phenomenon of resonance, it refers to both physical and psychological processes, sometimes both at the same time (see Chapter 2). Foulkes also used the concept of resonance in his theory on group analysis, and it describes and helps us to understand the complex psychological processes of relationships and mutual neurological influence that happens between the group members (Lindvang *et al.*, 2018).

Conflicts in groups

In the training group, students have the chance to experience the potential power of being a part of a group as well as to learn from overcoming difficulties in a group. During the three courses, students allow their differences to be more or less visible and audible. Though rarely, it happens that discomfort or conflicts move beneath the surface to a degree that complicates the process. For example, mutual competition connected to performance in musical skills can dominate a group process, or a few group members' resistance in working with body awareness may spread as a tense atmosphere in the whole group until it is possible to share and investigate this in the open.

The British psychoanalyst Wilfred Bion developed his thinking in the same period as Foulkes, but Bion was not as optimistic about the potentials of the group as Foulkes was. Bion formulated the theory that every group is alternating more or less between the group as a 'work group' and the group as a 'basic assumption group'. The work group describes rational group functioning where the members collaborate in a realistic way and with attention and energy invested in the primary task of the group. In the basic assumption group, tacit emotional and conflictual states unconsciously affect the group process, and the group is characterized by, for example, diffuse boundaries between the members. A basic assumption group has a tendency to keep the individual in certain roles and it is difficult to stay grounded and hold on to differences in the individual experiences (Bion, 1961; Nielsen & Sørensen, 2013). To support the training group in GTT to stay primarily as a 'work group' it is essential that the training therapist intervenes to ensure that the group adheres to the educational goals and is clear when informing the students about their roles and their tasks. In addition, a clear description in the curriculum helps the groups to stay on the expected learning track. Still, every training group may have its difficulties that need caring and creative resources to get through.

Morris Nitsun, a South African-born artist and psychoanalyst, has contributed to the field of group psychotherapy with concepts and theory that further explain the possible negative dynamics in a group. According to Nitsun, these dynamics *can* be contained and thereby lead to a mobilization of the group's creative processes (Nitsun, 1996). Nitsun points out the importance of the therapist's intuitive, imaginative, and attuned empathic skills when containing difficulties in a group. The therapist needs to encourage the group to move towards greater 'beauty' by allowing the 'raw, darker and disruptive aspects' of self and others to emerge (Nitsun, 2014). In GTT it is intended that each group gets at least a tinge of the creative power of music and other artwork to contain opposites and embrace pain, as well as transform conflicts or negative energy into something that bears hope and new possibilities for the individual and the group. Sometimes the music is an indispensable co-therapist to the training therapist. For example, a simple musical play-rule like 'allow contradictions' (see Table 5.1; A10) can support a nonverbal cautious approach to one another in the group.

Group dynamic thinking

The American psychiatrist and psychotherapist Irwin Yalom is a central figure within group dynamic thinking, and a great inspiration for GTT in the Aalborg programme.

According to Yalom, a strong therapeutic factor of group therapy is the 'group cohesiveness'. The cohesion lies in the fact that members accept each other on a deep level and cohesiveness supports self-disclosure and risk taking. However, it takes time and effort to build up a highly cohesive group (Yalom, 2005). Yalom's theory underpins the amount of work in GTT that focuses on building trust and cohesion.

Yalom states that the therapy group demonstrates the existential paradox that we are on one hand *apart from*, but on the other hand always *a part of* (Yalom, 2005). The music therapy training groups strongly mirror this paradox – the dynamic between the individual and the group is always at stake through the courses. It is important that the students learn that they are not the only ones with problems or low self-esteem. In Yalom's terminology, the group members experience 'universality,' which is a 'welcome to the human race'-feeling. Yalom emphasizes the interpersonal learning as one of the most important therapeutic factors in groups that supports personal growth of the members. Through a dynamic interplay between the group members, a social microcosm is created – and with more spontaneous interaction this microcosm will develop in a quick and authentic way.

Concerning the relationship between the group and the therapist, Yalom emphasizes that the therapist is not the fulcrum of the therapy – rather the therapist facilitates the processes and has a role as a midwife for the group. Yalom's work has revealed how much the interaction between the members means to the individual (Yalom, 2005), which supports the intention in the training group to engage students with each other. Through exercises and spontaneous interaction, the group members become active helpers for each other in an authentic microcosm.

Mentalization-based group therapy – an integration

From the perspective of GTT and the applied integrative approach, it is interesting that the Norwegian professor S. Karterud has brought European and American thinking together within psychodynamic group therapy. Inspired by Yalom's American group psychotherapy model, Karterud formulated the need for interventions of a supportive character in groups. This includes the need for an active group therapist and a more structured approach to strengthen interpersonal learning and understanding (Karterud, 1999).

Karterud has published a manual for mentalization-based treatment in groups (MBT-G) (Karterud, 2015), which builds on Fonagy and Bateman's work (Bateman & Fonagy, 2006; Fonagy & Bateman, 2008). (See also the theoretical section about mentalization in Chapter 3.) Even though GTT does not follow this manual, the contribution is an important theoretical and methodological inspiration for GTT, for example the clear structure of group sessions, as well as a clear relational focus on interpersonal events of the participants either within or outside the group. Further, MBT-G uses elements and concepts from the group analysis, including matrix, mirroring, and resonance, as well as integrating Bion's and Nitsun's thinking. This means that the approach integrates Foulkes' idea about the group as harmonizing and socializing with the understanding of the possible negative tendencies a group can have, and acknowledges that therapeutic processes in the group are complex and happen on both conscious and unconscious levels (Karterud, 1999, 2015; Nielsen & Sørensen, 2013). The role as training therapist resembles the therapist in MBT-G, regarding having a conducting role in order to facilitate interaction and keep the group on the right track as a working group. As in MBT-G the training therapist strives to attain a high level of transparency as well as being a trustworthy, authentic, and professional person and not an omniscient expert (Lindvang, 2015).

Closing
Evaluation of the three courses in GTT
During the first and second course, the students must attend 80 per cent of the therapy sessions. If students do not live up to the criteria for participation and attendance, they will have to write a report at the end of the course about their experiences in GTT to pass the course. When terminating the third course of GTT the students have to pass an exam, which consists of writing a final assignment (5–8 pages) that covers many different aspects of the training therapy process in the group. Here the students describe the learning processes and reflect about how the course has contributed both group development and personal development, as well as at a basic level, such as assessing own resources, boundaries, and development potentials in relation to becoming a music therapist. The student delivers the assignment anonymously and an external examiner evaluates it. Writing the assignment provides the students with an important reflective level of learning.

Building blocks for further learning
The learning areas and the developmental themes of the three courses in training therapy presented in this chapter *do* overlap each other in practice, for example students do use and develop their empathic skills from the very beginning and a theme like self-discovery is present all the way through and not only in the first

course. The separation in the nine themes has been an analytic tool to embrace a huge and complex amount of material (see Table 5.2). These developmental themes illustrate the learning progression in GTT. However, the themes are also taken forward for further investigation, learning, and development in the students' coming years of studies in music therapy.

With the intention of creating concrete links between the different therapy courses in the curriculum, the students write a one-page summary of their final assignment on learning process in GTT and hand it over to their supervisors when they enter their internship in the sixth semester (see Chapter 12) in order to inform the supervisor about the most important personal learning areas. The experience of being in the client position and the familiarity with listening and expressing in music and in verbal dialogues are some of the building blocks that students bring from their initial group experiences in the GTT process. When the students enter the group conductor role in later group disciplines (see Chapters 7 and 9), or enter the therapist role in their internship as music therapists in the sixth semester, the earlier group experiences in GTT will help them to be grounded in themselves and to continue developing an open minded, investigative, musical, and empathic approach to the specific tasks and dynamics they meet.

References

Bateman, A. & Fonagy, P. (2006). *Mentalization-Based Treatment for Borderline Personality Disorder: A Practical Guide.* Oxford University Press.

Badenoch, B. & Cox, P. (2010). 'Integrating interpersonal neurobiology with group psychotherapy.' *International Journal of Group Psychotherapy, 60*(4), 462–481.

Bechgaard, B. (1994). 'Gruppeanalysens baggrund [Background of group analysis].' In S. Aagaard, B. Bechgaard, & G. Winther (eds), *Gruppeanalytisk psykoterapi [Group analytic psychotherapy].* Hans Reitzels Forlag.

Bion, W.R. (1961). *Experiences in Groups and Other Papers.* Tavistock Publications.

Coutinho, J.F., Decety, J., & Silva, P.O. (2014). 'Neurosciences, empathy, and healthy interpersonal relationships: Recent findings and implications for counseling psychology.' *Journal of Counseling Psychology, 61*(4), 541–548.

Cozolino, L.J. & Santos, E.N. (2014). 'Why we need therapy – and why it works: A neuroscientific perspective.' *Smith College Studies in Social Work, 84*(2–3), 157–177.

Davies, A. (2015). 'Experiential Groups on Music Therapy Trainings.' In A. Davies, E. Richards, & N. Barwick (eds), *Group Music Therapy. A Group Analytic Approach.* Routledge.

Dewey, J. (1938). *Experience and Education.* Collier and Kappa Delta Pi.

Fonagy, P. & Bateman, A. (2008). 'The development of borderline personality disorder: A mentalizing model.' *Journal of Personality Disorders, 22*, 4–21.

Foulkes, S.H. (1948/1983). *Introduction to Group-Analytic Psychotherapy.* Heinemann.

Hannibal, N. (2014). 'Implicit and Explicit Mentalization in Music Therapy in the Psychiatric Treatment of People with Borderline Personality Disorder.' In J.D. Backer & J. Sutton (eds), *The Music in Music Therapy.* Jessica Kingsley Publishers.

Hart, S. (2017). 'Introduktion til neuroaffektive processer i musikterapi [Introduction to neuroaffective processes in music therapy].' In C. Lindvang & B.D. Beck (eds), *Musik, krop og følelser. Neuroaffektive processer i musikterapi. [Music, Body and Emotions. Neuro-affective processes in Music Therapy]*. Frydenlund.

Karterud, S. (1999). *Gruppeanalyse og psykodynamisk gruppepsykoterapi [Use the group]*. Pax Forlag.

Karterud, S. (2015). *Mentalization-Based Group Therapy (MBT-G) – A Theoretical, Clinical, and Research Manual*. Oxford University Press.

Lave, J., & Wenger, E. (1991). *Situated learning - legitimate peripheral participation*. Cambridge University Press.

Lindvang, C. (2013). 'Resonant learning: A qualitative inquiry into music therapy students' self-experiential learning processes.' *Qualitative Inquiries in Music Therapy, 8*, 1–30.

Lindvang, C. (2015). 'Group music therapy – a part of music therapy students' training at Aalborg University.' *Group Analysis, 48*, 36–41.

Lindvang, C. (2017). 'Udvikling af samhørighed og mentaliseringskapacitet gennem læreterapi i grupper [Development of coherence and mentalization capacity through group training therapy].' In C. Lindvang & B.D. Beck (eds), *Musik, krop og følelser. Neuroaffektive processer i musikterapi. [Music, Body and Emotions. Neuro-affective processes in Music Therapy]*. Frydenlund Academic.

Lindvang, C., Pedersen, I.N., Bonde, L.O., Jacobsen, S.L. *et al.* (2018). 'Collaborative resonant writing and musical improvisation to explore the concept of resonance.' *Qualitative Studies, 5*(1), 4–19.

Nielsen, J. & Sørensen, P. (eds) (2013). *Brug gruppen [Use the group]*. Hans Reitzels Forlag.

Nielsen, K., & Kvale, S. (2004). '*Mesterlære som aktuel læringsform [The scholastic paradigm and mastery]*' In K. Nielsen & S. Kvale (eds), *Mesterlære. Læring som social praksis [Mastery. Learning as social practice]*. Hans Reitzels Forlag.

Nitsun, M. (1996). *The Anti-Group: Destructive Forces in the Group and their Creative Potential*. Routledge.

Nitsun, M. (2014). *Beyond the Anti-Group. Survival and Transformation*. Routledge.

Orlinsky, D.E. & Rønnestad, M.H. (2005). *How Psychotherapists Develop, a Study of Therapeutic Work and Professional Growth*. American Psychology Association.

Pedersen, I.N. (2002). 'Self-Experience for Music Therapy Students. Experiential Training in Music Therapy as a Methodology: A Mandatory Part of the Music Therapy Programme at Aalborg University.' In: T. Eschen (ed.), *Analytical Music Therapy*. Jessica Kingsley Publishers.

Rosenørn, S.M. & Petersen, A.H. (2012). 'Kan vi føle hinandens smerte? – et indblik i det neurale grundlag for empati [Can we feel each other's pain? An insight into the neural basis of empathy].' In A. Gade (ed.), *Den sociale hjerne [The social brain]*. HjerneForum.

Yalom, I.D. (2005). *The Theory and Practice of Group Psychotherapy* (5th ed.). Basic Books.

CHAPTER 6

Therapy-Related Body and Voice Work

Sanne Storm

Introduction

'Therapy-Related Body and Voice Work' is a discipline focusing on self-experiential learning, based on body and voice awareness and experiences. It is important to emphasize that body and voice in this discipline is considered the client's or music therapist's possible choice of instrument in a music therapeutic setting at an equal level to other instruments. The basic teaching approach and understanding of the discipline 'Therapy-Related Body and Voice Work' is that body and voice are one united instrument (in sounding), but the body may also function as an instrument by itself (body movement without giving sound).

Since 2004, the content of this course has been developed and undertaken in a collaboration between Ass. Professor Inge Nygaard Pedersen and the author. As described in Chapter 4, the course runs over 25 hours which are split into five hours in the first semester and 20 hours in the fifth semester. The progression of the course as a whole is that the first 10 hours focus on 'Three Personal Being and Communication Spaces' as described in detail in Chapter 4. The purpose and content, as well as the approach and theoretical understanding of the last 15 hours of the discipline 'Therapy-Related Body and Voice Work', will be described in detail in this chapter.

The purpose and aim of the course

The course is a basic tuning of the student through body and vocal exercises that supports a grounding sensation of the music therapist's identity with *listening perspectives* and *listening attitudes* underpinning the whole approach. Listening perspectives and attitudes are described and defined in Chapter 3, but can broadly be defined as a 'training in learning not only to listen in order to analyse the client or the client's music, but also to listen to oneself listening to the client' (Pedersen, 2002, p.170). In the present discipline the 'music' is expressed through the body and voice, focusing on primary modes of expression.

The course functions as a bridge between a functional training of the voice and a tuning of the music therapy students towards a psychological awareness and understanding of how the voice is inextricably interwoven with the personality, the person's emotional life, and state of being as a whole. The overall purpose is to broaden and deepen the music therapy students' understanding of their primary instrument – the human body and voice – as well as to develop an awareness and consciousness about the possibilities this instrument can offer in clinical practice. The course aims to awaken implicit body knowledge, which is derived through one's lifetime, and to support a growing awareness and consciousness about how the individual music therapy student can be present with their body and voice as an instrument in the meeting with others. The purpose and aim are to tune the students' ability to distinguish cognitive reactions from affective reactions, and to tune the possibilities of regulating arousal levels consciously. Furthermore, it aims at awakening a sensorial, emotional, and cognitive vocabulary connected to body and voice.

At the end of the course, it is required that the students write a 5–8 page report on their experiences through participation in the discipline. This report is evaluated internally. The given structure of the report requires the student to focus on two selected key self-experiences, to make descriptions of and self-reflections on bodily and vocal experiences from the course related to these experiences, and to relate relevant theory to their descriptions. The report includes the students' reflections on the applicability of the experiences for their further psychodynamic development, for their participation in CGMS (see Chapter 7), and for their future clinical practice.

The teaching approach – an overview

In this section the teaching approach and overall theoretical understanding of the approach will be described.

The human voice

In contrast to other instruments within music therapy, body and voice together is the one instrument that is always present and active in the meeting with others.

It is an inborn instrument which has been used since birth. As human beings we *are* this instrument. From the very first breath, the human being – the baby – expresses its needs, frustration, or satisfied sensation of its state of being with body movements and vocal sounds in the meeting with others and the world (Malloch & Trevarthen, 2009; Stern, 2000; Trevarthen & Malloch, 2000). It is an expression with different *dynamics*. These dynamics will always be present and colour the vocal sound – even though words are added while speaking or singing with words – and reveal what is unconsciously hidden behind the words spoken. This teaching approach focuses on awakening a knowledge and consciousness towards this primary and non-verbal modality and elements.

The understanding is that the human voice is influenced by inheritance, the culture, family pattern, and environment, as well as the personal journey and dynamic interplay with the world through life. Thus, the voice is a reflection of a human being's 'way of life' as a whole. The voice is inseparable from our emotional life and our contact with the world around us. Thus, the vocal expression is an 'imprint' of the individual human psyche and action patterns – a *vocal gestalt*. In this teaching approach an awareness towards the entire human being is therefore applied.

Listening perspectives and listening attitudes
As mentioned above, the *listening perspectives* and *listening attitudes* underpin the whole approach. Listening is understood in a broad sense and introduced as a way of orienting yourself towards yourself and others. It is furthermore a discipline for the perception and awakening of an awareness towards the possibility of tracking bodily sensations and characteristics of the vocal sound, as well as connecting physical and vocal actions to emotional experiences. This includes studying and exploring the relationship between physical sensations, postures, movements, and the quality of the vocal sound. The theoretical understanding will be described in more detail later in this chapter.

The 'bottom-up' and 'top-down' processes
The teaching approach applies both *bottom-up* and *top-down* processes, which is the description of the two directions of information flow. These processes and the interplay connected to them hold significant implications for how 'Therapy-Related Body and Voice Work' operates. Damasio (1999) writes: 'Physical actions are creating the context for mental actions; bottom-up processes are affecting upper level processes. [This is] the feeling of what is happening' (p.27).

The teaching is based on body and vocal interventions – a sensorial stimulation – putting the human being in motion and releasing a response/reaction in the body, emotionally or on a cognitive level. The next step is to develop a sensorial, emotional, and cognitive vocabulary. Drawing is an integrated part of the training and deliberately used in this process of capturing something essential, and of finding words to describe it, and to make the experience take form and structure. Drawing is also supporting the student in being in dialogue with themselves. When using the top-down processes our emotions (mammalian brain), heart rate, sensations, breathing, and impulses (reptilian brain) can be examined; and our thoughts or conclusions (neocortex) can, as a result from carrying out a remediated action, capture the essential of the experience as a whole expressed in a drawing. These processes aim at awakening and tuning the listening perspective. This is a necessary first step in order to be able to define, observe, and describe the body and vocal parameters by either describing the present state of being or a change.

The conditions for tuning the listening perspectives

In the course the students meet each other and share an intersubjective space, a *sounding* or *movement space,* or a combined *sounding movement space.* In other words, the sounding space is a space of existence – *being* – *living.* In the meeting with others, a self-motivated action is created and takes form as the intention to engage, grow, and expand into a *field of play* (Kenny, 1989) and existence is explored and shared by the students through movement and/or sound.

To give sound is both something subjective and objective. Subjective, because it reflects the inner life, feelings, thoughts, and experience of the person giving sound. Objective, because the sound created by the human being is also an external object – something possible to observe and react to. The sounding movement space can therefore be considered a *resource pool* to the individual and the other (Kenny, 2006). The listening perspective gives access to this resource pool of sound and movement in many ways. To mention a few, it can be a key to the understanding of *patterns*, *dynamics*, *moods*, *feelings*, or *images*. The listening perspectives are based on principles about the process of meeting, being present, listening to, and using this resource pool of sound with empathy, respect, and wisdom (see Chapter 3). It is a holistic phenomenon representing both objective and subjective elements. The listening discipline is shared subjectivity and very different from a standard verbal psychological setting because the training primarily is nonverbal and deals with the primary mode of engagement, sound, and music (Kenny, 2006).

The structure and setting of the course

'Therapy-Related Body and Voice Work' training is conducted in a block of three days, which makes it an intensive workshop. It gives the student the opportunity to immerse themselves during participation.

The setting requires a large room with the possibility of creating an open space and being able to move freely in big movements. Additionally, oil pastel colours and paper are at the students' disposal. The students are furthermore asked to dress casually so it is comfortable for them to move around, and bring colours and logbooks, because drawing and taking notes is an integrated part to support the students to register their self-experiences.

The teaching starts with very basic body and vocal exercises, awakening the body, voice, and inner experiences. The very basic exercises have a centring and grounding purpose and will be repeated continually along the course. Most likely they are known to the students from functional training of the voice or from other courses. However, in this course, the focus is towards awakening an awareness regarding tracking the inner sensations while working. The attention and focus are turned towards how it is possible nonverbally to prepare body and mind for something emotionally challenging.

The further progression of the course aims at intensifying the possible ways of how the students' bodies are put in motion. Although the body and vocal exercises may seem simpler as the course progresses, the exercises in other ways grow in complexity and intensity of inner experiences.

All the exercises presented during the course are applied by the author in clinical practice.

In general, the teaching is carried out so that the students first try out the exercises, which provide them with some self-experience. Then they are asked to draw their self-experience, ending by composing a sentence or choosing three words that capture the essence of the experience as a whole. The rationale behind this process will be described in more detail in connection with Vignette 1 below.

Then follows a group reflection and sharing of experiences, ending with the author linking the exercise to clinical practice. The sharing of experiences and reflections is an important part that deepens the understanding of how exercises can be experienced differently, but also supports the finding of themes common within the group.

In the following, four vignettes will be presented. They will present a sensorial description and a picture of the progression and prototype of exercises in the course. The vignettes are built on descriptions from students who have provided permission for the author to share their experiences and pictures. The exercises are presented in a way that both describe the exercise and the student's way of approaching and experiencing the exercise. After each vignette there follows a description of the theoretical approach underpinning an understanding of the exercise, ending with a quotation from the student.

Vignette 1: Awakening the body through movement without music

Sara is part of a group of music therapy students. They are sitting on the floor in a big room free from instruments. Alongside the wall are yoga mats, logbooks, papers, and colours. The teacher has just asked everyone to rise and spread out in the room. Sara finds her spot, a bit to the side, but still close to the centre of the room. The teacher asks everyone to allow themselves to close their eyes for a moment. Noticing, without judgement, what kind of body sensations, emotions, and state of being are present right now in this moment. Sara registers a sensation of tiredness in mind and body, as well as low energy. She cannot really grasp or describe any emotions right now.

The teacher continues the guidance and asks everyone to put the registered sensations aside for a while, and to now direct their full attention towards the feet and start a movement on the spot with the feet in full contact with the floor, while moving one foot at a time in outward circles. Sara starts the circle movement with her right foot in a very slow tempo. Her eyes and breathing are following the movement, and she starts to shift between moving the right and the left foot. Sara registers that they now are allowed to move in the space. She starts a slow skating movement across the floor. Her eyes keep following the movement of her feet. Still, in full contact with the floor. Sara stays with her slow tempo, and mirrors and matches the movement with the sensation of low energy and tiredness in the body. Moving in and out between her fellow students, but without making eye contact.

Then the teacher asks the group to explore the many ways the foot can be in contact with and move across the floor. Sara starts by lifting the foot and sliding the upper part of the foot across the floor and continues the exploration. She moves across the room on the side of her feet, on the heels, turning the feet inwards and outwards – her eyes following every movement. Suddenly her feet become alive, and she has an experience of the feet talking together, expressing themselves in different dynamics. At the same time, Sara experiences a change in body-sensation and energy. She feels grounded and her energy is growing. Sara starts to feel a curiosity towards her body, alongside being guided by the teacher to take the contact to different body parts and to have each body part lead the movement. She begins to sense a happy feeling inside and a gratitude in discovering every single body part by giving it her full attention. A strong feeling of centre is present as well as a growing playfulness, and Sara goes with it surprised by how fast she is able to move. She feels wild, impulsive, and yet in control. In the background of her attention, she is noticing the other group members moving much slower, and staying in the same spot in the room, and Sara realizes that her urge and impulse to move is stronger than wanting to fit in. She skates in between the others at a high pace, with a sensation of being grounded and flying at the same time. She keeps following the impulses awakened in the body and experiences and senses new ways of moving her body and she is astonished by what is possible and the potential variety of ways to move her body. A growing intense feeling of a free body in motion is appearing. Sara starts to explore different dynamics and intensities. It is as if the whole body is awakening and playing. Every body part is sensed and in motion, at the same time as a strong feeling of a present centre is present. The hands are lifted to the sky, fingers spread and folded, and it is as if Sara grasps energy in the air, which then arrives in the body with a tingling sensation. The feet make rhythmic patterns of movement, and a feeling of pride appears. The movements are big and powerful and imperceptible. Sara's appearance becomes big, strong, and powerful. She feels like a dancer or maybe like a strong martial artist.

Finally, the teacher asks the group to stop and, while staying on the spot, asks everyone for a moment again to close their eyes and without any judgement register the present body sensations, emotions, and state of being. Then follows the instruction of carrying out a remediated action capturing the wholeness of the experience and expressing it in a drawing. Sara moves across the room and quickly picks

up a green colour and starts drawing her sensation. She senses how the body leads her way of drawing. At the end Sara chooses three words capturing the wholeness of the experience: Energy – Dancer – Big.

Awakening through movement

This vignette presents a key basic exercise, nourishing an awakening of the body through improvised movement without music. When the students are moving freely, the teacher will make a choice of either bringing the exercise to a close or expanding it and incorporating the human voice, based on an empathic attention towards the students' response to the intervention. When merging sound with movement the instruction of the teacher encourages the students to follow and match their movements. This supports an awareness towards listening to an impulse and, furthermore, to awakening a variety of dynamic ways of sounding within the human voice. The exercise facilitates an embodiment of the movement and sounding of the individual student's inner states and *dynamic forms of vitality* (Stern, 2010). In other words, it supports a connection to spontaneity and *being a live body*. A reconnection to something preverbal. This ultimate statement will be explained further theoretically later in this chapter.

The connection to 'Psychodynamic Movement'

In Chapter 4 Inge Nygaard Pedersen describes the history of Psychodynamic Movement. The exercise 'Awakening the Body through Movement Without Music' arises from this tradition and is based on listening perspectives. The beginning still includes a body scan. Then, however, the improvised movement differs in that it is based on an ongoing inner dialogue. In this dialogue the student is listening for and tracking body sensations, inner states, and dynamic features, making an affective attunement to their Self and expressing it through body movement. At the same time, in the exploration of gesture and movement, the student is putting their Self in motion. In matching and exploring the dynamic features in improvised movement, impulses are awakened and followed. Inevitably over time, while moving, change will happen. The individual student is tracking, registering, and reflecting upon this, and then finally sharing the experience in the group and reflecting further ahead.

Being present

The body scan is an effective way of beginning a practice in general. The students tune in to the body and reconnect to physical experiences, and are instructed to notice any sensations without judgement, and to stay with the body. This nourishes the awakening of the students' awareness towards themselves and towards being present. Furthermore, this first body scan will function as a baseline to track and follow the change and development over time.

A sensory stimulation

The skating movement is a sensory stimulation that sets an arousal in motion and puts the human being in motion. The basic principle in the movement makes the foot have full contact with the ground while being in motion. This literally establishes adequate contact with the ground and supports the person in getting a sensation and feeling of contact with the ground and the feet, instead of only having a mechanical sense of contact to the ground. This is supporting a grounding sensation, as well as an experience of being present and staying mindfully attentive with the body.

Freeing the body; freeing the voice

There is a strict guidance in the intervention on focusing both on individual body parts, but also including the body as a whole. The exercise always starts with a focus on the feet, moving the attention towards many parts of the body and ending with a free improvised movement. The expression through movement starts from an inner state of being and then grows through exploration of the body parts. The stepwise development, of making contact to and integrating other body parts and ending by having the whole body moving, has the purpose of freeing the students from interfering thoughts. This furthermore supports being present. There is a conscious choice in using the word *movement* instead of *dance*. Just like the word *sounding* instead of *singing*. The words dance and singing are easily connected to expectations and self-criticism. Additionally, the words movement and sounding are very concrete and basic. When exploring the movement, it is about exploring the body part and providing an entrance to being in body motion as a whole. By valuing an aesthetic beauty in all kinds of movements and sounds, it will support the student in freeing their movements and sounds and enable them to dance and sing their Self alive. The idea is to have the students establish an inward contact with the body and to allow body sensations to be put in motion by body movement. This supports an awareness of how the body movement is connected to emotions, possibly setting these free. In the ongoing dialogue thoughts will appear, which inevitably will challenge the students in the allowance of following their impulses or in feeling comfortable and safe enough to follow the impulses.

Sensorial, emotional, and cognitive vocabulary

The students are instructed to listen to themselves in a broad sense of listening (see Chapter 3 concerning listening perspectives). They are invited to explore the relationship between their physical sensations and movements, and how the interplay affects both their emotional and inner states, as well as influence the words they choose to describe their self-experience. The transition of translating the self-experience and putting it into words and capturing the essential part of the wholeness can be a difficult task.

As mentioned earlier, drawing is an essential part of the tuning process within this teaching approach, and this functions as a stepping-stone in developing a sensorial, emotional, and cognitive vocabulary. Drawing has the potential to capture the sensory experience as a whole, and to be experienced by the viewer as a whole. At the same time an internal experience is visualized and provides the possibility of being in a dialogue with the Self. When translating the essential part of the self-experience into words, the students are asked to either compose a sentence or choose three words that capture the wholeness and include the sensorial, emotional, and cognitive vocabulary. The combination of drawing and words supplements each other and can illuminate the inevitable change of the dynamic features over time. This procedure documents that change is possible, and it also documents the fact that the students have an influence on their state of being, and this will bring to consciousness which actions can support or challenge the individual in an uncomfortable situation. All of this is connected to tuning an awareness of connection between body, mind, and mental health.

Quotes from Sara

It was cool to feel every single body part and let one body part at a time lead the movements of the rest of the body. It's a completely different way of moving, which you might never do otherwise. Especially with body parts like knees and elbows, as it is usually not so natural to have them lead a movement. You discover that they actually can move a lot. I almost felt gratitude and pride towards my own body in this exercise, because of how much it is capable of. This contact to the whole body provided me with a feeling of freedom and a lot of energy. When there was free play at the end of the exercise, I danced around with great force and great movements. I felt like a dancer, or maybe like a martial artist.

The exercise gave me a feeling of being present in my body in a way that I can sometimes miss in my everyday life. When I get a little insecure, I tend to 'pack my body together' and not feel so much. It may give a feeling that I am not completely free in my own body, and here for me there is a close connection between body and psyche, where it is not entirely possible to say what is what. When I am able to relax in the body, I also become calmer in the mind and vice versa.

Vignette 2: Awakening the inner 'tumbler' by sounding a 'sigh'

Peter is part of a group of 12 music therapy students standing in a circle with a good distance between each other, all facing the centre. The teacher has just guided the group to place their feet parallel to each other with a distance between the feet, so they match the size of their hips. Then they are instructed to sense the front part of the foot, placing and holding all the body weight in this position for a little while without lifting the heel while breathing and gently and slowly letting go of a sigh. Then follows an instruction of an opposite position with all body weight placed on the back part of the foot without lifting the toes, still while breathing and gently and slowly letting go of a sigh. Peter listens and follows the instructions carefully. The teacher now instructs the group to start a small movement between these body positions, focusing on bringing this little movement in flow and not losing balance, ending the movement by stopping in the middle where a sensation of the whole foot is captured. Now taking a deep breath and giving sound while bouncing up and down in the knees. When stopping this movement Peter and the group follow the further instructions of not having a posture of overstretched knees, but letting go in the knees in order to create a sensation of flexibility or elasticity in the knees. Peter realizes that this posture feels different and unknown, and therefore not as safe as had he taken his usual posture where he is locking his knees. However, he decides to try out the proposed posture.

Now the teacher gives instructions about beginning a movement in the legs putting the hips into motion. The hips are supposed to swing from side to side as if a gentle belly-dance were performed on the spot. Peter finds it difficult to loosen up in his hips, and he feels awkward. He becomes aware that this kind of movement is not something he is used to doing at all. Peter takes a quick look around in the circle and notices, to his relief, that everyone is doing the same thing. He notices that he is not the only one struggling, and he realizes that he is not alone, and the fact that everybody is doing the same thing makes the awkward feeling less awkward to him. Peter again focuses on keeping the motion going and then he rather quickly notices that his body sensation is changing. He realizes that this rocking swaying movement is affecting his whole body in such a way that a growing feeling of pleasure is emerging.

The teacher asks the group to keep the hips in motion and now focus on the breathing in through the nose and allowing themselves the uttering of the natural sound of a sigh – an open Ah-h-sound. Peter immediately starts to think about his uneasy experience of his voice and body and gets an uncomfortable feeling. But Peter carries on and begins to give sound to the sensation of a sigh. He notices that he is not starting in as high a pitch as he usually does, and to his surprise the intonation and sound is unstable and not so powerful. As Peter's sound is sliding down from his highest pitch in a fluent movement of a descending glissando, he registers that the sound quality grows in power, and then fades again when he is sounding more low pitches. The teacher is instructing the group to allow the sound of air to be present while emptying the lungs in order to start a new round of breathing in through the nose and so forth.

Already the second time Peter is sensing that the glissando movement is more pleasant to carry out, at the same time as he experiences that it is less forced. But he is still having this sensation of body and mind setting up a barrier for his sounding. He becomes aware of tension in his shoulders and in his body and directs his attention to his movement in the hips. He tries to give in to the movement and allows the muscle tension to release. Peter realizes that the rocking swaying motion in his hips is kind of shaking the body so it can let go. His shoulders are now more relaxed and the movement in the hips feels more natural. This body-sensation propagates to Peter's voice, and he hears and notices how the sound is changing and becoming richer. The starting point for the descending glissando movement is getting higher and higher in pitch and he observes a more even sound all the way through the glissando. Peter starts to feel comfortable, and everything seems easier, and a new sensation emerges from within.

Awakening and tuning a centring and grounding sensation from within – the 'tumbler-effect'

A repeated phenomenon kept in focus during the course is to tune the student not only to know something about the effect of a centring and inner grounding sensation, but to recognize as a body sensation to trust. Vignette 2 describes one of the very basic body and vocal exercises supporting this phenomenon.

The body-mind connection is clear. The information flow and how it affects the state of being goes both ways.

Maintaining a position where the knees are slightly bent creates a sensation of flexibility or elastic movement in the knees. This supports a more even distribution of muscle tone, and an economical use of body tension instead of using too much force and energy into holding the body position. This provides a physical experience of centring and grounding that creates the basis for an inner psychological experience of feeling safe and secure.

Tension in the knees, feet, and legs will create an illusion of security and diminish the experience of feeling grounded. Furthermore, this will have an impact on how free, flexible, or rich the vocal output and expression is (F.M. Alexander in Heirich, 2005). Locking the knees creates a tremendous pull on the whole torso, and simultaneously it inhibits the body from having an energetic flow (Lowen, 1975). The inhibition of an energetic flow in the body will suppress the feeling of being centred and grounded. A human being overwhelmed by emotions like anxiety seems to have a tendency to stabilize oneself through tension and rigidity rather than through a flexible, integrated body with solid support through the legs (Lowen, 1975; Ogden, Minton, & Pain, 2006).

The exercise intends to make students (or human beings) get in contact with this inner feeling and sensation of centredness, flexibility, grounding, focus, and balance, and to know it and be able to recognize it. A grounding and centring body sensation will also foster an experience of being in contact with an inner psychological 'platform' or foundation within – a kind of inner private base or 'private space' following Pedersen's definition of the 'Three Personal Being and Communication Spaces' (see Chapter 4). In order to feel safe and secure enough to dare to explore the possibilities or opportunities as well as the internal experiences, thoughts, and feelings, it is essential to establish and have contact to this 'private space'. A good analogy for the 'state' of the body and the function of this exercise is that it is kind of a 'tumbler-technique' where the principle is just like this type of toy that can tumble over and then straighten up by itself, because it has a weight in the base, a good centre, and flexibility.

So, within this exercise is a tuning of an awareness of how to affectively regulate yourself and create conditions that make it possible to stay with difficult feelings without losing your Self.

The rocking and swaying motion

Keeping a rocking or swaying motion moving while sounding a sighing descending glissando movement keeps the body from finding its habitual posture, which is blocking the body and its flow of energy. At the same time, it is a sensorial stimulation which activates the autonomous nervous system while, on an unconscious level, making contact to the limbic system. The body can recognize this positive sensation and it can be compared to the feelings evoked in a child receiving compassion by its primary caregivers when calming the child.

Breathing, natural sounds, and intentional sounding

The breathing and intentional sounding of a 'sigh' – a descending glissando movement as described in the vignette – can support a more subtle sensation of the inner 'tumbler'. Breathing is both an autonomous act and something that can be regulated by the power of will. A sigh is defined as a *natural sound* and is often involuntary, spontaneous, and springs from emotions (Austin, 2008; Brown, 2004; Dayme, 2009). The natural sounds are part of a whole pattern of responses involving the body and mind in a holistic way. As an example, the breathing pattern of anxiety or a panic attack is characterized by the respiratory system failing to maintain a stable rhythmic pattern (Hart, 2008). In other words, the breathing becomes irregular. Thus, a regulation of energy and arousal is directly associated with the breath, and it is very natural that the breath also reflects traumatic reactions (Levine, 1997; Ogden & Minton, 2000).

The intentional sounding of the descending glissando movement – an over-dimensional 'sigh' – requires slow exhalations, and this calms the nervous system and promotes a calm physiological state mediated by the vagus nerve (Porges, 2017). When inhalation and sounding of the 'sigh' has found a regular rhythm, then the glissando exercise in its entirety will be in flow, and then within quite a short time it will provide an inner experience of a calm state of being as well as a feeling of safety (Porges, 2017). In this act the whole body is being synchronized (Hart, 2012) and the body, via the nervous system, is given a message that it is okay to let go of tension, and thus an affect regulation is supported. Thus, the process of sighing can both turn on and off the 'vagal brake' (Porges, 2017). The sounding of a 'sigh' then provides a concrete tool and opportunity to reduce the arousal level and 'balance' the nervous system and balance a breathing pattern without force and strain (see below).

Additionally, a reflex of automatically taking deeper breaths is naturally supported by emptying the lungs completely, which is supported in the exercise by allowing the sound of breathing being present at the end of the sounding of the 'sigh'. The whole act furthermore supports the client to naturally empty the lungs completely of air and thus activate a reflex that automatically supports a deeper breath. Over time, this can support freeing the vocal expression.

The sounding of the descending glissando movement

When sounding a 'sigh' in an exaggerated descending glissando movement, with all the elements of a natural sigh maintained, it will literally be a possible tool for an 'instant sedative' when stress and anxiety arise. It is a very simple technique that has several advantages:

- It instantly helps to reduce the intensity of tension in the body

- It gathers attention and focuses on something concrete and self-soothing

- Doing it regularly strengthens the ability to let go of stressful thoughts and feelings and supports being present in the moment

- The vicious circle of inner stress build-up is interrupted

- It provides a concrete tool to be able to act actively instead of being passive

- The design of the exercise will gradually loosen the tendency to hold your breath or not get ventilated

The hypothesis is that sighing as an action has both a physiological and mental impact and opens a window for resetting body and mind.

A quote from Peter

I have always had a difficult relationship to my own voice and body. Maybe that's why I responded to this exercise. I felt it was a very basic exercise, that could calm my body. Basic, but still with many opportunities for experience and reflection. I felt it as a movement or transition, from a sense of insecurity to security. I have done the exercise several times since. We did the exercise several times over the different days, and it was very comfortable and straight-forward. I had a great benefit from an easily accessible exercise, and it had a noticeable effect on me every time we did it.

Vignette 3: The CoreTone growing to a CoreMelody (Song of the Self)

Tony and Andrew, and the rest of the group, are sitting back-to-back on two chairs placed in connection to each other. In this position they establish a very close body contact to each other's backs. They are instructed to start a rocking motion moving the bodies while the backs are in contact in order to find the balance of being supportive, but not carrying the other. Without asking for or receiving verbal confirmation, Tony and Andrew find the spot and stay with it.

Now the instructions are to place the hands above the chest bone and focus the attention on the breathing, following the breathing pattern mindfully, and if possible, to allow themselves to close their eyes. The breathing is guided to happen through the nose and the exhalation is happening through the mouth by putting a little resistance while sounding a tiny ssh-sound. When the exhalation is coming to an end they are instructed to be aware of emptying the lungs before taking another breath. Breathing and sounding without compulsion.

Hardly noticeable to Tony and Andrew, their breathing adjusts to each other and they synchronize, and together they are finding a breathing and sounding rhythm in flow. Their body contact grows and supports the subtle feeling of not being alone and feeling safe. The doing of their breathing and sounding allows it to become deeper, easier, and more relaxed.

The instruction continues and they are asked to keep their hands placed on top of the chest bone, and to close their eyes and direct the attention and awareness towards an imaginary private space existing behind their hands. They are asked to imagine how the breathing is reaching and growing from this private space.

Tony is now deeply focused and concentrated. He experiences that he *is* the breathing, and his body becomes more relaxed.

Then follows an instruction about listening into this private space and allow the talking voice to grow from this space. In the doing of the talking, Tony is listening for a single tone, a fundamental repeated tone his talk is spinning around. Right now, in this moment. He quickly senses a tone and allows this single tone to sound within the body. An easy humming with closed mouth. Tony senses how his body is reacting and how a vibrating sensation is thriving. Then follows an allowance of the tone to be sounded by opening the mouth and finding a suitable volume, which makes sensation of the sounding of the single tone easy. The breathing and sounding are coming into a flow by repeating the sounding of the single tone over and over again. After a while follows the instruction of taking a little pause and allowing the single tone to fade away alongside the resonance of the tone in the body. Tony senses how his breathing now is deep and realizes that it is much deeper than it has been for a long time. He becomes aware of how the stressful summer is leaving the body, and how he becomes more and more relaxed.

Then follows a second round. The instruction is to reconnect and start the sounding of the single tone again, and then allowing it to grow into a little melody finding a form and structure of a melodic ostinato. This phrase is instructed to be repeated over and over again for a while. Tony starts the sounding of his chosen single tone again, and he easily finds the breathing sounding pattern and surrenders to it. To his surprise he, without any effort, finds a little ostinato to sound, and he allows himself to lean on to this tiny melodic phrase and repeats it over and over again. Tony is keeping his deep breathing and sounding pattern in flow now including the tiny melodic phrase. After a while follows the instruction of taking a little pause, having the melodic phrase fade away alongside the resonance of the little repeated melody in the body. Tony senses that his body still is very relaxed.

The instruction for the third and last round is to reconnect to either the sounding of the chosen single tone or the tiny ostinato, coming into a breathing sounding pattern in flow, and then allow the tiny melody to grow in every sense, allowing it to wander leisurely along. Tony keeps his eyes closed and his hands on the chest bone. His thoughts are silenced and, as the exercise develops, he *becomes* the breathing and sounding, and his little melody starts to wander without any effort. All Tony's theoretical musical thoughts are gone. It is like the melody freely wanders along exploring all kinds of things without taking any notice of harmonic structures or the fundamental frequency. After a while of sounding freely follows the instruction of coming to a closure and staying with the sensation of the free melody's wandering in the body.

Tony's whole body is resonating, and he becomes overwhelmed at the same time as he is experiencing a very liberating emotion inside. Somehow, he has managed to let go of control. He cannot remember when this has happened to such a degree as now while improvising. He realizes how much it means to him to be embodied in the breathing and the sounding, and what this can provide him with. He understands that he is so much more embodied now than before the exercise. Furthermore, he becomes aware of the fact that when this embodiment happens his possibilities grow in being spontaneous and intuitive in sounding his vocal improvisation. Tony experiences how his voice and vocal free wandering melody somehow is supporting his worries and tension to leave his body and mind. He is aware of a body sensation very grounded and heavy in a good way.

Tony and Andrew let go of the body contact through their backs slowly and turn around and face each other, ready to share their experiences and reflect.

Sitting back-to-back resonating from within

The vignette illustrates the establishment of a safe sensation, which facilitates the student to allow them to reconnect to a breathing pattern coming naturally from the person's own instinctual source – the body. This empowers the vocal expression further and it is resonating with full power and resonance. Sitting back-to-back supports a physical sensation of being close to another person without being intimidated. By allowing yourself to reconnect to your instinctual source, the body will naturally give a synchronization in breathing pattern. This synchronization is supporting a sensation of being close but not alone – to have a safe haven. From here the CoreTone and the CoreMelody is growing and being sounded.

The CoreTone and the CoreMelody (Song of the Self)

In asking the students to find and choose the pitch themselves, an awareness towards their Self is supported and is nourishing the awakening of listening and sounding their Self and sharing this. Listening for the CoreTone naturally leads to the pitch resonating the most and with most richness. This will be the tone most easy to sense physically on top of the chest bone. Furthermore, the person will, when sensing how the sound vibrates and resonates in the body by being in physical contact with these vibrations with the hands placed on the chest bone, have access to a more subtle sensation of body and Self, as well as of the ability of being more fully present in the moment.

The CoreTone comes from a *core centre feeling* within the student – *a private space*. The names *CoreTone* and *CoreMelody (Song of the Self)* are related to the psychological understanding of what the effect of sounding the CoreTone or CoreMelody brings and represents. This is connected to Daniel Stern's (2000) theory and definition of the Core Self. The CoreTone is not a fixed pitch, but will change in relation to mood, energy, or state of being. In other words, the CoreTone is a *dynamic* phenomenon. And so is the CoreMelody.

Another key section of the teaching approach is about how very simple and basic vocal exercises gradually incorporate and awaken the human voice ending with a *free improvisation*, that could be called a CoreMelody or 'Song of the Self'.

The conditions for exploration and growth of creativity

As described earlier, there are some conditions which need to be met in order to feel secure and safe enough to dare explore the bodily and vocal creative possibilities and opportunities as well as the internal experiences, thoughts, and feelings. In the acceptance and allowance of the sound quality *to be*, a *living space* – a concept drawn from the understanding of Merleau-Ponty (2002) – is provided, and the person sounding is *living* the CoreTone or CoreMelody in the here and now, having it vibrate and sound while connecting to a subjective experience as it is lived pre-theoretically and pre-reflectively (Stern, 2010). This provides a starting point for working with the vitality forms and the feeling of being alive (Stern, 2010).

The setting for exploring the *living space* in Therapy-Related Body and Voice Work is offered in a so-called *musical space*, mentioned earlier, which Kenny (1989, 2006) defines as a field of existence explored and shared by the client and the therapist through sound. In Therapy-Related Body and Voice Work it is a *moving sounding space*. In the meeting a self-motivated action is created and takes form with a self-healing force driving the intention to engage, grow, and expand into the *field of play*, as well as to develop wholeness.

When working together two and two, the students are, from a Polyvagal Theoretical point of view, doing a 'neural exercise' (Porges, 2017). To enhance the co-regulation of a physiological state to promote the neural mechanisms involved in supporting the sensation of safety, the interactive play requires training in a synchronous and reciprocal behaviour between the students, in order to necessitate an awareness of each other's social engagement system. The self-experience of each student will both tell the student something about themselves in this specific situation, requiring a specific attention and presence, as well as something about the other. The exchange of self-experiences will furthermore support a growing consciousness about how the sympathetic activation involved in the mobilization may react.

Quotes from Tony

I think a lot about what goes on in the music theoretically during improvisations and I have a hard time turning off my 'theoretical' ears. But in this exercise, I really managed very well to be present with my own tone and my own melody. I also experienced that, at times – especially in the last part of the exercise – I 'forgot' to think about which key I was playing. It was as if I let go of the feeling of the basic tone. It was a hugely liberating feeling. After the exercise was completed, the whole body was buzzing. I was really all the way down in my body. One of my reflections was that the reason I was able to turn off my theoretical thinking perhaps was related to me being so much present in my body. The more deeply rooted I am in my body, the greater opportunity I have to be more spontaneous and intuitive in my voice improvisation.

Usually, I have a little difficulty with familiarizing myself with such exercises, where it is about finding 'my' tone or 'my' sound. But in this discipline, I experienced getting some tools that can be very helpful for me, in my work of getting more in touch with my body and letting go of the head and the theoretical, analytical ears a little more.

Vignette 4: The dyadic CoreTone

Around Lisa and Karen, who are standing face to face, at a comfortable distance, the rest of the students are sitting in silence on the floor with paper and colours ready. Their full attention is focused on Lisa, while they are preparing an open listening attitude in order to closely follow and colour the sounding of her CoreTone.

Karen is also preparing and already listening. She has placed her hands on top of each other above her chest bone, listening and studying Lisa while being willing to meet, follow, and stay with her while she is in the sounding of her CoreTone.

Lisa is a bit nervous, but also sceptical and questioning the intervention. How should it be possible for one single tone to make her feel anything at all and how should she locate her single tone? However, Lisa decides to give it a trial, and she starts to listen to the teacher, who in a soft, steady, and calm but still clear voice is guiding her to place her hands on top of each other above her chest bone, focusing all her attention on the sensation of the breathing rhythm and movement. By following this sensation of her breathing, Lisa finds and experiences an inner peace growing. At the beginning, her thoughts circle around a single tone she has chosen beforehand in case she cannot find a tone. This happens to be unnecessary. With her eyes closed, Lisa continues listening to the teacher's specific guidance, which supports her to listen to herself and find a specific tone to sound. Lisa realizes that her voice seems to have a will of its own and, in that moment, she becomes aware of the fact that her mind wants something, but her voice something else. Lisa chooses to listen to her voice and trusts this impulse coming from deep within. Lisa starts to sound the CoreTone and is guided by the teacher to establish a stable attachment to her CoreTone and, when ready, to meet Karen through her CoreTone. The teacher assures Lisa that Karen is ready when she is ready.

As a sign to Karen that Lisa is ready to meet her, she opens her eyes, and meets Karen by making eye contact while sounding her CoreTone. Karen, who readily is there with her full attention, starts to sound together with Lisa. In the meeting of the two in the sounding space, Karen consciously establishes a rhythmic and dynamic synchronicity and flow in the sounding and breathing of Lisa's CoreTone. Karen adjusts her own quality of the tone and attunes in a way that mirrors Lisa's quality of her CoreTone closely.

Lisa reacts to this with her whole being. Thoughts and emotions are awakened, and they all move Lisa and put more life into Lisa's sounding of her CoreTone. The tone seems to grow in every sense and becomes more alive at the same time as Lisa experiences a secure and strong grounding sensation within. Lisa has a growing sensation of her CoreTone filling out the space, at the same time as she senses and feels how Karen is staying very present with her, being her safe base and faithful travel companion. Lisa realizes that her body and voice are in control, and for once her mind and self-consciousness do not manage to take over. At one point Lisa experiences that she has no choice but to follow the will of her voice, allowing it to sound the way it wishes to sound. The thoughts and emotions gather and, to Lisa's surprise, they find a form and structure that lead to the memory of a very dear person she had lost. Contained in the strong sounding and grounding sensation, she feels her grief and sorrow, as well as a very deep warm feeling and an emotional connection to this person.

The group of students are listening, drawing, and picking colours. The colours are warm and strong, and many of the students pick the same colours. At the end, the students choose three words or make a sentence that captures the wholeness of the listening experience. Many words are synonyms of one another or describe qualities alike. Lisa receives all the drawings as presents from her fellow students. One drawing has a very essential little something extra. This fellow-student does not know Lisa well due to a leave from the study. She presents her drawing to Lisa and explains how she did not control what she was drawing. She simply just followed her impulses. In the drawing, there is a little butterfly within all the warm colours. Lisa gets emotional. This is the symbol she and her family carry when their thoughts and feelings are gathered about their lost dear person.

The dyadic CoreTone is an exercise constructed specifically for the setting of teaching music therapy students. However, the exercise contains many elements which are presented during this teaching approach, and also have been used by the author over many years in clinical practice. The spectrum of client population ranges from hospitalized psychiatric patients to people looking for self-development. Although there is a simplicity to this exercise, it is very intense in other ways. The work with the CoreTone exercise contains many possibilities and it is experienced by the author as an exercise that brings many elements into play, which then becomes very concrete to reflect upon for the students. The exercise also contains elements which tune the student for another course they later enrol in called 'Intertherapy' (see Chapter 10).

The students' different positions during the exercise

Resonance and synchronization – 'the CoreTone' and
your own free melody, 'the Song of the Self'

When the dyadic interplay is based on a single tone, the principles of creating a neuroaffective attunement and synchronization between two human beings are simplified and based on the primary intersubjective principle of attunement in the reciprocal subject–subject format of proto-conversation. It is an interpersonal communion, in which the student attends and attunes to a co-student's emotive expressions and gesture – and sound – producing movements, inviting semblant re-enactment and affect attunement (Bråten, 2009; Bråten & Trevarthen, 2007; Stern, 2000). Bråten (2007) describes this as an altercentric mirroring and self-with-other resonance in an intersubjective matrix.

The perception of a feeling of being met by another human being is based on purely sensorial experiences created by the meeting of two sounds in a common sounding space.

The attunement is not merely towards the pitch of the voice, but also towards the timbre, compression, and intensity of the voice. Thus, the student perceives the attentiveness and presence of the attuning co-student. This is a basic circumstance to be able to synchronize and perform neuroaffective attunement.

In the role of a supporter, the co-student engages in mirroring another person; they usually involve themselves in the other person's sound and try to understand it from the centre of the other person's body and mind (Bråten, 2009). The co-student tunes in, and functions as a sounding mirror, matching and meeting the co-student's sound quality in the sounding space, adding a little extra, enriching dimension to the sound. This creates a variant of the tone and facilitates and supports beneficially in different ways, following the principle of interpersonal communion. In order to do so, the student will have to know how to make their sound resonant, as well as how to awaken a sensitivity towards listening for a certain ring and detecting the resonance. Here the student can be open to a strong acoustic reflection occurring in the common sounding space (harmonic higher rings) where the overtone swarms out. Tongeren (2004) describes how intersubjectivity is reflected in the sounding space, as well as the intensity of the meeting, in the following way:

> This is first of all so because of the fundamental frequency, which usually carries most of the sound energy. But if these are perfectly attuned, then so are the harmonics above them. This synthesis of two tones on a higher plane reinforces the convergence of the two voices, which now fuses on many levels and not just on the ground level. ... The effect can be so strong that it leads to intense experiences of bliss or rushes of energy taking hold of the body and mind. (Tongeren, 2004, p.43)

If the sound meeting is perceived as positive and safe for the student, an automatic response is that the common sound is growing in all aspects. This phenomenon can also be described as the performance of a limbic attunement, causing the two students to open up for a mutual field of resonance and thereby enable a holistic experience of one another. This intersubjectivity becomes important for the establishment of a neuroaffective attunement and development. Through living experiences here and now during a dyadic voice exercise, as the one described above, emotional competences are implicitly developed and learned.

A very attentive way of being present together with another human being will inevitably set all aspects in movement: cognitive, bodily, emotional, cultural, and social aspects. To listen to and meet another human being, where the total sound being present in the room is growing, can be the ultimate meeting between two human beings, and if simultaneously they have eye contact, the meeting reaches deeply into some very primary intersubjective attunement patterns from the first mutual dialogues (Bråten & Trevarthen, 2007). Bråten and Trevarthen call this an 'alter-centric mirroring' and a self-with-others resonance in an intersubjective matrix.

The listening perspectives

To see a World in a Grain of Sand

William Blake (1803)

The dyadic CoreTone exercise puts the listening perspectives in play in many ways. The listening attitude and perspectives are essential to the act of interpretation. Intuitive listening is something which remains unconscious, subjective, and not verifiable by others. It causes a growing consciousness about how the sound of the voice changes accordingly within different actions and relationships. Drawing, while listening intensively with the body without thinking, may support the movement from something unconscious to something becoming more conscious in relation to what was 'heard'.

This listening attitude and perspective must be trained in order to perceive, to remember, and to interpret.

1. The first impression – subjective spontaneous associations – open listening – drawing. This act requires being able to place yourself in the openness – let go of thoughts – not think and not try to understand during the act, but rather take a position of *being in the listening attitude*. This position provides the possibility to hear a whole life-story in one single tone, but to know the path of this listening position requires training. The interventions before the dyadic CoreTone exercise prepare the students for this intenseness in the listening attitude. Thereby, the

201

openness in listening capacity is awakened and growing alongside every couple performing the dyadic CoreTone exercise in the whole group.

2. The couple in the dyads. In order to meet the other in the sounding and provide a *sounding space* the supportive student will attempt to equalize their aesthetic conditions through *tuning in* and *matching* the leading student's sound. This serves to attune to emotive expressions and to gesture and sound producing movements. This act is also about tuning the student's awareness towards listening to how the other's sound is sensed and felt in their own body. Within this act the possibility exists to be aware of how the body reflexively adjusts itself to the other's sound. This way of listening can be defined as an *audio-kinetic examination* of the human voice, where the listener is 'sensing' their reflexive muscular reactions and recognizing those spontaneous and sympathetic kinaesthetic sensations, which occur in the muscular functions of the listener's apparatus. It is a bodily oriented way of listening.

3. The whole exercise is completed by first having the couple describe their experiences and then having the opportunity to ask each participant mutually about how specific actions during the dyad were experienced by the other. This is very similar to what the students will meet in the course 'Intertherapy'. It is a unique possibility.

This is followed by the rest of the group presenting their individually open listening experiences, which offer the opportunity to become aware of how the sound space was perceived from outside.

The listening perspectives as related to the vignette about the dyadic Core-Tone exercise – as an open listening – open your self to the sound – has over the years proven to me that: *'in one single tone a whole life story can be told and heard'* (Storm, 2013, p.93).

Quotes from Lisa

Before the start of this exercise, I had a tone in my head which I could sing, then at least I had something to offer, but this did not at all become necessary for me. For me to be guided – to have my eyes closed, to speak a little and slowly raise the sound provided, that I found a certain tone (not the one I had chosen beforehand), one tone that dominated my inner landscape. Already at that point, I was positively surprised by the exercise. I really got the feeling that my consciousness wanted to do one thing, but my voice wanted something different.

I was overwhelmed by thoughts and feelings, which touched me very much and gave further life to my tone. At this time, I had a sensation of filling out the whole room with my sound and I had, as a safe ground, my supporter – the co-student. In the same moment as I was in the middle of this exercise my thoughts were very deep inside me.

…aside from the natural sorrow and the feelings of missing him, the thoughts further contributed to a deep warmth in my body, that I have seldom experienced. This warmth must have come to expression in my voice because several of the listeners had heard and painted this warm feeling. One drawing really took me. On this drawing a butterfly was painted on top of a lot of warm colours. The painter had no intention to draw a butterfly, but the impulse came when I was singing, and the sound was audible in the room. What the painter did not know was that in my family – since my brother passed away – we have used the butterfly as a symbol of him. The painter had indirectly been painting my brother at the same time as he was in my thoughts.

My voice had simply chosen to lead the 'unfolding of the battle', and my consciousness did not have a chance to follow, which I simultaneously experienced as moving and scary. Scary in the way that you as a human being often want to have control over yourself and the world around you, but your voice does not hide anything for the surroundings.

This exercise gave me an insight into which kind of fear and nervousness the clients can experience before an exercise, that can seem barrier-breaking and involve improvisation. Normally I am not affected in this way in other training situations, but I was very touched in this situation. From a professional point of view, this was a positive experience for me in terms of becoming a future music therapist. I now feel more ready to understand those clients who feel like being pushed into an improvisation exercise. Using your voice to express what is happening behind the mask – inside the body – has meant a lot for my future work in music therapy. For many years, my voice has been an instrument that had to be used beautifully and in the right way as a tool for entertainment. Through both exercises here I have experienced how the singing voice can describe a state of being at the same level as words and sometimes better.

The theoretical understanding underpinning the teaching approach

In this section the theoretical understanding underpinning the teaching approach will be presented.

The lived body and the corporeal body: An existential theory

When applying Therapy-Related Body and Voice Work within music therapy the process can be described as a 'bottom-up', nonverbal approach including sensory stimulation of the body (Bonde, 2009; Hart, 2012; Panksepp & Trevarthen, 2009; Van der Kolk, 2014). Furthermore, using the *human voice* can be understood from the polarity of the *lived body* and the *corporeal body* as described and presented by the French phenomenological philosopher Merleau-Ponty (1908–1961). Merleau-Ponty (2002) focuses on the body and the embodied being-in-the-world, and, according to him, you act through the body, perceive, and exist through it, even without explicitly reflecting on it. In that way the body is an unconscious centre of thoughts and actions. This means that the body in any given situation has sensed and created a meaning before a conscious reflection is made upon it or a thought occurs in the mind. Therefore, from an ontological point of view, body and mind are not separated, but one and the same – *a lived body*. This worldview is integrated in the teaching approach by body and vocal exercises in order to provide the student with self-experiences illustrating/describing how the body and the human voice functions as an instrument and medium within Therapy-Related Body and Voice Work.

In orienting yourself towards the sound of the voice, the voice suddenly can display a human being *in balance* or *out of balance* and can be understood as a representation of the human state of balance, as the human voice dynamically changes according to emotional states. Our psychological (mind) and physiological (body) state of being as well as our 'way of life' is reflected in the quality of our voices. One example of this is how a person suffering from severe depression often presents a cracked, rusty, thin, flat, unharmonic, or out-of-balance voice. Through voice work the client is *living* a path towards recovery and wholeness, and the sound of the voice reflects the client's process in how the voice grows. A full harmonic or balanced sound usually reflects a vital and balanced state of the human being (Storm, 2013, 2019).

This understanding and approach becomes very concrete during teaching, where the students mutually move in the common space and in and out of each other's spheres, in a meeting with the other or more others. Therapy-Related Body and Voice Work explores how to grasp and trust the impulse and how to make it grow. It is this deep impulse resonating and growing from within which is connected to a person's wish to live and be, and to explore the individual allowance of expression being present. The students are exploring the talking space with body and voice nonverbally and they learn how it feels when you are growing from deep within. They also come to know how these experiences differ from more cognitive thoughts and wishes.

Inherent in this worldview is also the psychodynamic understanding that a state of being is not static, but dynamic, and it can change, either by your own force growing from within or by being affected by a force coming from outside. This means that our thoughts, feelings, beliefs, and attitudes can positively or negatively affect our biological functioning. In other words, these elements can set the human being in motion emotionally, bodily, and cognitively (body and mind).

Arousal, dynamics, and forms of vitality

Arousal is the fundamental force in any kind of sensory stimulation in the nervous system, being the basis for the feeling and sensation of *vitality, empowerment, energy,* or a manifestation of *being alive*. Arousal can be conscious as well as unconscious. It can happen to anyone – even comatose patients. The arousal system is important in that it supports the human being to think, feel, perceive, or move voluntarily (Damasio, 1999; Stern, 2010). Stern (2010) describes arousal as follows:

> To be aroused is 'to be put into motion' or 'stirred up' or 'excited into activity', physically, mentally, or emotionally. It is synonymous with 'to animate'. In more scientific terms, it is the force behind the initiation, the strength, and the duration of almost everything we do. (Stern, 2010, p.58)

The sensory stimulation of the body and voice work sets the body, mind, and feelings in motion and may be explored and studied in the 'here and now'. An encounter, interaction, and meeting with other people will always arise and effect an arousal, which forms itself into vitality affects and gives an unconscious sensation of pleasure or displeasure. Both cause bodily sensations. The process is implicit and shapes what Stern calls *vitality affects*, and the philosopher Susanne Langer's (1956) notions of *forms of feelings*. Damasio (1999) links the vitality affects to his definition of *background feelings*. Background feelings are not always conscious to our mind, and in these situations, there is a tendency to focus on other mental matters or content. Background feelings are more internally directed and may be observable to others in myriad ways, like body postures, the speed and way of moving and taking space, and even in the tone of our voices and the prosody in our speech as we communicate thoughts that may have little to do with the background emotion.

According to Stern (2010) the form that the energy, strength, and power take in the movements is defined as 'dynamic forms of vitality' and can best be described and explained through kinaesthetic terms such as rushing, relaxing, sliding, tense, trembling, weak, accelerating, and bouncing.

> Vitality is a whole. It is a Gestalt that emerges from the theoretically separate experiences of movement, force, time, space, and intention. It is not analysed in any conscious way piece by piece, any more than a familiar face is, even though each separate element could be taken aside and studied in isolation. (Stern, 2010, p.5)

When relating the above quote to the human voice, the overall expression of the voice as a whole could be understood as a *vocal gestalt*. The vocal gestalt is a complex phenomenon of many parameters such as the duration of the sound, the range of tones used, the fundamental tone of frequency, volume, resonance, compression, timbre, amount of intensity, and active overtones present in the sound produced (Storm, 2013, 2017). Research suggests that selected vocal parameters can describe and evaluate vocal sound and its expression, including evaluating the dynamic forms of vitality, and provide relevant information about a client's state of being (Storm, 2013, 2017). In the course of Therapy-Related Body and Voice Work the students are trained to tune themselves towards nonverbal parameters in body and voice starting by exploring their own experiences, finding words to describe these, and deepening the understanding by sharing their individual experiences throughout the course.

'The body keeps the score'

Life leaves traces on our minds and emotions, on our capacity for joy, and intimacy, and even on our biology and immune systems (Van der Kolk, 2014). Breathing and sounding are deeply rooted in the psyche and reflect when emotions are blocked or inhibited (Austin, 2008; Lowen, 1975; Van der Kolk, 2014). Conversely, when the body and voice can be observed as unconstricted movement in the doing – *in flow* – it reflects that the human being is opening up both body and mind. If, however, the rhythm is abrupt and constricted, it may reflect that the human being is closing off, withdrawing, holding in, or holding back whatever is difficult to handle and be connected to emotionally in the situation. This understanding is supported by Lowen (1975) and Ogden *et al.* (2006). In that way breathing and sounding may be viewed as a barometer for the psychological states of being. The voice will reflect when emotions are blocked or inhibited.

Body resonance

Fuchs (2005) further mentions another dimension of body and space, which is the quality of the felt atmosphere, the expression and impression of our affective engagement and participation in the world.

There are descriptions such as *There is something 'in the air'* or *a gloomy atmosphere*, which are used to describe the space around us and grasp the sense of a felt atmosphere, a so-called emotional space, where the body physically experiences that it widens, tightens, weakens, trembles, and shakes, and becomes an *instrument* that starts to act congruently with the feelings and atmospheres experienced. According to Fuchs (2005) the body in a broad sense could be described as a 'resonant body'. In many ways, Fuchs' definition of *body resonance* is similar to Langenberg's (1988) definition of the *resonating body function*. A loss of body resonance will furthermore result in a desynchronization (Fuchs, 2005, 2009).

'The window of tolerance'

According to Siegel (2012), our mental experience and arousal level during specific emotional experiences will have a tolerance range where the person functions optimally. Within this range of tolerance, which Siegel describes as 'the window of tolerance', a person does well. Outside the window, the person is pushed beyond a tolerable and manageable arousal level and moved to either an experience of chaos or rigidity. Thus, the adaptive and harmonic function is also lost.

For example, when a person is afflicted with anxiety, the window will narrow, and the person will more easily experience an arousal level that is too high. If a person experiences becoming increasingly anxious during the conversation, the music therapist can start centring and grounding exercises targeting stepwise movement of sensory stimuli. This has the purpose of getting an experience of dealing with anxiety and maybe even experience something different and new in relationship to oneself and one's way of being present with oneself.

Our autonomic arousal naturally fluctuates between high and low levels throughout the day. Changes in arousal reflect the innate capacity of our nervous systems to instinctively evaluate whether we are at risk or safe and then help us achieve the arousal level – high, low, or in-between – that would support adaptive behaviour.

Somatic resources are physical functions, actions, and capacities that provide a sense of well-being and competency on a physical level and in turn positively affect how we feel. Movement of our bodies is inextricably linked with our emotions, beliefs, and general sense of competency; working with posture, movement, and gesture and our senses can directly support our well-being.

Movement as somatic resource for self-soothing – notice how the body reacts to the movement

With body movement and sounding it is possible to provide a sensory stimulation functioning as an external somatic resource with the purpose of supporting an inner sensation of feeling safe, centred, and grounded. Body and voice can be used as interventions to calm the nervous system. Body movement, descending glissando sounding, and a focus on tempo of breathing can be ways to regulate high arousal such as anxiety.

Listening

On an unconscious level, we draw on our lived experience with this primary function of body and voice, and we still listen, relate, and act in response to the way the voice carries the words when speaking or singing. Among many other things we listen to the *timbre*, *harmonic quality*, *rhythm*, and *way of movement* or melody in the speech or song, as well as the *dynamics* of the voice like the *intensity* and *loudness* of the voice. This is the *music* of the human voice, and it colours our perception of the person sounding. Together with the meaning of the words this determines how we interpret what the person just said and gives us some clues to a person's self-image and emotional health. The sound of the voice can therefore be a tool – a mirror giving us an opportunity to 'perceive' the person sounding more clearly.

The principal teaching approach of *listening* is therefore so much more than *hearing*. It moves us on every level and allows us to get in contact with images, patterns, moods, textures, feelings, and processes. Therefore, it is important to notify that the students during this course are tuned towards an awareness of the several layers of attention that are actively in play at the same time. Pedersen (2006, 2007) defines this as an *allocentric way of listening*. An allocentric state of listening requires an extra sensitive and attentive way of 'being present' in the situation and being able to oscillate in and out of the shared field. Pedersen (2006) defines the allocentric attitude as follows:

> Here the therapist listens with her full awareness directed towards the patient and resonates deliberately and authentically with the patient's physical presence

in the room (the foreground). Gradually she then makes it possible for small 'sparks' of emotion from the patient's split reality (the background) to become a part of their relationship (both within the music and outside of it). (Pedersen, 2006, p.124)

The listening, furthermore, includes a spatial body sensation connected to the quality of the sound, both towards one's own sound and when tuning in and matching another person's sound. It is a listening to how the body reflexively adjusts itself to the other person's sound quality and a listening towards kinaesthetic information of a felt inner-body sensation. Listening for the subjective experiences and studying the muscular as well as the bodily reactions will support a growing body-awareness as well as a growing consciousness of the related emotional code. This way of listening is a very primary stage of listening, based on a primary mode of engagement. This action could overall be described as listening for the sounding gestalt. The definition of a gestalt is that it is an organized wholeness perceived as more than the sum of its parts.

References

Austin, D. (2008). *The Theory and Practice of Vocal Psychotherapy. Songs of the Self.* Jessica Kingsley Publishers.

Bonde, L.O. (2009). *Musik og menneske. Introduktion til musikpsykologi [Music and man. Introduction to music psychology]*. Samfundslitteratur.

Bråten, S. (ed.) (2007). *On Being Moved. From Mirror Neurons to Empathy.* John Benjamins Publishing Company.

Bråten, S. (2009). *The Intersubjective Mirror in Infant Learning and Evolution of Speech (Advances in Consciousness Research)*. John Benjamins Publishing Company.

Bråten, S. & Trevarthen, C. (2007). 'Prologue: From Infant Intersubjectivity and Participant Movements to Simulation and Conversation in Cultural Sense.' In S. Bråten (ed.), *On Being Moved. From Mirror Neurons to Empathy.* John Benjamins Publishing Company.

Brown, O.L. (2004). *Discover Your Voice. How to Develop Healthy Voice Habits.* Singular Publishing Group, Seventh Singular Printing.

Damasio, A. (1999). *The Feeling of What Happens. Body and Emotion in the Making of Consciousness.* Harcourt Books.

Dayme, M.B. (2009). *Dynamics of the Singing Voice* (5th ed.). Springer-Verlag.

Fuchs, T. (2005). 'Corporealized and disembodied minds. A phenomenological view of the body in melancholia and schizophrenia.' *Philosophy, Psychiatry & Psychology, 12*(2), 95–107.

Fuchs, T. (2009). 'Embodied cognitive neuroscience and its consequences for psychiatry.' *Poiesis Praxis, 6* (3–4), 219–233.

Hart, S. (2008). *Brain, Attachment, Personality. An Introduction to Neuroaffective Development.* Karnac Books Ltd.

Hart, S. (2012). *Neuroaffektiv psykoterapi med voksne [Neuroaffective psychotherapy with adults].* Hans Reitzels Forlag.

Heirich, J.R. (2005). *Voice and the Alexander Technique. Active Explorations for Speaking and Singing.* Mornum Time Press.

Kenny, C. (1989). *The Field of Play: A Guide for the Theory and Practice of Music Therapy.* Ridgeview Publishing Company.

Kenny, C. (2006). *Music & Life in the Field of Play: An Anthology.* Barcelona Publishers.

Langenberg, M. (1988). *Vom Handeln zom Be-Handeln [From Action to Treatment].* Gustav Fischer Forlag.

Langer, S. (1956). *Feeling and Form. A Theory of Art.* Routledge & Kegan Paul Limited.

Levine, P.A. (1997). *Waking the Tiger. Healing Trauma.* North Atlantic Books Berkeley.

Lowen, A. (1975). *Bioenergetics.* Penguin Compass.

Malloch, S. & Trevarthen, C. (eds) (2009). *Communicative Musicality: Exploring the Basis of Human Companionship.* Oxford University Press.

Merleau-Ponty, M. (2002). *Phenomenology of Perception.* Routledge Classics.

Ogden, P. & Minton, K. (2000). 'Sensorimotor psychotherapy: One method for processing traumatic memory.' *Traumatology, 4*(3), 3.

Ogden, P., Minton, K., & Pain, C. (2006). *Trauma and the Body. A Sensorimotor Approach to Psychotherapy.* W.W. Norton & Company.

Panksepp, J. & Trevarthen, C. (2009). 'The Neuroscience of Emotion in Music.' In S. Malloch & C. Trevarthen (eds), *Communicative Musicality. Exploring the Basis of Human Companionship.* Oxford University Press.

Pedersen, I.N. (2002). 'Psychodynamic Movement: A Basic Training Methodology for Music Therapists.' In J.T. Eschen (ed.), *Analytical Music Therapy.* Jessica Kingsley Publishers.

Pedersen, I.N. (2006). 'Counter transference in music therapy.' PhD dissertation. Aalborg University. Accessed on 09/12/21 at https://vbn.aau.dk/ws/portalfiles/portal/70261290/inp_2007.pdf.

Pedersen, I.N. (2007). 'Musikterapeutens disciplinerede subjektivitet [The disciplined subjectivity of the music therapist].' *Psyke & Logos. Dansk Psykologisk Forlag, 1,* 358–384.

Porges, S.W. (2017). *The Pocket Guide to the Polyvagal Theory. The Transformative Power of Feeling Safe.* W.W. Norton & Company.

Siegel, D.J. (2012). *Pocket Guide to Interpersonal Neurobiology. An Integrative Handbook of the Mind.* WW Norton and Co.

Stern, D. (2000). *The Interpersonal World of the Infant. A View from Psychoanalysis and Development Psychology.* Basic Books.

Stern, D. (2010). *Forms of Vitality. Exploring Dynamic Experience in Psychology, the Arts, Psychotherapy and Development.* Oxford University Press.

Storm, S. (2013). 'Research into the development of a voice assessment profile in music therapy.' PhD dissertation. Aalborg University. Accessed on 09/12/21 at https://vbn.aau.dk/ws/portalfiles/portal/316401121/Sanne_Storm_Research_into_the_Development_of_Voice_Assessment_in_Music_Therapy.pdf.

Storm, S (2017). 'Den Menneskelige stemmes stimulering af krop og psyke – psykodynamisk stemmeterapi mod prænatal angst og depression [The stimulation of body and mind by the human voice – psychodynamic voice therapy towards prenatal anxiety and depression].' In C. Lindvang and B.D. Beck (eds), *Musik, Krop og Følelser. Neuroaffektive Processer i Musikterapi [Music Body and Emotions. Neuroaffective Processes in Music Therapy].* Frydenlund Academic.

Storm, S. (2019). 'The Voice Assessment Profile.' In S. Jacobsen, E. Waldon, & G. Gattino (eds), *Music Therapy Assessment. Theory, Research, and Application.* Jessica Kingsley Publishers.

Tongeren, M.C. van (2004). *Overtone Singing. Physics and Metaphysics of Harmonics in East and West.* Fusica.

Trevarthen, C. & Malloch, S.N. (2000). 'The dance of well-being: Defining the musical therapeutic effect.' *Nordisk Tidsskrift for Musikkterapi, 9*(2), 3–17.

Van der Kolk, B. (2014). *The Body Keeps the Score. Mind, Brain and Body in the Transformation of Trauma.* Penguin Books.

CHAPTER 7

Clinical Group Music Therapy Skills (CGMS)

Niels Hannibal & Stine Lindahl Jacobsen

Introduction

CGMS is a multi-layered module that runs for two semesters with a focus on building skills in planning and running group music therapy for a variety of client groups and users. The module is taught to 3rd-year BA music therapy (5th and 6th semester) students, who know each other well as they participated in Group Music Therapy in years 1–2 (see Chapter 4).

Professor Tony Wigram developed CGMS, and the first course was introduced in 1992 (Wigram, 1996). Since then, CGMS has been an integrated part of the BA programme. The students experience themselves as therapist for the first time as they have to plan, run, and reflect upon a training session with a specific client group. The CGMS teacher and facilitator supervises the student-therapist prior to the training session and guides them in connecting needs, goals, activities, and interventions. Fellow students roleplay clients, thus giving the student-therapist a semi-realistic and safe group to work with. The student-therapist enters into a real-time experience of having to adjust/attune the musical and verbal interventions accordingly, facilitates the dynamic process of the group, and follows the process of each individual client. After every training session the student-therapists continue to reflect and are encouraged to reflect on their performance and level of presence as experienced by themselves. In an in-depth dialogue facilitated by the teacher, the student-therapist receives constructive feedback from fellow students and the teacher on what happened in the training session, including the interventions used, adjusting to needs in the moment, how the client reacted (and felt), the connection between needs, goals, and activities, etc.

Professor Tony Wigram, who introduced CGMS in the curriculum at the Aalborg music therapy education, was focused on some of the challenges in 'teaching' students how to intervene and act as a therapist. Theoretical-based knowledge is necessary but also has limits when it comes to learning 'how to' – the procedural level of learning. In relation to using theoretical models in teaching, Wigram wrote: 'what [students] frequently don't find in any of the literature on clinical music therapy or the books on music therapy training that have been produced are clear procedures' (Wigram, 1996, p.1). Procedures are not fixed, and students therefore have to learn to adjust and be flexible when it comes to procedures in music therapy. Reading about being flexible and adjusting in the here-and-now is not enough. You must also try it out, experience it, and learn through these experiences. CGMS is a module that aims to facilitate training in learning the balance between knowing about theoretical-based procedures and experiencing how they may be applied in a semi-realistic music therapy setting. Every user and client group has unique and specific needs, and every music therapist adjusts to this challenge in clinical work. In this module, the students' theoretical understanding is based on analytical, existential, and humanistic orientations, but also includes more behavioural, neuropsychological, and functional approaches when relevant. In that sense, CGMS provides the students with an opportunity to approach the planning of the session as pragmatic and integrative as they see fit (Wigram, 1996).

Integrating theoretical and experience-based knowledge

CGMS aims to begin the transition from student to therapist and builds on modules taught in the 1st and 2nd BA year. The students have had many different courses to prepare for the transition: experience-based modules include Group Music Therapy, Applied Musical Performance, Music Instruction Level 1 and 2, Voice Work, Clinical Body and Voice Work, and Improvisation. Theoretical modules include Problem-Based Learning, Music Psychology, Observation and Description of Clinical Practice, Developmental Psychology and Neuropsychology, and Theory of Music Therapy and Research 1–3. Theory of Music Therapy and Research 1–3 includes a focus on a variety of clients such as clients with physical and psychological disabilities (4th semester), somatic and neurological disabilities including clients with dementia (5th semester), and social and psychiatric challenges (6th semester). All this comes into play when the student has to prepare, carry out, and reflect upon their CGMS session. The students are expected to utilize their theoretical knowledge in planning the sessions and understanding the clients and integrate experience-based knowledge in understanding themselves and their own actions and reactions. In order for student-therapists to navigate in the therapeutic process, they need to experience phenomena like attunement, matching, mirroring, and framing, as well as resistance, defences, transference-related experiences, and other psychodynamic-related experiences. They need to encounter, and experience and explore, those phenomena in their own process of becoming a therapist (Chapter 5). Building on these combined and diverse competences, the students are ready to have their first practical experience as therapist.

Study curriculum

In the study curriculum the learning goals include the following:

- Basic knowledge about aetiology and pathology relevant to clinical practice

- Application of music therapy for specific clinical populations

- Strategies for preparing, conducting, and evaluating group music therapy sessions

These goals reflect a classic approach to treatment. Every condition or issue a client is dealing with has its own specific aetiology and pathology. From a therapeutic point of view, our understanding and knowledge of the condition or issue is reflected in the way the therapist understands, plans, and executes the music therapy intervention in the session. This might have a focus on deficiencies, resources, or both, as both symptoms and resources are approachable in a music therapy context. Theoretical knowledge and practical training are utilized in CGMS when it comes to learning how to prepare, conduct, and evaluate. This is also in line with the core didactic and educational approach of the PBL model (see Chapter 2) at Aalborg University.

The learning goals include many different skills and competences developed during the CGMS course. They can be organized into four larger groups (musical skills, process skills, organizing skills, and analytic and reflective skills).

Musical skills

- To use musical material and create musical frames in group therapeutic work

- To be able to recall and describe musical material from group music therapy activities

- To use expressive (i.e., improvisation, song writing, and music performance) and receptive music therapy methods (i.e., guided relaxation, movement or imagery to music) attuned to the needs of the specific clinical population and their developmental potentials

Process skills

- To read/sense the client's expressions and attune to the needs of the client
- To appear authentic in the therapeutic relationship

Organizing skills

- To prepare, conduct, and evaluate a music therapy session, as well as to consider the needs of the specific clinical population and their developmental potentials

Analytic and reflective skills

- To analyse and reflect on the clinical population's needs and potential for development in relation to the choice of music therapy method/intervention
- To reflect on the future role as therapist
- To analyse, document, and disseminate the therapeutic process in a professional way according to the clinical population's needs and potential for development

Users and client groups

A wide range of physical, psychological, social, existential, cognitive, and neurologic challenges are explored during the two semesters, including clients from psychiatry, children and adults with intellectual disabilities/learning differences, and more general medicine. CGMS aims to prepare students to undertake group work with a variety of clients, and to focus on how to make use of musical material and musical frameworks for the purpose of group therapy work in child, adolescent, and adult settings. The groups should always reflect current society and are therefore frequently updated. Client groups covered include:

- Blind clients
- Clients with autism/on the autistic spectrum
- Clients with learning disabilities
- Clients with schizophrenia (paranoid)
- Clients with schizophrenia (thought disorders)
- Clients with anxiety
- Clients with depression
- Clients with bipolar/affective disorders
- Clients with borderline personality disorders
- Clients with dementia/Alzheimer's
- Clients with substance abuse
- Clients with eating disorders
- Clients within social psychiatry
- Users within family therapy
- Clients with cancer
- Refugees with PTSD
- Employees on sick leave with work-related stress/burnout
- Kindergarten children with attention and social challenges
- Clients with acquired brain injury
- Clients with COPD (chronic obstructive pulmonary disease)
- Clients with ADHD (attention deficit/hyperactivity disorder)

Progression throughout the two semesters

The level of vulnerability and complexity in the client groups also increases from the 5th to 6th semester and each student is meant to work with both verbal and nonverbal groups as well as both children and adults to increase the student's set of skills and self-insight (Wigram, 1996). In connection with the wider set of modules and tasks during the 5th and 6th semester, CGMS in the 5th semester is meant to prepare the students for the first internship in the 6th semester. The students need preparatory experiences to help them understand both their role as a therapist and achieve deeper insight into the experience of the client. The students need to acquire these experiences in order to develop their own ability to recognize and assess what is 'happening' in their therapeutic work and to get a sense and understanding of the session from the clients' point of view.

The CGMS format provides a progressive learning experience as tasks increase in complexity and the demand for independency from the students increases during the two semesters. In the 5th semester, the therapists work in couples, while they manage the same tasks alone in the 6th semester. During the first semester of CGMS, the students work together in pairs when planning with the supervisor, performing with four clients roleplayed by their co-students, and reflecting upon the training session together with the group and the teacher. The first time, the aim is primarily to manage the session while being observed by the group and teacher/supervisor, as the transition into the therapist role puts a lot of stress on them. When they realize that 'mistakes' or 'mishaps' are not treated as right or wrong, but as opportunities to learn and improve, they become more relaxed. In the 6th semester, they work solo with three roleplaying client-students, and they mature quickly. During the 6th semester, they are expected to increase their ability to adjust their actions and interventions according to what is happening. This is seen as a result of not only engaging in the process as student-therapist, but also of student-clients having experienced many different ways to utilize music, and of observing each other's performance and reflections in the group.

When reflecting during feedback after the training sessions, the perspective of the clients is the starting point giving the therapist-pair more time to understand and respond. In the second semester of CGMS, the student-therapist independently begins the evaluation and connects aims, activities, interactions, and interventions and afterwards follows feedback from the co-student-clients and the teacher.

Facilitating and teaching CGMS

The teacher and facilitator have a complex role to fulfil. The role has two layers: one is as a teacher who advises and supervises in the preparatory phase. The 'teacher' creates the structure of each session before and after the student-therapists have conducted their session. The second role is a sort of combined facilitator and supervisor. This is a function where it is important to create the necessary environment for feedback and reflection. It includes balancing the learning process in a kind of learning circle. Each part of the sessions may reveal situations, actions, and events that are interesting, relevant, and potentially can offer new insight and ideas for different solutions. This material unfolds in real time and is multi-layered. The facilitator's most important task is to motivate and support the students to allow them to engage in and investigate all these sequences that the sessions have provided and extract as much knowledge as possible during the session, and afterwards when they review the recordings.

Since CGMS involves a great level of unforeseen events and unpredictability, it is essential that the teacher facilitates and helps establish a safe and contained environment from day one. The sessions in CGMS are introduced as training therapy sessions with closed doors, no interruptions, supervision times before and after the sessions, and ethical agreements with the students about the confidentiality of material emerging in these sessions.

It can be helpful to the teacher and the student if the teacher has specialist knowledge and therapeutic experience with the specific client-groups. However, this is not a must. Tailored facilitation, however, is always required.

The teacher has many tasks and responsibilities during the many elements of CGMS, including introducing CGMS and building a safe environment, supervising students, providing a safe frame just before the training session, ensuring ethical standards for the student-therapist and student-client during and after the training session, facilitating feedback dialogues and constructive reflection, and giving respectful and nuanced feedback to all students.

It is a very multi-layered and complex task, and often, as teachers in CGMS, we get close to the students' personal reflections about themselves. They share pain and joy with the group and with the teacher. Sometimes we celebrate great accomplishments together with the students and sometimes we help contain, acknowledge, and respect painful disappointments. It requires good insight into your own values and identity as a therapist to make sure you do not unconsciously project or expect the same from the students. It is a privilege to be part of the students' personal and diverse journeys.

Structure of the module

The CGMS module consists of an introduction lecture, dyad, or individual pre-supervision before every training session, the training sessions themselves, and one last lecture as preparation for the exam. Each training session has its own structure: First, a dialogue about the client group and creating a safe environment, then the training session itself, and finally a feedback dialogue and reflection in the group facilitated by the teacher.

Getting started

Introducing the course and the learning goals to the student takes a full lecture, as much needs to be explained and organized. The different roles (therapist, clients, videorecorder, making minutes, etc.), responsibilities, and tasks are explained and distributed, and some examples of simple instruction are tried out; this also helps set the right mode and concentration for the group. The teacher focuses on building a safe environment for the students, by making sure everybody is aware about their task and by role-modelling the seriousness and focus that is needed before entering a complex space for learning.

Preparation prior to training sessions

Before every training session the students are required to read and study background information about the client groups with whom they will be working. This includes looking into the aetiology, pathology, and difficulties of these client groups.

The student-therapist is presented with a client group of three or four clients and has three major preparatory tasks.

First, the students have to prepare 2–3 pages of written information about the client group, including typical characteristics, symptoms, needs, behaviour, general treatment, music therapy treatment, etc. This information is shared with the whole group and provides the client-students with information about the client they have to roleplay.

Second, the student-therapist has to prepare a plan for the training session, based on needs and aims for the client group and how they want to organize the session and the musical activities with a specific population. The plan includes reflections about the needs and challenges in the specific group, suggestions for structure and interventions applied, and a description of the students' strengths and weaknesses.

Third, the students have a pre-supervision, where they receive feedback on their written descriptions about the client group as well as on their plan for the training session, including supervision on their worries and insecurities about being the therapist and also their thoughts about their own strengths and potentials, such as general confidence specifically related to the musical activities and interventions. Special attention is given to identify the most appropriate therapeutic approach and musical material to meet the needs of each client individually and the group as a whole. Each activity should be connected to a specific need and the overall aim for the session. Often students spend time unlearning the tendency to choose the activity before focusing on the needs of the client and the connected goal of the session. Need, goal, and activity should be strongly interconnected. Based on the didactic methods of Tony Wigram (1996), the students are therefore encouraged to define their approach based on the client's needs according to three levels: general needs (feeling safe, exploration, etc.), needs related to pathology-specific challenges (challenges in interaction or emotion regulation, etc.), and individual needs (personality, personal history, etc.).

Roleplaying clients

The group of roleplayed student-clients is understood as a group where the individuals have met each other at least a few times, so it is already an established group, where a little sense of trust and familiarity can be expected to have been developed among the clients. The student-clients are expected to learn and memorize a brief description about the client that they have been assigned to. The information about the client includes personal ways of behaving, their relationships within the group, and some of the challenges that they are experiencing. The level of information is not too rich as the student-clients cannot be expected to remember a whole history of a person's life. Instead, the student-clients can be creative in the training session and bring their own ideas into the role they are undertaking, perhaps adding some aspect to the client. The student-clients are always given a different name and, during the training session, this name is written on a white label, which they wear. Having a new name is quite important for the process in order to have a sense of a change of identity.

The student-clients are going through two processes. First, they have to identify and empathize with the role of the client and the different challenges of this person. Second, they are also trying to explore how such clients would act and interact in music therapy sessions. This is a very demanding task and requires total commitment and trust in the student-therapist, student-client, and the teacher.

Here are two examples of group and client information provided to aid the student-clients and to inform the student-therapist:

Example 1: Area of focus: Clients with autism – moderate

Context: The clients live in an institution in the municipality. The regular staff are social workers. Their parents visit but are unable to manage them at home. The clients have received music therapy in this group for four months.

Henrik is an eight-year-old boy with autism. He does not have any language, except echolalia with a few specific words. His IQ is low. He has been a resident in the institution for three years. In music therapy, he shows interest in using instruments. His playing is monotonous and automatic.

He also produces sounds with his voice. He does not seek contact with other people, but he does not react or reject when someone approaches him. He shows stereotypical hand movements, and he sometimes moves his fingers in front of his face.

Example 2: Area of focus: Clients with schizophrenia with thought disturbances

Context: All the clients have difficulty with concentration and attention. They receive neuroleptics, a medical treatment that influences the central nervous system. They are all in a state of mind where they have lost their sense of reality.

Johan is a 27-year-old male. He believes that his thoughts are being taken out of his mind by an external force or power. He often stops mid-sentence and explains that his mind is empty. He becomes anxious when he loses his thoughts. He shows little affect and it is often difficult to get in contact with him.

Prior to training sessions, the teacher readies the student-clients by refreshing knowledge about the client group based on the written material produced by the student-therapist and based on personal encounters in the entire group of students. Often the personal encounters and experiences of the student group are a great way to tune into the client group and create a safe environment prior to the training session.

When the students start to behave like a client, they begin to experience a different sense of reality, sinking as deeply as possible into the role, frequently withdrawing and then emerging as the client. The student-clients are encouraged to react as authentically as possible to the interventions and activities provided by the student-therapist, trying to be true to the client at hand. Even though they do not believe they have become the client in question, the roleplaying sometimes triggers feelings, anxieties, despair, and loneliness coming from the clients they are portraying. This client experience in some cases is very deep, and the student-clients may sometimes retain feelings from their experiences as clients, which continue during the rest of the day and perhaps into the following day. In taking on the role of a client, students may find out about a part of themselves which is quite near to the difficulties described in the client's personality. It is an incredibly valuable experience in forming a therapist identity and a way of reaching into a possible sense of the client's inner being and understanding them on a different level. If it is difficult for a student to let go of the experience, the teacher (supervisor) will always assist in a debriefing immediately after the training session and/or in the following hours/days if necessary. However, it happens very seldom, as the teachers always assess and talk briefly with each student who has played a client.

Student-therapists in the training sessions

A CGMS session is complex and much goes on simultaneously. The student-therapist performs the role as authentically as possible and treats the 'clients' as real clients. The student-therapist for each of these groups also perceives the group they are working with as clients rather than their fellow students and responds with great sensitivity and a therapeutic approach. After the session begins, everyone stays in character. This is a challenging learning experience, and the student-therapists experience 'what it is all about' to be a music therapist in a safe environment. Introducing the students to how to roleplay and short descriptions of the clients gives the student-clients a setting for the training session. What the student-clients try to do in the training session is addressed afterwards in the feedback dialogue facilitated by the teacher. Because the nature of the therapeutic setting is chaotic and unpredictable by nature, the only way to prepare for this is to experience it in the here-and-now, and CGMS is meant to provide a sense of this experience to the student-therapist and the student-clients. Besides planning the training session, the student-therapist also needs to realize that there is no certainty in a music therapy session. Each session will (hopefully) develop in the way that most appropriately meets the needs of the clients (Wigram, 1996, 1997, 2004). Many layers are active in the training sessions: the student-therapists train their ability to attune to the complex set of needs of the client in the moment both verbally and musically, as well as keeping track of time and ensuring the requirements of the room. Ensuring the requirements of the room includes choosing instruments to be available and visible, chairs vs. sitting on the floor, who sits where, where to place a camera, etc.

Other student tasks during the training session

Students who do not play clients or who do not run the sessions as therapist are all observers and have important tasks. They need to make careful notes of the musical and verbal interactions going on in the training session, the way the student-therapists are approaching and working with the group at a musical level, and at an interactive, personal, and verbal level, and the way the clients are responding. All aspects of the group process need to be observed, and in the feedback dialogue the observers play a significant role in giving a somewhat objective and reflective view of what has just occurred. One student is responsible for video recording the training session and feedback dialogue. This is of great value to the student-therapists, who can revisit what happened and get deeper learning retrospectively.

Feedback after training sessions

Immediately after the training session, all the students and the teacher have a feedback dialogue. The intention is to explore how 'the clients' experienced the session, what actions were taken by the student-therapist(s), interventions, therapeutic value, and any relevant feedback about episodes and events that have occurred. The student-clients stay in contact with the client role and provide and share their experiences of how it was to be this person in this session. Despite the roleplaying nature of their experience, it gives valuable information to the student-therapist about how other people (and clients) might experience them in the event that just unfolded. As a therapist it is unique (as it is mostly impossible and unethical) to be able to get in-depth feedback from your own clients, and this is where the students develop a sense of how to get to know their own resources and potentials and can start building a therapist identity.

As mentioned above, there is a progression to how this feedback unfolds. During the 5th semester, the feedback dialogue begins with the student-clients' experience and feedback, accompanied by the teacher and, if relevant, the observation group. Sequentially, the student-therapists engage in the feedback dialogue, and if needed a specific element of a training session may be rehearsed or re-enacted; for instance, paying attention to a musical parameter (e.g., tempo, dynamic) in a specific exercise or activity and/or trying out how a small intervention change sometimes can make a huge difference. The students practise critical reflection using their own experiences and the experiences of their peers as an information source aiming towards including all elements of the learning objectives: remember, understand, apply, analyse, evaluate, and create.

In closing the feedback dialogue, the student-therapists are encouraged to update their written portfolio on matters such as new insight into the client group, scheduling and planning a session, their own verbal and musical interventions, sense of time, pace in relation to client group, ability to adapt to the present/to be flexible, leadership role, collaborating with a co-leader, ability to remember and reflect after the session, etc.

Training session vignette

This description is a summarization and partly a fictive description of one session with a dyad of students working together. To bring the experience to life we have written it in the perspective of one pair.

One pair of student-therapists (5th semester) were in charge of a session with a group of student-clients roleplaying people with dementia. They had organized the session around reminiscence and arousal regulation through musical activities. The music therapy session included some physical activity to music at first to stimulate engagement and participation, as well as to regulate arousal to an optimal level. This was followed by singing in the group, using familiar songs chosen by the therapists. This was done to enhance cognitive and emotional responses from the participants, and to perhaps also evoke memories (reminiscence) and offer the possibility for verbal dialogue, meaningful communication, and contact. In general, the session went as planned, but one of the student-clients was in a restless state of mind, and she kept getting up walking around in the room during the group singing. The first time she got up, one of the therapists stood up and walked over to her, establishing contact through singing and engaging with her by gently putting a hand on her arm. The student-therapist tried to establish eye contact guiding the client to sit back down again. However, after a short while the client once again stood up and walked around in the room. This time the student-therapist decided to leave her be for a longer time and concentrate on the other student-clients. In the feedback dialogue with the student-clients and the teacher, this situation came into focus. What were the therapists' reactions to this client's behaviour? What was the client's experience of being in the session? Different approaches were discussed. Was it possible to continue the music with the rest of the group and at the same time help the woman who was a bit agitated and hyperaroused? It was suggested to try an approach of keeping the song they were singing going, while at the same time contacting the client and carefully lowering the tempo and dynamics of the music, as a means to facilitate the student-client being more at rest and able to participate, instead of being left alone by herself. The student-clients went back into roleplaying, and the situation was recreated. The student-therapists carefully changed the dynamics of the singing, and one student-therapist went over to the student-client, who was again walking around in the room, initiated contact, and the student-client responded. Together they walked over to the student-client's chair, and she sat down. This is a situation where the student-therapist consciously can try out interventions they did not do in the session, and they can experience the difference between not intervening, and intervening, and having their attention at both the whole group and the specific client. In the reflections after the exercise, the student-therapists described how they became aware of their own agenda and how it to some extent kept them from taking action in the here and now situation. They experienced how the change of musical dynamics can make a big difference in the group dynamic, and they became more aware of adapting to the individual need of clients and the ability to intervene in a chaotic and unpredictable environment.

Evaluation

This course is evaluated at the end of the 6th semester with an external examiner. The method of evaluation is similar to the process of the training sessions during the year. The students choose client groups one-to-two weeks before they have to submit a written plan about the exam session. No later than two weeks before the exam, the students submit the written description (2–3 pages). This contains a short description of the needs of the specific client group, including the needs of the individuals and the group as a whole. The students must include a presentation of the overall rationale, planned structure and activities, musical material, and most importantly connect needs, aims, activities, and interventions. Furthermore, the written description should also include a short description of the student's expectations of the session and possible personal challenges. The exam session lasts 25 minutes. After the session, the student has five minutes to prepare for a feedback dialogue with the examiner and external examiner that lasts for 15 minutes. The students are expected to focus on the perception of clients' needs in the session, musical and verbal interventions, and overall reflection about their role as therapist. The evaluation takes five minutes, and the evaluation feedback lasts for 10 minutes. In total the examination lasts for one hour. The focus is not on success and how 'well' the session went. The outcome is not the focus in evaluating the student; instead, the evaluation focus is on the student's ability to:

- Integrate theoretical understanding/knowledge

- Understand what went on in the session

- Show clinical and musical skills in the session

- Reflect on future role as therapist (personal strengths and challenges)

- Reflect about future 'working areas'

The primary goals are evaluating the student's observational skill, their ability to use experience, reflect about the experience, and discuss what happened in terms of 'this went well, and this didn't'. In a sense it is the ability to administer their responses to the unforeseen and sometimes chaotic nature of a therapy session and their reflections about this process that is important. It is not expected that the student prepares and conducts a 'perfect' session.

Theoretical underpinnings

In his teaching and his therapeutic approach, Wigram was inspired by UK music therapist Juliette Alvin and her individualized approach focusing on client need and the concept of free improvisation and adapting to the here-and-now. Individual need and adapting through improvisation are cornerstones in the theoretical underpinning of CGMS developed by Tony Wigram for the music therapy BA education at Aalborg University. Alvin proposed the potential to use different approaches in different situations and she mainly worked from a humanistic and developmental point of view (Alvin, 1975, as cited by Wigram, 2002).

According to Bruscia, Alvin believed that every music therapist should be an experienced musician as well as have the basic psychological knowledge about how musical experiences can (and cannot) help clients. Furthermore, among other personality traits, the therapist should be able to share and observe, to show sympathy and understanding without being emotionally involved, to have a sense of humour, and to be patient and tolerant whatever happens. Music creates 'infinite kinds of relationships', and this forms the cornerstone of music therapy. Music therapy can be implemented within the framework of various psychological theories including both behavioural and analytical directions. According to Bruscia, Alvin described the preparation for sessions in much detail and she plotted out the goals and needs for each individual and/or each group and this guided the course of therapy (Alvin, 1975, as cited by Bruscia, 1987).

Wigram was explicit about how he was inspired by Alvin and individualized, free improvisation in developing CGMS and other modules at Aalborg University

(Wigram, 2002). Wigram's massive and inspirational set of clinical musical skills without a doubt developed into an important cornerstone for music therapy at Aalborg University for the future. In the mid-1990s, he developed a module placed in the 7th and 8th semesters focusing entirely on clinical musical improvisation skills, and in 2004 he published his book *Improvisation*. The book is a practical and comprehensive guide to learn musical techniques and therapeutic methods for students, teachers, therapists, and musicians (Wigram, 2004).

Problem-based learning

As described above, CGMS is the first module where the students experience the role of being a therapist. Until this point, they have not had this opportunity. It is also the first time they have to empathize with and impersonate a client. Both experiences possess an option for essential learning before their first internship in the following semester. In many ways, CGMS is at the centre of the didactic principles of Aalborg University in general and music therapy education specifically.

Primarily, CGMS is a module that utilizes the problem-based learning model (PBL) (see Chapter 2). This model focuses on teaching within a realm of real-world issues, and CGMS attempts to deal with real-world issues. In the 5th semester the students only meet their fellow students as 'clients', but in the 6th semester the course is taught parallel with them being in their first internship as student music therapists. The parallel learning in the internship with real-world clients and the safe environment of CGMS provide an excellent context for exploring and developing their therapeutic identity. It brings forth the importance of earlier training.

Experiential learning

The experiential dimension of CGMS is of utmost importance. As described above, the students prepare training sessions twice: first during the 5th semester and again in the 6th semester; first in collaboration with another student and the second time on their own. When the training session starts, the students must stay in character throughout the session no matter what happens. Both student-therapists and student-clients experience the session as if it was a real-world situation, even though they are roleplaying. The value of this experience cannot be underestimated. From a theoretical perspective, CGMS is the first step in tuning the students to the therapist role. It is experiential training (see Chapter 1).

The students develop the following competences in CGMS:

- Their attention towards themselves, their fellow therapist, the group, and the individual group members

- Their responsiveness towards actions and events that unfold in the here and now

- Their ability to apply their musical skills and competences

- Their ability to contain and cope with planning a session according to the client's needs and facing the chaos of reality where the 'here and now' may overrule any planning

- Their ability to differentiate between wanting to help and comfort someone and perhaps meeting a person who is not able to receive what is offered

CGMS is their first experience of the concept of phronesis: ethical know-how (see Chapter 1). The teaching at the candidate level provides a lot more of this type of learning, and it is a skill that is tuned in many different ways in the following semesters. Bloom and colleagues' (1956) taxonomy is integrated in all subjects taught in the music therapy education, and CGMS illustrates all elements of learning objectives in Bloom and colleagues' taxonomy, which are activated in this teaching: referring, understanding, applying, analysing, evaluating, creating, and critically reflecting/evaluating (Bloom *et al.*, 1956).

The role of the teacher/facilitator

The whole structure of CGMS relies on tailored facilitation done by the CGMS teacher. In a student-centred setting and PBL teaching approach, the ability of the student to take control of their own learning is seen as a source of motivation and as a qualification in itself. Student-centred learning requires facilitation, and the teacher in CGMS can be understood as a facilitator in a PBL environment. Being a facilitator suggests openness toward the perspective of the student and points to a more equal power relationship between teacher and student. The teacher facilitates an open space where the students are free to act, even though they as teachers still perform the tasks of guiding, advising, and teaching the students to tolerate insecurity and guide them in appropriate directions. The facilitator has to appropriate their practice to a mix of student needs and identities and to secure a group-based learning progress. Facilitating is complex and diverse and can be described as a kind of chaos-management at the micro level – for each new situation that unfolds in the here and now a custom-made facilitation is needed.

As a facilitator in a custom-focussed setting, it is possible to act like a group member, focus on facilitating dialogues, and/or perform the role as a consultant (Kolmos *et al.,* 2008). Another important task for the facilitator is to ensure peer feedback and peer dialogues for the students. Studies suggest that peer facilitation is very effective as students function as role models for each other and can be soft leaders towards each other due to the shared tacit knowledge about being a student (Hmelo-Silver, Bridges, & McKeown, 2019). These aspects can be understood as active during CGMS teaching specifically in pre-supervision and in the feedback dialogue facilitated by the teacher.

Facilitator vignette

This vignette is a summarization of many students' experiences written from a first-person perspective.

The student-therapist was planning to work with a group of people with depression and met with the teacher in the pre-supervision to discuss the plan. She wanted to work with movement and body activities with the aim to strengthen the body awareness of clients. The teacher asked her how she understood the needs of the clients, and she moved her focus to each individual. One of the clients was described as very shy and timid and she reflected that the activities might have to be instructed in ways where the clients on their own could decide how much they wanted to move. Although this was a good reflection, the teacher asked again about the specific need of this particular client. She thought about it and became silent for 10 seconds.

Student-therapist: 'He needs to feel secure and understood; he does not need to feel like a failure or not good enough... So, I can't work with body awareness?'
Teacher: 'Yes you can, but you need to start with the need – not the activity or aim. Not feeling good enough...okay...what does he need?'
Student-therapist: 'To feel good enough... In his body?'
Teacher: 'Yes, this a different way to look at it. To feel good in his body. How would you try to facilitate this?'
Student-therapist: 'Then I would make a sitting body guide with some calm music focusing on breathing exercises.'
Teacher: 'Great. How would you choose the music and what role would it have?'

After this shift from activity to need, the student carefully planned the session focusing on a cohesion between challenges, needs, aims, and activities. In the training session, the student carefully tailored her interventions to the needs of the clients, and it seemed to fit the clients to have a calm body focus where no one could fail in the activities. However, in the feedback dialogue afterwards with the other students, the student-therapist reflected on a different matter:

Student-therapist: 'I don't know what happened. I did what I planned. It seemed to fit the client. They all did what I asked them and guided them to, but I did not intend for them to almost fall asleep. It's like the energy was gone somehow.'

Student-client: 'Yeah, it was good meaningful exercises but somehow I just got so tired. I felt very safe with you, but it was all very quiet.'

Teacher: 'Did you notice how you instructed the guiding? Your timbre and tempo when talking?'

Student-therapist: 'Mmhhh – no, not in the moment but I can see now that I was very low in volume, it was airy and slow. I think I did it to make the clients feel safe?'

Teacher: 'Okay, yes it seemed they felt safe with you. Could anything else in the room have affected you? How was the group of clients when they entered the room?'

Student-therapist: 'They were very low on energy and very quiet... Hang on... Are you talking about transference? Mmmmaybe...so the low energy of the group might have affected me somehow?'

Teacher: 'Maybe – you could also understand this as countertransference.'

Student-therapist: 'I see. So, I could have been more energetic to help the group be more active instead of copying their level of energy?'

Student-client: 'Yes, my role could probably have benefited from some more energy from you as the therapist. Then "Hans" would probably have talked more about his experiences and his feelings afterwards.'

Teacher: 'How did you perceive your role as a therapist in terms of being supportive vs. confronting or directing?'

Student-therapist: 'I guess I was mostly supportive, but I also wanted them to try to connect with their body and reflect upon this, which I know is difficult for them. It is difficult to manage the balance.'

Teacher: 'Yes, it is difficult. It is still difficult for me and for all therapists I presume. The main thing is to acknowledge the difficulty, monitor yourself and your "default" tendencies, and give room to manage the balance between being supportive and confronting constantly.'

In this example, it is clear that CGMS enables many layers of reflections for the students. The teacher plays a crucial role in facilitating supervision and feedback dialogues and doing so with respect and acknowledgement of the student to keep them engaged and motivated in their journey.

Situated learning

CGMS is situated learning (see Chapter 2) with a bottom-up approach. Besides being the student-therapist in the training session, the students prepare information about the client group and discuss ideas about how to use music in supervision. The students carry out the session, and finally, yet importantly, they participate in self-reflection and a peer-feedback dialogue. This is part of a culture where reflection and critical thinking are essential for any therapist's future performance and development of identity.

Finally, CGMS includes a bodily knowledge part (see Chapter 1) related to experiential learning. Even though this is not something they can master in their first try, the CGMS format allows for a beginning development of the ability to listen to the impulses, sensations, and reactions in their own body while engaging in the therapeutic process. In CGMS, the students might experience phenomena such as countertransference and transference in the dynamic process (see Chapter 3), not as an intellectual understanding, but as a relational phenomenon that unfolds here and now. This is why roleplaying is so important. Other important learning processes are related to the roleplaying of the client. When the students enter the room in the role as a client, they have an opportunity to experience how it might be to live with such challenges and difficulties. One student questioned the value by asking: 'Is this really how it is in real life?' The reply to this question is both yes and no. Roleplaying is a form of impersonation, and every student does this differently. Nevertheless, it always has elements of the issues at hand, and it is always a personal impersonation, so the student-therapist does not know what to expect. This provides an element of unpredictability and surprise. The answer to the question about degree of reality might be: Yes, this is as unforeseen as real life, and no it is not real life, it is a training setting, which is sufficient as preparation for the internship in the 6th semester. The unforeseen element and the whole situation strengthen their empathic skills and their ability to identify with and understand future clients. Another important element of this exercise is that, as long as the sessions are in motion, the roleplaying students are obliged to stay in character and that gives the situation a strong sense of reality. There is no intermission, and it is serious. This adds to the element of reality and thereby makes it a situated learning environment.

In our opinion, CGMS is a powerful way to create an environment where the students can begin to develop their personal therapeutic identity and receive and achieve experiential knowledge they can transfer and unfold in the internship in the 6th semester. CGMS helps the students to begin identifying situations in therapeutic endeavours where they are 'not in tune' yet (see Chapter 1). This is a way to help them view themselves as an upcoming therapist, realizing and acknowledging situations and events where they were in tune and were not in tune with themselves, and/or the client's needs or situation. Knowing when you are and when you are not in tune are important steps of building therapist identity and clinical skills.

References

Bloom, B.S., Engelhart, M.D., Furst, E.J., Hill, W.H., & Krathwohl, D.R. (1956). *Taxonomy of Educational Objectives: The Classification of Educational Goals. Handbook. Cognitive Domain.* David McKay Company.

Bruscia, K. (1987). *Improvisational Models of Music Therapy.* Barcelona Publishers.

Hmelo-Silver, C.E., Bridges, S.M., & McKeown, J.M. (2019). 'Facilitating Problem-Based Learning.' In M. Moallem, W. Hung, & N. Dabbagh (eds), *The Wiley Handbook of Problem-Based Learning.* Wiley Blackwell.

Kolmos, A., Du, X., Holgaard, J.E., & Jensen, L.P. (2008). *Facilitation in a PBL Environment.* AAU Online Publication.

Wigram, A.L. (2002). 'Free Improvisation Therapy? The Alvin Model.' In T. Wigram, I.N. Pedersen, & L.O. Bonde (eds), *A Comprehensive Guide to Music Therapy. Theory, Clinical Practice, Research and Training.* Jessica Kingsley Publishers.

Wigram, T. (1996). 'From theory to practice: Role playing clients as an experiential technique to develop music therapy skills with advanced level music therapy students.' Paper to the 8th World Conference of Music Therapy, Hamburg, Germany.

Wigram, T. (1997). 'Musicoterapia: Estructura y flexibilidad en el proceso de musicoterapia [Music therapy: Structure and flexibility in the music therapy process].' In F. Palacios & P. del Campo (eds), *La Música como Proceso Humano Amaru Ediciones. Colección Música, arte y proceso [Music as a human process].* Bind 1.

Wigram, T. (2004). *Improvisation.* Jessica Kingsley Publishers.

CHAPTER 8

Individual Training Therapy

Charlotte Lindvang

> *Be patient to all that is unsolved in your heart and*
> *try to love the questions themselves...*

Rainer Maria Rilke (1929)

Introduction

This chapter focuses on the mandatory course of individual training therapy (ITT) that students follow during the fourth year of their training in music therapy at Aalborg University. The study curriculum sets a common starting point, a list of learning objectives, and a uniform framework for the course. Nevertheless, each student has a unique process with personal authentic themes as a focal point. The students enter a therapeutic relationship, experience the client position in music therapy on their own body, and reflect on the feelings and thoughts that emerge. Training therapist and student mutually reflect on the process as a whole in relation to the student's future professional life as a music therapist. The chapter presents a section on ethical considerations on this learning process and concludes with theoretical contributions and a perspective related to lifelong learning as a therapist.[1]

Since the start of the music therapy programme at Aalborg University in 1982, ITT has been a mandatory part of the curriculum. ITT is a short-term psychotherapeutic music therapy course of 8 sessions, placed at the beginning of the Master's degree level (4th year/7th semester).

---

[1] The chapter builds on the study curriculum, the author's former experience as an individual training therapist, as well as student interviews (Lindvang, 2010), and an interview done by Hannibal in 2018 with the current individual training therapists who have as well proofread this chapter.

Few students have experienced individual music therapy when they reach the Master's level and the course of individual training therapy. In most cases, students are ready for further development and ITT has a strong impact on them. ITT is a room of continuity in which the students can concentrate on personal and relational themes that may have surfaced during the preceding years of music therapy training.

As students begin to study at the Master's level, their feeling of responsibility grows, and the learning processes become more personal and at the same time more professional. ITT facilitates that students engage in therapy sessions as a student-client in order to grow as a person – in their own unique way. Closely connected to that, the common focal point is an elaborated formation of a future ethical and professional music therapist.

Individual Training Therapy seen in context and relation to other learning areas

On entering the Master's level, students take a quantum leap in relation to theoretical, musical, and therapeutic learning. At the Master's level, the students are more aware of the upcoming complex tasks in music therapy that lie ahead. ITT provides a continuation of learning experiences from being in the client position as well as the therapist position in past and present learning processes. Chapter 2 presents a figure that gives an overview of the curriculum. Parallel to ITT, students also follow advanced courses in Music Therapy Theory, Clinical Improvisation, and Music Therapy Assessment (an optional module), which all together constitutes a new and advanced level in the training. On the one hand, it is a huge task to enter individual therapeutic processes, while you are at the same time advancing in the academics. On the other hand, students report that ITT is like having a safe place that supports you while being in a demanding process of navigating between all the different subjects and exams on the expert level of training (Lindvang, 2010).

In the Group Training Therapy (GTT) students had the possibility of learning through the resonance and mirroring that took place between peers in the group. In GTT, the training therapist structured the steps of the learning process and facilitated specific themes of the group work. Now in ITT the students have the possibility of taking up the whole space, allowing the intensity of an individual focus and receiving the full attention from the training therapist.

The individual training therapy process prepares the student for participation in the therapy courses that follow ITT. This includes Intertherapy (8th semester; see Chapter 10), BMGIM level 1 (Bonny Method of Guided Imagery and Music – an optional module), in which the students work in dyads as both 'guide' and 'traveller' (8th semester; see Chapter 11), and the long internship with accompanying individual and group supervision (9th semester; see Chapter 12).

Overall learning objectives of Individual Training Therapy

The Aalborg curriculum divides the learning objectives of ITT into three domains: knowledge, skills, and competences. Overall, the students gain knowledge about short-term psychotherapy based on a psychodynamic theory ground. Students get to know how it feels, and what it means, to be in the client's position in a short-term therapy and they gain insight into their conflict-material as well as their resourceful, creative, and relational potentials. Students also gain knowledge about the importance of the therapist's ability to self-care in the context of music therapeutic work.

Concerning skills, ITT aims at building students' ability to open up, share, investigate, and reflect on their own experiences. Students develop their level of reflection concerning the role of the music in the therapeutic process as well as their ability to describe their musical experiences and the therapeutic process adapting a professional terminology.

Altogether, ITT aims at increasing students' awareness and extending their tolerance. Students are learning to explore their own feelings and needs, to register and regulate their own energy and emotional states, to access their own musical and creative capabilities, and they prepare themselves to apply these competencies in the future work in a position as music therapist.

The setting of Individual Training Therapy
Time and space

At the time of writing Aalborg University has employed three individual training therapists. For some of the students ITT takes place in a private clinic in the town outside the programme, and for some students in the therapy room at the Music House where the music therapy programme is located.

It is important to plan the ITT sessions in a way that secures the right rhythm in the process and, at the same time, considers the planning of other teaching courses and exams. There must be sufficient space between the sessions without spreading them too much. Usually, the first sessions are closer than the rest of the sessions for the training therapist and the student to get to know each other and build a therapeutic alliance. Each of the eight sessions lasts 50 minutes. Students are required to participate in all eight sessions and training therapists find alternative dates in case of illness.

Recording

Both training therapists and students record the sessions or parts of the sessions – for their own use – and with the obligation to keep the material safe according to GDPR. At the beginning of their music therapy training, students sign a consent form concerning recordings in various teaching courses during the Bachelor's and Master's level. The consent includes allowing training therapists to use the recordings for general preparation for sessions, as well as for sharing recordings if needed in supervision. Training therapists consent to delete all material after the course has terminated.

Ethical considerations and precautions

The study board requires that the training therapist is a member of the Danish Association for Music Therapists and complies with the ethical guidelines prescribed by the association. Furthermore, training therapists must be members of the Danish Association for Psychotherapists *or* have the amount of session experiences from practice, the amount of supervision hours, and of personal therapy sessions equivalent to the requirements for admission to the Psychotherapist Association.

ITT is an indispensable stepping-stone and an integrated part of the music therapy programme as a whole. The training therapists know and refer to the curriculum in meeting the students in ITT. Thus, each student receives the course of individual music therapy under the same terms and conditions. ITT is at the same time a confidential space for the students and the training therapists do not report anything to the teaching team at the programme about the students' processes. However, training therapists have a duty to report, in agreement with the student, to the leader of the study board if a student has serious problems that prevent them from learning and thriving as a student. It also happens on rare occasions that a student, on the training therapist's recommendation, applies for permission from the study board to extend the course of individual music therapy with one or two more sessions to be able to round off ITT in a proper way. On other occasions the training therapist advises a student to seek a long-term individual therapy when the process in ITT has finished. This may happen if for example traumatic experiences seem to need more support than the coming Intertherapy can provide.[2]

Training therapists who take care of ITT know that the student can continue

---

2   Music therapists employed in the university do not offer private additional therapy to students during the time that they are students.

the therapeutic learning processes in Intertherapy, GIM Level 1, and in supervision in relation to the coming internship. Even so, it is of great importance to make a student aware if there is a heavy issue that needs further processing. Training therapists give feedback to the students about 'blind spots' and the responsibility when working with future clients, i.e., the ability to take care of their own countertransference. Students will gradually get to know, through experiences in training therapy, that every professional music therapist needs to get supervision occasionally or regularly during their future professional work.

The employed training therapists who take care of ITT only do training therapy; they do not have any other teaching tasks at the music therapy programme. This boundary ensures that the students will not meet one of the individual training therapists in an evaluating role at any point during the education.

The music therapy milieu in Denmark is small and the students will most likely meet the training therapist on other occasions in the years to come, for example at the annual national meeting for music therapists. The training therapists inform that they will keep confidentiality and always leave it to the students how their future contact can be.

Training therapists receive supervision but do not seek supervision from educators in the music therapy programme in order to keep the duty of confidentiality. The short course of individual training therapy places great demands on supervision, since the training therapist needs to be quick in the processing of emotional material as well as cognitive or existential questions raised in the therapy. Supervision is an essential element to staying present in each unique student-process and at the same time keep in mind the framework and learning objectives of the training therapy. In supervision, the training therapist practises, in line with the psychodynamic approach, what we want to teach students: to be continuously open for investigating the relationship, to be aware of own contributions, transference and countertransference, and for new opportunities to support the therapeutic learning processes in the best possible way.

The combination of music and verbalizing elements in the sessions

Music therapy students are ready to enter the musical interaction in ITT. With three years of training, they are able to apply music for self-expression, and to orient themselves in the many layers that are present in the musical interaction in ITT. Music therapy students have different, and often particularly good, prerequisites than many other clients in music therapy – still during ITT they have the possibility to explore themselves through music and to experience from within how it feels to step into something unknown and undefined. Some students are musically trained to an extent where it can be difficult to let go of what they have learned and to be investigative in the music. Sometimes training therapists suggest that students close their eyes while playing, to support an inward attention and thereby be acquainted with a minor loss of control.

Self-development in ITT happens through music-making, body-movement, and image-producing processes in music. It is an important learning objective that students feel comfortable about such explorations, since a part of their future job will be to be able to work exploratively in a creative field and to motivate others to do the same. As a part of that, it is a further learning objective to expand the ability to stay present in the music and be in resonance with whatever is present in the mind or feelings or in the body. It is an important part of the learning process to connect the inner authentic feelings with the extrovert musical expression – to remain listening while playing and keep searching for their own tonal language.

In ITT, both active and receptive music therapy methods are applied – with most weight on the active improvisational domain. Sometimes the training therapist plays a piece of pre-composed music or provides a piece of music in a recorded version, for example, in order to calm down a student who is highly stressed. By regulating the nervous system, the student is more ready to focus on concrete themes at stake. It might also be exactly what the student needs to develop: the ability to regulate the nervous system with support from music listening.

During ITT the music can be seen as an agent or catalyst that connects students to deeper layers of their personality, their values, and their problems and longings. Every time music is applied, the process is deepening, and the landmark moments often happen in the music. Music opens the senses, opens an inner experience space, opens the shared space between student and training therapist, and paves the way to aesthetics – and students do not always have to verbalize an understanding of the experience – sometimes the nourishment lies in the silence that follows the musical expressions.

However, it is, as mentioned above, also an essential learning objective to be able to reflect verbally and the training therapist invites students to describe their experiences and dive into investigative dialogues about the experiences in the music. In each individual therapy, the training therapist and student will find a unique balance between musical and verbal contact and communication.

The sessions in ITT last 55–60 minutes. If a session starts with a verbal conversation, the training therapist is aware of the time and suggests moving into the music after 10–15 minutes to provide enough space for the musical investigations and interactions and prevent the participants from thinking too much and possibly getting lost in a long conversation. It is always a delicate balance between therapeutic learning objectives at stake. Trust in the nonverbal art-based and intuitive process should go hand-in-hand with a developing consciousness, awareness, and growing understanding.

On a metacognitive level, the training therapists sometimes apply psycho-educative elements during sessions. For example, the training therapist can draw a simplified model to illustrate dynamics in relational patterns that the student now starts to realize. However, it is a short course with only eight sessions, and if possible, the training therapist lets the therapeutic process move organically until the last couple of sessions – before suggesting looking at the process from an analytical meta-perspective. In the last session, training therapist and student review the course of sessions and reflect together about the most prominent learning elements and outcomes.

It is worthwhile to mention that it sometimes happens that a student is aware about important issues on the level of sensation and musical interaction, but only much later, a conscious and coherent understanding emerges (Pedersen, 2019).

As the training therapists navigate between various elements in each ITT session, they need a broad spectrum of music therapy methods and verbal techniques in their toolbox as well as a well-developed trust in the process, trust in their own and the students' intuition, and not least a good sense of timing.

Progression of the course of Individual Training Therapy
Preparation
When music therapy students arrive at the individual therapy, they have built a basic understanding of the relevance of learning the profession through a personal experience through music therapy. They get an introductory letter from the training therapist in order to prepare for the course. The letter explains the formalities around the course, such as timeframe and schedule. The training therapist advises the student to make time and space around the sessions to be able to tune in before, and digest and integrate the therapy experiences afterwards.

The course of individual training therapy requires that the students prepare for the process by re-reading their therapeutic portfolio (personal logbook) and their final assignment from GTT as well as notes from CGMS and from the internship in the 6th semester, including their report on supervision. Going through the former learning processes will support the students in being aware of where they are in their ongoing process of formation and support them to be able to decide an appropriate and authentic starting point or focus for the Individual Training Therapy. Students' preparation and ongoing commitment is extremely important and valuable in order to benefit as much as possible from this short-term therapy.

The curriculum contains a relevant list of literature about training therapy, therapists' listening perspectives, relational, analytical, and existential approaches to therapy, etc. that students read in their own rhythm. Training therapist and student usually do not discuss this literature during the therapy sessions where the learning is embedded in and embodied through intuitive and relational processes.

Building a therapeutic relationship and alliance

It is obvious that even though the individual course is a part of the curriculum and has the same structure and learning objectives every time, each training therapist and each student is different and therefore each individual therapy course is unique. For example, some students have many work and life experiences as their reference points during ITT, whereas some students are young, and not that experienced. Students have different ideas about what it might be like to enter ITT. Some students are uncertain about stepping into an individual therapy and others have a complete plan concerning the therapeutic process that is about to take off. The training therapist does not know anything about the student before starting the course. When they meet for the first time, it is a new situation for both of them.

It is the therapeutic relationship that provides access to the unique learning, and students have expressed how they learn to think less and relate more during training therapy. During ITT, the student has a chance to realize that building a relationship takes time and the training allows the student to explore the meeting and realize that human relations to a great degree are communicated in tacit ways (Lindvang, 2010).

In ITT, the student has a safe and confidential space where they can expose vulnerable themes, and feelings of insufficiency or shortcomings in the music or therapeutic skills. They also have the possibility to explore incidents from their life history that they have chosen not to share in the group training therapy or in other training contexts.

Getting started

In the first couple of sessions, the training therapist forms an impression of who the student is. It is important that the student feels safe and likes to attend the sessions to make it a resonant field of learning.

In the first session, the training therapist informs the student about the frame, setting, methods, and ethical guidelines but takes care not to overload the student with too much information. Furthermore, the training therapist interviews the student in order to identify a main theme for the course. Usually, this interview is very open and directed by what the student would like to share and finds important to say.

It is a priority to improvise together already in the first session. It helps the training therapist and student to be present and to meet each other in a different way. Either it can be a non-referential improvisation, or student and therapist will decide on a play-rule related to the themes they have discussed. The training therapist will support the student in the musical interaction through matching, accompanying, amplifying, etc., and investigate the student's flexibility, listening capacity, expressiveness, etc.

Defining an overall theme for the individual therapy course

An overall theme for the short course varies from student to student. For example, the theme can be related to a general existential problem like anxiety, identity, or loneliness, or it can be related to a concrete emotion that the student needs to investigate more, like anger or joy, or a concrete event from the internship that the student experienced as a possible key to development. Close relationships to, for example, parents, siblings, partner, or fellow students often emerge during the course, either as an explicit theme for the students or as an integrated part of their whole being.

The trainee therapist can want to address challenges that have come up for them as part of their role as therapist during the internship, such as a fear of doing harm or a fear of not being good enough to fill out the role as therapist, or the need to build more trust in their own musical skills or in their own intuition. It could also be that the student has identified a relational pattern, like a marked withdrawal, when feeling misunderstood or a significant ignoring of their own impulses, both of which could be counterproductive in a future position as therapist.

Sometimes a student brings a theme of a more traumatic character, for example loss of a parent, abuse, or psychological illness in their close family. Such private shocking or sad events may be crucial to process in order to be equipped for future tasks as a music therapist. Furthermore, self-care is a recurring issue – students often have a stressful everyday life, and it is common that it takes some time to become present and grounded in the therapy session. Many students (and music therapists) feel an urge to help others and they risk ignoring their own needs, which could be exhausting and reduce their professional ability over time.

Even though the student and training therapist agree on a main theme, it may very well transform or lead into unforeseen directions during the process. Each student has a different progression. Still a theme is an important point of reference also later when the student looks back and reflects on the therapeutic learning.

Therapeutic learning outcomes

The student learns from being in the client position and, at the same time, the competencies as a future therapist are in focus. Accordingly, the learning outcomes are both personal and professional. It is important that students actually get the experience of a unique therapeutic space, of a therapeutic relationship, and an authentic therapeutic process including the unpredictability that comes with it – within the structures and frames of the curriculum.

It is a consistent underlying theme during ITT that students get insight into what it is like to sit in the client's chair and into the client perspective in relation to music therapy and specifically music therapeutic improvisation as a therapeutic medium. They learn about music therapy at an intensive and personal level in order to recognize and possibly change reactions and action patterns that could complicate their future therapist function. The more specific outcomes of ITT will vary from student to student. Students often uncover hidden resources, or they make already conscious resources more explicit and more in circulation through the interaction with the training therapist. Sometimes students may be at risk of feeling pressure of what they believe is the expected personality development and change, and they need to realize that becoming a therapist is not an ideal of perfection they must live up to – rather it is essential to discover what it means to be authentic, honest, and present.

In most ITT courses, there are special moments, pivotal moments (Grocke, 1999): these moments are transformational. In an interview study with students close to graduation (Lindvang, 2010, 2013), it was found that these moments usually emerge in nonverbal experiences, in music or in close relation to an experience in music. The student may experience the self at another age, may get intense experiences of inner images, may get a completely new sense of grounding, may feel and receive support from the training therapist for the first time, or may have a transcending, spiritual experience. A new perspective.

ITT motivates students to let go of the mask and let the underlying emotional layers emerge and become shareable, which often has a liberating effect and provides renewed energy to meet new personal and professional challenges. Sometimes, students may be nervous that their own wounds from life experiences might be a burden in the therapeutic work in the future. However, through ITT, they begin to realize that overcoming difficulties and learning to tolerate, take care of, and listen to their own vulnerability can turn out as empathic recourses as a therapist.

One student, who analysed the themes of their own processes in training therapy (both group and individual) in their Master's thesis, identified that several key areas had developed and led to the following outcomes:

- From now on, I feel more equipped for new challenges and an upcoming job

- I no longer have the same reservations about new and unknown situations

- I feel better equipped to handle counter-transference in relations with future clients

- I have become much freer in improvisations

- More peace of mind about being who I am and being able to do what I feel like

(Pedersen, 2019, p.45)

Vignette

One student shared how her former job required that she work very fast, effectively, and flawlessly. She suffered from burnout symptoms, decided to change career, and started her music therapy training.

The student was surprised to find out that exactly what had given her the burnout symptoms was still prevailing and difficult to get rid of. The student improvised together with the training therapist and allowed herself to practise slowing down and to investigate without knowing the exact outcome – trying to be open to what would emerge in the intersubjective field. In the beginning, this was quite uncomfortable and challenging for her. The student's peer group had also been responding to her that she was 'pushing' a little in the process of being a group-leader in the group-leading exercises, like insisting on a specific outcome, rather than just listening and being open towards the dynamics of the group. She was happy that the group had the courage to mirror her, and that she could return to ITT and investigate this theme further. She recognized that she needed to heal deep emotions stemming from the past: she always had 'to be perfect and clever' in order to be accepted as a child. She also recognized that she had continued the pattern as a grown-up in her former job, where she had the breakdown.

The student found out that it is not enough to know what you need to change in your life – you have to experience the change deeply, which became possible for her in the music improvisations and through the therapeutic process altogether in ITT.

The student pointed out that it was essential that the training therapist followed her closely in the process. When practising letting go of perfection in the improvisations, she needed support to let go. However, in the end she found a completely new strength in the ability to be open and came to accept this new part of her as something very precious for her future therapy identity.[3]

Between the sessions

Students do important work between sessions by reading their notes and listening to or watching their recordings, that is, watching the experience 'from the outside'. One student experienced each individual therapy session as a process in three parts: being in the session, 1) feeling the body and being present in the music, 2) with a part of the mind being aware of what was happening; at home after the session, 3) playing back the recording of the session, reflecting on the process (Lindvang, 2010, p.158).

Moreover, training therapists motivate students to follow up on the process by, for example, making a drawing to illustrate an important experience or to write a poem or a song that expresses and acknowledges the insights from the session. Both the preparation for the coming session and the post-session processing are likely to enhance the benefits and learning outcomes for the student.

The student's final assignment

The student keeps a personal diary (logbook) of all sessions, partly to promote the ability to reflect as part of the therapeutic learning process, and partly to have notes available for the final assignment required at the end of the course.

In the final assignment, the student describes and reflects on the most

---

3   The vignette is fictitious – fabricated based on many students' similar processes.

important change and developmental processes the individual course has initiated for the student, with an emphasis on the role of music. Moreover, the student includes an in-depth analysis of their own resources and developmental potentials in relation to a future music therapist identity and future work with clients.

The assignment has to be between three and five pages. Thus, the student needs to give a condensed description of the therapy. It is also emphasized that the student is able to use relevant music therapeutic and psychotherapeutic terminology, including using concepts within the psychodynamic and existential framework of understanding.

An examiner outside the teaching team evaluates the assignments as passed or not passed. It is the dissemination of the process that the examiner evaluates – and *not* the therapy itself, the content, or the themes. If an assignment does not pass the examiner informs the student what is missing, and the student re-writes the assignment. For example, if the student has not communicated about the role of the music, the assignment will not pass. The curriculum describes the requirements for dissemination.

The final assignment is an important part of the student's personal portfolio.

Theoretical underpinning

The course of individual training therapy is not a theory-driven process. However, an integrated theoretical framework based on a modern psychodynamic approach constitutes the foundation of the therapy. The first three chapters of this book thoroughly describe the theoretical foundation of the therapeutic track in Aalborg. In the following sections, further theoretical contributions will briefly point out, in addition to the introducing chapters, what training therapists in the Aalborg programme draw upon theoretically.

In contemporary psychoanalysis and psychodynamic tradition, the relational perspective is central. The characteristics and quality of the therapist's contribution to the relationship are crucial, as well as what the client brings, and moment-by-moment negotiation of relatedness takes place. The unconscious of both persons is at stake and transference and countertransference is happening in the co-constructed interactive processes in therapy. Thus, a richer understanding of dynamics between participants in therapy requires an awareness of the therapist's specific way of being and contributing, not only an understanding of the client's history and way of interacting (Binder *et al.*, 2006).

Mary Priestley – who founded the analytical music therapy orientation – developed the idea of offering training therapy in music therapy to music therapy students. In the early 1970s, Priestley offered private music therapy training to students: both individual training therapy and Intertherapy (see Chapter 10). Priestley emphasized the need to experience a therapeutic process as a client with the same tools that the future therapist is supposed to offer future clients (Priestley, 1994).

The American clinician, professor emeritus in psychiatry, and author Irvin D. Yalom recommends student-therapists seek personal therapy for at least three reasons. First, student-therapists must know themselves, also their dark sides, to be able to empathize with future clients. Second, students' experience of the therapeutic process from the client's seat are important, including, for example, the need for acceptance and warmth from the therapist. Third, Yalom mentions the fact that working as a therapist can be a demanding enterprise and student-therapists need to build awareness, inner strength, and coping strategies related to that (Yalom, 2003).

Building trust

When the course of individual training therapy begins, it is a primary task for the training therapist to establish a safe and trusting contact between student and training therapist. This is a common factor in most psychotherapy traditions (Hougaard & Østergård, 2021). Music therapy students will carry the therapeutic learning of building trust, and of sensing the affective attunement from the therapist, into the future work with clients in the field.

Apprentice training

Even though students are in the client position during ITT and dive into their personal developmental process, they observe how the training therapist works – with a part of their mind – and internalize methods and types of interventions that the training therapist applies.

As presented in Chapter 2, an individual course of training therapy may resemble apprenticeship learning. In an interview study (Grimmer & Tribe, 2001) the participants experienced personal therapy during their training as a socialization experience – as part of a rite of passage into the professional role. This type of learning happens in relationships and through practical experiences i.e., learning through modelling – it is a 'bottom-up' type of learning – without formal teaching (Nielsen & Kvale, 2004). A 'bottom-up' type of learning is also known as an 'implicit to explicit' learning, a wording that refers to processes where knowledge firstly emerges as a bodily experience, then it connects to affect and cognition (Hart, 2012).

Carl Rogers emphasized the need for empathic understanding of the client in his classic article 'The necessary and sufficient conditions of therapeutic personality change' (1957). Still today, there is an agreement across different psychotherapy theories that an empathic attitude of the therapist is a central issue. Clients profit enormously from the experience of being seen accurately and fully understood. As the training therapists are empathic to the students, they will teach them to be empathic to others. Being empathic is an everyday phenomenon – however, the trainee therapist needs to discover that 'it is extraordinarily difficult to know really what the other feels; far too often we project our own feelings onto the other' (Yalom, 2003, p.21). This is the reason that training of the 'mentalizing muscle' is highly relevant during ITT.

Developing mentalizing capacity

As emphasized in the introductory chapters, experiences of being adequately emotionally attuned and regulated in the (mentalizing) consciousness of trusted others are of great importance. To get a response and to repair possible misunderstandings is necessary in order to develop into mature autonomous individuals, with the ability for self-regulation and mentalization (Bateman & Fonagy, 2012).

Students in training therapy work on integrating not only their thoughts, feelings, and bodily reactions but also their past, present, and future in an expanded empathic self-understanding. The ability to mentalize makes it possible to tune into the mind and state of others, such as future clients, which is a help when trying to understand or even anticipate their actions and reactions (Hart, 2012). Openness to discovering oneself and others in new ways, and to being surprised and enriched by the process, are essential components in a mentalizing capacity, which is needed in order to offer ethically responsible therapy (Fonagy & Allison, 2014).

Here-and-now in focus

Mentalization theory builds on the psychodynamic understanding that early attachment, past life circumstances, and life events influence who we are today. Nonetheless, the primary focus of mentalization-based therapy is in the here-and-now: what is happening in the here-and-now and how it feels to investigate the here-and-now (Bateman & Fonagy, 2012). In ITT this means that student and training therapist may go back to 'there-and-then' in the student's past, but only to come back to 'here-and-now' and the intersubjective field in the music and in the verbal conversation.

Individual Training Therapy is primarily an experience-based therapy. The student is creatively experiencing and expressing through playing and moving in an intersubjective space together with the training therapist in the here-and-now. The exploration and new insights are partly happening tacitly.

The here-and-now focus is also present in the experiential therapy tradition stemming from Rogers and Perls (Elliott & Parthyka, 2005). It is the concrete phenomenological reality of the client and the concrete emotional experience in the therapy, as well as the mirroring from the therapist, which is interesting, and not the past in itself. Experiential therapy applies phenomenological experiments during the sessions in order to work through, for example, ambivalent emotions in a close relationship (Elliott & Parthyka, 2005). In music therapy, it is possible to stage the issues in the music. In ITT the training therapist can represent, for example, a relative, or let different instruments represent certain affects, situations, family members, etc.

The American psychologist Daniel Stern holds that therapeutic change takes place in the relationship in the here-and-now interactions and in the implicit domain (see Chapter 3). For example, in an improvisation in training therapy the student can experience new ways of being together and 'present moments of meetings' (Stern, 2004). In fact, Stern advocated for music therapy and other arts-based psychotherapies as important ways of working therapeutically in the nonverbal domain (Stern, 2010 [**AQ**]). Stern states:

> The basic assumption is that change is based on lived experience. In and of itself, verbally understanding, explaining, or narrating something is not sufficient to bring about change. There must also be an actual experience, a subjectively lived happening. An event must be lived, with feelings and actions taking place in real time, in the real world, with real people, in a moment of presentness. (Stern 2004, p.xiii)

Corrective emotional experiences and creating new narratives

A caring therapeutic relationship in itself may become a corrective emotional experience if, for example, the student in earlier close relationships has experienced being scolded or even abandoned when expressing emotions. If a student during ITT experiences empathic resonance from the training therapist, in either shared music or in a verbal conversation or both, it may be an important step towards acceptance of their own feelings and maybe towards an expanded tolerance of feelings in general.

During ITT, students investigate more or less intensively their own life story, and through the training therapist's listening, witnessing, and mirroring, the students gradually reformulate (parts of) their narrative. The training therapist and student together apply music in order to expand the personal narrative. Through musical explorations, it is possible to add new memories, details, emotions, and perspectives of the narrative and thereby manifest, reinforce, or change the story. The student may have had a certain narrative incorporated from early childhood, for example of being too noisy and dominating. Going through an investigative process reveals that this tells more about the family situation than about the student's personal character, and the student can then build up a more congruent and authentic narrative (White, 2007). A new narrative can lead to a release of guilt and bound energy. This process empowers the student and opens the gate to courage and new opportunities in relationships.

Psychoeducational elements

According to Yalom (2003), an important axiom for education and for therapy as well is that people learn best through personal participation in interaction, combined with observation and analysis of that interaction. When the training therapist includes psychoeducational elements by taking a meta-perspective and explaining to the student how it is possible to see and understand the student's thoughts, feelings, and psychological process, it can help the student to understand what is happening. This is a metacognitive approach, which is an element in many different theoretical orientations and in music therapy and music therapy training therapy as well (Jeppesen & Sørensen, 2013). The new understanding may further motivate the student and increase trust and giving in to the therapy ('top-down learning'). The activation of an intellectual understanding is a way to cast light into the process and not an isolated intervention. From gaining new understanding, student and training therapist may move on into music again, in order to translate for example a body sensation into music or express how it feels to reach a new insight, or simply to sense the contact between them in music.

Yalom presents the Johari window as a useful model in groups as well as in individual therapy. The model consists of four quadrants/domains. One domain – known to self as well as known to others – is called the 'open area'. Another domain is known to self but unknown to others and is called the 'hidden area'. A third domain is unknown to self but known to others – the 'blind area'. The fourth domain is both unknown to self and others and is named the `unconscious area' (Yalom, 2003).

The model is just a simple map compared to the complexity of the reality and the inner life of each student. However, during ITT the model can serve to help the students expand their self-knowledge. To know and understand that all four quadrants are human may, for example, prevent the student from feeling wrong or stupid when discovering some of their blind spots. During ITT, the students often grow the size of the open area quadrant because of becoming able to share with the training therapist (and as a result, a growing openness in other relationships). The size of the other three quadrants may be appreciably diminished, as the students explore themselves in the interactional music and verbal exchanges and gradually become acquainted with deeper levels of themselves as well as acquainted with mentalizing processes.

Tolerance for uncertainty

The present chapter began with a quote from the Austrian poet Rainer Maria Rilke (1929). The quote points to the value of patience – it invites us to love the unfixed, tolerate the unknown, and find courage to be open-minded, present, and enduring in relation to difficulties in therapy as in life. The students' processes in ITT may lead to greater tolerance for uncertainty, which could seem a very humble outcome. However, due to the complexity of humans and of therapy, 'an important point in therapist and counselor development is when students begin to realize that entering into this knowledge world leads to questions as much as answers and that uncertainty keeps pace with certainty' (Skovholt, 2012, p.12). Maybe the quote can support the (coming) music therapist to look beyond acquiring skills, tools, and treatment plans during training, which in its worst case may result in a professional mask that blurs the authenticity and potential value of therapeutic relationships.

A lifetime of learning

Conducting music therapy will always require much more than technical proficiency. According to Rogers (1961), working as a therapist requires a lifetime of learning and a continuous process of 'personal becoming'. Students do not arrive at a terminus when the Individual Training Therapy course is over, nor when they complete the training programme after five years.

The therapeutic learning processes during training are just a starting point aiming at preparing for a professional life after graduation in which the novice music therapist is confident about the value of seeking support, inspiration, and professional growth in supervision, personal therapy, or other relevant contexts.

Priestley recommends music therapists find a lifestyle that balances with the demanding professional area of therapeutic work. She also recommends that music therapists, when needed, continue to work with their own difficulties in life through music therapy (Eschen, 2002).

References

Bateman, A.W. & Fonagy, P. (eds) (2012). *Handbook of Mentalizing in Mental Health Practice*. American Psychiatric Publishing.

Binder, P.E., Nielsen, G.H., Vøllestad, J., Holgersen, H., & Schance, E. (2006). 'Hva er rela-tionell psykoanalyse? Nye psykoanalytiske perspektiver på samhandling, det ubevisste og selvet. [What is relational psychoanalysis? New analytical perspectives on interaction, the unconscious and the self]'. *Tidsskrift for Norsk psykologforening [Journal of the Norwegian Psychologist Association]* 43(9), 899–908

Elliott, R. & Parthyka, R. (2005). 'Personal Therapy and Growth Work in Experiential-Human-istic Therapies.' In J. Geller, J.C. Norcross, & D.E. Orlinsky (eds), *The Psychotherapist's Own Psychotherapy*. Oxford University Press.

Eschen, J.T. (2002). *Analytical Music Therapy*. Jessica Kingsley Publishers.

Fonagy, P. & Allison, E. (2014). 'The role of mentalizing and epistemic trust in the therapeutic relationship.' *Psychotherapy, 51*(3), 372–380.

Grimmer, A. & Tribe, R. (2001). 'Counselling psychologists' perceptions of the impact of man-datory personal therapy on professional development – an exploratory study.' *Counselling Psychology Quarterly, 14*(4), 287–301.

Grocke, D.E. (1999). 'A phenomenological study of pivotal moments in Guided Imagery and Music (GIM) therapy.' Doctoral dissertation. Faculty of Music, The University of Mel-bourne. Accessed on 10/12/21 at www.wfmt.info/Musictherapyworld/modules/archive/stuff/papers/ErdoGroc.pdf.

Hart, S. (ed.) (2012). *Neuroaffektiv psykoterapi med voksne [Neuroaffective psychotherapy with adults]*. Hans Reitzels Forlag.

Hougaard, E. & Østergård, O.K. (2021). *Kort og godt om psykoterapi [On psychotherapy – in short]*. Dansk Psykologisk Forlag.

Jeppesen, L.A. & Sørensen, L.V. (2013). *At leve sin terapi [To live your therapy]*. Mindspace.

Lindvang, C. (2010). 'A field of resonant learning: Self-experiential training and the development of music therapeutic competencies.' PhD thesis. Aalborg University. Accessed on 12/05/22 at https://vbn.aau.dk/da/publications/a-field-of-resonant-learning-self-experiential-training-and-the-d.

Lindvang, C. (2013). 'Resonant learning: A qualitative inquiry into music therapy students' self-experiential learning processes.' *Qualitative Inquiries in Music Therapy, 8*, 1–30.

Nielsen, K. & Kvale, S. (2004). 'Mesterlære som aktuel læringsform [Apprenticeship as current teaching approach].' In K. Nielsen & S. Kvale (eds), *Mesterlære. Læring som social praksis [Apprenticeship. Learning as a social practice]*. Hans Reitzels Forlag.

Pedersen, K.E.V. (2019). 'Nonspecific, relational competencies.' Master's thesis, unpublished. Department of Communication & Psychology, Aalborg University.

Priestley, M. (1994). *Essays on Analytical Music Therapy*. Barcelona Publishers.

Rilke, R.M. (1929). *Letters to a Young Poet*. Harvard University Press.

Rogers, C.R. (1957). 'The necessary and sufficient conditions of therapeutic personality change.' *Journal of Consulting Psychology, 21*(2), 95–103.

Rogers, C.R. (1961). *On Becoming a Person*. Constable.

Skovholt, T.M. (2012). *Becoming a Therapist. On the Path to Mastery*. John Wiley & Sons, Inc.

Stern, D.N. (2004). *The Present Moment in Psychotherapy and Everyday Life*. W.W. Norton & Co.

Stern, D.N. (2010). *Forms of vitality: Exploring dynamic experience in psychology, the arts, psychotherapy and development.* Oxford University Press

White, M. (2007). *Maps of Narrative Practice.* W.W. Norton & Co.

Yalom, I.D. (2003). *The Gift of Therapy. An Open Letter to a New Generation of Therapists and Their Patients.* Piatkus.

CHAPTER 9

Psychodynamic-Oriented Music Therapeutic Group Leading

A LEARNING SPACE WITH MULTIPLE LEVELS OF EXPERIENCE AND REFLECTION

Bolette Daniels Beck

In the unfolding human encounter in a group, spontaneous expression, interaction, and dialogues occur, where past and present psychological material blends and where new patterns emerge.

Introduction

The experience of carrying out sessions and getting feedback in a reflexive learning environment is indispensable and highly qualifying for the music therapy student. This chapter describes the course Psychodynamic-oriented Music therapeutic Group leading (PMG) in which each of the students carries out a music therapy session under direct supervision from the teacher with a group of peer students who are working with their own authentic material. The students prepare a focus and a structure for their session, they receive a pre-supervision, and after the session they evaluate the session and get feedback from the group members, student observers, and the teacher. The learning focus is on improving flexible group leading skills in psychodynamic group music therapy with healthy clients. There is also a specific focus on facilitating verbal processing of experiences of receptive and active music therapy exercises, and on evaluating and reflecting on emerging group dynamics in the session. The group training format is complex and multidimensional, and a model of three levels of reflection is presented.

The Aalborg music therapy education subject PMG is an advanced course, where the students take turns to lead a group music therapy session with a group of fellow students, under direct supervision. The framework for the course was created by Inge Nygaard Pedersen in 1991 with the purpose to train the students in music and verbal therapeutic work with normal clients in group dynamic forms (Pedersen, 2002). The course is informed by psychodynamic therapy theory, which means that there is an emphasis on the intrapersonal and interpersonal relational processes and dynamics in the group as it plays out in both musical and verbal interactions. Over the years, the course has been developed and refined, but it still contains the same basic elements. This chapter will describe the overall framework and goals of the course, exemplify the learning processes through case vignettes, and discuss theoretical aspects underlying the practice and teaching.

Placement in the education

The PMG course is placed in the first year of the Master's degree in music therapy (fourth year of the full course), where the students are trained in becoming music psychotherapists in clinical settings. As part of the Bachelor programme, the students have been taught the fundamental theoretical concepts of psychodynamic therapy theory, have acquired improvisation skills and techniques, have been trained in how to reflect on their own practice, and have participated in music therapy training therapy in groups in the first one-and-a-half years (see Chapter 5). Furthermore, they have been trained in the application of active and receptive music therapy techniques in another group leading subject, Clinical Group Music Therapy Skills (CGMS; see Chapter 7), a training format where the students take turns to be the music therapist for groups of peer students who are roleplaying as clients with different types of diagnoses and problems. In their Bachelor internship, some of the students have worked with verbal processing with clients.

This subject is the first in the Master's programme to work with therapeutic relationships and reflect on therapeutic processes with non-clinical clients using concepts and theory from the psychodynamic therapy framework. Instead of playing roles as in CGMS, the students now enter a client position contributing with their own authentic reactions, themes, and problems. Instead of focusing on the facilitation of musical processes as in CGMS, the students are here specifically trained in leading a therapeutic verbal discussion with a minimum length of 30 minutes.

Following the PMG course, the students continue to experience individual training music therapy, where they can go into depth with themes that came up during the PMG sessions, and Intertherapy where they work as a music therapist for a fellow student under direct supervision.

Competencies

During the PMG course, the students learn to work out a session plan, carry out the session independently, and evaluate it afterwards. In the curriculum of the course, the following competencies are described:

- To independently lead a music therapy group by following a predefined structured plan and be more flexible by relating to the group dynamics

- To use the group members' resources and developmental potential and their mutual transference relationships professionally

- To direct complex and unpredictable music therapeutic work and development situations demanding new models of solutions

- To receive and give feedback to support the development of the individual student's music therapist identity

Furthermore, the course aims to develop new competencies, such as basic use of verbal processing skills, presence, and authority as a therapist, ability to tolerate their own emotions and help others to work with their emotions, and trusting oneself as a group leader.

Structure and content of the course

The PMG course begins with a theoretical introduction session covering psychodynamic therapy theory and verbal therapeutic communication skills, with small dyad exercises where the students are trained in basic verbal techniques, such as using open questions versus directive/closed questions, repeating important words/phrases of the client, and the ability to recognize and reflect on the clients' metaphors.

The course contains a weekly three-hour-long teaching session, and each of the students is responsible for one session in which they are the student music therapist and group leader. Each student group leader prepares a one-and-a-half-hour group music therapy session for a group of four to six of their fellow students. They structure their session programme around a self-chosen focus or theme related to adult self-development. The students can include theories, exercises, and approaches stemming from psychodynamic (music) therapy or from other therapeutic frameworks as long as they can name and reflect on their practice. Each student receives an individual pre-supervision with the teacher on their planning.

Planning the session

Concerning the session's structure, the students are asked to plan an opening activity (tuning in or warming up), one or two main activities (such as instrumental or voice improvisation, movement or music listening), a mandatory verbal reflection period of at least 30 minutes, and a closing activity. They can add several shorter verbal reflection periods if needed. As part of the preparation, the students consider timing, physical arrangement of the therapy room (placement of instruments, mattresses, and chairs), preparation of art materials, and check up on the sound equipment. Before their pre-supervision with the teacher, the students are required to describe their session in a written form (1–3 pages), including a description of their reflections on their therapist role as a group leader. An example of a session plan with the focus 'Grounding' could be:

- Body exercise to pre-recorded music (5 min.): Guiding to feel the body and imagine roots going downwards into the ground from the feet

- Presentation of the theme (5–10 min.): All group members briefly reflect on the theme

- Working through exercise (20 min.): Musical improvisation over two themes: a) feeling ungrounded, b) feeling grounded. The music therapist provides the shift with a bell

- Drawing (5 min.)

- Verbal reflection (30 min.)

- Closure (5–10 min.): Voice improvisation standing in a circle

In an investigation of student session plans in the period 2012–2020, I found that the themes fell into three categories: 1) sessions planned around a concept or theme that the student is engaged in personally at the moment, such as coping with stress or exploring self-esteem, balance, or strength; 2) sessions planned around roles in the musical improvisation (and subsequent perspectives in life), such as exploring oneself in the group, being a leader/follower, taking initiatives, supporting others, or receiving care; and finally, 3) themes related to more existential concepts, such as love, being versus doing, or loneliness. A few students chose to work with an open focus letting the group unfold its own themes through improvisation or imagery to music.

Pre-supervision

Around one week before the session, the students receive 45 minutes of individual supervision on their programme. The choice of activities related to the theme and the use of improvisation play-rules and exercises are discussed. The student is prepared to focus and present the theme and the exercises/activities clearly. Possible scenarios that could be played out in the group according to the chosen theme are imagined. The students also reflect on their therapist role and the type of leadership they plan to carry out. They are invited to reflect on concerns and fears related to the session and strategies to handle them during the session. For example, one student group leader thought about where to be placed in the room during an improvisation exercise. The example shows a deep sensitivity for the student-clients and also a novice's sensitivity about taking one's place in the room as a therapist:

> It is wildly problematic where to place myself when they are improvising! I should not play with them because of the imbalance in the therapist/client relationship. However, where could I be? I cannot sit in the middle of the circle or behind someone's back?[1]

The choice of pre-recorded music (for relaxation, movement, or imagery exercises) is closely examined in the supervision. After the supervision, the students often re-work their programme. The group participants do not see the programme in advance.

The teaching session

The structure of the three-hour PMG teaching session includes a brief introduction with the whole group together, the student-led one-and-a-half-hour group music therapy session, a break, and finally one hour of evaluation.

The introduction takes place in one great circle where all the students in the class participate, and where 5–10 minutes is used to 'check-in' and establish a safe learning space. One to three students are observers, and they are placed in the corners of the room. They are instructed to observe and take notes regarding the student-therapist's body language, use of voice, clarity of instructions and guiding, verbal, and musical interventions, leadership and presence, and the interaction with the group. The student-therapist carrying out the therapy session is responsible for time-taking and framework. The teacher stays in the

---

1   The quote is included with permission from the student.

room during the therapy session and is available for the student-therapist or participants if needed. One student videorecords the group therapy sessions and the post-session evaluation.

The process of a group music therapy session: Balancing flow and structure

To facilitate the therapeutic processes in a psychodynamic-oriented music therapy group, an overall goal for the group leader is to balance between flow and structure: being in the flow of music, emotions, and processes with the group and at the same time providing a structure and direction of the work. The session's theme and structure make it safe for the participants to explore themselves and their issues. The structure provides boundaries and grounding, and the theme can direct the attention so that the group members can work together on the same topic. At the same time, given the fluent character of music improvisation and group processes that are opening up unconscious layers of the psyche, it is also important for the group leader to be able to provide space for the unknown. The group leader is asked to try to resonate and empathize with the group, to let the process move in an unplanned direction and to find new solutions to the needs of the group here and now, also when that means that the original focus, programme, or timeframe must be changed on the spot. To enable a fluent balance between structure and emergent themes, the group leader can try out different kinds of leadership roles, with more or less structure, guiding, and participation.

The following example from the above-mentioned session with the theme Grounding illustrates the balance between preparation and unfolding of the session. The example is composed by the author with inspiration from different PMG sessions.

During the *non-grounded* part of the musical improvisation, the music was fragmented and out of pulse, and in the *grounded* part, the group found a common rhythm and ended up in a shared expression of energy and joy. The drawings reflected these two experiences, where the joyful and grounded part for some was represented by orange and red colours, and the non-grounded experience was expressed with thin black and blue lines. In the verbal reflection, all the group members described their drawings one by one. Several group members experienced a sense of insecurity and loneliness, not being connected to the group, and not being answered in their music by the others in the non-grounded part of the improvisation. The student-therapist had planned to discuss how grounding could be connected to personal self-confidence and music therapist identity but chose to follow the group's theme and invited the participants to discuss how non-grounding and grounding were related to the feeling of loneliness versus belonging to the group. The discussion was lively, and the group members affirmed each other's perspectives. One group member disclosed that he did not feel grounded in the body because of the stress in his life. Furthermore, he said that he generally disliked moving his body to music. The student-therapist expressed acceptance of this, and the session ended with a vocal improvisation with the whole group standing in a circle.

The evaluation and feedback after the session will be described below.

Evaluation

After the PMG session, the chairs are put back in the big circle for a round of feedback conducted by the teacher. During the feedback and evaluation rounds, an open atmosphere of shared learning is established by the teacher. The student-therapist is the first to reflect on their experience and can disclose any experience of failure, insecurity, fear, or other difficult emotion, as well as experiences of calmness and feeling at home in the therapist role.

The students are trained to give a useful and constructive peer evaluation. The group members, and after them the observers, give constructive peer feedback one by one, and they typically talk about the overall experience of the group leader's presence and authenticity in the role, the use of body language and voice, and the verbal interventions. If student feedback comes out in a hurtful way (which happens very rarely), the teacher has the responsibility to interfere, stop the feedback and process the reactions, and, if possible, harvest the potential learning of the feedback.

As part of the evaluation, the student-therapists are asked to reflect on their own dynamics and their perception of the group dynamics. The students must take a new role with group members they might know much about and some of whom might be their close friends from daily life. Even though they can fear their ability to balance peer roles, friendship, and a professional role, the group members' closeness can sometimes bring about sincere and valuable reflections. For example, in the evaluation round after a session, the friend of a student-therapist remarked:

I think you were very authentic. I really could feel you as being you, but you also

*managed to take a new kind of authority. It felt very safe to be in the group
with you.*

The composed case of the Grounding session is used to shed light on some
of the underlying transference processes that can happen in the group and the
therapist.

In the feedback from the student-clients, the student-therapist was praised for
shifting her focus and expanding on the themes of loneliness and belonging in
the verbal dialogue, because it helped them to be clearer about their need of
support and connection with others in their lives as students. While the student-therapist reflected on the verbal dialogue, she found out that even though
she managed to express acceptance of the student-client who expressed that
he disliked movement, she on a deeper level felt a bit criticized. She identified a
feeling of insecurity and vulnerability that she associated with a general fear of
inadequacy, a feeling she linked to critical remarks from her father. Some of the
other students revealed that they could feel the atmosphere change between
the training student and the client student in that moment, and that it did not
seem as if the dialogue was rounded off. One student-client said that she had
felt an impulse to defend the student-therapist. Another student disclosed that
she also did not feel good about moving in music therapy sessions but had kept
that to herself. The teacher said that one could think that the student who told
about his dislikes in the first place might have felt that the student-therapist
provided a safe enough space to share this. The student-client thought this was
a good way of thinking for her that helped to think better about herself. The
teacher also remarked that it seemed like the reflection was bringing some of
the underlying 'rules' and insecurities of the group matrix to the surface and
helped to negotiate what to share and what to hide.

Several group members agreed and stated that they had felt a relief in the
session when the group moved on to the vocal improvisation where everybody
felt at home.

Teacher feedback

At the end of the teaching session the teacher sums up the feedback and provides an overall evaluation. The teacher summarizes and validates the student's
strengths as a therapist (for example, clarity of instructions, a warm and open attitude, ability to keep an overview in an emotionally laden atmosphere, a well-ar-
ticulated and sonorous guiding voice, courage in the use of verbal questions,

etc.). Then the teacher mentions some areas where the student could develop as a therapist and group leader (for example, to trust themselves and their intuition more, to sit with a more open bodily posture, to use more open questions and avoid leading questions, to be more directive, etc.). The teacher can carefully go back to situations and issues from the therapy session that have not been fully discussed during the student feedback and can inquire about group dynamics and possible transference/countertransference as well as provide theoretical perspectives. On some occasions, a specific situation from the therapy session is replayed with the teacher at the student-therapist's side, working as a direct supervisor and possibly suggesting verbal interventions. This can, for instance, be beneficial if the music therapy student was stuck in a specific situation or did not yet have the skills to find a suitable verbal intervention. The active replay where the student tries to express themselves in new ways provides a more profound learning experience than solely theorizing about it (Lindvang, 2015).

Students' home evaluation

A video recording of the whole session, including the evaluation session, is taken home by the student-therapist. Post-supervision time with the teacher is accessible for the student if they need to process difficult experiences, themes from the feedback, or other issues related to their session.

The evaluation of the course consists of a written report (5–8 pages), where the students summarize their session and reflect on their theoretical therapeutic approach, leader role and forms of governance, ways to relate therapeutically, musical and verbal interventions, and developing identity as a group music therapy leader. They also sum up what they have learned about their own resources as a therapist, as well as areas where they need development. There is an extensive literature list for the course, and the students are asked to integrate a selection of relevant theoretical aspects in their written report. The names and personal information of the peer students are anonymized. The report is evaluated and graded by another teacher of the PMG subject.

Ethics

In this course, it is the first time in the education where the students take a therapist's position for their peers working with authentic and actual material and processes during the group sessions. The students are informed about keeping confidentiality, taking responsibility for themselves and their own boundaries, and choosing how much they would like to share in the verbal rounds. They are asked to comply with GPDR regarding the storage and deletion of the video recording after completion of the report.

Aiming for a career as a music therapist, the students are often eager to try to work 'for real' as a music therapist in a self-development setting, but at the same time, they can fear not performing well enough or finding themselves in some form of 'cliché'-role as a therapist, not being able to find a way to stay authentic and present. Especially the long verbal reflection round is often seen as a big leap into the unknown by the students. To embrace the students' insecurities, the teacher must create a safe learning space and be prepared to name and normalize these feelings in an empathic way. One way to deal with it is to clarify that it is a learning experience and that the students will learn more from a session with challenges and 'errors' than from a smooth and 'successful' session. Another important thing to mention is that they only have one session each and not a series of sessions. As such, the learning situation is not comparable to real-life group therapy, where the therapist would have several sessions to get to know and understand the dynamics of a group and get back and repair possible mismatching situations or misunderstandings.

The students are very concerned about how to react when their fellow students are getting into contact with emotions such as sorrow or anger during their session, and they are often in doubt whether they should let the group member avoid showing any feelings in the group or help them to stay with and express the emotions. When reflecting on this in the evaluation round, the underlying 'rules' and fears in the group often come to the surface, and it becomes possible to discuss the benefits of emotional outlet versus the protection of boundaries and fear of losing control. The development of the professional ability to witness, validate, stay with, and contain painful feelings in others, and find suitable ways to express verbally when helping others process emotions, is an essential part of the teaching.

The teacher role

The teacher is navigating in a highly complex learning situation, and it is beneficial if the teacher has a solid experience as a group music therapist, good mentalization skills, and a well-developed ethical sensitivity. Pedagogical supervision for the teacher is an important part of teaching in a psychodynamic setting. In the music therapy programme, we have found it beneficial to have two teachers working in parallel, each with their PMG group, enabling ongoing peer support and supervision.

Levels of reflection: A learning space model

The learning space can be seen as a developing system, with increasingly higher levels of complexity (Lindvang, 2015). To clarify the complexity of the experience and help the students and the teacher navigate the complex field of learning, a learning space model was created.

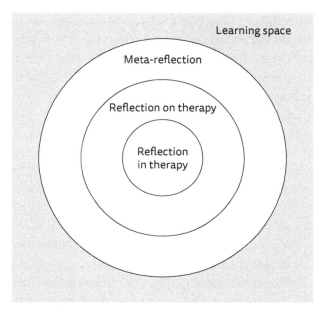

Figure 9.1: The learning space. Levels of reflection in Psychodynamic-oriented Music therapeutic Group leading

The model shows three different reflection spaces that are unfolded in the learning space: reflection in therapy, reflection on therapy, and meta-reflection. All levels contribute to an overall development of the students' reflexivity and mentalization capacity.

Reflection in therapy mainly takes part during the one-and-a-half-hour therapy session, where the students participating in the session reflect on their experiences individually and as a group, primarily in the verbal sections. The student-therapist might establish an 'inner supervisor' and (inside) reflect on choices of interventions and how to carry out the session. The students might reflect inside as well when improvising and listening to each other in the verbal parts of the session.

A reflection on therapy is unfolded in the evaluation phase after the therapy session has ended, where the group leader reflects on the session, the student-clients, and the observers, and the teacher provides feedback. Part of the reflection on therapy can also be the teacher's introduction of theoretic concepts relevant to the therapy session process. The planning of the session, pre- and post-supervision, reflection while watching the video, and writing up the report also belong in the reflection on therapy learning space.

The meta-reflection most often takes place at the beginning of the teaching session and at the end of the teaching session – where the teacher offers the students an opportunity to reflect on the learning space and course setting. The meta-reflection serves as ethical safeguard for the students and their integrity in the complexity of the learning situation. Defining the meta-reflection as distinct from the other two reflection spaces provides an opportunity for the teacher and the students to address the learning situation as a whole and to comment on the student/teacher interaction that can play out as a parallel process to the therapeutic group processes during the course. The meta-reflection space also serves to reflect on the session at another level – such as the ongoing formation of therapist identity, concepts related to the profession as a music therapist, and the attempts to integrate the continuous development of new skills during the course.

Even though the model is distinct between three spaces, in reality a moving in and out of the spaces and activation of several reflection spaces can happen simultaneously. For example, during the therapy session, the observers or teacher can momentarily be absorbed in the music and carried away in a dream state or engaged with their own relationship with the session's theme resonating on a more bodily level, moving in and out of conscious reflection. In the evaluation phase, the students might still be in the resonance of the session (reflection in therapy). The teacher is responsible for taking care that the therapeutic process is not continuing in the feedback situation. The students might also be observing how the teacher gives feedback to develop their own way of providing professional peer-to-peer feedback (meta-reflection).

The growing complexity of the learning space may illustrate the group's accumulated experiences, as the latter group leaders learn from the first group leaders' experience. The learning seems to take place across sessions, and themes seem to jump from session to session. With the complexity of processes and experiences in a music therapy group, not everything is remembered with a conscious mind, not everything is reflected upon, and only a small part is verbalized. For example, whole parts of a therapy session are often not reflected upon until the teacher speaks about it. The teacher has a key role in providing transparency and facilitating a therapeutic learning space. However, it is also crucial that the teacher is aware of the unconscious processes and can protect the group, as there can be vulnerabilities in each participant, the group, and the group dynamics that are not yet ready or suitable to be confronted or talked about in the present context.

Theory: Psychodynamically oriented music therapy

In PMG, the students are expected to operate within a psychodynamic-oriented framework, based on previous learning about inter- and intra-relational processes with music that the students have acquired theoretically and through self-experience. A short definition of a music therapeutic psychodynamic-oriented framework from the *Oxford Handbook of Music Therapy* is:

> The basic underlying assumption in psychodynamic music therapy is the existence of, and dynamic processes within, an unconscious part of the mind, which has an influence on intrapsychic and interpersonal processes within and outside of the musical activity between the therapist and patient. (Metzner, 2016, p.1)

Some of the main authors inspiring the students' psychodynamic-oriented approach are Bruscia (1998), Hadley (2003), Pedersen (2019), Priestley (1994), and Stern (1985/2010). Chapter 3 of this book, and its nine basic assumptions for modern psychodynamic music therapy, describe the fundamental ideas. The psychodynamic-oriented approach is here described as broad and inclusive with many theoretic layers and clear differences from the original Freudian psychoanalysis. One of the most important things in psychoanalysis' birth when Freud published his first paper on dreams (1900) was the attention to the reality of the inner subconscious world. The Norwegian psychiatrist Sigmund Karterud described this as something that cannot be reduced to cognitive-affective schemata or learned strategies: 'The inner world is alive! Here there is form and colour, time and space, birds and animals, music and talk, and a myriad of persons and situations' (1999, p.333, author's translation). This also means that the unconscious is far more than a place of repressed conflicts; it can be seen as the origin of creative impulses, ideas, and psychic energy. Working in a psychodynamic-oriented framework means to be open to the unconscious material that surfaces in the group. The therapist must be aware of inner and outer processes in the therapeutic space and must try to contain and make space for the bodily and emotionally intense musical experiences as well as imagery and associations. In the unfolding human encounter in a group, spontaneous expression, interaction, and dialogues occur, where past and present psychological material blends and where new patterns emerge.

As Kim (2016) wrote: 'The capacity to bear and accept uncertainty is required of any therapist working from psychodynamic perspectives' (p.12), and the student-therapist is challenged to work with uncertainty while facilitating the unfolding process in the group and the individual student-client.

From a psychodynamic perspective, the group offers a possibility to play out personality parts such as the inner child (Priestley, 1994) and work with inner dynamics created in childhood. Transference and countertransference issues can occur in both music and verbal parts of the session (Bruscia, 1998). In PMG, the student-therapist is encouraged to try to identify their own countertransference as a group leader and student-client transference issues, if relevant and possible. Furthermore, the student is encouraged to learn 'to deal with projections, introjections, and self-containment in practice' (Pedersen, 2002, p.175). This means that different psychological defence mechanisms can be played out in the therapy group, and the student-therapists (as well as participants and observers) will have the opportunity to experience such self-protective acts during the therapy session and be able to try to find ways to deal and work with such mechanisms while staying grounded and self-contained.

As the student-therapists usually are very focused on the session's facilitation, transference issues and self-protective defence mechanisms are often only identified in the evaluation after the session or later when the student is watching the session recording during the work with the report.

Group music therapy – the group matrix

The familiarization with the theory on group dynamics is part of the PMG course, and the course has an extensive list of reading. For an elaboration on group dynamic theory, please see Chapter 5. In the introduction to PMG, the students are taught fundamental group therapy theory, such as Foulkes' concept of the group as a dynamic matrix, where the so-called Foundation Group Matrix is created by past familiar, cultural, social, and lingual experiences and the Dynamic Group Matrix emerges through the interactions and the relationships growing during the group process (Foulkes, 1990). There are three windows through which to work with the group: with the individual in the group, with the connection between the members, and with the group as a whole. According to Foulkes, a therapeutic group, through the connections between the participants, amplifies mirroring processes, recognition, acknowledgement, identification, and relationships as a process of resonance. Focusing on the group as something more than a sum of participants, the student-therapist can begin to pay attention to and sense the underlying unconscious group atmosphere and stay open to the group's emerging themes as a whole, as seen in the example with the Grounding theme earlier in the chapter.

The students are also presented with the work of Ahonen-Eerikanen (2007), who describes how a music therapy group provides a specific possibility to tell one's own story as it is known, as it is re-known, or as it can be shaped in the form of a new narrative. She describes how the group music therapist can be aware of different perspectives of music: the group members and their music and/or listening, the therapist's own music and/or listening, the musical atmosphere in the group, and the music itself with all the musical parameters and elements. The student-therapists often apply instrumental or vocal improvisations in their sessions, and they often take the role as a listener. When listening to the group improvisation they get a sense of the atmosphere of the group, and intuitively begin to tune into the group matrix.

Leadership perspectives

According to Foulkes, the group therapist has a 'conductor's role' – the person who sets the scene and opens for all the instruments of the orchestra to play their part. The group therapist conductor is not following a composer's score but tries to give every client a space to express themselves, perform dialogues and contrasts, and enables the whole group to find their own sound and rhythm, whether it is a staccato rhythm with lots of silences or a more fluent state with harmonic interaction.

The student-therapists are expected to be conscious about their role in their session and reflect on it in their evaluation and report. They are exercising the art of disciplined intersubjectivity (Pedersen, 2007; see Chapter 3), where they are working with their relationship with the group consciously and professionally. Basically, they can choose between a directive versus a non-directive approach, and to get more experience, they are encouraged to try out a role that they are not usually and naturally taking.

Verbal interventions

The students are already trained in using communicative musicality skills such as matching, reflecting, imitating, and resonating with others in the music (Wigram, 2004). In PMG, they have to combine their musical and non-verbal skills, including the conscious use of tone of voice, timing, and body posture, with words and language. From participating in group music therapy at the Bachelor level, the students have multi-layered experiences of going back and forth between music – and maybe other artistic modalities such as drawing and movement – and verbalization and meaning-making. Now they are applying this knowledge as therapists. One of the important elements in the PMG training course is to enable the students to facilitate a process where experiences taking place in the music on an implicit level are verbalized on a more conscious and explicit level, and where the group members are making meaning out of the shared musical experience. The art of including the verbal part of conducting psychotherapy is approached with humbleness so that the student as a novice can take the first steps and try out basic types of questions and types of reflections without too much pressure.

According to Gardstrom (2007), verbal processing in music therapy at a basic level enhances the group dynamics by enabling the clients to find commonalities and validate each other's experiences during the music improvisation. However, words can also be used to avoid contact and to intellectualize, or in some cases, to judge or hurt oneself or others. It is the group leader's role to manage verbal communication in a way that creates safety and openness in the group and benefits the ongoing process.

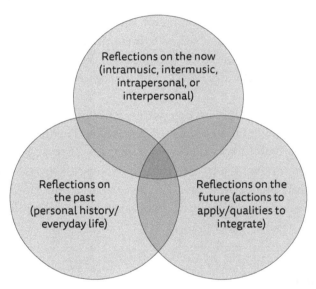

Figure 9.2: Therapist verbal processing of music experiences related to time

As suggested by Bruscia (2014) four levels of interaction can be explored: intra-musical (the individual inner experience of music and expression), intermusical (the shared music experience during an improvisation), and psychological intra-personal and interpersonal processes. Based on the student-therapist's sense of the student-clients in the group and the information they have gathered by observing the music improvisation, listening, movement, or drawing, they can pose questions that are open to any of those four domains and to cross over and mix the domains. Related to the intra- and intermusical processes the student-therapist can inquire about the experience of the music, the choice of instruments, the dynamics, the interplay, emotions, and sensations during the improvisation/music listening, etc. (Ahonen-Eerikanen, 2007). The exploration and reflection on the here-and-now experience includes going deeper. exploring bodily senses and emotions related to the music, the relationship with the other group members, and even reactions and processes to the actual experience of sharing. The student-therapist can also choose to move back and forwards in time, and for instance ask about possible associations or parallels between the actual experience and the client's personal history (upbringing) or everyday life outside the therapy room, or focus on the future, asking what the student-client can do (differently) based on this experience or which quality or essence to bring with them into their future life when they leave the therapy session.

In the PMG introductory session, the students are provided with inspiration for the questions they can pose in their mandatory 30 minutes of verbal processing during their therapy session. The course includes Gardstrom's eight types of questions, including direct and indirect types of questions:

- Probes (starting a conversation, asking open questions about experiences)

- Reflection on emotions (trying to reflect the emotional content underlying statements, validating emotions)

- Clarifying questions (to clear up diffusion and clarify understanding)

- Checking out (asking the clients if one's intuition, fantasy, or hunch about a feeling, dynamics, or pattern is right)

- Self-disclosure (using one's own experience or story as a parallel, as a mirror)

- Summing up (concluding on the themes and process of the session, leaving it open to clients to make final remarks)

Another framework used in training is Metze and Nystrup's (2004) meta-communicative response model. The model is construed as pairs of opposite types of questions: opening–closing, vertical–horizontal, expanding–narrowing, cognitive–affective. The vertical questions ask for details in the single clients' story, whereas the horizontal questions ask for generalizations, larger views, or suggestions about the overall (group) process. Cognitive questions ask for facts and data, whereas affective questions open up emotional aspects. Finally, they are introduced to making use of metaphor inspired by Tompkins, Sullivan, and Lawley (2005), where use of metaphor is understood as something central to how people create meaning and take decisions. The students are asked to pay attention to the client's spontaneous use of metaphors in the dialogue, and to repeat the metaphoric language, and with a curious and sincere attitude inquire about the metaphor, for example by asking 'And as you are leaving a part of yourself outside the door, which part of you is this part outside the door?'

Most students choose to establish a verbal reflection round where they ask one person at a time about their experience. Doing this, they must give everybody an equal amount of time, so that there is a balance in the group. As the course progresses, the students are increasingly working with the group resonance and response on each other's material and with the facilitation of group reflection, where the student-therapist takes a less directive role, observes, and provides reflective comments to the group (mirroring).

In the following example of a replay situation, a student-therapist was provided with direct supervision to help to facilitate an unprocessed emotion in one of the student-clients and to use the group as a mirror. This example is not related to the Grounding session but is composed from elements of actual experiences from different sessions by the author.

> In the verbal round, after a music improvisation focusing on 'Being oneself in the group', a group member shared that she felt that she had taken too much space and played far too loud in the improvisation. After saying this, she looked down and did not meet the eyes of the student-therapist. The therapist asked her about her feelings right now, and she said she was feeling uneasy. The therapist gave an empathic sound and asked if she would like to say more, and she responded 'no'. The conversation moved on to the next group member.
>
> In the post-session evaluation, the student-therapist told that when the student-client said 'no', she experienced a moment of freeze and went empty in her head. She felt that something was not finished, but she could not find any words to say. With the student-client's consent, we organized a replay of the situation, where the student-therapist could explore her 'emptiness', could invite the student-client to go a little deeper, and to also expand on how to work with the group validation and reflection. The teacher sat next to the student-therapist. We agreed that both the student-therapist and student-client could ask for help and that the teacher could suggest interventions. The student-therapist felt her empty head for a while, and then asked if the student-client recognized the feeling of uneasiness from her life story (Reflection on the past). The client said that she was normally careful not to take up too much space, and she related it to the fact that during childhood, her mother was suffering from depression, and she had tried to keep quiet and to not disturb her. The student-therapist empathized with the client but could not find the words and asked for guidance. The teacher helped her to continue by acknowledging that

considering the student-client's history, she found it very courageous to try out to play loud in the group. The student-client gave a spontaneous sigh of relief, and the student-therapist mirrored the sigh and kept a silence for a moment. Suggested by the teacher, the student-therapist asked the student-client if she would like to look around in the group and see how the others reacted. She looked around and saw the warm smiles of the other group members. The student-therapist asked how the student-client felt now. She said that it was surprising but nice. The teacher suggested that the student-therapist ask if the student-client would also like to hear what the other group members thought about her playing loud in the improvisation. She was interested in that. The other student-clients said: 'I was happy to hear you playing loud', 'I did not hear you at all, I only heard my own music', and 'yes, you played loud, but I liked it and was inspired to play louder myself'. The student-client was reddening and looking up and down several times, and the teacher asked the student-therapist to recognize this as a sign of emotional reaction and check if there was a change inside. The student-therapist asked her how she felt about hearing this from the others, and she said that it was 'kind of affirming' with a crooked smile. There was a light shared laughter in the group. The student-client now looked up and around and sat straight up.

In the following didactic discussion, we talked about how the therapist can give some more time for the client to process on a bodily and emotional level during the conversation, and in this co-regulation also get enough time to get out of moments of pressure or freeze as a novice therapist and think about what kind of intervention to choose. The student-therapist commented that she thought the suggested interventions were elementary, but she did not yet have enough overview to get into the flow of verbal interaction. We talked about how easily one can feel insecure as a student when guided by the teacher like this, and the group thanked the student-therapist that she was willing to be in this didactic situation for the benefit of the whole group's learning.

The replay served as a learning experience of how to use the group to mirror new behaviours, when a pattern from the foundational matrix is tested and restructured in the dynamic matrix. The replay also demonstrated how the therapist's sensitivity to signs of shame in the client (looking down, reddening, contracting body) is important to regulate the process of group validation and mirroring. According to Yalom and Leszcz (2005) the impact of being mirrored in an empathic way by the group seems to be valuable for the client in another way than being mirrored only by the therapist.

Learning perspectives

During the PMG course, the whole group is developing as a practice learning community (Lave & Wenger, 1991; see Chapter 2). The learning is taking place on multiple layers in a complex structure on both conscious and unconscious levels. The learning is focused on self-experience in different roles with several dimensions in the same teaching session. It includes a long therapeutic session with in-depth work, reflexive discussions between the therapist, clients, observers, and teacher, and meta-reflections on the learning space and teacher/student relationship. The relationship between students and teacher is both constituted as a student–supervisor relationship and partly as a master–apprentice learning relationship. The whole process is deepened and supported by theoretical perspectives and reading as well as writing of a report. The PMG course demands integration of all the former subjects and pieces of training that students had during the music therapy programme, the engagement needs to be high for both students and teacher, and the successful outcome of the course process is an exciting and effective step in the tuning of the students into reflexive and skilled psychodynamic-oriented music therapists.

References

Ahonen-Eerikanen, H. (2007). *Group Analytic Music Therapy*. Barcelona Publishers.

Bruscia, K. (1998). *The Dynamics of Music Psychotherapy*. Barcelona Publishers.

Bruscia, K. (2014). *Defining Music Therapy*. Barcelona Publishers.

Foulkes, S.H. (1990). 'The Group as Matrix of the Individual's Mental Life.' In S.H. Foulkes, *Selected Papers*. Karnac.

Freud, S. (1900). *The Interpretation of Dreams*. PBS.

Gardstrom, S. (2007). *Music Therapy Improvisation for Groups: Essential Leadership Competencies*. Barcelona Publishers.

Hadley, S. (ed.) (2003). *Psychodynamic Music Therapy – Case Studies*. Barcelona Publishers.

Karterud, S. (1999). *Gruppeanalyse og psykodynamisk gruppepsykologi [Group analysis and psychodynamic group psychology]*. Pax.

Kim, J. (2016). 'Psychodynamic music therapy.' *Voices: A World Forum for Music Therapy, 16*(2), 1–10.

Lave, J. & Wenger, E. (1991). *Learning in Doing: Social, Cognitive, and Computational Perspectives. Situated Learning: Legitimate Peripheral Participation*. Cambridge University Press.

Lindvang, C. (2015). 'Kompleksitet i læreprocesser og terapi [Complexity in learning processes and therapy].' In T. Hansen (ed.), *Det ubevidstes potentiale: Kybernetisk psykologi i anvendelse* [English edition in review: *Potentials of unconscious intelligence: Redefining the unconscious in psychotherapy, creativity and learning*]. Frydenlund.

Metze, E. & Nystrup, J. (2004). *Samtaletræning. Håndbog i præcis kommunikation [Training in dialogue. A handbook in precise communication]*. Gyldendal.

Metzner, S. (2016). 'Psychodynamic Music Therapy.' In J. Edwards (ed.), *The Oxford Handbook of Music Therapy*. Oxford University Press.

Pedersen, I.N. (2002). 'Self-Experience for Music Therapy Students.' In J. Eschen (ed.), *Analytical Music Therapy*. Jessica Kingsley Publishers.

Pedersen, I.N. (2007). 'Musikterapeutens disciplinerede subjektivitet [The disciplined subjectivity of the music therapist].' *Psyke & Logos, 28*(1), 27.

Pedersen, I.N. (2019). 'Analytical and Psychodynamic Theories: Classical Psychoanalysis.' In S.L. Jacobsen, L.O. Bonde, & I.N. Pedersen (eds), *A Comprehensive Guide to Music Therapy* (2nd ed.). Jessica Kingsley Publishers.

Priestley, M. (1994). *Essays on Analytical Music Therapy*. Barcelona Publishers.

Stern, D. (1985/2010). *The Interpersonal World of the Infant. A View from Psychoanalysis and Developmental Psychology*. Basic Books.

Tompkins, P., Sullivan, W., & Lawley, J. (2005). 'Tangled spaghetti in my head: Making use of metaphor.' *Therapy Today. Journal of BACP*. Accessed on 18/01/22 at https://cleanlanguage.co.uk/articles/articles/30/1/Tangled-Spaghetti-in-My-Head-Making-use-of-metaphor/Page1.html.

Wigram, T. (2004). *Improvisation*. Jessica Kingsley Publishers.

Yalom, I.D. & Leszcz, M. (2005). *The Theory and Practice of Group Psychotherapy*. Basic Books.

CHAPTER 10

Intertherapy

Inge Nygaard Pedersen

Introduction and history of Intertherapy

The term Intertherapy was first defined by three English music therapists all from London and educated at Guildhall School of Music and Drama by Juliette Alvin, namely Mary Priestley, Peter Wright, and Marjorie Wardle, back in the early 1970s. They were colleagues at St Bernard's Hospital (a mental health hospital) in London, and they used Intertherapy in a peer form as a therapeutic ongoing learning possibility for educated therapists where they took turns in being the client, the therapist, and the observer taking notes. The aim was twofold – ongoing individual therapy for the therapist and trying out new therapeutic methods in music before they were applied in music therapy clinical work in mental health. Thus, Intertherapy was initially understood as an excellent tool (as a nonhierarchic music therapy for music therapists) for taking care of the mental well-being and flexibility of music therapists (Priestley, 1975).

Intertherapy gradually became an important part of Priestley's training disciplines in her Analytical Music Therapy (AMT) approach developed during the 1970s (see Chapter 2; Priestley, 1975, 1994).

The peer form of Intertherapy, as described above, thus was developed into an educational form of Intertherapy, in which two AMT students worked together taking turns in being the client and the therapist under live supervision from a trained AMT therapist. Personal therapy in the form of individual or group music therapy in AMT was from the beginning a prerequisite for starting Intertherapy. At the Aalborg programme today, we have more disciplines as a prerequisite for Intertherapy (see Chapter 2).

Professor Johannes Theodor Eschen from Germany was one of the two students in Priestley's first educational Intertherapy dyad in AMT. In this initial form of Intertherapy both students were present when one of them had supervision on the role of being the therapist in the dyad as part of the learning process.

Eschen transferred the experiential disciplines individual and group music therapy and Intertherapy as integrated parts of a two-year full-time music therapy programme in Germany in 1978 – the Mentoren Kurs Herdecke (see Chapter 2).

I participated in the discipline of Intertherapy during my two years' full-time training at the Mentoren Kurs Herdecke (1978–1980) for 12 sessions, where Benedikte Barth Scheiby was my student-therapist. Colleen Purdon (trained by Priestley) was our live supervisor. In the last semester of our training in Germany, after we had finished our Intertherapy training, Benedikte and I took off for an internship period in London for seven weeks at St Bernard's Hospital, where Priestley did her clinical work. During this period, we took 12 additional Intertherapy sessions privately with Priestley as our live supervisor. Shortly after we returned to Denmark in 1980, we started Intertherapy in the original peer form among music therapy colleagues, with a Danish colleague Torben Moe (TM) as our peer participant every second week for almost one year.

In our Master's thesis, based on experiences from the Herdecke programme, Scheiby and I (Scheiby & Pedersen, 1999) reflected on this integrated model, where therapeutic, musical, and theoretical disciplines in a programme were taught simultaneously, with equal weight, and were integrated. We defined the most important learning processes and concluded that these were very beneficial for the future clinical work of music therapy students. We were convinced that this model should be replicated at the music therapy training programme at Aalborg University. When I was the first person employed to build the new programme, I expressed clearly that that was what I intended to create.

In this chapter, I will briefly describe the theoretical platform and teaching aims for the discipline of Intertherapy and describe how the discipline has developed over the years at the Aalborg programme. These descriptions will be illustrated with short vignettes, the most detailed covering how the students learn from disseminating their Intertherapy case in an internal evaluation of being the student-therapist. As a university discipline, Intertherapy has to be evaluated, and it has been an ethical challenge to develop an evaluation form that fulfilled ethical rules for the students.

A theoretical platform for Intertherapy

Eschen built his theoretical platform for the three disciplines from AMT he integrated into the two-year full-time post-graduate music therapy education in Herdecke on, among others, Rycroft (1972) and Ammon (1974). They had introduced into the psychoanalytical literature a so-called *tertiary process thinking*, which is derived from a:

...dream-like thinking or (following Freud) primary process thinking...[and which] displays *condensation* and *displacement*, [wherein] images tend to become fused and can readily replace and symbolize one another...[and wherein they] ignore the categories of space and time... [In contrast], secondary process thinking obeys the law of grammar and formal logic...and is governed by the reality principle. (Rycroft, 1972, p.124)

Reflecting further on these two very different thinking processes, Eschen (2002) explains: 'Thinking in creative processes is (following Ammon 1974) conceivable as "tertiary process thinking," a state of mind where we can easily oscillate between primary and secondary process thinking' (p.17). This state of mind I think many music therapists recognize in improvising music, playing composed music, or in listening to music. In opposition to classical psychoanalysis, personal growth in music therapy for the person is not understood as a movement from mainly primary process thinking and acting to primarily thinking and acting through secondary processes. To be mentally healthy and creative is understood as being able to easily oscillate between primary and secondary thinking and acting. These ideas can be seen as forerunners for contemporary theories, such as, for example, the supramodal space. I also see these ideas from Eschen as a simple first step of what we offer in this book where we describe the more complex difference between basic assumptions in the classical psychoanalytical orientation, assumptions 1–6, and basic assumptions for a modern integrative psychodynamic music therapy, assumptions 4–5 (for more information, see Chapter 3).

Intertherapy as a training discipline today

Intertherapy takes place in the eighth semester and is the last discipline in which students are trained in music therapy methods through mutually being client and therapist to one another. Simultaneously, it is the first discipline where this training is continued with the same student dyad during a series of sessions. The structure of the sessions is that A is a therapist to B for 40 minutes. Then B is a therapist to A for 40 minutes. Then therapist A receives supervision for 20 minutes while therapist B takes notes in a separate room. Finally, therapist B receives 20 minutes of supervision. In the form we apply today, the students do not join the supervision of one another as this space is solely for the student-therapist. The possible length of the course today would be seven Intertherapy sessions and one feedback session. The discipline is placed just before the students enter their comprehensive internship.

In Intertherapy, the work is about personal problems and resources within the students and is similar to counselling work or to self-developmental work in music therapy.

The aims for this discipline at the Aalborg programme are primarily:

- To be able to work psychotherapeutically, both as a client and as a therapist, and to integrate the client perspective and client experiences into the development of a therapist identity

- To work from a fixed working theme (inspired from theme-based short time psychotherapy) and at the same time meet the client's need and follow the process of the client

- To apply relevant methods (reconstructive and progressive) musically and verbally in relation to a music therapeutic frame and the need of the student-client

- To use the supervision appropriately and to apply music therapy theoretical reflections and personal experiences to demonstrate an understanding of the role of being a music therapist student, including an understanding of transference issues (see Chapter 3), leading styles, and approaches during the Intertherapy course

Supervisor's preparation of the students for the Intertherapy course

Comprehensive information is given to the students about professional and ethical considerations from the supervisor before they start the Intertherapy course. They are informed that being in the role of the student-client here has two purposes: 1) to be a helper for their student-therapist for them to exercise being a future professional music therapist, and 2) to be able to work further with personal issues that have been brought up and have been worked through and reflected in group and individual teaching therapy disciplines and which they may have noted in their personal logbook. Each student is guided to keep track of important personal developmental processes during all five years of training in an ongoing logbook (see Chapter 2), or to be able to work with other issues that may appear in the therapeutic process.

Before the start of the Intertherapy course the students are asked to create dyads among themselves if in any way possible. If it is not possible the whole group will meet with a supervisor before the start, to come to an agreement.

At an introductory meeting just before the first Intertherapy session the dyads are informed by their supervisor about the duty of confidentiality and that they are not expected to talk with their student partner about the Intertherapy processes outside the course. Second, they are informed that all sessions where they are the therapist are video recorded, so that the student-therapist can watch the recording between the sessions and learn from it and bring questions from this observation to the supervision. The dyads are further informed to write careful notes from the experiences of being a client in the Intertherapy course to benefit more reflectively from the learning processes and to be able to give careful feedback to their student-therapist under live supervision after the course is terminated. Finally, the students are informed to take turns in being the first and the second therapist in the dyad (see below).

Information on the role and responsibility of the supervisor before the start of the course

As already described, the supervisor plays an important role in preparing the students for this discipline before the start. The Intertherapy students are also informed about the role and responsibility of the supervisor during the course. The supervisor is present in the room during the entire course and takes comprehensive and careful notes. The supervisor is responsible for the frames of Intertherapy and for ethical considerations throughout the entire course. The supervisor will not interact during the therapy processes if there is no ethical reason for interference. My own experience over 35 years is that this has never been relevant, as the students have learned ethical considerations of therapeutic training through the integrated training of the therapeutic track being part of the graduate training already in previous semesters. The student-therapist can choose to ask for support from the supervisor if the student urgently feels that a therapeutic situation calls for this. This has been relevant a few times. The supervisor's notes have to be so comprehensive that musical expressions, verbal formulations, therapist's attitudes, and relational challenges in the therapeutic process can be mutual and concretely reflected, and alternative suggestions can be created. Further the role of the supervisor is to give a bird's eye perspective on the therapeutic process and to suggest directions and further possibilities for the student-therapist.

Structure for the first and last session

There is a given structure for the first and last session. The structure for the first session was originally developed by Priestley, but in my experience, it is still relevant. For the very first session the student-therapists are instructed to conduct a semi-structured interview with their student-client in a question or dialogue style they can identify with. The areas that they are informed to cover during the interview and which they are given in writing before the session are as follows:

- The client's relation to parents/brothers/sisters

- The client's relation to partner – sexuality

- The client's relation to friends – interests – group memberships

- The client's relation to religion – taboos

- The client's relation to death – eventual previous experiences of passing away of close relationships

- The client's self-report of current problems/resources

The student-therapists are also informed that they have the responsibility to come to an agreement with the student-client on an overall working theme for the whole course of Intertherapy in the first session (see above). They mostly address this agreed theme again in the second session to confirm or correct it. The application of an agreed working theme is to ensure a red thread in the work. During the process, many other different issues arise and are coped with, and they can be reflected towards the working theme to give an integrated understanding. Finally, they are asked to meet in music with the student-client in the first session either through improvisation (mostly applied), or in listening to or playing pre-composed music. For some students, who know each other very well before starting collaboration in Intertherapy, it can be experienced as artificial to ask for information, because they already know about their student-client. They are guided to ask all the questions anyway, because the most important thing for the work here is to have the student-client's narrative as the common ground of information and not the picture of the student-client, which the student-therapist may have created beforehand. The Intertherapy process unfolds in line with the identified working theme under close supervision after each session.

The supervisor also provides a specific structure to close down the process in the last session. For the last session the student-therapists are guided to read through their comprehensive notes for all sessions and to watch relevant video excerpts again before this session to write a summary of all the sessions by highlighting the different issues they have been working with and by relating these issues to the overall working theme of the Intertherapy course. They are further informed to check out if their way of formulating these issues is understood and recognized by the student-client. Finally, the student-therapists are asked to give as much space as possible to musical interaction in the last session and to bring in a preliminary terminating ritual to emphasize that in this last feedback session they are giving mutual feedback as future colleagues, not in a therapist-client relationship.

Supervision of Intertherapy when started

After student A has been a student-therapist for student B for 40 minutes and after they have changed their roles for another 40 minutes, student A has 20 minutes of individual supervision, while student B write notes of the process of having just been a student-therapist in another room (see above). As the change from being a client to being a therapist to a supervisee usually takes a couple of minutes, the whole setting is scheduled for two-and-a-half hours. The students are informed before starting that they need to take turns in being the first therapist and the first client. Being the first therapist means that you will also be a student-client, before you have to quickly switch back and reflect on your previous experiences of having been the student-therapist for your individual supervision. Students mostly do this smoothly, but deep processes from having just been a client might call for a few minutes' transition, which of course will be accepted by the supervisor. Being the second student-therapist means you have 20 minutes to write notes and reflect on your role as a therapist before you enter your individual supervision. These circumstances provide different settings and different learning situations for supervision. So turn-taking is needed. The aim of the quick shifts is to prepare the students to be able to function as a professional music therapist also on days where they might have distracting experiences that need to be temporarily contained in order for the therapist to be fully present for the client and the therapy process.

Themes brought up for supervision are manifold. After the first Intertherapy session, most students reflect on the artificial situation of suddenly being a therapist to a co-student, with whom they normally relate differently and often as friends. Most students are surprised that they can actually transcend former relationships to the student, and that they thought they knew the student-client quite well, but the semi-structured interview/dialogue of the first session mostly brings up new and unknown information for the student-therapist. A typical issue for the first supervision is the mutually developed working theme for the course work, and reflections on how this theme might mirror the student-client's personal narrative or not. Student-therapists are always asked in the first supervision session to bring up the working theme again in session two of the

Intertherapy course to ensure that this is what the student-client really wants to focus on. Often it needs a further polish to resonate what was really meant by the student-client. Another theme often brought up by the student-therapist in the first supervision is the student having felt extremely nervous and having the feeling of being slightly dissociative and not adequately coping with the situation. Most students do cope adequately with the situation already in the first session, and it is not visible from outside that they may feel slightly dissociative, even if they may feel very nervous inside. Here confirmation and acknowledgement from the supervisor is of value to them. Further possible techniques that could be appropriate in clinical work with their student-client, where they have agreed on a specific working theme, and how to start the second session, are also central issues for the first supervision. It is always the primary task of the supervisor to both push and support the development of challenges and resources of each single student. But the most important task, I think, is to offer an open and containing space for and encourage the disclosure of whatever thoughts, feelings, sensations, and reflections that the student might want and need to bring in.

Vignette from Intertherapy supervision

This example is fictional based on different experiences from supervision after the first Intertherapy session.

Student-therapist: I feel like this working theme of *becoming better at expressing myself emotionally to my partner and close friends* is a huge issue, which is also kind of my own problem. I feel inferior to work with this.

Supervisor: Can you tell me what you imagine could be helpful for you personally to get on with this issue?

Student-therapist: I need someone who in a kind way does not let me get away with not expressing my feelings.

Supervisor: You just put into words what could be your most distinguished task for your student-client here. Could you think of some play-rules or other artwork that could underpin this task?

Student-therapist: I could imagine suggesting that we play out certain emotions in music as a follow up of what the student-client tells me and to offer myself as a reinforcing partner in the music.

Supervisor: Yes, sure. This is a possibility. You might also later in the course find some music to listen to for your client, when you have a deeper feeling of what the client is not expressing – music that you feel could meet the emotions of your client and eventually let your client draw when listening.

> Be aware in your verbal interventions how you acknowledge what your client is telling you – and may not tell you – as a first step, before you move into more explorative techniques. As an example, you might feed back: 'I hear you and I understand how important it is what you are sharing with me just now. I wonder if there are some emotions connected to what you just told me, and if you feel like exploring these together with me? You may also want to play alone with me as a careful listener.' If the client chooses interplay, be aware of finding a way to ask, and to get information from the client about the following: 'Do you want me to reinforce what you are playing or to accompany you and thereby allow you to play more as a soloist? Is there any preferred instrument you want me to play?'

Despite whatever comes up in the second Intertherapy session, the second supervision is mostly about how the student-therapist copes with interventions both in musical interplay and in verbal dialogues. Specific verbal formulations are at the centre of supervision in Intertherapy, as the students have previously had several semesters of teaching in musical improvisation and in taking different roles in clinical music improvisations (Wigram, 2004). They have had teaching experiences in verbal dialogues for single sessions but not in a music therapy course running over several sessions, where the process is continued from session to session and where live supervision is offered in all sessions.

The supervisor makes comprehensive notes during the Intertherapy sessions, writing down direct verbal interventions by the student-therapist, and an overall analysis of the musical interplays and of the role of the therapist in the music, to be able to dive into concrete material in the supervision. Watching video clips is a possibility, but not so often applied, as it takes time to find the moment of the specific intervention. Concerning supervision on verbal interventions, a specific verbal phrase often asked for by the student-therapist is how to tell the client to maybe exercise or be aware of something that calls for a change without sounding authoritarian as a therapist. One way of coping with this which I have often applied myself as a music therapist working with private clients for 35 years, and which I often bring in as an example in my role as a supervisor, is to phrase a sentence: *Would it be possible for you to allow yourself to...?* And then wait; and if the student-client answers *yes maybe...*then reinforce that you think it could be a very important step. If the student-client answers *I don't think so...*it could be appropriate/not appropriate to ask if the student-client could allow that they explore together in music why this seems not to be the case. The wording *allow yourself* raises other inner imaginations by the student-client of a personal issue, rather than the wording *you need to...*or *I want you to...*from the therapist. If a student-client expresses *I do not want to allow myself to...*then it is a choice by the student-client that should be respected. In this process, the student-client comes to reflect on the issue anyway. The issue mostly comes up later in the Intertherapy course, and here it most often will be visible if it was a question of the wrong timing by the student-therapist bringing it up, or if the student-therapist had a perception that seemed not to be important to the client. It is an ongoing task for the student-therapist as a part of this learning process (supported by the supervisor) to be able to perform psychodynamic (see Chapter 3) individual music therapy, to be able to remember and consciously carry over experiences from previous sessions to later sessions, and to be the one who can bring coherence for the student-client into the joint experiences of the Intertherapy process.

Transference issues are important in supervision

An issue which arises repeatedly in Intertherapy supervision is transference and countertransference (see Chapter 3). Almost all students at some point raise the question of how to know if it is their own emotions/sensations the student-therapist is experiencing – or if it is emotions/sensations coming from the client. Because of the quick shift between being a client and being a therapist, often experiences from being the client merge into being the therapist for the same student. Simultaneously, the therapist is consciously coping with containing their own emotions in a way so that they can be there fully open and empathically for the client.

In the history of countertransference there have been different ideas about how to identify and how to cope with countertransference. Overall, there has been a movement from 1) the idea that countertransference is something the therapist should overcome, and if the therapist is overwhelmed by emotions they needed more therapy (analysis), to 2) countertransference counts all emotional experiences and reactions from the therapist to the client and this is the most important source of information one can get as a therapist (Pedersen, 2007). In cases where clear and strong emotions are experienced by the student-therapist, I have very often heard the student express 'Oh now I know what countertransference is about and how much information it can bring'.

Also, parallel processes are a part of Intertherapy supervision (Jacobsen, 2000). An example here is a student-therapist, who is very hesitating in the narrative for supervision after having just worked with a very hesitating student-client, and the supervisor feels the same degree of tension in the body as the student-therapist did in the previous Intertherapy session. Here the learning process most often is that the supervisor discloses this parallel process and reflects with the student so the student can learn from this experience and find a personal way to be aware of similar processes in the future work.

Student-therapist gets feedback from student-client

After the students have finished the Intertherapy course, and before they start preparing for the oral examination, they come together for an extra teaching block to give mutual feedback under direct supervision. Here the role of the supervisor is to ensure that the therapeutic process is not continued. Before providing the feedback, students are required to go through their notes from being a client in the Intertherapy course and to write responses to the following given questions:

- Did I feel understood by my therapist – in what way (how/how not)?

- Did I feel like been heard and seen by my therapist – in what way (how/ how not)?

- Could I use the playing rules emerging in our joint process – in what way (how/how not)?

- Could I use the musical interventions applied by my therapist – in what way (how/how not)?

- Could I use the verbal interventions applied by my therapist – in what way (how/how not)?

- Which issues and improvisations do I most easily remember?

- Did I experience changes in the way my therapist was functioning along the course?

- Did I miss something?

- Is there anything I would like to tell my therapist concerning being a future professional music therapist?

At the beginning of the feedback session, student-clients are guided again to ritually step back from the role of being a client and to try to give feedback to their former student-therapist by observing their own therapy process as objectively as possible. The main aim of the feedback is to help the student-therapist develop their clinical skills to the fullest.

The supervisor is present during the feedback and intervenes if a student-client starts to express frustrations about a specific therapy situation instead of telling the former student-therapist what was helpful or not helpful during the therapy course. The supervisor also intervenes if the former student-therapist – who is receiving feedback – starts to ask the former student-client (outside the questions) what they felt like when the student-therapist coped with a specific situation in this specific way. The aim of this learning process is not to repeat a process from the student-client being in the client position or to confirm an insecurity of the student-therapist being in the therapist position. It is a chance for the student-therapist to have a formalized feed-back from a client (which is normally not possible in clinical practice) about what was helpful or not so helpful of what they performed as the therapist in the Intertherapy course. It might sound complex but during the many years I have intervened quite a few times and corrections have been easily understood and implemented.

Examination of Intertherapy

Since 2003, this discipline has been subjected to an internal, ungraded examination where the student-therapist has to present the course of Intertherapy as experienced by the therapist (Pedersen, 2003). The students are prepared by the supervisor on the structure of and ethical considerations concerning disseminating a case with vulnerable data. The demands of this examination have shifted during the years due to political reasons at the university (Pedersen, 2013). In 2021, we had the possibility to move back to an internal ungraded examination with a person, not known to the students, as the censor. We have kept the structure, as it has been for the last 18 years, as it seems to function well, and the students confirm that this examination gives them a new layer of understanding of their role as a therapist and of the therapeutic processes of Intertherapy. Furthermore, it gives them a trial of how to present case material with relevant ethical concerns in the future. Aims for the evaluation process are:

- To document the student-client case through video excerpts and written material that are ethically responsible and professionally relevant

- To reflect and integrate one's own self-experiences and learning processes into the development of a therapist identity

Preparation for the oral examination

The oral examination is scheduled for at least three weeks after the feedback session. This gap gives the students an opportunity to digest their own process as a client, as well as the process of having been a therapist dealing with a deep process of another student. The student-therapists must watch all the recordings carefully and identify phases in the Intertherapy process. They also have to select relevant music excerpts as illustrations for the examination. All musical excerpts must be approved orally by the former student-client before they can be used for the examination.

The student-therapist gets a schema developed by the supervisors to enhance the self-learning process and to facilitate the organization of clinical material gathered during the Intertherapy and supervision sessions. Table 10.1 shows an example of a completed schema from the evaluation of Intertherapy, where one student A, having been the therapist for another student B, has filled out the schema in preparation of the oral examination.

Table 10.1: Schema for Intertherapy evaluation

	Phase 1: ses. 1–3	Phase 2: ses. 4–5	Phase 3: ses. 6–7	Phase 4: ses. 8
Working issues **Sub-issues**	To create space for the inner child. Set boundaries. Be playful.	Rebirth.	Integration. Primitive forces transform vulnerability to sensitivity.	Consolidation of tools to stay grounded in the body in spite of restlessness/ chaos.
Content	Improvisation through vulnerable voice qualities. Express anger (drums). Try to stay in the body in spite of chaos.	Enlarge sensitive sensations – contain my self in an imaginary space. Restlessness transformed.	Firm and still floating. (Drum/ voice.) Care for the sorrow of an inner infant. (Cello/voice/ metallophone.)	Djembe + voice. Pain, sensitivity, and primitive force integrated.
The role in the music	Encourage changes in the process. Offer symbiosis. Create a bridge from anger to vulnerability.	Companion and container. Following X in her explorations.	Listening. Being present. Seeing/ hearing the client. Being very confirming. A safe base.	Witness, mirror. I see you and know that you are conscious of your integration process.

cont.

	Phase 1: ses. 1–3	Phase 2: ses. 4–5	Phase 3: ses. 6–7	Phase 4: ses. 8
Role as therapist	A good enough mother. Holding/ matching. Playmate.	Companion/ witness, who can mirror the experience of the client. Midwife.	Positive father. A protector around the client being a careful mother to her inner infant. Be present in distance.	Mirror: sum up the issues and create a coherence of the symbols in the process. Makes the client's self-care visible.
Own process being a therapist	A little insecure. Too fast. Can I sufficiently and carefully contain this process? Enjoy finding a balance in being present in a disciplined subjective way.	Surprised and happy that therapy work can be funny and beautiful. Laughter can be releasing.	Aha! Experience. I could offer the quality of being a positive father. It is accessible to me.	Satisfied with the work. Thankful to be allowed to follow this beautiful process in a positive way. Satisfied in experiencing a better balance in doing and being in my own self-image and understanding of identity.

Source: Pedersen, 2013

Note how the schema requires the student-therapist to retrospectively divide the case material into phases, but these phases are mostly not conscious for the student-therapist or student-client during the process. In the above case, four phases are identified, where therapist A has to document the content of the case of student-client B, the jointly agreed working issue, and how this is worked through during the different phases of the therapy. In the second horizontal row, A has to summarize the content of B's process in a generalized way, so that it does not involve biographical details, but still shows the important psychodynamic events and progression of the case. As this example is some years old, the schema today has changed the content of the case to the therapist's beings and relationships as well as strategies in each phase, so the emphasis is more on the therapist's learning processes.

The student-therapist mostly selects one piece of music, most often improvised, from each phase of the case, and illustrates the psychodynamic progression through a brief description of these examples for the oral presentation. It can also include music listening. The musical examples are intended to be chosen from the criteria, that they show core material from each phase of the case related to the overall working title.

In the lower three rows of the schema, the experiences and developments of student-therapist A are documented concerning the role of and reflection by the student-therapist.

Filling out this schema and choosing the music examples are the main part of the preparation for the evaluation, and it is a huge challenge to all students. They look through all video recordings and search for the most important events from both their recordings and written notes from seven therapy sessions, supervision sessions, and one feedback session from their client.

This is a learning process in how to apply the experiences from being in the therapist role to retrospectively look back on your process work and to select and reflect on your work at a level where you can disseminate the therapy process for others due to certain structures and thus how to reduce meaningfully a big amount of data within a given structure.

The oral examination

The oral examination lasts for 30 minutes and involves the student presenting the case based on this schema and based on playing and reflecting on the chosen music examples. The schema is submitted to the examiner and the internal censor beforehand. During the 30-minute examination this schema has to be presented meaningfully and clearly, accompanied by the music excerpts, which have to be clearly explained, and the evaluators need clear instructions of what to listen for.

To best illustrate how the oral examination can be used to evaluate the Intertherapy experience, I will present how the specific presentation of student-therapist A is formulated as found in Table 10.1 and also describe shortly the various music excerpts. The schema presented in Table 10.1 presents the working theme for the student-client (B) as follows: 'To create space for the inner child part of the student-client. To develop the ability to set necessary boundaries and to allow herself to be more playful.'

This topic was created mutually between the student-therapist and the student-client from knowledge of biographical details from the student-client's life, showing that she had to be the responsible adult at a very early age, and she had to be a parent for her own parents. Also, the story mirrors a life situation where the natural boundaries of the child were not always respected. The client thus developed a life strategy of always expecting herself to serve other people's needs and not to be sufficiently aware of her own.

She also developed a very high level of sensitivity towards the surroundings (never really knowing the state of her parents as a child), which made it difficult for her to feel grounded in her own body feelings and body sensations. The topic was also created on the basis of her previous therapeutic experiences at the music therapy programme before entering the Intertherapy training course.

Through the musical excerpts, the following working processes were shown through the chosen musical improvisations (A is the student-therapist and B is the student-client).

Presenting musical excerpts at the oral examination[1]

Musical excerpt one

This example is from phase one. B plays the drum sets and A plays the piano. At first B shows frustration in her body language, beating in a rather inward way, crying as if she cannot get through or cannot be heard, until she suddenly expresses very clearly and openly a lot of anger. A accompanies these expressions, being careful of not dominating B in the music at any moment. B seems to fight with herself in frustration, before she gets increasingly direct in her attacking way of beating the drums. Gradually she seems to be playing intentionally, as if she is beating someone or something through her drum playing. This part is finally followed by a calm reflective body expression and a very sensitive touching of the cymbal with her fingers.

A interpreted from the dynamic of the music and from the verbal discussion of the experience with B that B allowed herself to be really angry with her parents. She had always been split between being angry and feeling sad for them. She realized that strong feelings were held back in the anger and she felt released after the attacking music, as if, for the first time, she had allowed the real emotions of her inner child to come out without these emotions being mingled by the adult part of her feeling sad for her parents. She put it into words like this: 'I feel I can remain better in my feeling of my body even if I do face a lot of chaos just now. ... Normally, I have felt like leaving my body when these emotions came up as if they were not allowed. Here I could defend myself against being overwhelmed by the feeling of leaving my body.'

Musical excerpt two

This example is from phase two. On the basis of the experiences in phase one, B is now exploring the newly recognized sensations of trying to stay in the

---

1   This section is reprinted from Pedersen, 2013

body – even when conflicting emotions or ambivalent emotions emerge. She literally tries to create an imaginary space for her new body sensations by playing the piano, being supported softly by A on a second piano. B is experimenting in her playing in both the upper and lower part of the piano (spaces between the hands), and she is playing very open textures in the sound, as if she is softly and carefully examining if there is a sound space for her to be present in: Is it allowed? Am I invited to stay?

A tries to follow the character of the music, simultaneously remaining very stable in creating an open inviting bass sound picture – supporting and inviting at the same time in her interplay. B did not have many words for this experience. She just commented that it was new and nice to be there in the open sound space.

Musical excerpt three

This example is from phase two and shows B improvising alone with her body and voice. A is very carefully listening to her and she is giving her full attention. B starts with vocal utterances combined with movements with her arms and hands, as if she is pushing things away from herself, from her body. The sound develops into the quality of the sound of a bee combined with trembling movements and she ends up creating very clear and direct intentional cries combined with body movements where her whole body seems to accompany the sounds.

After the improvisation, B said that she felt as if she was trying to push her restlessness away from the body, as if she tried to create space for more embodied voice expressions such as the cries. She also felt restlessness being transformed afterwards into a feeling of calmness, space, and containment in her body sensations. She mentioned the importance of having been so clearly and convincingly seen and heard by A.

Musical excerpt four

This example is from phase three in the Intertherapy course and it shows B allowing herself to be expressive, and to recognize and be in touch with a very sensitive and vulnerable part of herself. She is sitting with the cello embracing the top of the cello while sensitively and very softly plucking the strings. She has closed eyes and puts her forehead towards the top of the cello.

She seems to care for a vulnerable part of herself through her cello playing. A plays very softly on the metallophone and she creates a safe sound space around the 'mother–infant dyad' of B's cello music. It seems as if A represents a 'positive father', making sure the scene is safe for the careful meeting of a mothering part and a vulnerable child part of B.

B reflects verbally that it was very dangerous for her to allow these vulnerable sounds to be expressed and that she was afraid of not being understood or being really heard. She also said that she had felt totally safe here in the presence of, and the musical environment of, A.

Musical excerpt five

This excerpt is from the last session in phase four. B is playing alone. She is playing a djembe (African drum) and using her voice. In this improvisation she seems to combine and integrate the forces of her real anger and her sensitivity is transformed from being very vulnerable. She plays very flexibly and dynamically, and her body language seems to flow in a very integrated way with the music.

Her comments after the music were focused on feeling more integrated in her body now, as if she could allow herself to stay present physically both in being angry (feeling her strength) and in being vulnerable (feeling her sensitivity).

A commented, as you can follow in the schema in the third row in phase four: 'I feel like being a witness who mirrors that I see you and know that you are conscious of your integration process.'

One could also say that during the therapy process B had once more, and at a deeper level, internalized a positive mother and father figure representation in her self-understanding. Thus, she has stabilized her identity of being very sensitive to others at the same time as she can stay in her own body. She can now stay present in her body, and she can also allow herself to express strong emotions directly. Further, she can now oscillate more freely between a primary process (her inner child being mad at the parents) and the secondary process (I feel sad for my parents), which gives her an opportunity to cope more creatively with her past. She had started this working process already in her individual therapy at the programme, but here it became more stable and clearer to her.

A, the student-therapist as found in Table 10.1, reflected in supervision on her learning process of being a listening playmate at the beginning and gradually being more holding as a 'midwife' and as the most foreign position for therapist A: she experienced clearly being able to move into a positive father figure for B. A stated at the examination that this was a new and very important learning process for her. She learned that as a therapist you can be active as a holding person, but you also can be aware when the client is in a self-healing process, where you as the therapist can just witness and support.

Learning from being a client and a therapist with the same partner[2]

This student-client (B), whose process we have just followed through the Intertherapy examination of her student-therapist partner (A), also had to go through an examination, having been a student-therapist to her student-client A. I want to present some reflections this student brought in a written form alongside her filled-out schema in her examination situation to disseminate her further reflections on the learning process.

She listed what she called her problems and insecurities being a student-therapist during the Intertherapy training. She tried to verbalize how she felt that her insecurity (which she identified being a therapist) and vulnerability (which she faced and worked through being a client) were gradually transformed into resources. This transformation for her was useful in her development of an identity as a student-therapist on her way to become a professional music therapist. Here is how she presented the connections she found between her problems and resources as a student-therapist at her oral examination.

Problem: Feeling inferior to my client, being slower, not so well-formulated.

Resource: I am connected to my emotions through my body. I am decoding through my body, very sensitive to my client's body changes, and invite her to trust her body.

Problem: I feel like being passive in the verbal parts. I am using all my energy for empathic listening.

Resource: I give space to let the client's expressions unfold between us. I enjoy the privilege of being a witness and trusting that I will intuitively intervene when it is necessary for the client process.

Problem: I feel like being a follower; I feel the need to smooth out, to create harmony and coherence.

Resource: I am spontaneous and authentic in my mirroring of the client. I create an empathic 'parent space'. I support and connect to our joint working theme. I use humour in my way of gathering and focusing her topics.

Problem: I would like to be able to relieve my client from her problems.

---

2   This section is reprinted from Pedersen, 2013

Resource: I contain the client's frustration and give the possibility to go into dialogue with her problems and to create personal changes herself.

Problem: I feel a chaos inside from experiencing both my own feelings and those of the client.

Resource: I look very calm (on the video). I am able to contain feelings and I am not acting them out; in the situation I am able to let what I perceive by the senses inform me how and when to intervene.

Transformation from student-client to student-therapist[3]

In summing up this student, from her training in the discipline of Intertherapy, followed by an oral internal examination, it is evident that she first experienced and later reflected on her own therapeutic identity. She realized that her learning processes had been the following.

From being a student-client

- I can now take better care of a 'repressed' inner child

- I am transforming vulnerability to sensitivity

- I can now stay grounded in my body instead of flying out of my body

From being a student-therapist

- I can accept self-identified problems such as being slow, being passive, having a need to smooth out, and feeling a chaos inside, in a way so they can act as resources in the role of being a therapist

- I am learning to better cope with countertransference experiences and to trust intuition and sensitivity

In becoming a professional music therapist

- I can incorporate self-identified problems and learning processes from being a client in creating a sensitive and more clear music therapist identity

In the Intertherapy case documented in this chapter, these exact processes seemed to help the student to transform vulnerability into resourceful sensitivity. It is

---

3   This section is reprinted from Pedersen, 2013

important to add that the personal learning processes in the Intertherapy course are different for each student. Added to these learning processes is the challenge of quick shifts from being a client to being a therapist, where the students have to learn to be present in two parallel processes running simultaneously. The first process is the formal one following the prescribed turn-takings of being in the therapist and the client role. The second process running underneath is the therapeutic relationship influencing both the therapist and the client. To contain another person's intimate material can encourage one to trust the situation and open up. Of course, it can also be the opposite. Meeting defences by the partner in one role can make it more difficult to be trusting and open up in the other. Therefore, this quotation from 1999 is still relevant:

> From a supervisor's perspective, it is somewhat of a balancing act to be part of such intensive processes of the students. It presupposes that the supervisor sensitively balances the role of pushing/challenging and supporting in the supervision to help the student contain and develop their identity from this specific training involving sudden shifts of being client and therapist. Most students realise how important an understanding of one's own client's issues is, as basic tools for being a therapist. (Scheiby & Pedersen, 1999, p.69)

An international perspective on Intertherapy

Intertherapy as described here is also part of the training of postgraduates at Molloy University, New York, today as part of an advanced Analytical Music Therapy training programme. One difference from the Danish model is that the student dyads are created by the programme leader. MacRae (2019), in her PhD thesis, has examined the discipline of InterMusicTherapy (IMT) at Molloy University, and she describes the aim of the discipline as follows: 'IMT is an experiential learning method in which the therapist-in-training constructs his own understanding of the therapeutic music experience by engaging in it, and then processing it, with the AMT trainer in individual supervision' (MacRae, 2019, p.32). This training includes 15 Intertherapy sessions which invite a deep personal development for all involved students. In a survey (see Chapter 1), a couple of European training programmes responded that they were offering Intertherapy as a discipline in their programme, but it was not with live supervision. The students were working by themselves, and the supervisor had the recordings for comments after a number of sessions.

From this perspective, the Intertherapy course at the music therapy programme at Aalborg University seems to be the only one integrated in a graduate programme and with live supervision in each session.

References

Ammon, G. (ed.) (1974). *Gruppendynamik der Kreativität [The Group Dynamic of Creativity]*. Kindler TB.

Eschen, J.Th. (2002). 'Introduction.' In J.Th. Eschen (ed.), *Analytical Music Therapy*. Jessica Kingsley Publishers.

Jacobsen, C.H. (2000). 'Parallelprocesser i psykoterapi og supervision. Nogle refleksioner over fænomenet og dets psykologiske mekanismer' [Parallel processes in psychotherapy and supervision. Some reflections on the phenomenon and its psychological mechanisms].' *Psyke & Logos, 21*(2), 600–630.

MacRae, A. (2019). 'A phenomenological inquiry into intermusic therapy: An "experiential meeting place".' (Publication No. 27665970) [Doctoral dissertation]. Temple University. ProQuest Dissertations.

Pedersen, I.N. (2003). *Evaluation of Intertherapy*. Teaching Report. Department of Communication. Aalborg University. Unpublished.

Pedersen, I.N. (2007). 'Counter Transference in Music Therapy. A Phenomenological Study on Counter-Transference Used as a Clinical Concept by Music Therapists Working with Musical Improvisation in Adult Psychiatry.' Unpublished PhD Thesis. Institute for Communication and Psychology. Aalborg University. Accessed on 12/05/21 at www.mt-phd.aau.dk/phd-theses.

Pedersen, I.N. (2013). 'The Integration of a Self-Experience Track in the Education and Training of Danish Music Therapists: The Aalborg Model.' In K. Bruscia (ed.), *Self-Experiences in Music Therapy Education, Training, and Supervision*. Barcelona Publishers.

Priestley, M. (1975). *Music Therapy in Action*. Constable.

Priestley, M. (1994). *Essays on Analytical Music Therapy*. Barcelona Publishers.

Priestley, M. & Eschen, J.Th. (2002). 'Analytical Music Therapy – Origin and Development.' In J.Th. Eschen (ed.), *Analytical Music Therapy*. Jessica Kingsley Publishers.

Rycroft, C. (1972). *A Critical Dictionary of Psychoanalysis*. Penguin Books. (First published by Nelson, 1968.)

Scheiby, B.B. & Pedersen, I.N. (1999). 'Inter Music Therapy in the training of music therapy students.' *Nordic Journal of Music Therapy, 8*(1), 58–72.

Wigram, T. (2004). *Improvisation: Methods and Techniques for Music Therapy Clinicians, Educators and Students*. Jessica Kingsley Publishers.

CHAPTER 11

Guided Imagery and Music (GIM) in the Aalborg Therapeutic Training Programme

Bolette Daniels Beck, Charlotte Lindvang, & Lars Ole Bonde

The music is pivotal to evoking the feelings, memories, hopes and inspirations of the clients, rather like a wave that moves over and through the mind and the body. ... Therapists need to be present alongside the client on their journey both emotionally and physically, without turning away or feeling overwhelmed...

In the Bonny Method of Guided Imagery and Music (GIM) and in music and imagery experiences, it is the music and skill of the therapist, that holds the session in place.

(Kilham & van Dort, 2019, p.665)

Introduction

Guided Imagery and Music (GIM) is a psychotherapeutic model of receptive music therapy, where programmes of specially selected classical music pieces are applied to create inner experiences and imagery in altered states of consciousness. GIM, often called the Bonny Method of Guided Imagery and Music (BMGIM), was developed by the American music therapist Helen Lindquist Bonny in the 1970s. Originally, the method was created for in-depth exploration of the consciousness to access transformative and transpersonal experiences (Bonny, 2002). Today, GIM is used worldwide for a wide range of target groups and with a range of adaptations and modifications to meet different clients and their specific needs in therapy (Grocke, 2019; Grocke & Moe, 2015). 'GIM' was labelled an umbrella term for a spectrum of different techniques (see figure, Grocke & Moe, 2015, p.24). One widely applied modification of GIM has been named Music and Imagery (MI) and is characterized by a focused short music listening experience (just one piece, or 2–10 minutes of music) in a slightly altered state, where verbal interaction between therapist and client only takes place before and after the music listening. The method can be used both individually and in groups, for both resource-oriented and problem-oriented purposes (Grocke & Moe, 2015).

GIM is a well-researched model, and two systematic reviews have demonstrated the efficacy of the method in both clinical and non-clinical populations (Jerling & Heyns, 2020; McKinney & Honig, 2017). More information about the GIM method can be found in, for example, Grocke (2019, parts 1, 3, and 5) and Bruscia (2015).

GIM in the Aalborg curriculum

In 1998, GIM training was included in the Aalborg university curriculum to provide the music therapy students with basic knowledge of a model that has its roots in the humanistic therapeutic tradition, and that is also well integrated with psychodynamic theory (Bruscia, 2019), and thereby goes hand in hand with the students' psychodynamic training (see Chapter 3). The GIM course in Aalborg takes place as one intensive five-day course with 30 hours of teaching with groups of 6–14 students. It is carried out as a retreat every other year at the nearby Ørslev mansion, a former medieval nunnery, now used as a work refuge for artists and scientists, as well as for special courses such as GIM. The thick walls and atmosphere of the old nunnery provides a special framework for the deepening work of music and imagery, where the students are given the possibility to enter a deeper level of interaction with music and their inner world. Every other year, the course is held at the university, so that students who have small children or other reasons that they need to stay in the city can take the course.

The training is the first level of the GIM education, an introductory course taught by a music therapy professor who is also a 'primary trainer' accredited by one of the international GIM organizations (AMI or EAMI), together with an assistant trainer, who has completed the GIM training. The advanced GIM training (Levels II and III) is offered in private settings outside the university curriculum to candidates with a minimum of two years of clinical experience.

The trainers have many years of experience of training music therapists, as well as years of experience as GIM therapists, and the two teachers work together as a team, and combine their unique competencies.

As a preparation for the course the students are required to read several articles and book chapters from the GIM literature, and they get a compendium of approximately 50 pages that serves as a basic text for the course. The training is a fine-tuned combination of theory and practical exercises, and the practical exercises include three to four different group GIM experiences and several dyadic experiences where the students are working in pairs.

Placement in the curriculum

Students in their 8th and 10th semester are invited to enrol for the GIM course, which figures as an elective. This means that the group of students participating in the course are in different phases of their Master's level training. However, they have all completed their individual music therapy training course (see Chapter 8) as well as the course in psychodynamic-oriented music therapy group leading (see Chapter 9). The GIM course functions as an inspiration and deepening of students' former experiential training, and for the 8th semester students, the GIM course can be an opening to deeper layers and themes, that they can work with in Intertherapy and supervision that follows the course in the curriculum.

An important precursor is of course the receptive music therapy training, which is embedded in both experiential training and theoretical teaching preceding the GIM course.

Previous training in receptive methods

The Aalborg University music therapy curriculum has included teachings in receptive methods in several ways over the years. Currently, the students are taught basic receptive music therapy for two whole days (one day of the 6th and one of the 7th semester). These one-day courses build on several years of practical experiences from the three courses of group training therapy (GTT), where the students have experienced a wide range of receptive music therapy techniques guided by a training therapist, such as breathing to music, guided fantasy journeys to music, music listening and movement, drawing after deep listening, etc. (see Chapter 5). In CGMS (Clinical Group Music Therapy Skills) and PMG (Psychodynamic-oriented Music therapeutic Group leading) (see Chapters 7 and 9), they have applied receptive group music therapy exercises with peer students and some of the students have used receptive methods in their BA and MA internships. During all these previous experiences the students have received supervision on music choice, level of intervention, and how to facilitate the integration of the music listening experience with clients.

In the two course days of receptive music therapy, the students are given

an overview of different receptive music therapy methods, and they are introduced to and trained in basic Music and Imagery methods, such as guiding
their co-students into a relaxed state, facilitating a short listening experience,
and guiding back to a normal state of consciousness. They are also trained in
relaxation techniques such as Jacobsen's Progressive Relaxation (Jacobsen, 1957),
and Schultz's Autogenic training (Schultz & Luthe, 1959), including mental image-
ry-based guided relaxation types such as the 'ball of light' (Grocke & Wigram,
2007). After having tried several types of relaxation scripts with calm music as a
background, the students are given feedback on the sound and quality of their
voice, rhythm, and pacing, and they learn how to create a safe and protected
space for the relaxation experience with voice and music.

The basic receptive training is based on Grocke and Wigram's (2007) comprehensive book on *Receptive Methods in Music Therapy*. The students are introduced
to the 'Taxonomy of therapeutic music' developed by Wärja and Bonde (2014),
providing a framework to select music with (a) supportive, (b) mixed support-
ive-challenging, or (c) challenging intensity profiles. Furthermore, Summer's
continuum model of supportive-reeducative-reconstructive levels of therapy is
presented (Grocke & Moe, 2015, p.347).

During the training in receptive music therapy, including the two full days
dedicated to receptive methods, the learning objectives are that students experience music as an evoker of imagery in many modalities, and as an inducer of
bodily states of tension and relaxation. It is also important that students experience and understand that there is no 'right' or 'wrong' music listening experience,
and even difficult ('negative') experiences can have meaning and value.

Overall learning objectives of GIM

The course in GIM aims to provide the students with an extended learning of
theory and practice in receptive music therapy in general as well as providing new
knowledge about GIM specifically. The teaching programme is in accordance
with the international standards of GIM Level 1 training, and it is endorsed by
the European Association of Music and Imagery (EAMI).[1]

The theoretical parts of the training include an introduction to the Bonny
method, its core elements (music, imagery, altered states of consciousness,
guiding, and processing), the application of the Bonny Method with different
client groups, and contraindications. The students also are familiarized with
the historical background of GIM, and they get a brief introduction to relevant

---

1   www.music-and-imagery.eu

theory and research in GIM. At the end of the course, they are informed about ethical guidelines, and standards of practice.

Furthermore, students are taught selected psychological theories and international research that highlights the therapeutic benefits of GIM. Students develop their skills concerning basic relaxation techniques and inductions and they develop their ability to master basic techniques in guiding short travels to music, including the ability to make qualified choices of music for specific clients and for specific contexts and purposes.

Drawing a circle-shaped image, a mandala, after the return from the music listening experience, is part of the GIM method (Bonny, 2002). Mandala drawing is used for the immediate processing of the music and imagery experiences and, while sharing and reflecting upon the mandala in the dyad and in the group, students learn how to integrate this element on a supportive level, both as a client ('traveller') and as a therapist ('guide').

Formal competencies

The GIM Level 1 course is seen as introductory to GIM, which means that students are not sufficiently skilled to be allowed to call themselves GIM therapists nor to facilitate guided GIM sessions after the course. However, the combination of advanced self-experience and theoretical didactics deepens their knowledge and understanding of the power of music in general. The training upgrades their insight into what music listening can set in motion and thereby improve their professional and ethical sense as future music therapists who apply receptive methods.

After the course the students are allowed to facilitate Music and Imagery (MI) group and individual work with healthy clients/peers, and closely supervised MI work with selected client populations with which the student has a profound knowledge and experience.

Group experiences

During the course, the students go through several group music and imagery experiences guided by one of the trainers. The group has a common focus for the listening experience and the trainer guides the students before and after the music. All students lie on mats and an induction helps students to enter an altered state of consciousness. In most group experiences the students listen uninterrupted, but one of the group experiences is a so called 'talk-over' exercise, where the trainer continues to guide the students into a specific imagery or a specific focus, leaving time in between to let the music help to form the imagery. Each student can allow their own personal version of the story or theme to emerge, or they can go in another direction than the guide suggests. At the end of the listening session each student draws a mandala, and the group gathers to share, one after the other, the experiences and imagery that occurred.

One of Bonny's basic talk-over music and imagery experiences is 'The Meadow' (Bonny & Savary, 1973/1990, p.55). Here the trainer invites students to imagine themselves in a beautiful meadow (or garden) at their favourite time of the year and to let the music lead them to explore the meadow in all its details. The music can be for example *Fantasia on Greensleeves* by Vaughan Williams or the 2nd movement of Beethoven's 5th *Piano Concerto*.

During the course, students are exercising how to guide each other in a clinically adapted format of MI (Beck, 2019a). In small groups, they are taking turns in being the therapist and the client, and from a short conversation where the client is sharing their current state of mind, the therapist chooses a short piece of music to match the client. This music can be any style or genre that the guide finds suitable. While the music is playing the client is guided to paint a spontaneous picture (it may or may not be a mandala). After the music they round off with a short conversation about the experiences of the music listening and the painting.

Demo-session

At least one demo-session takes place during the course in which one of the students voluntarily enters the client position and the primary trainer is the GIM therapist. The other students enter the position as observers. Usually, the observers are separated into one group which has the task of focusing on the training therapist and another group which has the task of focusing on the student-client. The observers write notes during the session, and they are instructed to note verbal as well as nonverbal expressions and episodes.

The structure of the session is comparable to a normal GIM session, starting with a verbal conversation where the trainer and the student-client talk about the client's present situation and together identify a theme that the client would like to work with in the session. This prelude can take place outside the group if the student-client and trainer decide that is preferable. The client lies down on a couch and the training therapist guides the student-client into a slightly altered state of consciousness to be ready for the music listening phase. Often the trainer and the student-client will have agreed on an imaginative starting point for the inner imaging, and the training therapist will guide the client to the starting point before the music begins (Grocke, 2019). The trainer selects the GIM programme, which is usually a maximum of 30 minutes due to the overall time-frame. While listening to music, the training therapist follows and gently guides the student-client's experiences as they are carrying out a dialogue during the music. The session ends with a short dialogue in a normal state of consciousness, in which the trainer and student talk about the mandala drawing, and if the student accepts, the trainer supports the student-client in finding meaning in the experiences in relation to the initial conversation and focus for the session.

After the GIM session, the whole group gathers to describe and discuss what happened in the session. It is a unique situation where it is possible to ask the trainer about the considerations, for example, behind choice of music and the applied interventions. Furthermore, the group can have a meta-reflection about the images that the student-client had, and about the specific musical content of the chosen music. The discussion is structured and facilitated by the other trainer.

To ensure an ethical framework, the student-client is offered an individual conversation with the trainer who did the demo-session later during the course. The post-conversation safeguards the student's possibility to process the experience, since the student needs to contain both her own personal process in the session as well as the other students' reactions, comments, and questions.

Vignette[2]

One student-client found in the initial conversation that her life situation was characterized by a painful feeling of loneliness on one hand, and on the other by experiences of contemplation and peace of mind when she stayed in nature – which she did a lot. The student-client shared a traumatic experience she had many years ago where she was physically injured but didn't reach out for help. The training therapist and the student-client agreed that the focus of the session was to explore feelings of loneliness. The training therapist chose the GIM programme Solace, without the Shostakovich piece. During the first movements (Haydn's *Cello Concerto in C, Adagio*, and Sibelius' *Swan of Tuonela*), the student-client experienced a deep connection with nature at the beach, and she flew with the seagulls. While she listened to Boccherini's *Cello Concerto No. 9 in B-flat major (Adagio)*, she saw herself climbing in a tree with her brother. She said: 'He is good at climbing trees... He is a good friend. An excellent friend, who makes me feel completely safe [sighs].' The student-client felt touched, tears

---

2   Re-written with permission from the student-client from Beck (2019b).

running down her cheeks, and told that when they were children, she felt much freer, whereas growing up and being an adult was difficult and associated with being hurt or injured in some way. Listening to a Russian chorus singing *The Joy of Those Who Mourn*, the two different feelings of being child and adult merged in her. The guide asked her to let this feeling sink into her. While listening to the Dvořák piece *Serenade in E major (Larghetto)*, the student imagined herself and her brother sitting apart on each branch in the tree; she felt a deep concern for her brother. The guide asked her if she could say something to her brother, and she said aloud, 'I love you, it is going to be alright.' While the music came to a minor peak at 5:30–6:00 minutes, they hugged each other for a long time, and she felt her brother's hands on her back.

The student-client drew a mandala of herself and her brother as tiny figures in a huge tree. In the postlude, which was carried out in the group, the client found that the experience represented a polarity to her focus of loneliness and gave her a new way of thinking about herself and her connectedness with her brother, and maybe also with other people in her life.

After the demo-session the student-client stepped back and listened as the group had a conversation where the students described their observations and raised questions that felt relevant to them as they tried to understand how the GIM therapist works, how the interventions influenced the process, and how the music stimulated the imagery formation. The meta-reflection also gave rise to the group expressing empathy with the student-client and putting into words how it resonated with themselves. Later during the course, the student-client had one more talk with the trainer about the demo-session.

A case example from another student dyad is presented in an article including a transcript of the verbal dialogue, mandalas, and follow-up interview with the student three years later (Bonde, 2004). More than ten years later, the imagery was still vibrantly alive in the traveller.

GIM dyad work

Following the first music and imagery experience in the group, the introduction to basic guiding techniques as well as the demo-session, the students are ready for working in dyads. The training therapists create the dyads, and the students are matched from criteria such as age and life experiences, and similar ways of processing or common themes in the initial group music and imagery experience.

To create a safe and supportive environment, the dyadic GIM experience is modified for training. The music programme is shortened from the usual full range of 30–45 minutes to a duration of 20–25 minutes, and the 'working pieces'[3] are excluded.

While working in the dyads, the student guides are instructed to adopt an attitude of presence and to try to use 'GIM language': sounds of affective affirmation with melodic contours mirroring the client experience such as 'mmm', and simple open questions such as 'what are you experiencing now?' In this way the students are improving their guiding skills and developing their ability to use their voice coordinated and tuned in relation to the music and the client (Short, 2020).

As a pre-entry to the GIM training sessions in dyads, the students experience 'body listening' (Bonny, 2002) and movement on the floor to a GIM music piece. One of the students from each dyad is moving and the guide is witnessing and taking care of the partner as the person moves with closed eyes and enters a slightly altered state of consciousness. This exercise also introduces the experience of travelling, such as trusting the guide, and experiencing the music on a bodily level.

The format of the training dyad is a little different from a normal individual GIM session, both because several journeys are taking place in the same room to the same music, and because the teachers decide the music programme for all the travellers based on all the travellers' choice of focus for the journey and starting image. A starting image is not always used in GIM sessions, but is suggested by Bonny to facilitate the entry into the flow of imagery in inexperienced travellers (Bonny, 2002), and to provide a safe place to start from and to return to in case the travel is moving into unpleasant or scary material (Beck, 2015). The music choice for the training dyads is selected from a list of shortened basic GIM programmes (see also Bruscia, 2014).

A schedule of the training dyads is presented in Table 11.1, showing the different tasks and their timing.

Table 11.1: Training dyad schedule – Guided Imagery and Music Level 1 at Aalborg University

Phase	Client's state of consciousness	Time	Task
Prelude	NSC	15 min.	Guide/traveller: Identifying focus and starting imagery

cont.

---

3   A GIM programme is structured as a series of 3–7 music pieces with the most stimulating/challenging pieces – 'working pieces' – often placed in the middle (Grocke, 2019). In many of the short GIM programmes, there is only one or no working pieces.

Phase	Client's state of consciousness	Time	Task
Interlude	NSC	15–20 min.	Guides and trainers: Pre-supervision/presentation of music Travellers: Pre-mandala
Induction	NSC ▸ ASC	6 min.	Guides: Guided relaxation and induction
Music journey	ASC	22–25 min.	Travellers: Music listening (same programme for all) Trainers: Onsite supervision
Return	ASC ▸ NSC	15 min.	Guides: Guiding back, mandala drawing, and short conversation
Postlude	NSC	60 min.	Dyads 1+2: Processing of guides and travellers' experiences together in one big group Dyads 3+4: Guides and travellers process separately in two groups

Note: NSC: Normal state of consciousness, ASC: Altered state of consciousness.

After the prelude the guides meet with the trainers to inform about the focus and the starting image of the travellers, and in some cases get a short pre-supervision if needed in relation to what the traveller brought up in the pre-conversation. This is called an interlude and is not a normal part of a GIM session. The trainers briefly introduce the chosen music programme by introducing the pieces, playing small music examples, and informing about peaks and length of the pieces. Meanwhile, the travellers are drawing a mandala related to their focus to keep in contact with the focus and to prepare for the music listening. When the guides return, they have a few minutes' conversation with the traveller about the mandala and how the traveller is feeling now. To help the travellers to focus and prepare for the music listening phase, the guides, all at the same time, guide a short relaxation that relates to the theme of their traveller. The trainers keep the time and start the music. Both training therapists are present in the room and follow the work of the dyads. The guides are asked to raise their hand to ask for help at any time, and the training therapist will come and listen and guide the process, for example, by writing a suggested verbal intervention on a piece of paper or whispering in the ear of the guide. On rare occasions the training therapist takes over and intervenes directly for a moment or for the rest of the session.

When the music has finished and the student travellers are guided back to a normal state of consciousness, the travellers draw a mandala and briefly process their experience in a verbal conversation.

The dyads work together four times, which gives each person two times as guide and two times as traveller. After the first two dyads the whole group gathers and each of the dyads share their experience as guides and travellers. Usually, after the third and the fourth dyad, the group is divided in two and the guides will get post-supervision with the primary trainer, while the travellers gather for a therapeutic sharing space in a smaller group together with the training assistant.

During these short GIM travels the students have all sorts of experiences, from strong and even peak experiences, over deeply moving memories, bodily sensations, abstract or aesthetic imagery, to unconnected fast changing imagery (stream of consciousness). The diversity of the experiences is eye-opening for the students, and a mutual understanding of the multi-modal and multi-sensory nature of music imaging is established.

The guides often verbalize a sense of wonder at being able to follow their travellers' inner journey, and they express a respect for the skills of guiding that they have experienced as beginners.

Students' reactions to the experiences from the dyads can be summarized and exemplified as follows:

- Surprise – that listening to or moving to the music can be so powerful

- Gratitude – that the music and imagery can be so touching and deeply rewarding

- Discovery – that music can be a path to new areas of the mind and body

- Affirmation – that entering the role of a guide can give a sense of personal competence and integrity as a music therapist

- Curiosity – students are inspired to learn more about the power of the music

- Bonding – students experience resonance and deep connections amongst them through the emerging themes and emotions that are shared

Evaluation of the GIM course

The students evaluate the course in an open oral discussion and by written feedback from the students after the course. The students underline the importance of self-experience, being 'clients' in different receptive formats, and of being 'therapists' responsible for the experience of one fellow student. With very few exceptions, the students identify the dyads in the GIM Level 1 course as the most intensive experiences.

The course as a university subject is passed by a minimum 80 per cent attendance, and there is no formal examination. The students have a final 10 minutes of individual conversation with the trainers to round off the personal learning process, and to give recommendations about future practice and readiness for continuing GIM training.

Ethics

It is a requirement within EAMI/AMI that the students get insight into the ethical guidelines regarding GIM practice. At the beginning of the course, the trainers inform the students about the confidentiality of the shared experiences during the course.

Entering the course, some students bring serious themes related to their specific life situation, and the possibility to process their situation in GIM allows students to experience the transformative power of the method. It may also happen that difficult material and strong emotions emerge within the dyad sessions – to the students' own surprise. The students are used to sharing their emotions in groups and with the trainers from their music therapy training. However, if a student is overwhelmed, the trainers give special attention to the person and the dyad-partner, and counsel the student before ending the course. A student can also ask for a consultation with the trainer about the experience in a private dialogue during the course. In most cases the dyads can handle challenging material that emerges during the music travelling. The students are moving closer to graduation when they participate in the GIM course, and they are eager to try the role as guide. However, the trainers are following closely and sometimes assist by sitting beside the student guide to support and give advice for the guiding process. On rare occasions, an unrecognized trauma can be evoked in a dyad, and the student can be unable to contain the experience within the didactic framework. In such cases, the trainers can take the student out of the dyad, and one of the trainers can give the student special attention, perhaps including a personal session.

The GIM course is not a personal therapy and not a group therapy course. However, as in other disciplines in the therapeutic track, the course is a mixture of method learning and self-experience. The students participate authentically and may as mentioned experience important steps in their personal development. Furthermore, the students influence each other a lot in the group. They inspire each other, they get emotionally involved and engaged in each other, and they may experience synchronicity in their images. Students' personal difficulties can sometimes create tensions in the whole group. It is important that students are willing to share in the group or with the trainers if they have any special needs or difficulties, and that they are willing to follow advice from the trainers both concerning their role as traveller and as guide.

The students take a role as a GIM guide in their dyads even though they are at a beginner's level and have not yet learned how to guide in altered states of consciousness. This represents an ethical dilemma, and entails a responsibility of the trainers, which requires a high level of experience and awareness during the course. However, the potential learning is huge, as the students get a first-hand experience of the intimacy and depths of a traveller's journey with music. By getting feedback from their traveller, the students adapt their responses and interventions in the dyad, thereby refining their therapeutic competencies.

Theory
GIM didactics
The founder of GIM, Helen Bonny, wrote briefly that the most important thing for a GIM trainee is to have self-experiences of GIM (Bonny, 2002). She also created the three phases in GIM training, with Level 1 as an introductory training. Further descriptions of pedagogics and didactics tied to GIM training are sparse. Clark and Keiser (1989) wrote about the experiential-didactic approach in GIM training. Bonde presented the schedule of the GIM Level 1 course in detail and reflected on the connection between training in receptive music therapy and GIM at Aalborg University (Bonde, 2014). Summer (2015) described her development of a GIM training programme based on the 'Continuum model', reflecting on the span from the full Bonny Method to focused Music and Imagery formats.

Furthermore, Summer has thoroughly described dyad work in GIM and illustrates with cases how students learn through dialoguing in the dyad and reflecting with the trainer (Summer, 2014). Summer refers to Rogers' humanistic view as she emphasizes the important factors for teaching GIM, which is the process of directing the students to reach a deep connection with music as well as creating a containing space of acceptance and empathy:

> Almost every trainee enters GIM training with a common misconception: to help a client solve problems, you must be skilled enough to use the 'right' verbal interventions and to choose the 'right' music selections. These misconceptions are corrected through experiential exercises that direct the trainees' attention to gaining the essential skills necessary for GIM: to listen deeply to music, to be genuine and empathetic; and to give unconditional positive regard when faced with a distraught client. (Summer, 2014, p.13)

The trainer role

Carrying out a GIM Level 1 training in the university, the trainers maintain a delicate didactic, balancing between teaching theory, guiding group exercises, and facilitating therapeutic processes in the dyads. On one hand, it is a didactic and ethical challenge to go deep enough to expand the students' existential horizon as well as to experience the ethical responsibility when working with clients in altered states of consciousness. On the other hand, students need to be in a condition where they are aware of their own limits and can take care of themselves during and after the course. As a trainer it is a special task to hold and contain diverse experiences in the group and at the same time maintain the learning objectives. The use of two teachers on the course is necessary due to the complexity of the training format, where there are many transitions back and forth between altered and normal states of consciousness, and where the deep processes of imagery and embodied learning can bring about pure music transference, and transference and countertransference among the students, as well as between the trainers and the students (Bruscia, 1998, 2019).

Further didactic reflections

As presented in Chapter 2, self-experiential music therapy training can be compared to principles of apprenticeship (Kvale & Nielsen, 2004). During GIM Level 1 the students learn from observing the demo-session(s) and from the way the trainers are guiding induction as well as facilitating and processing imagery experiences in the group MI sessions. By applying the guide role step-by-step, receiving feedback from trainers and co-students, and by experiencing sessions as clients they are 'learning by doing' (Dewey, 1931; Lave & Wenger, 1991, Lindvang, 2010). The GIM course is based on the constant interaction between theory and practice. Theoretic teaching is integrated in the experiential training, as the students ask questions about GIM during or at the end of exercises, that refers to the theories underpinning GIM.

The training in GIM Level 1 supports the student's ability to take on a phenomenological approach which means that they stay open and curious when participating in the lived experience of another person's lifeworld and inner journeys, and when inquiring about imagery experiences and personal processes in the dyads. This strengthens the student's attitude towards an embodied presence to witness the evolving imagery, and to allow and support the student-client to uncover their own meaning in the post-conversation. 'The allowing aspects of GIM lessen the need for imposed interpretation by an authority figure and place the burden of definition of uncovered symbols and experiences on the individual' (Bonny, 2002, p.96).

Theories informing GIM

Helen Bonny created the GIM method with inspiration from psychedelic therapy research and humanistic growth movement in the 1970s, referring to different theories such as Jung's and Assagioli's models of transpersonal realms in the human psyche (Assagioli, 1965; Jung, 1969), Maslow's pyramid model with the goal of reaching realization through peak experiences (Maslow, 1971), and Leuner's Guided Affective Imagery (1969). Bonny regarded GIM as a method for spiritual and transpersonal growth, where music as a 'catalytic agent' works together with the self-organizing principle in the psyche to bring about change, transformation, and insight (Bonny, 2002). Bonny conceptualized the music-induced altered states of consciousness through several cut-log models, describing the oscillation between ego consciousness and different types of expanded states (Bonny, 2002). Goldberg (2019) and Clark (2014) further developed new consciousness models to map the healing and integrative potential of the inner journey.

The role of the music

During the course the students are presented with classical music, in the form of different shortened basic GIM programmes and single pieces. Bonny emphasized that knowledge of the music acquired from continuous deep listening is imperative for the coming GIM therapist and described the role of the music in GIM as a container, a catalyst, a vehicle, and a co-therapist (Bonny, 2002). She pointed out that classical music 'presents a mood or feeling, then significantly alters it through the use of complex development sections, before the music finally comes to a resolution' (Bonny, 2002, p.181). This development of the musical structure allows for a transformation in the traveller. From a trainer's perspective, the power of music underlines the necessity of thorough training of the therapist.

Imagery formation in GIM

During a GIM session the body is apparently 'inactive', but imagery – including all inner senses, mental and bodily systems such as kinaesthetic and visual experiences, subjective feelings, and memories – is at work in the client. The close connection between music and imagery presents evidence for the collaboration of sensory, motor, affective, and cognitive systems in music perception (Perilli,

2019). These embodied imagery phenomena during music listening in an altered state of consciousness are mediators of meaning formation for the traveller (Bonde, 2005, 2017). A pilot EEG study on imagery types and 'neurophenomenology' (Hunt, 2011) documented that the full range of brain waves are activated at different times during the GIM travel, which also point in the direction of the integrative potential of GIM. While guide and traveller are working closely together in the 'music envelope' (Bonny, 2002), phenomena of entrainment and mirroring processes can be observed in GIM sessions, and in a dual EEG study Fachner and colleagues (2019) identified synchronization between guide and traveller in moments of highly charged emotional imagery. This provides a neuroscientific perspective on the therapeutic potential of music and imagery experiences.

Bridging the relational and spiritual dimensions

Bonny described that consciousness serves as a personal 'faculty' that integrates various perceptions of reality (Bonny, 2002), and this was confirmed by Goldberg: 'The entire psyche is resonated by the music, allowing the opening to psychodynamic and spiritual dimensions of the person. The music reaches all aspects of the self, the entirety of the person' (Goldberg, 2019, p.483).

As multimodal imagery experiences are *shared* between traveller and guide, it is relevant to include theories on intersubjectivity. The Swedish psychologist and GIM therapist Katarina Mårtenson Blom provided theoretical understanding of the general psychotherapeutic change process in GIM supported by current developmental and relational theory (Blom, 2011, 2014; Bonde & Blom, 2016). Blom constructed six categories in a theory-based analysis of several GIM session transcripts. The first three categories are basic ways of sharing: 1) attention, 2) intention, and 3) affectivity in the client–therapist dialogue. The last three categories are truly interpersonal, shared experiences of: 4) confirmation, 5) non-confirmation, and 6) surrender to the music and/or to transpersonal or spiritual experiences/states. Blom's contribution is important for the training because it integrates psychodynamic thinking with the transpersonal realms and theories of consciousness, opening the door to conceptualizing spirituality as a relational experience. In GIM Level 1, the students are supported to acknowledge how non-ordinary states of consciousness can be regulated with music and the therapist's presence. On a basic level they might have experiences of enduring moments of tension or difficulty (category 5) and following that surrendering into experiences of transpersonal and/or spiritual character, transcending duality (category 6).

An example of a surrender experience during a GIM dyad session took place for a male student while listening to the music (with permission from the student). During the music, he said:

I am floating, I feel weightless. I can see a huge eagle... At first, I only see the eye and the beak. I am a little scared, it has so much power... Now I become the eagle and I feel my wings and I can see all the details on the Earth below me... I feel free...I soar in large circles.

The experience gave the student a feeling of connection to something larger than himself and allowed him to expand his self-understanding. Later, he also used the image of the eagle to empower himself when working with patients in music therapy.

Closure

For the music therapy students, the GIM course adds an experience of working in profound levels of the psyche in altered states of consciousness. It also offers a possibility to elaborate their musical horizon when working intensively with classical music. Furthermore, it gives the students experiences with the therapist role on a new level, when guiding and assisting each other on inner journeys touching upon existential themes in life.

> Music holds the listener in the here-now of All-that-is. It is a language of immediacy, which helps us to stay with the moment, the now; it facilitates a total attunement to the present and constant focusing and refocusing on the unending nows of existence. (Bonny, 1987, in Bruscia, 2019, p.44)

References

Assagioli, R. (1965). *Psychosynthesis: A Manual of Principles and Techniques.* Hobbs.

Beck, B. (2015). 'Guided Imagery and Music (GIM) with Clients on Stress Leave.' In D. Grocke & T. Moe (eds), *Guided Imagery and Music (GIM) and Music Imagery Methods for Individual and Group Therapy.* Jessica Kingsley Publishers.

Beck, B.D. (2019a). 'GIM in Mental Illness and Mental Health Conditions.' In D. Grocke (ed.), *Guided Imagery and Music – The Bonny Method and Beyond* (2nd ed.). Barcelona Publishers.

Beck, B.D. (2019b). 'Sacred moments in Guided Imagery and Music.' *Approaches, 11*(1), 1–15.

Blom, K.M. (2011). 'Transpersonal and spiritual BMGIM experiences and the process of surrender.' *Nordic Journal of Music Therapy, 20*(2), 185–203.

Blom, K.M. (2014). 'Experiences of transcendence and the process of surrender in Guided Imagery and Music (GIM). Development of new understanding through theories of intersubjectivity and change in psychotherapy.' Doctoral dissertation, Institute for

Communication and Psychology, Aalborg University, Denmark. Accessed on 15/12/21 at https://vbn.aau.dk/ws/portalfiles/portal/316470580/Katarina_Martenson_Blom_Thesis.pdf

Bonde, L.O. (2004). "'To draw from bits and pieces a more supportable narrative". An introduction to Paul Ricoeur's theory of metaphor and narrative and a discussion of its relevance for a hermeneutic understanding of music-assisted imagery in The Bonny Method of Guided Imagery and Music.' *Canadian Journal of Music Therapy, 11*(1), 31–56.

Bonde, L.O. (2005). 'The Bonny Method of Guided Imagery and Music (BMGIM) with cancer survivors: A psychosocial study with focus on the influence of BMGIM on mood and quality of life.' Doctoral dissertation, Institute for Communication and Psychology, Aalborg University, Denmark.

Bonde, L.O. (2014). 'Music and Imagery in the Training of Danish Music Therapists at Aalborg University.' In K.E. Bruscia (ed.), *Self-Experiences in Education, Training and Supervision*. Barcelona Publishers.

Bonde, L.O. (2017). *Embodied Music Listening: The Routledge Companion to Embodied Music Interaction*. Routledge.

Bonde, L.O. & Blom, K.M. (2016). 'Music Listening and the Experience of Surrender. An Exploration of Imagery Experiences Evoked by Selected Classical Music from the Western Tradition.' In H. Klempe (ed.), *Cultural Psychology of Musical Experience. Advances in Cultural Psychology, 23*. Information Age Publishing.

Bonny, H.L. (2002). *Music and Consciousness: The Evolution of Guided Imagery and Music*. Barcelona Publishers.

Bonny, H.L. & Savary, L.M. (1973/1990). *Music and Your Mind. Listening with a New Consciousness.* (rev. ed.). Station Hill.

Bruscia, K.E. (1998). 'The Dynamics of Transference.' In K.E. Bruscia (ed.), *The Dynamics of Music Psychotherapy*. Barcelona Publishers.

Bruscia, K.E. (2014). *Discography of Guided Imagery and Music (GIM) Programs*. Barcelona Publishers.

Bruscia, K.E. (2015). *Notes on the Practice of Guided Imagery and Music*. Barcelona Publishers.

Bruscia, K.E. (2019). 'A Psychodynamic Orientation to Guided Imagery and Music (GIM).' In D.E. Grocke (ed.), *Guided Imagery and Music: The Bonny Method and Beyond* (2nd ed.). Barcelona Publishers.

Clark, M.F. (2014). 'A new synthesis model of the Bonny Method of Guided Imagery and Music.' *Journal of the Association for Music and Imagery, 14*, 1–22.

Clark, M. & Keiser, L. (1989). *Teaching Guided Imagery and Music: An Experiential-Didactic Approach*. Archedigm Publications.

Dewey, J. (1931). *Context and Thought*. University of California Press.

Fachner, J.C., Maidhof, C., Grocke, D., Nygaard Pedersen, I. *et al.* (2019). '"Telling me not to worry..." Hyperscanning and neural dynamics of emotion processing during Guided Imagery and Music.' *Frontiers of Psychology, 10*, 1–23.

Goldberg, F. (2019). 'A Holographic Field Theory Model of the Bonny Method of Guided Imagery and Music (GIM): A Psychospiritual Approach.' In D.E. Grocke (ed.), *Guided Imagery and Music. The Bonny Method and Beyond* (2nd ed.). Barcelona Publishers.

Grocke, D. (ed.) (2019). *Guided Imagery and Music. The Bonny Method and Beyond* (2nd ed.). Barcelona Publishers.

Grocke, D. & Moe, T. (eds) (2015). *Guided Imagery and Music (GIM) and Music Imagery Methods for Individual and Group Therapy*. Jessica Kingsley Publishers.

Grocke, D. & Wigram, T. (2007). *Receptive Methods in Music Therapy*. Jessica Kingsley Publishers.

Hunt, A.M. (2011). 'A neurophenomenological description of the Guided Imagery and Music experience.' PhD thesis, Temple University.

Jacobsen, E. (1957). *You Must Relax*. McGraw-Hill.

Jerling, P. & Heyns, M. (2020). 'Exploring Guided Imagery and Music as a well-being intervention: A systematic literature review.' *Nordic Journal of Music Therapy, 29,* 371–390.

Jung, C.G. (1969). 'The Archetypes and the Collective Unconscious.' In H. Read, M. Fordham, & W. McGuire (eds), *The Collective Works of C.G. Jung* (vol. 9, part 1). Princeton University.

Kilham, K. & van Dort, C. (2019). 'Self-Care for the Therapist: Creating a Strong Foundation for Ethical Practice.' In D.E. Grocke (ed.), *Guided Imagery and Music. The Bonny Method and Beyond* (2nd ed.). Barcelona Publishers.

Kvale, S. & Nielsen, K. (2004). *Mesterlære. Læring som social praksis [Apprenticeship. Learning as a social practice]* (5th ed.). Hans Reitzels Forlag.

Lave, J. & Wenger, E. (1991). *Learning in Doing: Social, Cognitive, and Computational Perspectives. Situated Learning: Legitimate Peripheral Participation.* Cambridge University Press.

Leuner, H. (1969). 'Guided affective imagery (GAI).' *American Journal of Psychotherapy, 23*(1), 7–23.

Lindvang, C. (2010). 'A field of resonant learning. Self-experiential training and the development of music therapeutic competencies: A mixed methods investigation of music therapy students' experiences and professional's evaluation of their own competencies.' Doctoral dissertation, Institute for Communication and Psychology, Aalborg University. Accessed on 15/12/2021 at https://vbn.aau.dk/ws/portalfiles/portal/316410062/6465_dissertation_c_lindvang.pdf.

Maslow, A. (1971). *The Farther Reaches of Human Nature.* Viking Press.

McKinney, C. & Honig, T. (2017). 'Health outcomes of a series of Bonny Method of Guided Imagery and Music sessions: A systematic review.' *Journal of Music Therapy, 54,* 1–34.

Perilli, G.G. (2019). 'Metaphor and Emotion Regulation in the Bonny Method of Guided Imagery and Music.' In D.E. Grocke (ed.), *Guided Imagery and Music. The Bonny Method and Beyond* (2nd ed.). Barcelona Publishers.

Schultz, J.H. & Luthe, W. (1959). *Autogenic Training: A Psychophysiologic Approach to Psychotherapy.* Grune & Stratton.

Short, A. (2020). *Exploring integral interactions in voice and music for GIM practice.* Paper at EAMI online conference, 24 September.

Summer, L. (2014). 'Case Vignettes Demonstrating Experiential Learning in GIM Seminars.' In K.E. Bruscia (ed.), *Discography of Guided Imagery and Music (GIM) Programs.* Barcelona Publishers.

Summer, L. (2015). 'The Journey of GIM Training from Self-Exploration to a Continuum of Clinical Practice.' In D. Grocke & T. Moe (eds), *Guided Imagery and Music (GIM) and Music Imagery Methods for Individual and Group Therapy.* Jessica Kingsley Publishers.

Wärja, M. & Bonde, L.O. (2014). 'Music as co-therapist: Towards a taxonomy of music in therapeutic Music and Imagery work.' *Music and Medicine, 6*(2), 16–27.

CHAPTER 12

Clinical Supervision for Internship Students

Inge Nygaard Pedersen, Ulla Holck, & Hanne Mette Ridder

Achieving self-awareness is a prerequisite to becoming an effective clinician, and a clinician cannot be effective without self-awareness. Thus, reflexivity is both the process and outcome of supervision.

(Bruscia, 2019, p.305)

In this chapter, we will present the discipline of clinical supervision as it is trained and developed with music therapy students during internship at Bachelor's and Master's degree level. It is an essential part of the therapeutic training track at the music therapy programme at Aalborg University, where clinical supervision is integrated as an important learning experience for the development of the students' professional music therapy identity. Based on our supervisor experience at the programme for decades, we describe how supervision can be performed at different levels of training from novice to experienced students, and with different foci on, for example, techniques, client perspective, therapist role, or relationship, and whether supervision is carried out in individual or group settings.

A psychodynamic approach to supervision

An overall understanding of supervision was formulated by Mary Priestley in 1975. She saw the client, the therapist, and the music as equal parts of music therapy work, and that all three parts play an equally important role in the reflection on and evaluation of the clinical work. In this understanding, the student-therapist (also named supervisee in some of the quotes in the following) is always an active part of the clinical work. Therefore, the dynamic processes of the student-therapist/client/music triad as well as the student-therapist/supervisor/music triad are simultaneously present in supervision and central to reflection and evaluation (Pedersen, 2009).

Our approach to supervision is rooted in a relational psychoanalytic understanding, which includes that unconscious as well as conscious mental processes are created and developed in a basically inter-subjective context. Music therapy practice is related to how the therapist and the client are present and understand themselves and others through repeated experiences of contact and communication in and outside music. These ideas are inspired from Stern (2004, 2010), Kohut (1990), and Winnicott (1971). They have been further developed and clarified through contemporary research in developmental psychology and neuro-affective processes in music therapy as described by Lindvang and Beck (2017) and in Chapter 3. An important perspective from these theories is the way in which client and therapist are present and mutually influence each other. Neuro-affective developmental psychology offers an integration of theories from developmental psychology, attachment theories, trauma research, and research in the affective structures of the brain. An underlying assumption is that the personality is biologically settled by both the character and the temperament of the single person, and socially shaped by close relationship experiences with attachment figures. In addition, the personality is modulated by psychologically overwhelming experiences through one's life. Thus, the psychodynamic approach highlights unconscious processes and self-awareness integrated with a biological, psychological, and social understanding of contemporary neuro-affective and developmental psychology (see Chapter 3).

For the music therapy student, who is expected to establish a music therapeutic process with a client for the first time, it involves many challenges, layers of involvement, self-awareness, and reflections. With a series of internship periods and increased responsibility for the student-therapist, the supervisor must be able to meet the different needs of the student-therapists, and to address the numerous ethical dilemmas that the student will need to relate to. We will unfold these different needs and levels of supervision processes in the view of a progression of internship periods.

Context and purpose of internship supervision

The purpose of internships and clinical supervision is to prepare music therapy students for ethically conducted clinical practice. This preparation is not just learning about client populations, clinical methods, techniques, approaches, and theories; it is also about ethical considerations and about how to tune oneself to the role of a therapist. This implies the competencies to take care of oneself, being prepared to tune into the needs of each single client, but also to understanding the overarching needs of client populations, of team members and health care systems. Supervision plays an important role in the process of achieving such rich awareness. In the following, we will describe three steps in internship supervision: first by prolonged observation of music therapeutic processes, second by supervised music therapy at a small scale, and third by entering a supervised role as a music therapist.

1. Observation at clinical setting

The first internship period takes place by the end of the first study year. Each student visits a professional music therapist at an institution for one month, solely *observing* the work of the music therapist. The aim is to observe and describe the work of an experienced music therapist and to learn to distinguish between personal beliefs and professional controlled subjective statements, in a way where the students develop the ability to understand situations from various perspectives. The students are expected to gather musical data and to analyse these from different perspectives in a written report (25 pages) and for an oral examination.

2. First-time internship

The second internship period takes place by the end of the third study year, mostly at institutions without music therapy professionals. For the first two weeks, the student-therapists observe daily practice at the institution, and then continue by offering individual music therapy sessions once a week for 10 weeks to one or two clients. The aim is to give the student first-hand experiences as a therapist within interdisciplinary collaborative teams and to understand their therapeutic work in relation to a specific client population. A contact person at the institution guides the student when they have questions about choice of clients, logistics, ethics, and specific rules, expectations, and approaches.

During this internship, the student-therapists take part in group supervision at the university training programme. As part of the supervision, the students are expected to gain knowledge about ethical principles and an active use of the supervision process. In the supervision, the students work on the formulation and modification of therapeutic working aims. At the start of the supervision, they reflect on techniques and methods to start up a therapeutic process and continue to work through and to terminate the therapeutic course of therapy in a responsible and ethical way. The abilities developed through group supervision include the ability to reflect on clinical matters and to identify and evaluate one's strengths and challenges in the clinical situation. The students must be able to evaluate their own influence on the therapeutic relationship and to start identifying which dynamic processes are evoked in the relationship. Further, the student-therapists learn to identify coherence between the needs and problems of the clients and the working aims created for a music therapy case formulation. Most student-therapists at this level are primarily concerned about which techniques can be applied and how to use them in 'the right way'. During the supervision process, they are introduced to and realize the importance of a broader perspective of the clinical process.

Prior to the first-time internship, the therapeutic training track at the university prepares the students to develop self-awareness, the ability to identify how they themselves influence interactions, and which dynamic processes they are part of in therapeutic processes. Disciplines in the musical training track prepare them to perform music, and to master musical techniques and improvisation styles during the therapeutic process, and finally disciplines in the academic training track prepare them to have a theoretical platform for their clinical work (for syllabus details, see Table 2.2 in Chapter 2). In addition, the student-therapists are required to collect comprehensive notes and audio/video data in an ethically responsible way, and in a format where data can be integrated in a documentation report and case formulation. Thus, the supervision process for the first-time internship students promotes a development of reflexive practice as a starting point for gradually building a music therapy identity.

3. Full-time internship

The third and last internship period takes place at the start of the fifth study year. For this internship period, the students spend four days a week over four months working as music therapists with clients in both individual and group sessions, and by taking part in the teamwork at the institution. The aim of this internship is to give the student-therapists hands-on experiences as a professional within an interdisciplinary collaborative team, and to understand their role as a therapist in the team as well as in the sessions with the clients. The aims for the supervision are at a more advanced level, training the students to use the supervision processes as a beneficial asset for the clinical work, and for their process towards a more stable music therapy identity. As a preparation for this comprehensive internship period, the students visit the place for an observation period of one week during the preceding semester and carry out a systematic literature review on the client population and/or relevant interventions. Further, the students are expected to re-read their notes, logbooks, and reports from previous internship experiences and supervision sessions.

At the institution, it is emphasized that the student-therapists see their role as a staff member and a real part of the team. Often the institution has never had a music therapist employed, and staff may not be familiar with music therapy as a treatment possibility with their population. This puts a strong demand on the student to disseminate not only their clinical work, but also music therapy as a discipline. During supervision, the supervisor works with the student-therapists to be adaptive to the treatment culture at the institution, to comply with the duty of confidentiality, and to be realistic in their aims and expectations for the therapeutic work. The student-therapists must – as a minimum – work with three individual clients and one group over a longer period. At some institutions, such as hospices and hospitals, it is not possible to meet even once a week or to have longer courses of therapy, as the clients may only stay for a short time. The student will adapt to these realities and will instead include more clients. The students can request an individual supervisor among the possible supervisors in the Aalborg team and their wishes will be met if in any way possible. The students are obliged to collect audio/video data and comprehensive session notes. When relevant, the students may add pre/post collection of data and other types of data during the internship. This gives the students the opportunity to integrate comprehensive and rich data for their Master's thesis. Thus, each student has the possibility to – step by step – be specialized within one client population during their last years of the five-year music therapy programme.

In preparation for this internship, the students have worked with trusting their sensations in relationship from the therapeutic learning track as disseminated through all the previous chapters in this book. This learning track also prepares the students to be aware of how to find a balance between identifying with the sufferings and needs of others, and still be grounded and able to listen openly to oneself in relationships. From the musical learning track, the students are trained in advanced clinical improvisation, where they learn to intuitively follow a direction in the music, and to choose the right technique with the right timing. In doing this, they must simultaneously be aware of what is happening in the music and how to terminate the improvisation. In the academic learning track, the students study advanced music therapy theory and research. Overall, the aim of this third comprehensive internship period and supervision processes is to train the student-therapists to reflect and to integrate implicit and explicit therapeutic, musical, and academic learning in order to create a future stable music therapy identity.

Individual and group supervision

In their third year, the student-therapists take part in group supervision, and then, in the fifth year, both individual and group supervision are provided. On top of sharing and often exploring techniques during musical roleplay between the students, the advantage of group supervision for the first-time therapist is the possibility to share frustrations and insecurities. By listening to peers, the students realize that others may struggle with the same problems and may find ways to transform their frustrations into new understandings and insights. They listen empathically to the challenges of their fellow student-therapists and apply creative media to give aesthetic feedback under the lead of the group supervisor, who ensures that the feedback is positive and appropriate. This supports the student-therapists to increase self-awareness as well as the ability to shift perspective. Countertransference issues are pointed out by the group supervisor to help the students become aware of these more complex processes, and gradually be able to recognize these themselves.

The individual supervision process allows for reflections on client selection, alliance building, session-to-session challenges, and clinical and ethical considerations. The advantage here is that personal challenges that influence the therapist role, and that the student prefers to share only with the individual supervisor, can be explored and dealt with in a more secure field. In the fifth year, in both individual and group supervision, it is expected that the student is able to address, for example, countertransference issues and to go more in depth in the exploration of challenges in the therapeutic relationship.

Creative media in supervision

Creative media is a cornerstone of music therapy supervision – both individual and in groups. During the supervision process, the supervisor or group members may give aesthetic responses in various ways (Ødegaard & DeMott, 2008). It allows for understanding a problem from more perspectives and may take form as, for example, 1) fellow students making drawings or poetic writings, while listening to the narratives of a student-therapist, and return these as feedback to the student and the group, 2) musical roleplaying, where the student-therapist is asked to roleplay the client and to choose another fellow student as the therapist and 3) the student-therapist is asked to play (improvise on) their sensations/impressions of the client or to instruct the supervisor or fellow students to improvise a specific client or a group of clients.

IDM: *The integrated developmental model of supervision*

We understand supervision as a continuum process, but also find it important to describe levels in the supervision, although these would be overlapping and flexible. We are inspired by the Integrated Developmental Model (IDM) describing levels in the supervision process, which we find useful for understanding student-therapists' learning processes through the internships. In the following, we will present the model, and use it as inspiration to understand and discuss music therapy internship supervision at different levels.

The IDM was developed by Stoltenberg, McNeill, and Delworth (1998) and expanded by Stoltenberg and McNeill (2010) and identifies three levels in the supervision processes. With clinical experience, level three can grow into an integrative level (Stoltenberg & McNeill, 2010). The levels are related to eight clinical domains and three overriding structures describing the therapist. The eight domains are: intervention skills and competence, assessment techniques, interpersonal assessment, client conceptualizations, individual differences, theoretical orientation, treatment plans and goals, and professional ethics. The three overriding structures are: 1) Self- and Other-Awareness, 2) Motivation, and 3) Autonomy. These structures are described with specific characteristics at the different levels. As an example, the structure of Self- and Other- Awareness is defined with a perspective on *cognitive* and *affective* characteristics. At level 1, supervisees cognitively tend to be more self-focused without self-awareness, which may lead to performance anxiety when it comes to affective characteristics. At level 2, supervisees cognitively show increased focus on the client and better understand the client's perspective which, when it comes to affective skills, means that empathy is possible but there's also a risk of over-identification with the client. When the supervisee at level 3 manages to accept their own strengths and weaknesses and also the strengths and weaknesses of the client, the affective characteristics are better awareness of their own reactions and increased empathy. Finally, at level 3i, the personalized understanding of the supervisee crosses all eight domains.

Processes of internship supervision towards a music therapy identity

In our supervision of music therapy students, we have experienced different levels similar to the three IDM levels, both as a linear progression in each student's experiences and learning process and as a circular movement, where the student continually moves back and forth between levels in their understanding and identification of themselves as a future professional music therapist. In the following, we will illustrate which kind of developmental processes the music therapy students go through inspired from the IDM and the three levels. As these reflections are related to student music therapists, we call them *Student Music Therapist* (SMT) supervision Levels 1, 2, and 3.

SMT supervision Level 1

At the first SMT supervision level, we experience that insecurity is prevailing for the music therapy students. Their focus is often on *What can I do to help this client?* They ask for tools, techniques, and ideas so they can (rather quickly) make the problems and symptoms disappear. If these do not disappear, the students call for other tools or techniques, or ask to be taught how to overcome the problems. In a chapter on music therapy supervision with students and professionals with focus on the use of music and analysis of transference experiences, Pedersen (2009) was inspired by the first edition of the IDM (Stoltenberg, McNeill, & Delworth, 1998) to describe how the student music therapists at this level are:

> ...occupied with acquiring techniques. The supervisees use much of their cognitive capacity to consider rules and guidelines for a concrete practice. Their self-concept is dependent upon how far they succeed in applying a technique; they are very concerned about themselves. This concern about their own performance often gets in the way of awareness of the patient and his material. Novices are mostly not aware of their own reactions to the patients. This can be reinforced by anxiety about being in the new role as a therapist, by insecurity and by negative self-evaluation of their own performance. Finally, supervisees at the novice level can be very preoccupied with thoughts about approval or disapproval by both patients and the supervisor. (Pedersen, 2009, p.48)

Based on this, we suggest that the role of the supervisor is to encourage the student-therapists, to give advice and ideas for tools and techniques, but also to share that problems and symptoms may not just disappear. The student-therapists' focus on techniques and attitude of wanting problems to dissolve quickly can stop the development of the working alliance, not only with the client but also with the supervisor. The supervisor's responsibilities for the student-therapists' ethical conduct towards the clients is important, and therefore the students learn to receive supervision as a part of professional development. At SMT supervision Level I, the supervisor is responsible for the structure of the supervision, which has a double impact as the student-therapist may model the supervisor's working style in their work with clients. Finally, at this level, Stoltenberg and McNeill (2010) suggest that transference issues should not be disseminated and verbalized by the supervisor. We experience that with students who have had more years of therapeutic training, transference issues may cautiously be shared and verbalized (Pedersen, 2009). Also, parallel processes in supervision (Jacobsen, 2007) most often have to be kept as implicit knowledge by the supervisor, or to be disseminated and reflected supportively.

SMT supervision Level 2

At SMT supervision Level 2, the student-therapists mostly have gained more confidence in being in a therapist's role, and now often seem highly concerned with the state of the clients. They strive at fully understanding the problems and sufferings of the clients and work hard to identify with these sufferings. Sometimes student-therapists feel that they are the only person who really understands the client, and in the music interplay or music listening with the client they develop unique ways of being together. Such situations may be very intense and helpful for the client, and surprising developmental steps may take place in the music therapy process. This is highly valuable for the student-therapist; however, it becomes a problem if the student-therapist expects to always be such a special contact and healer for all clients. Potentially, this will evoke a crisis the day the therapy process is not that successful. We may talk of beginner's luck; however, the first experiences as a therapist often build on strong – and helpful – enthusiasm. Pedersen, inspired by the IDM (Stoltenberg *et al.*, 1998), describes this level as follows:

> Supervisees have more trust in their work and their focus has moved from concern with the application of techniques to a focus on the client, which allows for deep empathic understanding of the clinical situation. There is a risk of over-identification with the client, followed by very strong countertransference reactions. The focus on the client might reduce the therapist's ability to be aware of herself and her own reactions towards the client. Often, the therapist is seeking a personal therapeutic style and a relevant theory to accompany it and might not want too much 'interference' from the supervisor. (Pedersen, 2009, p.49)

For other student-therapists, the reactions from the client may be aggressive, agitated, and difficult to understand. This may create a feeling of hopelessness in the students, leading them to conclude that the client is not ready for music therapy. It may also create a feeling of helplessness, which reinforces the insecurity from SMT supervision Level 1 and may provoke the idea of never going to be a proper music therapist.

The role of the supervisor at SMT Level 2 is to be aware of, and witness, such reactions and to remain supportive and flexible. It is still important to give advice, but also to offer alternative ideas and to support the student-therapist in finding the most meaningful way forward. It is essential not to kill the enthusiasm of the student-therapist, but to help them formulate their own ideas about interventions and to understand the sense of the relationship with the client, as well as with the supervisor. It is possible at this level to point at and clarify transference/countertransference patterns in the therapeutic relationship and eventual parallel processes in the student/supervisor relationship. For the supervisor, it is important to ensure that ethical principles concerning the work of the student-therapist are maintained, not only regarding closeness/distance in the relationship with the clients, but also in relation to the context of the institution.

SMT supervision Level 3

Supervision at SMT Level 3 is described by Pedersen, inspired by the IDM, as something that is:

> ...mostly first achieved after several years of clinical practice. When the supervisee has developed a consciousness of her own reactions, a varied understanding of the therapeutic process and a well-developed capacity for empathy and understanding are evident. Countertransference mechanisms are much more conscious, and the supervision is much more of a mutual interplay where both partners can reflect at an equal level. It is to be expected that any confrontation will be met at an analytic reflective level and seen as the basis for further investigation. (Pedersen, 2009, p.49)

At the Aalborg music therapy programme, due to a comprehensive experiential and resonant training in the therapeutic learning track, the students in their last study year with the full-time internship are supervised at SMT Level 3, also with processes where they are moving back and forth between Levels 1, 2, and 3. As an integrated free flow between sensing, feeling, and thinking is still in process, the student music therapists may still be concerned with what they can or cannot allow themselves to play and to say in the therapist role. The students may also find specific interventions artificial and fight to find a way to intervene that is both meeting the situation and the need of the client, and at the same time feels natural and embodied for the student music therapist to use.

The role of the supervisor at Level 3 is to be supportive and acknowledging the student music therapist. The supervisor must still be aware of and apply the roles from Levels 1 and 2 when needed, but needs to remain with a balanced view on the work even if the student music therapist is over-enthusiastic about or devaluing their work.

SMT supervision Level 3i

Added to Level 3 in the IDM is an advanced level, Level 3i, which is integrative of the other levels. This level is achieved after several years of clinical practice (Stoltenberg & McNeill, 2010). Overriding structures are in play when the therapist functions across domains and a fluidity in movement among the domains appears. The integrated Level 3i is not often fully achieved, and is where clinicians are considered experts by their colleagues. The growth to Level 3i may be experienced as movements that are less vertical (understood as moving up the levels), but more horizontal in spreading an integrated understanding across domains and by conceptually linking and organizing relevant learning and information into what Stoltenberg and McNeill (2010) term as schemata.

We find it highly relevant to be aware of SMT supervision Levels 1–3 for supervision of student music therapists, and in the following we will describe and discuss the possible developments of the student music therapists according to the SMT supervision levels, which are inspired from the IDM. We will therefore present examples from our supervisory practice described as three vignettes illustrating the different levels. The vignettes are based on generalized patterns of problems the students have brought up in supervision, and they do not refer to a specific student or a specific client.

Vignette 1: First-time internship: Everybody can sing a song!

The first vignette is from the internship period in the third study year, where the student-therapists for the first time are responsible for 1–2 clients during ten weeks at an institution. The supervision takes place in a group setting with four students, and the vignette is from the very first supervision session. The student in focus introduces the institution, a home for people with dementia, where he carries out individual music therapy with A, an 80-year-old woman with severe dementia.

Student-therapist: I have seen A twice, and she reacts positively when I sing and play her favourite songs. Last time I also improvised a little on the guitar, but she became restless, so I stopped playing. It is meaningful to sing A's favourite songs with her, but I cannot do this all the time. How can I progress this work?

Supervisor (smiling): First, A and you need to be familiar with one another!

Student-therapist: Yes, okay (laughs a little). I know I am a little fast, and of course I have to take into account A's arousal level, but I just want so much to apply what I have learned at the music therapy programme. Everybody can sing a song.

Supervisor: Tell me, what makes sense when you are singing a song with A?

Student-therapist: She is calm and seems to be attentive.

Supervisor: Yes, exciting! – and how does that affect you?

Student-therapist (looks a little confused): Well, that's fine.

Supervisor: Can you show a video clip from the session where you have a sense of meaningfulness inside?

The student-therapist shows a short video clip to the group of fellow students and the supervisor. They express empathy in the form of smiles and sighs.

Supervisor (while the video continues playing): When you watch this clip, can you then recall the emotion in the situation?

Student-therapist: Yes, it is a nice feeling… Mmm (thoughtful), A opens her mouth, maybe she actually tries to sing with me?

Supervisor (nodding): Your voice is soft and airy, and you make a small *ritardando* at the end of each melodic line. Is it on purpose?

Student-therapist (surprised): No, it just feels natural to do so. Maybe I could lower the tempo even more and see if that makes it easier for A to sing with me?

The video clip is shown again while the student-therapist together with the group and the supervisor reflects upon how he can use *improvisational elements within the frame of singing favourite songs* to increase synchronization and micro-regulations in order to increase A's possibilities to take part in the interplay. The student-therapist tries out different suggestions on the guitar and reflects upon the theory on Communicative Musicality (Malloch & Trevarthen, 2009) in the light of the interplay with A.

During the supervision process, the group members listen and respond with drawings or by catching the most important words or expressions and putting them poetically together. At the end of the supervision, these products are given to the student-therapist together with brief feedback from each group member.

Theoretical reflections

The beginning of the supervision is characterized by the student's frustration about not being able to improvise with A. He acknowledges and laughs at his own impatience, but he is nevertheless caught in a dilemma between him devaluing singing a favourite song as a music therapy method, and at the same time experiencing it as meaningful with A. We often see this dilemma with novice therapists and suggest that the supervisor explores the situation in a way that supports shifts in perspective. In this example, while watching video clips together, the supervisor guides the student-therapist by explicitly highlighting the client's reactions when the student-therapist is singing, and thus adding insights to the situation and validating the student's sensation of meaningfulness.

The video recording and the reactions from the group members may further enhance the sense of meaningfulness. The use of video to highlight situations that are successful adds to the learning process, which is also used in the Marte Meo-method (Aarts, 2000). Further, re-viewing the video clip helps the student to recall an *embodied sensed experience of meaningfulness*, close to what is described by Merleau-Ponty (2013). When the student recalls the experienced meaningfulness in the interplay with A, his fixed idea of separating song and improvisation is replaced by an improvisational, creative approach to use well-known songs. At the same time, the student becomes aware of his implicit use of communicative musicality in the way he sings with A (Holck, 2020), and he integrates this knowledge with his knowledge of meeting the psychosocial needs of people with dementia through musical micro-regulations (Anderson-Ingstrup, 2020; Ridder, 2019). From a learning perspective, a conscious bridge is created between the tacit and the reflexive knowledge the student-therapist has obtained during the internship, and during the therapeutic and academic training, leading him to see the situation in a new perspective and to create new ideas.

The supervision process starts at SMT supervision Level 1, as described above, where the student-therapist is primarily preoccupied by techniques he is longing to try out in clinical practice independent of the needs of the client. Through the supervision process, he acknowledges this tendency, and begins to validate the meaning of A's reactions, approaching SMT supervision Level 2. Although the student was confused when asked about his own sensations, he experienced the significance of being guided by these sensations in the contact with A, which touches SMT supervision Level 3. Thus, the supervision started at SMT supervision Level 1, but through a psychodynamic understanding of the goals of supervision, the supervisor moved flexibly between the levels.

The group setting in this example allowed the fellow students to function as a mirror and as a resonance board for both frustrations and meaningfulness. In group supervision a mixture of cognitive and arts-based feedback (e.g., drawings or poetic writings) is recommended in order to provide a space for resonance (Lindvang, 2010; Lindvang *et al.*, 2018). The arts-based methods help the group members to concentrate and to give resonant feedback in contrast to speculative interpretations. This increases both the feeling of safety and the courage to share what might not be successful the first time working with a client. Finally, the group format may raise the effect of learning, as the novice therapists will be able to recognize their own problems when the other group members share their work with other clients and client populations.

Vignette 2: Full-time internship: I am forgetting myself

This vignette is from individual supervision with a student in her last full-time internship in a kindergarten for children with learning differences. B is a five-year-old boy diagnosed with autism. He shows a strong interest in playing musical instruments, but he has severe difficulties in playing together with the student-therapist.

In the first six sessions, the student-therapist has repeatedly succeeded in synchronizing and matching B's fleeting play, when playing together with him. In these moments, he reacts with social facial and gestural signs such as smiles and glances towards the therapist. Nevertheless, the student-therapist comes to the supervision session with an attitude of giving up and seems to devalue her own capability. Even when the supervisor emphasizes the progressions with B, she keeps saying that it is difficult to get on with the case.

The supervisor changes the focus and asks the student-therapist to show two video clips from the last session with B, one video clip where the student-therapist experiences a relatively good interplay between them, and one video clip where she experiences the opposite. While watching the two short clips, the supervisor notices that the student-therapist in both clips is rather withdrawing in her musical expression, even when B is attentive and reacts socially in the musical interplay.

Supervisor: Let us focus on the first video clip where you experience a good interplay. When you watch this clip and recall the situation, how do you feel inside?

Student-therapist: I try to follow him so he can feel the connection between us. He smiles fleetingly, but still, I feel it is difficult. I don't know if the things we are doing have any value. B needs structure and the staff members tell me that... (the student continues to speak in a fast tempo).

Supervisor (develops shortness of breath and stops listening to the words): Try to stop for a moment...close your eyes, and allow yourself to breathe deeply...how are you feeling right now?

The student-therapist has tears in her eyes and expresses that there is a feeling of chaos inside. When she left home, just before supervision, her little son reacted with screams and kicks.

Supervisor: Let us give this issue attention for a moment.

In the following dialogue, it turns out that the student-therapist has a tendency to forget herself, but also to prioritize the internship over the family. As she becomes conscious of this, she rejoices that her son has the ability to respond to her mental absence, and the supervision again turns towards the case of B.

Supervisor: Let us watch the first video clip again. While we watch it, tell me along the way how you feel inside while you recall the situation.

Student-therapist (while watching the video clip again): I use all my attention to follow B. He reacts with a smile and his usual beats on the drum...but here (pointing to the screen) it starts running in circles, and I get a little mechanical and look tired. It is as if I am forgetting myself. I know it does not sound very ethical...but, actually, I become a bit irritated and feel bored (looks questioningly at the supervisor).

Supervisor: What do you feel like doing if you could allow yourself not to focus on B?

Student-therapist (eagerly): To play something chaotic, fast, and loud...

Supervisor: Like when your son screams and kicks?

Student-therapist: YES! (She laughs a little.) I wish B and I could play together, that he does not only react with fleeting smiles but stays in contact with me for longer periods.

The supervisor, now at the end of the session, suggests that the student takes a deep breath and turns her attention inward, when she is with B. This could help her to not so easily forget herself. In the following supervision, the student-therapist and supervisor perform a musical roleplay together, where the supervisor roleplays B's fleeting attention, while the student-therapist examines different ways of using music to contain it, and to stay creative in the interplay with B.

Theoretical reflections

The student-therapist knows that with children with severe autism it is recommended to use an approach where the therapist follows the child's lead while synchronizing and matching the child (Geretsegger *et al.*, 2015). Even though she gets responses from B using this approach, the student-therapist over time becomes irritated and bored. An explanation may be that the approach unconsciously triggers her personal tendency to forget herself and to be rather withdrawing in her musical expression.

The student is familiar with her personal issue from self-experience disciplines in the therapeutic track during the music therapy programme and from the first internship period. She has described the issue in her therapeutic training portfolio (see Chapter 2), which the supervisor read before the start of the supervision course. Therefore, the supervisor quickly spots the issue when watching the student's musical withdrawal on the video clip. The tendency to focus on the client's needs and forget her own feelings is described at SMT supervision Level 2, and when the supervisor feels her own countertransference (shortness of breath) she stops the student's explanations and asks her to feel inward instead.

When the student mentions the reactions of her son, the supervisor gives it space to unfold, but also takes on a more controlling role so that the parallel of the work with B becomes clear. The boundary between supervision and personal therapy is a thin line (Jacobsen, 2013) and the role between being a supervisor and a therapist has to be separated. Still, in psychodynamic supervision, it is important to make issues conscious if they prevent the student-therapist from being fully present with the client (Deurzen & Young, 2009).

In the work with clients with moderate to severe autism, the supervisor must be aware of personal matters in the student-therapist that affect intersubjective abilities. It may evoke strong reactions in the student-therapist, when experiencing the rapid shifts between 1) being able to sense the child's intersubjective abilities and 2) the feeling of not being able to reach the child (Holck, 2010).

In the supervision process, the student-therapist unexpectedly receives help from her little son, who with fully developed intersubjective abilities responds to his mother's absence. The student-therapist reacts similarly to B's fleeting attention and feels rejected when her son reacts to her absence. The parallel between the two situations is so obvious that the student came to laugh when she discovered the connection. The son became the key for the student to take her irritation and boredom seriously, and with the help of the supervisor, she became aware of what was happening inside her in the interaction with B. The student-therapist in the beginning showed a good understanding of the client's need (SMT supervision Level 2) and gradually in the supervision she reached a level (SMT supervision Level 3) where she became conscious of her own reactions, and showed a well-developed capacity for empathy and understanding of therapeutic processes. The supervision helped the student to stay empathic and creative, and B soon reacted with increased interest and joy.

Vignette 3: Full-time internship: Is my poor client that strong?

Student-therapist L is doing her full-time internship at a mental health hospital for four months. She is working with adults suffering from personality disorders, including borderline personality disorders and eating disorders. It is the first supervision for the group of ten internship students, and L is the first to present her topic or problem for supervision. She has been working with a woman, C, who is around 30 years old, for three sessions before this supervision. L feels that she is not able to make C play music, and she is concerned about the helplessness of C. The supervisor wants to explore L's perception of the client.

L: I am so worried about C – she is very helpless and keeps telling me that she is always misunderstood and not acknowledged by her surroundings. Therefore, she is not even able to play music.

Supervisor: Tell me more about your experience of C.

L: She talks about being in a terrible state. No one ever understands her or wants to be close to her. She doesn't want to express herself in words, as she expects that no one understands her or wants to answer her. I am so sorry for her, and I try to do my best to find a way to make her more comfortable so she can trust me and hopefully come to play with me. She seems so helpless.

Supervisor: Would you mind taking part in a roleplay where you play the client and you choose one of your fellow students to play the therapist? This might give you more information about her state of being.

L accepts this invitation and chooses a therapist among the fellow students. L and the fellow student start roleplaying, and the group supervisor keeps the time of approximately ten minutes and takes detailed notes during the roleplay. The rest of the group continues drawing or giving an aesthetic *response*.

Roleplay

Fellow student: Welcome. I want you to choose an instrument you like to hold. I will also choose an instrument I like to play.

She takes a metallophone, and after some time L puts a drum on her lap. The fellow student starts to play and invites L to accompany her if she feels like it. For the first five minutes, the fellow student plays for herself and now and then she looks at L and invites her with small melodies or rhythms, calling for melodic or rhythmical answers. L looks down and does not play at all. The fellow student expresses verbally while still playing that 'it is okay for me to be together with you, also when you do not want to play'. The fellow student continues playing, and all of a sudden, L bangs the drum very loudly. The fellow student answers back with a loud sound of her voice following her dynamic play on the metallophone. A musical fight between the two unfolds for a couple of minutes; then the music becomes more flowing, ending the music with mutual soft sounds.

After a long silent pause, the fellow student softly says: 'I really enjoyed playing with you.'

L: Didn't you think I was too noisy or too shouting?

Fellow student: Not at all. I enjoyed the forceful energy coming from you, and I really felt like being together with you at our mutual ending phrases. I felt you had a lot of strength.

L: I never experienced this before. Normally everyone thinks I am too noisy and too much, and I have learned to keep my mouth shut.

Fellow student: So how was it for you to open for this too-much-energy in our interplay?

L: I really enjoyed it.

The roleplay is terminated, and the group supervisor asks the two players to step out of their roles. The group supervisor invites L to talk about her experience.

L: I was so surprised how powerful it felt, when I was invited to play but didn't play. I really felt I was in charge of the situation.

Supervisor: You started the supervision by expressing how helpless you found C, and that you felt so sorry for her. How do you think about this now?

L: Yes, this is really surprising! That patients who do not communicate, and who seem helpless and misunderstood, may also feel powerful.

Supervisor: This sounds important. How was it for you when you banged the drum?

L: I felt so naughty and powerful. And a bit aggressive, but mostly naughty.

Supervisor: How was it for you to be met with a loud (maybe also naughty) response from your fellow student-therapist here?

L: I felt so released and it encouraged me to continue. I actually realized that shouting in music is less frightening than shouting with words; especially for me but probably also for my surroundings!! It was really important that the therapist told me that it was okay if I didn't want to play, and that it was okay for her to just play alone being with me. This encouraged me to break through the isolation and bang the drum that powerfully. I didn't feel any pressure or have a feeling of being sensed as helpless by her.

Supervisor to fellow student-therapist: How was it for you when your patient didn't answer your musical invitations?

Fellow student: First, I felt a bit rejected and felt like being left alone in my playing, but I tried to stay present in my private space and to play from there. And actually, this helped me feel okay with the situation, playing alone and having no answers to my invitations.

Supervisor: How was it for you when L banged the drum all of a sudden?

Fellow student: At first, I was frightened and surprised; then I felt like stepping out of my private space to the social space and even to the soloist space. I allowed myself to enjoy being in that fight with her and to feel her strength – like we were being two equal strong women playing together and continuing into a phase with mutual flow and mutual ending of the music.

Supervisor to L: How is it for you to listen to these experiences?

L: It really makes me thoughtful about my understanding of C as helpless. I realize that I have expanded my view of her a lot through this roleplay experience. I am also feeling released from a fixed position in the relationship with C. It really was an important lesson for me.

The drawings of the group members showed symbols like 'a volcano suddenly exploding', 'fighting between two warriors', and 'opening doors'. The aesthetic responses by the group members contained responses like power, liberty, 'you are okay', and 'we are both okay'.

Theoretical reflections

The roleplay is rather complex as there are many layers of experience:

- The student-therapist in relation to the group supervisor

- The student-therapist as client in a relationship with the fellow student-therapist

- The relationship between the three (supervisor, student-therapist, fellow student as therapist in the roleplay)

- The relationship between the student-therapist and the group

During the roleplay student-therapist L feels like being met by the fellow student and was offered a chance to step out of the fixed state of being. This transcendence of a fixed position may be understood from a perspective of relational psychoanalysis, where terms from the classical psychoanalysis like the unconscious, transference, countertransference, and resistance are still applied but in the understanding that:

...patient and therapist mutually have to fight to transcend their fixed subjective

335

frames of references to create a space together where they can observe what is happening between them. (Binder *et al.*, 2006, p.904) (See Chapter 3.)

This roleplay technique is chosen as the supervisor has the impression that L is overidentifying with C, the client (Level 2 of SMT supervision). Her strategy of deeply trying to understand C may not help C, who seems to be in a fixed position of continually experiencing that no one understands her. L seems to be experiencing a complementary countertransference (Binder *et al.*, 2006; Priestley, 1994), where she identifies with a fixed role, feeling sad for C in the same way as people surrounding C feel sad for her. As this is a fifth-year student, who is familiar with countertransference experiences, the supervisor trusts that she can better transcend a fixed position by an embodied experience emerging through the musical roleplay than by verbal reflection. Embodied experiences are important in learning processes according to Merleau-Ponty's theory of experience (1945) and in the understanding of authentic presence (Toustrup, 2006).

Thus, the supervisor intended to give L a chance to experience how a fellow student-therapist would offer a different reaction in the therapeutic relationship. The fellow student seemed to contain the feelings of being rejected by the client, and as she was informed about the client by L, it helped her to be prepared, to stay in, and to handle the situation in the roleplay in a more contained way. A roleplay situation including musical improvisation can be understood from a phenomenological perspective, where the art media (here music) is offered for the participants to bypass verbal reasoning by embodied experiences in order to open for transformation: 'It is through the music we offer the clients a chance of human transformation' (Lee & Khare, 2001, p.268).

L expressed a transformed perspective from being fixed in a certain relation to the client to a deeper and wider understanding of the client. In this process, she came to realize the strength of the client. L further reflected that feeling misunderstood or being too loud were also part of her own baggage in life. She could easily identify with the client and experienced a release when breaking through the isolation by banging the drum in the roleplay. It felt familiar and she had previously addressed this in other therapeutic learning situations. A further confirming learning process for L was the acknowledgement from the group supervisor and the group of fellow students when she expressed a transformed perspective of the client. In this way, the supervision moved to SMT supervision Level 3. The supervision process in many ways was similar to a therapy session, which made it important for the supervisor to keep the focus on the relationship to the client (Pedersen, 2009, 2013). In the here-and-now, the supervisor trusted the roleplay process being unfolded among the students and did not need to interfere; however, interference may be needed if a fixed relationship does not transcend during a roleplay process (Haugaard & Mortensen, 2013; Ødegaard & DeMott, 2008).

Reflections on the SMT levels related to the vignettes

In reflecting on the SMT supervision levels inspired from Stoltenberg and McNeill (2010), we clearly recognize different levels of supervision for internship students. As mentioned earlier, the development is not only linear but also circular between the levels. We have described several steps of development within each of the three levels, and also when the student music therapists moved back and forth between the levels during their supervisory processes.

Concerning SMT supervision Level 1, we have in Vignette 1 given an example of a student music therapist being concerned with applying the right tools and techniques in the therapeutic process. From there the student-therapist changed his perspective to being concerned with the right timing of interventions and aiming to meet specific needs of the client. The student was devaluing singing a well-known song as a music therapy method compared with musical improvisation. During the supervisory process, his viewpoint changed by watching the video clips and by the supervisor pointing at improvisational techniques in the singing performance. The positive responses from the group members contributed to the change of view. The student succeeded in being present in a freer flow to what comes up in the here-and-now with the client, creating a more fluid relational process through a feeling of the right timing of interventions.

Concerning SMT supervision Level 2, we have in Vignette 2 described a movement into a deeper sense of and understanding of empathy, by being aware of the various reasons for one's reactions. The student-therapist was only concerned about following the child's lead, and she forgot to listen to herself and to be present in the process. She realized through the supervisory process that her own son in fact helped her by reacting appropriately to her being non-present. This illustrated a parallel between her relations to the client and to the son, and she became aware of the importance of allowing herself to move back and forth between the client and herself in her attention and awareness.

Through the supervisory process, the student-therapist learned to be centred in and listening to herself, and at the same time to meet the needs of the client. She allowed herself to feel the impulses and to act upon and repair the fixed situation – so she could react more dynamically and be more present in an intense relational field.

Concerning SMT supervision Level 3, we have described a developmental process for the student-therapists, starting from not being able to identify transference processes at the one end of a continuum, to being able to take responsibility for complex contact and communication patterns at the other end of the continuum, as illustrated in Vignette 3. This includes the competence by the student-therapist of disclosing transference and countertransference patterns in a way that transcends fixed perspectives in a relationship.

When student music therapists are fixed in their view of clients, for example seeing a client being misunderstood and helpless, it is difficult to really understand and help the client. The supervisory process, through including roleplay in the vignette, shed light on and expanded the understanding of the client. The perspective, seeing the client as weak, shifted to seeing the client as surprisingly strong. Shifting perspective may lead to a more holistic understanding of a client or a situation. Embodied experiences, as here provided by roleplaying the client, are helpful in the process of learning how to be authentically present with a client and at the same time be centred in oneself.

Through embodied experiences and reflections, the student music therapists increase self- and other awareness and enhance their mentalizing capacities (see Chapter 3). They develop capacities to empathically understand clients and simultaneously understand their own influence on the state of the client, on the client–therapist relationship, and on the development of the music therapy process. In addition, the students enhance their knowledge of how to adapt playing and improvising music to the therapeutic needs of the clients. Finally, being a music therapy professional is only possible if you are able to be a team member, to work with other professionals, and to disseminate the music therapeutic work to others.

Summary of the complex processes of supervision

In this chapter, we have given our perspectives on a continuum process of supervision in a music therapeutic training context. We have presented how we apply the psychodynamic ground as described in Chapter 3 and the basic assumptions as an underlying understanding of learning processes in supervision. We have related examples from supervision practice to the three SMT supervision levels, inspired by the IDM (Stoltenberg & McNeill, 2010), and described developmental processes in the back-and-forth movements both within each level and between the three levels.

As we wrote in the introduction, supervision is a complex learning process. In music therapy supervision, learning processes are not only about the awareness of the relationship, of your own presence, and of how you yourself as a therapist influence the situation. It is also about how you communicate nonverbally and musically. We consider that being grounded and sensitive to embodied perceptions and experiences are basic qualities for the student music therapist, and, as well, to gradually be able to understand the complex processes of clinical practice. In supervision, important learning techniques for supporting these learning processes are the use of video clips, where students are supported in recognizing their bodily feelings in the situation. In Vignettes 1 and 2, video clips are used to recall the students' embodied experiences by, for example, focusing on selected clips where students feel most confident, or by helping students to explore what happened and realize new perspectives.

Further, the use of music or other artistic media for reflections in supervisory processes supports the understanding of unconscious dynamics (see Basic assumptions 4 and 5, Chapter 3). In Vignette 3, the musical roleplay gave the student-therapist an embodied experience of strength while roleplaying the client. This facilitated new perspectives on the client–therapist relationship.

We find it important to add that at the beginning of the supervision process of novice therapists the supervisor will take a more leading and controlling role, which is gradually loosened as the student-therapists achieve more self-awareness and reflexivity, which further may lead to advanced peer supervision processes in group supervision in the fifth year of study. However, it is always the responsibility of the supervisor to be aware of when structure and control is needed, or when it is safe to step aside and trust the process.

As part of the supervision process, the student-therapists write a report about their learning processes from individual and group supervision after each internship period. We have been surprised to see how integrated the student music therapists describe their own learning processes as being at all levels in these supervision process reports. After termination of the full-time internship at the fifth year of study, the students take part in an oral external examination of a case presentation – a so-called practice dissemination examination (in which the supervisors are not involved). After the internship and the examination, the students write their Master's thesis, which – with a few exceptions – is based on clinical data from the full-time internship. This gives the students a chance to deepen and explore experiences, knowledge, and theories at an advanced level.

As we state with the quote at the beginning of this chapter, reflexivity is both the process and outcome of supervision. Therefore, the supervision – together with the clinical learning processes – play an important role for the writing process of the Master's thesis. Academic reflections as well are based on the ability to explain, explore, and shift perspectives. This makes the supervisory processes vital for the development of the student's music therapy identity; a therapist identity that implies the competencies of self-awareness, being able to tune into the needs of clients, and of understanding the overarching needs of client populations, of team members and health care systems. This makes supervising music therapy students complex, as the supervisor has to be able to function as a gatekeeper, supporter, role model, and controller. The supervisor must ensure ethically conducted clinical practice, support the students in developing their own music therapy identity, act in a way that the students can copy in their work, and know when to lead and control, and when to trust the process. A supervisor (teacher) always has to conduct with disciplined subjectivity – there are constantly unconscious dynamics influencing the relationships between client-therapist and therapist-supervisor that need awareness, exploration, and reflection (Pedersen, 2007). Self-awareness and reflexivity, in this chapter, are described as developmental levels necessary for therapists, but they are values and virtues that need to be constantly nurtured. Thus, description of levels may be useful in understanding learning processes, but in relational processes learning never ends – which is where ethics starts.

References

Aarts, M. (2000). *Marte Meo: Basic Manual*. Aarts Productions.

Anderson-Ingstrup, J. (2020). 'A flexible fit. Developing a suitable manual framework for a person attuned musical interaction in dementia care through a realist approach.' PhD thesis, The Doctoral Programme in Communication and Psychology, section Music Therapy. Aalborg University. Accessed on 15/12/21 at https://vbn.aau.dk/ws/portalfiles/portal/400466935/PHD_JAI_E_pdf.pdf.

Binder, P.E., Nielsen, G.H., Vøllestad, J., Holgersen, H., & Schanche, E. (2006). 'Hva er relationell psykoanalyse? Nye psykoanalytiske perspektiver på samhandling, det ubevisste og selvet. [What is relational psychoanalysis? New psychoanalytical perspectives on interaction, the unconscious and the self].' *Tidsskrift for Norsk Psykologforening [Journal of the Norwegian Psychologist Association]*, 43(9), 899–908.

Bruscia, K. (2019). 'Five Levels of Supervision. A Model of Clinical Supervision in Music Therapy.' In M. Forinash (ed.), *Music Therapy Supervision* (2nd ed.). Barcelona Publishers.

Deurzen, E. van & Young, S. (2009). *Existential Perspectives on Supervision: Widening the Horizon of Psychotherapy and Counselling*. Red Globe Press.

Geretsegger, M., Holck, U., Carpente, J., Elefant, C., Kim, J., & Gold, C. (2015). 'Common characteristics of improvisational approaches in music therapy for children with autism spectrum disorder: Developing treatment guidelines.' *Journal of Music Therapy, 52*(2), 258–281.

Haugaard, C. & Mortensen, K.V. (2013). *Psykoterapeutisk praksis på psykodynamisk grundlag [Psychotherapeutic practice on a psychodynamic basis]*. Hans Reitzel Forlag.

Holck, U. (2010). 'Supervision af novicemusikterapeuter i arbejde med børn med betydelige og varige funktionsnedsættelser [Supervision of novice music therapists working with children with severe and chronic functional disabilities].' In K. Stensæth, A.T. Eggen, & R.S. Frisk (eds), *Musikk, helse, multifunksjonshemming [Music, health, multiple functional disabilities]*. NMH-publications.

Holck, U. (2020). 'Personafstemt sang i demensomsorgen – mikroanalyser af kommunikativ musikalitet [Person attuned singing in dementia care – micro-analysis of communicative musicality].' *Dansk Musikterapi, 17*(2), 35–46.

Jacobsen, C.H. (2007). 'Parallelprocesser [Parallel processes].' In C.H. Jacobsen & K.V. Mortensen (eds), *Supervision af psykoterapi. Teori og praksis [Supervision of psychotherapy. Theory and practice]*. Akademisk Forlag.

Jacobsen, C.H. (2013). 'Grundlæggende elementer i supervision af psykoterapeutiske arbejdsområder [Basic elements in supervision of psychotherapeutic working areas].' In I.N. Pedersen (ed.), *Kunstneriske medier i supervision af psykoterapi [Artistic media in supervision of psychotherapy]*. Aalborg Universitetsforlag.

Kohut, H. (1990). 'The Role of Empathy in Psychoanalytic Cure.' In R. Langs (ed.), *Classics in Psychoanalytic Technique*. Jason Aronson Inc. (A reprint from: *How does Analysis Cure?* The University of Chicago Press, 1984.)

Lee, C. & Khare, K. (2001). 'The Supervision of Clinical Improvisation in Aesthetic Music Therapy: A Music-Centered Approach.' In M. Forinash (ed.), *Music Therapy Supervision* (1st ed.). Barcelona Publishers.

Lindvang, C. (2010). 'A Field of Resonant Learning: Self-experiential Training and the Development of Music Therapeutic Competencies.' PhD thesis, the Doctoral Programme in Music Therapy, Aalborg University.

Lindvang, C. & Beck, B.D. (2017). *Musik, krop og følelser. Neuroaffektive processer i musikterapi [Music, body and emotions. Neuroaffective processes in music therapy.]* Frydenlund Academic.

Lindvang, C., Pedersen, I.N., Jacobsen, S.L., Ridder, H.M.O. *et al.* (2018). 'Collaborative resonant writing and musical improvisation to explore the concept of resonance'. *Qualitative Studies* 5(1), 4–23.

Malloch, S. & Trevarthen, C. (eds) (2009). *Communicative Musicality: Exploring the Basis of Human Companionship*. Oxford University Press.

Merleau-Ponty, M. (2013). *Phenomenology of Perception* (9th ed.). Routledge.

Ødegaard, A.J. & DeMott, M.A.M. (eds) (2008). *Estetisk veiledning. Dialog gjennom kunstuttrykk [Aesthetic supervision. Dialogues through artistic expressions]*. Universitetsforlaget.

Pedersen, I.N. (2007). 'Musikterapeutens disciplinerede subjektivitet [The disciplined subjectivity of the music therapist].' *Psyke & Logos, 28*(1), 358–384.

Pedersen, I.N. (2009). 'Music Therapy Supervision with Students and Professionals: The Use of Music and Analysis of Transference Experiences in the Triadic Field.' In H. Odell-Miller & E. Richards (eds), *Supervision of Music Therapy. A Theoretical and Practical Handbook*. Routledge.

Pedersen, I.N. (2013). 'Kunstneriske medier i supervision af psykoterapi. Et metateoretisk perspektiv [Artistic media in supervision of psychotherapy. A meta-theoretical perspective].' In I.N. Pedersen (ed.), *Kunstneriske medier i supervision af psykoterapi. Indsigt og vitalitet [Artistic media in supervision of psychotherapy. Insight and vitality]*. Aalborg Universitetsforlag.

Priestley, M. (1975). *Music Therapy in Action*. Constable.

Priestley, M. (1994). *Essays on Analytical Music Therapy*. Barcelona Publishers.

Ridder, H.M. (2019). 'Music Therapy for People with Dementia.' In S.L. Jacobsen, I.N. Pedersen, & L.O. Bonde (eds), *A Comprehensive Guide to Music Therapy* (2nd ed.). Jessica Kingsley Publishers.

Stern, D. (2004). *The Present Moment in Everyday Psychotherapy and Every Day Life*. W.W. Norton & Co.

Stern, D. (2010). *Forms of Vitality: Exploring Dynamic Experience in Psychology, the Arts, Psychotherapy and Development*. Oxford University Press.

Stoltenberg, C.D. & McNeill, B.W. (2010). *IDM Supervision: An Integrative Developmental Model for Supervising Counselors and Therapists* (3rd ed.). Routledge.

Stoltenberg, C.D., McNeill, B.W., & Delworth, U. (1998). *IDM Supervision. An Integrated Developmental Model for Supervising Counselors and Psychotherapists*. Jossey-Bass Publishers.

Toustrup, J. (2006). *Autentisk nærvær i psykoterapi og i livet [Authentic presence in psychotherapy and in life]*. Dansk Psykologisk Forlag.

Winnicott, D.W. (1971). *Playing and Reality*. Tavistock Publications.

Postlude

Inge Nygaard Pedersen, Charlotte Lindvang, & Bolette Daniels Beck

As editors, we are happy to look back at many years of teamwork and reflections about the training therapy in Aalborg and the shared efforts to complete this anthology. When looking through the book, several perspectives stand out as common themes across the chapters.

Concerning what the therapeutic disciplines train, one formulation is repeated: 'a growing awareness and consciousness', which is related to the student's self-perception and self-understanding concerning bodily, emotional, and cognitive levels.

One of the core aims of the therapeutic track is learning the art of 'listening'. It is not only listening to distinguish the quality of sound, structure, dynamic, or intensity of the music. Nor is it only listening to verbal formulations or understandings of other students (-clients). It is about listening to one's body experiences and becoming aware of resonating perceptions and emotions while interacting in the therapeutic relationship. Surrendering to this kind of listening can gradually raise the students' consciousness about their contribution to the relationship, the clients' contribution, and the quality and nature of the implicit and explicit interaction. In other words, the students gradually develop the ability to 'listen to myself, listen to the other'.

The therapeutic track offers training in being fully present in the here-and-now and orientating oneself in the nonverbal field of experiences. The training intends to motivate the students to keep on being curious about the mutual influence in the interaction they are taking part in and finding their way of containing whatever experiences they perceive in the musical interaction. The students learn to use these experiences as information channels to guide their interventions and musical initiatives during the interplay.

Overall, the disciplines in the therapeutic track aim at increasing students' awareness and extending their tolerance. Students learn to explore their feelings and needs, register and regulate their energy and emotional states, access their own musical and creative capabilities, and prepare themselves to apply these competencies in future work as music therapists.

Conducting music therapy will always require much more than technical proficiency. It is also preparing for seeking a lifestyle that can balance the involving and demanding area of serving as a professional music therapist. During training, the therapeutic learning process serves as a starting point to prepare for professional life after graduation, in which the novice music therapist is confident about the value of seeking support, inspiration, and professional growth in supervision, personal therapy, or other relevant contexts.

Through this book, we have tried to draw inspiration from and disseminate 40 years of experience teaching different disciplines in the therapeutic track of the music therapy programme at Aalborg University. Looking ahead to the next 40 years, we keep the vision that these disciplines will figure as mandatory disciplines in music therapy training programmes, even though the single disciplines might slightly change in form and structure over time. We hope that these basic embodied steps in developing a professional music therapy identity will continue, no matter which approaches will further develop within music therapy as a profession, and no matter how many new populations might come on the list for whom music therapy will be relevant and beneficial.

Contributors

Inge Nygaard Pedersen, PhD, is an Associate Professor Emerita (since 2021) at the Department of Psychology and Communication, Aalborg University (AAU). She had the first position at the five-year music therapy programme at AAU in 1981 and was head of the programme from 1982 to 1995. Since 1995 she has been head of the Music Therapy Clinic for clinical work and research at Aalborg University Hospital, Psychiatry. Her research and publication areas are training of music therapists at all levels, supervision of clinical music therapy, and music therapy in psychiatry with different populations.

inp@hum.aau.dk; www.vbn.aau.dk

Charlotte Lindvang, PhD, is an Associate Professor at the music therapy department, Institute for Communication and Psychology at Aalborg University; GIM therapist (EAMI); and Psychotherapist MPF. She has been employed as music therapist for many years in psychiatry, as well as in palliative care and in private praxis. Her research areas are in education, training therapy, GIM, and music interventions in medical settings.

chli@hum.aau.dk; www.vbn.aau.dk

Bolette Daniels Beck, PhD, is an Associate Professor at the music therapy department, Institute for Communication and Psychology at Aalborg University; MA in music ethnology and music therapy; and GIM therapist, supervisor, and primary trainer. Her research areas include RCT studies on GIM with stress and trauma populations, music and health studies, university pedagogics, and qualitative inquiries in embodiment, nature, and spirituality in music therapy. She works at the Music Therapy Clinic for clinical work and research at Aalborg University Hospital, Psychiatry.

bolette@ikl.aau.dk; www.vbn.aau.dk

Søren Willert is today a Professor Emeritus at the Department of Culture and Learning, Aalborg University. During the period 1968–2006 he was attached to the Department of Psychology, Aarhus University. Psychosocial helping practice in its many forms – psychotherapy, counselling, supervision, coaching, organization consultancy, action research, etc. – became his main teaching, training, and research area. During this period he also served as external examiner at the Department of Music Therapy at Aalborg University.

swi@hum.aau.dk; www.vbn.aau.dk

Helen Odell-Miller, OBE, PhD, is a Professor and Director of the Cambridge Institute for Music Therapy at Anglia Ruskin University. A pioneer for early development of the music therapy profession in the UK, she developed international research, especially in the fields of adult mental health and dementia, including a psychoanalytically informed approach in music therapy. She led one of the largest Arts Therapies National Health Service mental health departments in the UK (1981–2006), where she still holds an honorary contract. She is currently the UK leader for HOMESIDE, a five-country research project for home-based people living with dementia.

Helen.Odell.Miller@aru.ac.uk

Sanne Storm, PhD, is an Associate Professor, part-time, and guest researcher at the Music Therapy Department, Aalborg University. Her research, teaching, and clinical work are focused on her approach and method – Psychodynamic Voice Therapy as well as VOIAS, a voice assessment profile. She is a member of the International Music Therapy Assessment Consortium (IMTAC). From 2014 to 2020, she was a member of the research committee of the National Hospital, Faroe Islands, and led an interdisciplinary perinatal team at the Psychiatric Center, the National Hospital, Faroe Islands, focusing on affective disorders, anxiety, and perinatal health.

stormsanne@gmail.com

Niels Hannibal, PhD, is an Associate Professor at the Institute for Communication and Psychology, Aalborg University, and head of the music therapy clinic at Aalborg University Hospital – Psychiatry since 2021. His main research area is music therapy in psychiatry, with a focus on people with psychiatric illnesses such as personality disorder, depression, and schizophrenia, and he has published on the theoretical understanding of music therapy processes, such as preverbal transference in musical improvisation and mentalization in music therapy.

hannibal@hum.aau.dk; www.vbn.aau.dk

Stine Lindahl Jacobsen, PhD, is an Associate Professor, head of the Art, Health and Technology Study Board, and head of the Music Therapy Knowledge Group, Aalborg University, as well as an Assessment of Parent-Child Interaction (APCI) developer, researcher, and trainer. Clinical and research areas mainly include arts and health, families at risk, child protection, effect studies, and assessment.

slj@hum.aau.dk; www.vbn.aau.dk

Lars Ole Bonde, PhD (in music therapy), was a Professor in Music Therapy at Aalborg University, 1995–2018. From 2008 he was Professor II at the Center for Research in Music and Health, the Norwegian Academy of Music, in Oslo, Norway, where he is now emeritus. He is a primary trainer in GIM (Guided Imagery and Music) and a certified clinical Supervisor. His current research projects are in GIM, music education, and opera. He has numerous publications on music therapy, music psychology, music education, and music theatre.

larsolebonde@gmail.com; www.vbn.aau.dk

Ulla Holck, MA and PhD in Music Therapy, is an Associate Professor at the Music Therapy Programme, Department of Communication and Psychology, Aalborg University; involved in the four years training programme in Existentialistic Body Psychotherapy and the two years training programme in Psychodynamic Clinical Supervision; and Head of the Center for Documentation and Research in Music Therapy (www.cedomus.aau.dk), Aalborg University. She has 25+ years of experience with research, teaching music psychology, music therapy theory, and research methods, and in academic and clinical supervision at Bachelor's, Master's, and PhD level at Aalborg University.

holck@hum.aau.dk; www.vbn.aau.dk

Hanne Mette Ridder, PhD, DMTF, is a Professor and Coordinator of the Doctoral Programme in Music Therapy at Aalborg University. She has long clinical experience in dementia care, leads research on music therapy in dementia and neurocognitive disorders, and is engaged in various international research networks. She is an approved clinical supervisor, and past president of the European Music Therapy Confederation (2010–2016).

hanne@hum.aau.dk; www.vbn.aau.dk

Subject Index

Author Index